MW01148997

CONTAINING HISTORY

CONTAINING HISTORY

How Cold War History Explains US-Russia Relations

STEPHEN P. FRIOT

University of Oklahoma Press : Norman

Publication of this book is supported in part by the generosity of Edith Kinney Gaylord.

Library of Congress Cataloging-in-Publication Data

Names: Friot, Stephen P. (Stephen Perley), 1947– author.
Title: Containing history : how Cold War history explains US-Russia relations / Stephen P. Friot.
Other titles: How Cold War history explains US-Russia relations
Description: Norman : University of Oklahoma Press, [2023] | Includes bibliographical references and index. | Summary: "Scours the history of the Cold War, from the end of World War II to the end of the Soviet Union, for clues as to why Americans and Russians think about each other the way they do and how the Cold War's legacies affect present politics and popular consciousness in both countries"—Provided by publisher.
Identifiers: LCCN 2022040092 | ISBN 978-0-8061-9190-4 (hardcover)
Subjects: LCSH: United States—Foreign relations—Russia (Federation) | Russia (Federation)—Foreign relations—United States. | Cold War. | BISAC: HISTORY / Modern / 20th Century / Cold War | POLITICAL SCIENCE / International Relations / Arms Control
Classification: LCC E183.8.R9 F73 2023 | DDC 327.47073—dc23/eng/20221026
LC record available at https://lccn.loc.gov/2022040092

The paper in this book meets the guidelines for permanence and durability of the Committee on Production Guidelines for Book Longevity of the Council on Library Resources, Inc. ∞

10 9 8 7 6 5 4 3 2 1

To Nancy Robin Friot,
now more than ever

Contents

Preface

February 24, 2022

The past is never dead. It's not even past.
—William Faulkner, *Requiem for a Nun*

At 5:00 a.m. on February 24, 2022, Russian forces, acting at the command of President Vladimir Vladimirovich Putin, launched a brutal and unprovoked attack by land, sea, and air on Ukraine and its people. Putin's dual motive was to prevent a thriving democracy from developing in Ukraine—lest life in Russia suffer by comparison—and to upend the post–Cold War Euro-Atlantic security order. Putin's decision to attack Ukraine was, regardless of the ultimate outcome on the ground, an epochal miscalculation. At this writing, Putin has succeeded in unifying NATO to a degree not seen in decades, in bringing larger numbers of NATO forces closer to the Russian border, in giving NATO members the political will to substantially increase defense spending, in fortifying the Ukrainians' sense of their own national identity, in permanently cementing Ukraine's alignment with the West, and in undercutting any perception of Russia as a first-rate military power in any conflict short of a full-on nuclear war. Of equal significance, the war will leave Russia an economically stagnating (at best), diplomatically isolated, and dangerous pariah state, with a population increasingly possessed by a sense of historical grievance, which has thousands of nuclear warheads and a veto in the UN Security Council. No conceivable benefit that could flow to the

Russian people from Putin's war will outweigh the consequences the Russian people—to say nothing of the Ukrainian people—will have to bear.

The challenge now confronting the West is to hold Russia in check while bearing in mind George F. Kennan's 1951 dictum: "The ways by which peoples advance toward dignity and enlightenment in government are things that constitute the deepest and most intimate processes of national life. There is nothing less understandable to foreigners, nothing in which foreign influence can do less good."[1]

On the long flight home from one of my early trips to Russia, I found myself wondering how the people of the two nations could be so much alike in so many ways yet in other ways so different. Searching rather randomly for clues to this mystery, I picked up my copy of *The Federalist Papers* and read that incomparable collection of essays again. That helped. Then I started reading Russian history. That helped even more. The short answer to my question is, of course, that Russian civilization has had formative experiences not shared with the American or other Western societies, and American civilization has had the benefit of formative experiences (some predating the founding of the United States by hundreds of years) that were not shared by Russian society. Over time, I realized that there is a book to be written that will shed light on why we think about the Russians in the way that we do, and why the Russians think about us in the way that they do. This, I hope, is that book.

As fate would have it, the Cold War era was the period in which hundreds of years of history, on both sides of the East-West divide, were fused into historical memory and popular consciousness with consequences that undeniably persist to this day. In the wake of Putin's disastrous Ukrainian adventure, this subject deserves attention if we are to make headway against two developments that portend nothing good. First, in terms of US-Russian relations, the high hopes that accompanied the end of the Cold War have been dashed. Those hopes, though perhaps unrealistically high in the first place, at least provided the impetus for a reengagement that served the interests of populations on both sides of the divide. Second, in terms of multilateral relations in the third decade of the twenty-first century, we have seen from some leaders and commentators on both sides of the divide a waning commitment to a rules-based international order. Reversal of these trends requires, among other things, an understanding of how we got here. The Cold War years have much to do with how we got here. Those years still have much to teach us.

ALTHOUGH THE LITERATURE OF THE COLD WAR is enormous, one thing that is little understood in the United States is the extent to which public attitudes in Russia are—in the twenty-first century—the product of a thousand years of history, including searing experiences in the twentieth century that have no counterpart in US history. Contemporary Russia has been shaped in part by the forty-five years of the Cold War and in part by the seventy years of the Soviet era, all against the backdrop of the millennium that unfolded after Christianity came to the Kyivan Rus. Likewise, the attitude of the American people toward Russia and the Russian people has been and will continue to be influenced by the Cold War and more broadly the seven decades of the Soviet era. Why is this important? Oleg Barabanov answered that question quite well: "Historical memory and how it is understood play a major role in forming civic solidarity, creating links between generations and making citizens feel like they have a personal stake in the state of affairs." For that reason, whether any given citizen—voter—understands it or not, "historical memory is a value that drives social and political behaviour in a meaningful way."[2]

It must be understood, too, that the effects of the events explored here—World War II and the Cold War—are different in Russia than in the United States. The politics of history and the politics of remembrance (not to be confused with nostalgia), rooted in historical memory, are real forces in the Russian polity and cannot be simply dismissed as tools for political opportunists such as Putin.

THE VIEWS EXPRESSED IN THIS BOOK do not necessarily represent the views or policies of the US government, any agency thereof, or any judicial organization.

Acknowledgments

This work would not exist without the advice and encouragement of a lot of friends and colleagues, both in the United States and in Russia. The wise counsel, steady hand, and good humor of Kent Calder, editorial director at the University of Oklahoma Press, have made all the difference. My judicial colleagues have served as invaluable sounding boards as this project has progressed—doubtless on many occasions when they would have preferred to talk about other things.

My Russian friends and colleagues—in academia, the judiciary, the legal profession, and elsewhere—deserve special mention. On countless occasions, you have been generous beyond any reasonable expectation in helping me to learn about your nation, its incomparable culture and people, and the challenges it faces. In your own way, you have made this a collaborative work. You know who you are. I am very much in your debt. And I must add that I have learned at least as much from my students in Russia as I have taught them in the lectures and seminars I have been privileged to conduct (and hope to resume, though we cannot know when that might be possible). Their energy, curiosity, and willingness to ask hard questions have been an inspiration.

Here in the United States, my friends and colleagues who have contributed their time, without compensation, to read individual chapters have helped sharpen my writing (and, in some cases, my thinking). The ideas and comments of Robert Henry, Anna Kazantseva, Maria Lvova, David Russell, Jay Shanker, Alexey Tarasov, and Ralph Thompson have contributed much to this work. All I can say is that I am ever more in your debt for your insights and encouragement. The same goes for invaluable counsel and priceless words of encouragement from Barbara Snow Gilbert, an award-winning author. Those words came when they were most needed. And without Lyn Marshala's expert assistance (to say nothing of her patience and unfailing good cheer), I never would have had a presentable manuscript.

The Harry S. Truman Presidential Library and Museum deserves special mention. Its staff was unfailingly responsive, even amid a pandemic lockdown, in providing materials not yet generally available.

I would be guilty of serious ingratitude if I failed to thank George F. Kennan (1904–2005), the author of the doctrine of containment, for inspiring the title of this work. Kennan's intellectual contributions to our national security are as relevant now as they were when he wrote so perceptively about "the Russians" nearly eight decades ago.

Finally, not out of mere sentiment is this work dedicated to my wife, Nancy. Her many hours of work, both by way of editing and substantive critique, have much to do with any value (to say nothing of readability) this work may have.

Prologue

Why the Cold War and Its Origins Still Matter

Alexis de Tocqueville told us in 1835 that "there are today two great peoples on earth, who, though they started from different points, seem to be advancing toward the same goal: the Russians and the Anglo-Americans." Writing about nations ruled by Tsar Nicholas I of the Romanov dynasty and by President Andrew Jackson, of decidedly less royal lineage, Tocqueville's conclusion was no less striking. Each nation "seems called by a secret design of Providence some day to sway the destinies of half the globe."[1]

So it was, 115 years later when the authors of NSC-68 (a US National Security Council document that, more than any other, defined the American military doctrine for the Cold War) observed that "the defeat of Germany and Japan and the decline of the British and French Empires have interacted with the development of the United States and the Soviet Union in such a way that power has increasingly gravitated to these two centers."[2] Tocqueville told them this is how it would be.

It is fitting that the temperature in Moscow rose to a few degrees above freezing on December 25, 1991, because the Cold War ended on that day, a date as crystalline a turning point as August 6, 1806, when Emperor Francis II, under pressure from Napoleon I, formally ended the Holy Roman Empire. On that evening in December 1991, the flag of the Soviet Union was lowered at the Kremlin for the last time, marking the end of the Soviet Union and its empire. Where there had been one nation, there were now fifteen. Vladimir Putin was later heard to say, in a much-misinterpreted declaration, that the collapse of the Soviet Union was the greatest geopolitical catastrophe of the twentieth century.[3] He had a point, but his point was (and is) poorly understood in the West, as discussed later in these pages. It would be misleading to call the present East-West relationship a new Cold War. For one thing, the present-day adversarial relationship, bitter though it is, is not ideologically driven. In some ways that is unfortunate, because ideology, one of the main drivers of the Cold War on both sides, helped to give the Cold War a certain predictability—what Acting Secretary of State Lawrence Eagleburger called "the familiar discipline and order of the Cold War."[4] On some issues, it was almost as if both sides had a script, each side knowing with reasonable certainty what the next line from the other side would be. Ideology, thus, did much to facilitate the development of rules of engagement for the Cold War, rules of engagement that may have saved hundreds of millions of lives.

To be sure, the Putin regime's attitude toward the West has taken on an ideological cast of sorts in recent years. If Putin's ethnonationalism, with an overlay of smoldering resentment toward the West, can be called an ideology, it is not an ideology in anything like the same sense that communism was, with its strong international messianic component, during the Cold War. The twenty-first century version may be more dangerous, because though Putin's brand of social conservatism positions him as the guardian of Russian values in the face of encroachments from the decadent West, we don't now have anything resembling the ideological drivers that helped keep East-West relations from spinning out of control during the Cold War.

The rules of engagement, to the extent that they still exist at all, are decidedly less clear now, especially in cyberspace. That makes the Cold War relevant. In both East and West (perhaps a bit more so in East than in West), the popular consciousness examined in this book is a unifying force. It goes far to determine what the constituencies expect of their leaders, what risks they will consider acceptable, what they will and will not tolerate, and what they are willing or unwilling to sacrifice in the service of the national interest as they see it, and as their leaders seek to define it.

When We Talk about "Popular Consciousness," Just Whose Consciousness Are We Talking About?

On the Russian side, the question—central to Russian popular consciousness—is, as Wright Miller put it in 1973: Who are the Russians?[5] This raises the touchy question of ethnicity, but it is a question that cannot be ignored.

An understanding of *Russia* requires an understanding of *Russians*. In turn, Russians cannot be understood without looking at Russian ethnicity and its essential components—race, language, culture, religion, and history. Although the Soviet Union was commonly referred to as Russia, today's Russia is in some important ways vastly different from the Soviet Union. This, again, requires us to address ethnicity. The Soviet Union was, within its own borders, a multinational empire, a fact of which the Kremlin from Lenin to Gorbachev was keenly aware. Individuals from scores of non-Russian minorities were woven into Soviet society and leadership. Save for a few situations in which it was expedient to emphasize the "Russianness" of Soviet society (as Stalin did at some crucial junctures during World War II), Soviet leaders cultivated what has aptly been called an "affirmative action empire"[6] in which Great Russian chauvinism was not encouraged. All of this had its effects on Soviet actions in the international arena. (And, by the way, to refer to the Soviet nation as "the Russians" during the Cold War, as US politicians almost invariably did, made it a vast oversimplification.)

The point is this: there is much more than a passing chance, as Michael Kimmage has observed, that Russians born after 1991 "believe in the distinctiveness of Russian culture more than their parents or grandparents ever did."[7] The ethnicity now shared by about 80 percent of the Russian population nourishes a common culture and, in a variety of situations (especially where there is a perceived external threat), can produce an uncommon sense of solidarity. This is not racism (and does not readily lend itself to cross-cultural comparisons). This is history and culture doing what history and culture will do in a relatively homogeneous society. These influences affect Russians' sense of their own interests, as well as their fundamental worldview. These realities, combined with the ascendant social conservatism of the ethnic Russian population, make Russia a force to be reckoned with in ways that are poorly understood in the United States. So, on this touchy subject of ethnicity (and its ramifications), it is perhaps best to start with objective facts.

As counted in the 1989 census, the population of the Soviet Union was 286.7 million.[8] Ethnic Russians made up a bare majority of this 1989 population—50.8 percent. The other half included more than a hundred specifically identifiable ethnicities.[9] In 1979 the Muslim population of the Soviet Union (mostly of Turkic extraction) was one-sixth of the total Soviet population, but it accounted for fully half of the increase in that population between 1979 and 1989. The rapid growth of the non-Russian population in the Soviet Union was primarily driven by increases in Kazakhs, Uzbeks, and Tajiks.[10] Great Russians were not just a bare majority in the population of the Soviet Union; they shared a nation with an array of other ethnicities that were increasingly animated by ethnic consciousness and aware of how different they were from the ethnic Russian population.

There was little room for doubt in the final years of the Soviet Union that the stability of the Soviet system depended on whether the Kremlin leadership could deal successfully with its "nationality problem,"[11] which was both a demographic reality and a political challenge. At the Twenty-Sixth Congress of the Communist Party of the Soviet Union (CPSU) in 1981, general secretary Leonid Brezhnev put it delicately yet unequivocally: "The dynamics of the development of a large multinational state like ours gives rise to many problems requiring the Party's tactful attention."[12]

There the matter sat when the USSR ceased to exist. In one stroke, the population governed from the Kremlin went from 50 percent Russian to 80 percent Russian. The Kremlin's constituency got much smaller—it shrank by at least 145 million people—but it became much more ethnically Russian. Russia was (and is) more ethnically homogeneous than Spain or the United Kingdom.

Why does this matter? This matters because, as the journalist Hedrick Smith accurately observed during the Soviet era, Americans misunderstand the meaning and underestimate the importance of ethnicity. Unlike asking Americans about their home state, asking Soviet citizens about their Russian, Armenian, Uzbek, Latvian, Ukrainian, or Jewish identity "goes much deeper. It is a fundamental form of identity. It communicates language, tradition, culture, value, heritage."[13]

This observation remains true of the Russian Federation of the twenty-first century. To be sure, the minority populations are still there. But the common ethnicity now shared by about 80 percent of Russian citizens is a critical ingredient of the affective identification—a feeling of solidarity based on ethnic and cultural similarity—that has contributed to cohesiveness in Russian society for a long time and, most notably, in the worst of times. Because it plays to some basic propensities of the human spirit, this ethnic affinity will endure for many generations to come.[14] This, again, is not racism. This bond sustains Russian patriotism (especially in the face of external challenges), patriotism being, as the British historian Elie Kedourie put it, "affection for one's country, or one's group, loyalty to its institutions, and zeal for its defence . . . a sentiment known among all kinds of men" and women.[15]

Thus, it is worth remembering that Tolstoy was not just telling us a quaint story when he told us about Natasha's dance. In *War and Peace*, Tolstoy wanted us to understand one very important thing about the irrepressible Countess Natasha Rostova. Although she was raised by a French governess, and was, by any standard, a worldly young woman, when Natasha quite unexpectedly found herself in Uncle and Anisya's humble cabin and heard the sound of a beloved folk song on the balalaika, she required no coaching to dance the dance that made it quite clear that she understood "all that was in Anisya and in Anisya's father and mother and aunt, and in every Russian man and woman."[16] Tolstoy's message was that, for Natasha and the reader, to be Russian was all that was necessary.

Some observers, both within and without Russia, are uneasy to the point of bristling when Russia is characterized, sometimes with a chauvinistic overtone, as a unique civilization. Aside from that, Timothy Frye has argued persuasively in his 2021 book, *Weak Strongman*, that Russia is not so very different from other countries (such as Hungary, Turkey, and Venezuela) that have decidedly illiberal regimes but don't share Russia's unique history and culture. His argument is that other, more salient, characteristics that Russia shares with those other countries go far to explain Russian attitudes and Russia's domestic political situation.[17] Fair enough. But the fact remains that Russia is, indeed, a unique civilization. It has been so for a long time and will remain so for a long time to come. That will make a difference to Russia's relations with the West especially as East and West engage—as they eventually must—with the task of finding a new way forward in the wake of the catastrophic war in Ukraine.

Chapter 1

It Took Centuries to Get to Yalta

On February 9, 1946, exactly a year after the Yalta conference, Premier Josef V. Stalin, the general secretary of the Central Committee of the Communist Party of the Soviet Union, standing for re-election to the Supreme Soviet, gave a speech—now known as the "election speech"—at the Bolshoi Theater. Acknowledging that "the Communist party is ready to receive the verdict of the voters," Stalin had every reason to be confident about the outcome of the election.[1] Given the time, place, and political context, Stalin had absolute freedom to choose what to say and how to say it. It is noteworthy, therefore, that he took this opportunity to survey what he thought to be the causes of the war just ended and of the wars he said were sure to come. The twin culprits were "monopolistic capitalism"[2] and the impossibility (reiterating basic Leninist doctrine) of peaceful distribution of capital and markets by the capitalist countries.[3]

To put it mildly, Stalin's message was not well received in the West. On February 10, 1946, the day after Stalin's speech, the *New York Times*, taking Stalin quite literally, reported that he had asserted that "the present capitalist system sets the stage for war."[4] Undersecretary of State (and future secretary of state) Dean Acheson took the speech as expressing a conclusion on Stalin's part "that no peaceful international order was possible."[5] Supreme Court Justice William O. Douglas, known for florid expression at times but assuredly not known to be a warmonger, pronounced the speech to be "the Declaration of World War III."[6]

On March 5, 1946, less than a month after Stalin's speech, Winston Churchill answered in kind, with his famous Iron Curtain speech.

> From Stettin in the Baltic to Trieste in the Adriatic, an iron curtain has descended across the Continent. Behind that line lie all the capitals of the ancient states of Central and Eastern Europe. . . .
>
> From what I have seen of our Russian friends and Allies during the war, I am convinced that there is nothing they admire so much as strength, and there is nothing for which they have less respect than for weakness, especially military weakness.[7]

Stalin's response: "Beyond all question Mr. Churchill's aim is a war aim, a summons to war against the USSR."[8]

The Cold War was on. The Cold War unfolded over more than four decades. Its antecedents unfolded over centuries.

The History

When the Napoleonic Wars ended in 1815, no nation in the world possessed more military might than Russia.[9] There was a good reason for this. Russia was then (and remains) the most invaded nation in the world. Although Russian history assuredly includes Russia as an invader, the collective memory of the Russian people is much more the memory of a people invaded with remarkable regularity from every direction except the north.

We will ignore the centuries of rule by the Mongols and the nearly 250 attacks by Tatars, Swedes, Poles, and Lithuanians on the territory of the historic Rus between 1055 and 1462.[10] Ignoring, for that matter, all invasions of Russia before the beginning of the seventeenth century, we have:

The Poles (again). In 1611, Polish forces burned all of Moscow except the Kremlin and its immediate environs. For good reason, Russia's National Unity Day, November 4, commemorates the popular uprising that expelled the Poles from Moscow.

The Swedes (again). Charles XII, of Sweden, was not happy with the founding of St. Petersburg by Peter I (the Great). Charles crossed the frozen Vistula with more than forty thousand Swedish troops in January 1708. Charles's Russian adventure ended with Russia's historic victory at Poltava in June 1709.

The Turks. Because Russia had controlled the Crimean Peninsula since the end of the Russo-Turkish War of 1768–1774, Catherine II (the Great) did not take kindly to a demand by the Ottomans in 1787 that Russia relinquish the peninsula. Though the Ottoman demand prompted Russia to declare war, the Ottomans took the offensive. This did not end well for the Turks. The end result was the Ottomans' final relinquishment of the Crimea to Russia in 1792.

The French. The East European Plain—less than 350 meters above sea level at its highest point in the Valdai Hills about midway between St. Petersburg and Moscow—was as inviting for Napoleon's Grand Armée as it had been for the Poles and the Swedes. This was the "space" of the "space, time and weather" that Tsar Alexander I said would be Russia's most reliable allies in the event of a French invasion.[11] Napoleon at least had the good judgment to start his Russian adventure at the beginning of summer (June 1812), as did Adolph Hitler 129 years later, in June 1941. On September 14, 1812, Napoleon entered Moscow. To his amazement, Russia did not surrender. This did not end well for the French, as is forever memorialized in the latter part of Tchaikovsky's *1812 Overture*, where the last, mocking echo of "La Marseillaise" signals the French retreat into the vast plain—and into the devastating Russian winter. The tsar's entry into Paris in 1814 required much less violence than the Red Army's entry into Berlin 131 years later.

The French (again) and the British (for the first time, but not the last). Strictly speaking, the Crimean War cannot be included in a list of invasions of Russia in conflicts in which Russia was not the initial armed aggressor. Russia did initiate the military action by sending troops into Turkey's Danuban principalities in mid-1853, a result (among other causes) of the displeasure of Nicholas I with Turkish concessions favorable to Roman Catholics in general and the French in particular in the Holy Land. (The Orthodox, backed mainly by Russia, had long enjoyed special privileges there.) The British, French, and Turks knew how to hit Russia where it really hurt: the Crimean Peninsula. The humiliation of the Crimean War resulted in Russian territorial concessions (but not of any land in the Crimea, Turkey having ceded Crimea for all time in 1792) and—worst of all—exclusion of Russian warships from the Black

Sea, barring Russia from access to the prized Crimean warm-water port of Sevastopol.

The British (again), along with the Americans, the French, the Greeks, and the Japanese. "For many months, American doughboys battled grimly against Red troops in Russia."[12] That line, in a 1951 issue of *Collier's* magazine, is from an American general's factual account of the deployment of US and Allied troops with the objective of effecting regime change in Russia in 1918–20. It was called the Allied intervention. The Allied intervention does not get more than a footnote—if that—in history books in the United States. The Russians remember it better than we do.

If we leave out the bit players, the aggressors in the Allied intervention were France, Great Britain, Greece, Japan, and the United States. Initially, the Allied intervention was motivated by a desire to see to it that Russian resources and war materiel would not fall into the hands of the Germans, who were still fighting on the western front.[13] But the Allied troops remained after the war ended in November 1918, fighting alongside the White Russians to defeat Bolshevism. Writing in *Harper's Magazine* in 1946, John Fischer stated that the objective of the Western powers was "to strangle the Bolshevik regime in its infancy."[14] Because winning was far more important for the Bolsheviks than for any of the Allies, Bolshevism outlasted the Allied intervention by nearly seventy years.

In the summer of 1979, a thirty-six-year-old US senator sat down in the Kremlin with Soviet Premier Alexey Nikolayevich Kosygin to discuss the US Senate's approach to the pending SALT II arms-control treaty. Before they got down to the business at hand, Kosygin set the tone: "Let's agree that we do not trust each other, and we have good reason not to trust each other. . . . [R]emember, you put American troops in our country to fight alongside the White Russians in 1917. We have never set foot on your territory."[15] It was a memorable conversation for thirty-six-year-old Senator Joe Biden.

The Poles (again). The Russo-Polish War, fought between April and October 1920, was but another chapter in the long, fraught history of relations between Russia and Poland. The Poles started it, but the Red Army ended it, mounting a counteroffensive which advanced to the gates of Warsaw. Those gains were reversed by Polish forces with the benefit of financing from France. This all ended with a treaty establishing a new boundary favorable, in some respects, to the Poles.

The Germans (again). Although the German advance on Petrograd (as it was then called) in early 1918 precipitated the humiliating Treaty of Brest-Litovsk, German forces did not penetrate deeply into Russia's historical homeland in World War I. But they made up for that in 1941.

Russians would be quick to point out that all the invaders listed here, save for Japan and Sweden, are members of NATO. (And as these pages are written, Sweden's accession—along with Finland's—is imminent.)

As historian Brian Moynahan puts it, "After 1914, apart from Russian fighting Russian in civil war, German, Austrian, Czech, American, British, French, Japanese, Hungarian, Rumanian, Italian, Finnish, Spanish and Chinese troops fought on Russian soil. The Spanish might amount to a division, the British and Americans to small units, the Chinese to a few border squads but all join the Russian roll call of invaders."[16]

Looking Back from 1946: The Hatreds and the Stakes

Hitler's hatred of the Slavs (worse yet, Bolshevik Slavs) had much to do with *why* the war on the eastern front was fought—and even more to do with *how* it was fought. The why and the how have not been forgotten in Russia. The racial and ideological backdrop, together with the sheer human cost of that epochal struggle, have much to do with the process by which the postwar global order was established beginning in 1945. As for the ideological component on the Russian side, Russians are, to this day, noticeably more apt to refer to the war on the eastern front as a war with the Nazis than as a war with Germany.

Hitler's primal racial hatred of the Slavs—*Untermenschen*—reminds us how important ethnicity and religion were to relations between Russia and nations lying to the west of the Eastern Slav heartland. An identifiable Slavic ethnos dates from as early as 600 BCE, centered in what is now western Russia.[17] Slavs are, thus, the dominant ethnic group in what Harrison Salisbury rather dramatically (but not unreasonably) called "Mother Russia, the eternal land of the Slavs."[18] Hitler did not just begrudge the Eastern Slavs the great expanses that had been their heartland since time immemorial—running from north of Novgorod to what is now Minsk and on to Kyiv and nearly to the shores of the Black Sea. He begrudged the Slavs their very existence.

The most vivid and tragic confirmation of the essential nature of the war in the East is that the siege of Leningrad was never intended to be anything but that: a siege resulting in mass starvation. Although Hitler ultimately planned to level Leningrad,[19] a kinetic assault for the purpose of reducing the living inhabitants of Leningrad to Nazi rule was not in the cards. Leningrad never surrendered, and surrender would never have been accepted. Hitler's intent was to starve the city out of existence.[20] As for Moscow, Hitler said, "I will raze this damned city to the ground and I will make an artificial lake to provide energy for an electric power station. The name of Moscow will vanish forever."[21] The Russians (as well as their Slavic brethren from the Ukrainian SSR and the Belarusian SSR) knew what the Nazis had in mind for them. As historian Timothy Snyder puts it, the Russians knew they were fighting Hitler's design to "create a vast frontier empire ruled by Germans, bereft of Jews, and scantly peopled by Slavs reduced to slavery."[22] The Great Patriotic War was a race war and a war for survival in a sense that was simply not present in the other theaters of war.

It is quite natural that World War II would evoke divergent collective memories—with divergent political ramifications to this day—in East and West. For one thing, in the West, those who care about these things remember quite well that as a result of Stalin's intimacies with Hitler in August 1939, manifested in the Molotov-Ribbentrop nonaggression pact and its secret protocols, Russia sat out the first twenty-two months of the war in Europe. Only Britain and Germany were in the war in Europe from the first day to the last. This had ramifications even in American politics, ramifications directly attributable to the diverse European national heritages found in the US population. For millions of Americans of Polish, Estonian, Latvian, or Lithuanian extraction, the Molotov-Ribbentrop pact is no mere historical footnote. But, for the Russians, the story of the Molotov-Ribbentrop pact begins in the Sudetenland—the heavily industrialized and largely German-speaking western cape of Czechoslovakia, as that country existed in the late 1930s. Hitler wanted, and got, the Sudetenland in September 1938, in the infamous Munich agreement he negotiated with prime ministers Neville Chamberlain of the United Kingdom and Édouard Daladier of France. Chamberlain's objective for his country, still aching with memories of the horrific British losses in the Great War, was simple: peace at almost any price. In the eyes of the Kremlin, the essential purpose of the Munich agreement was to induce Germany to look east, at least for the first phase of the conquests envisioned by Hitler.[23]

Stalin's problem, with Germany now having been induced to look to the east, was not an ordinary long-range military planning problem. The Great Purge had ravaged the Red Army's officer corps. Mindful of the effect the purge had had on Russia's readiness to withstand a German assault, Stalin knew that it was necessary to forestall that assault. But if Stalin was going to treat with the Nazis, some preparations were in order. In May 1939, he replaced Maxim Litvinov, his Jewish foreign minister, with Vyacheslav Mikhailovich Molotov, who served in that capacity for ten years. For good measure, Stalin also directed Molotov to purge all Jews from his new ministry.[24] All of this proves the accuracy of George Kennan's pungent observation, in the fall of 1944, that Stalin was "not learned, yet shrewd and pitilessly realistic."[25] And for the Germans, the "pitiless realism" lay in the fact that Hitler was not about to risk invading Poland without knowing what Stalin's response would be.[26]

When Ribbentrop arrived in Moscow on August 23, 1939, to negotiate a nonaggression pact, he could not but have noticed that the airport—in the capital of world communism—was bedecked with swastikas.[27] Nazi flags were in short supply in Moscow, so for Ribbentrop's benefit the Russians commandeered a supply of Nazi flags from a studio, interrupting the production of an anti-Nazi film.[28] To the everlasting disillusionment of both Nazi and communist true believers, the Soviet-German deal quickly fell into place. In short order, Ribbentrop and Molotov crafted the seven articles of the public pact and the four articles of the secret protocols. Stalin was quite pleased. So it was that, on August 24, 1939, the general secretary of the Communist Party of the Soviet Union raised a toast to Hitler's health in the Kremlin ceremonies. A few thin sheets of parchment were all that stood between Hitler's divisions and the Russian heartland.

The nonaggression pact consisted of an exceedingly straightforward public agreement—nonaggression between the USSR and Germany for ten years and neutrality in the event either party should be attacked by a third nation—and the secret protocols. The public agreement was released immediately; the secret protocols, dividing up Poland and the Baltic states like so many pieces of real estate, did not see the light of day until after the war. As late as 1983, Molotov denied the existence of the protocols, calling the protocol narrative "a fabrication."[29] Nevertheless, one of the great ironies of the nonaggression pact and the protocols is that Stalin bought an unknown amount of time by giving up a vast amount of space. In these pages, that space, a buffer in its various geographic permutations, is referred to metaphorically as the *glacis*, a sloping earthen belt protecting a fortress. By treating with Hitler, Stalin made it perfectly legal, vis-à-vis the Soviet Union, for the Wehrmacht to move to the very borders of Soviet-controlled lands stretching from the Baltic to the Black Sea. Although the six-year-long cataclysm that was about to unfold would ultimately lead to Hitler's demise, those who suggest that Stalin got the better part of the 1939 transaction must account for the fact that Hitler bought Stalin's neutrality with lands that Hitler didn't even own. In return for Stalin's neutrality, Hitler gave Stalin half of Poland, with Latvia and Estonia (and soon Lithuania) thrown in for good measure. For his part, Stalin could go to sleep late on that August night with a deep sense of satisfaction that the pact just signed would, at least for the time being, guarantee that Bolshevism's most persistent adversaries—Germany and the Western powers—would soon be at each other's throats. For their part, the British would not soon forget that, while Britain was going it alone, Russia was supplying much of the raw material—including more than 40 percent of the oil—that Hitler needed to support the blitzkrieg.[30] Aside from that, as Churchill put it, "Every Communist in England, under orders from Moscow, did his best to hamper our war effort."[31]

Within the US population, the secret protocols are, without doubt, the most odious part of the Molotov-Ribbentrop pact. Many in the substantial Polish American population, concentrated in the industrial northeastern and Great Lakes states, were surely disappointed that the Russians and the Germans were not slaughtering each other from the outset of the war, but the secret protocols (with territorial revisions negotiated in the fall of 1939[32]) doomed Poland to dismemberment and all three of the Baltic states to Soviet annexation—ultimately to become republics of the Soviet Union. It comes, therefore, as no surprise that Polish Americans, to say nothing of Americans of Baltic extraction, reserved special contempt for the secret protocols and the resultant obliteration of Poland and the Baltics as free states.

By Molotov's account (decades later), the effect of the Molotov-Ribbentrop pact was that "we delayed the war. This calmed the people a little."[33] Before daybreak on June 22, 1941, one year, nine months, and twenty-nine days after Stalin drank to Hitler's health in Moscow, Ribbentrop delivered a formal declaration of war to the Soviet ambassador in Berlin. With no warning from the Reich, but with ample warning from other quarters,[34] Germany hurled more than three million troops across a front stretching from the Baltic coast to the Black Sea. The people were not calmed. The advice from Secretary of War Henry Stimson to President Roosevelt was that it would take a minimum of one month, and possibly as much as three months, for Germany to defeat Russia.[35]

The Magnitude of the Struggle and Its Human Cost

The war of annihilation on the eastern front was fought on a scale and with a ruthlessness and savagery unknown in the West. The Soviet Union won the war in the East in large part because of the ability of that nation—singular among the combatant nations—to absorb enormous material and human losses. The Soviet Union, not Germany, had what was, for all practical purposes, an inexhaustible supply of compliant, fatalistic young men. In no other nation could so many millions of them die without causing the collapse of the ruling regime. The magnitude of the struggle and its human cost resonate to this day in Russian consciousness.

Although President Vladimir Putin can be relied upon to wave the bloody shirt of the Great Patriotic War, the enormity of the sacrifice and the glory of the victory, for crass political reasons, cynical political use of the collective memory of that war is not a predominant cause of present-day Russian consciousness of the war and the impact it had on every person at every level of society. The somber war memorials found in cities and villages throughout Russia are not the result of recent political calculation. For Russians, despite efforts to politicize the event, Victory Day is more personal—for most, rooted in their own family history—than political. It simply does not matter in the end whether or to what extent Russia's current collective consciousness of the war is in part the product of political opportunism. What does matter is that this consciousness does exist and still makes a difference. As President John F. Kennedy put it, "No nation in the history of battle ever suffered more than the Soviet Union suffered in the course of the Second World War."[36]

Assault and Occupation

Launched on June 22, 1941, and conceived of by Hitler long before he set plans in motion by signing Directive No. 21 in December 1940, Operation Barbarossa was (and remains) the most massive invasion in the history of warfare. Although several nations had informed the Kremlin of strong intelligence indications that Hitler was preparing to attack to the east, it is fair to say that the launch of Barbarossa, with its audacity and sheer scale, stunned the world. But, for some in the United States, the invasion was not without its practical aspects. Harry S. Truman, then the junior US senator from Missouri, undoubtedly echoing the views of millions of Americans, commented that "if we see that Germany is winning we ought to help Russia." He went on to say, "and if Russia is winning we ought to help Germany, and that way let them kill as many as possible, although I don't want to see Hitler victorious under any circumstances."[37] Four years later, Truman, as president of the United States, sat across the table from Marshal Stalin at Potsdam.

By the end of June, thousands of Red Army aircraft had been destroyed by the Luftwaffe—mostly as they sat on the ground. The Wehrmacht quickly overran lands that had been home to 40 percent of the Soviet population, a territory which had produced 65 percent of the USSR's coal and nearly 70 percent of its iron.[38] Ninety million people were trapped in territory controlled by the Germans.[39] Proportionately to the US population as measured by the 1940 US census, the equivalent number of Americans trapped in occupied territory would have been fifty-three million. By the end of November, more than a thousand factories were dismantled, to be reassembled in the Ural region, Central Asia, and Siberia. The occupied lands remained in German control until they were reclaimed at a cost of millions of lives.

Moscow, Leningrad, and Stalingrad

Moscow. Even though the Barbarossa invasion was mounted along an exceptionally long front, taking Moscow was the linchpin of Hitler's strategy for defeating the Soviet Union in a short war. Hitler was right that Moscow was important. Moscow was so important that thousands of women, shovels in hand, dug anti-tank trenches to defend the capital from the panzer divisions. Fittingly, on the highway from central Moscow to Sheremetyevo Airport, there is a sculpture of a giant tank trap, marking the closest the Wehrmacht got to the center of the city—fourteen miles from the Kremlin. Hitler discovered what Kennan would later describe as "the impossibility of combatting simultaneously both the Russian people and the Soviet Government."[40]

On December 5, 1941, the Red Army went on the offensive at Moscow. Wehrmacht troops tasted real defeat for the first time. The illusion of a short war—a promise all too frequently made by general officers to national leaders—evaporated. For the Germans, there would be no more huge territorial gains at minimal cost.

The Red Army's victory at Moscow did not come cheap. Soviet losses in 1941 (from the beginning of Barbarossa to the end of the year, encompassing the Battle of Moscow and the fighting as the Wehrmacht pressed east to the outskirts of Moscow) came to 4.5 million, including those who were killed in action, died later of wounds, or were missing in action or prisoners of war.[41]

Leningrad. In describing the overall human cost of the Great Patriotic War, Leningrad, where Putin was born and raised, is a special case. The immense human cost of that battle was not a byproduct of the war. In Leningrad, the human cost was *the purpose* of the war, so, in that sense, the human cost is inseparable from the rest of the story.

The siege of Leningrad started in September 1941 and was lifted nearly nine hundred days later in January 1944. No major population center has ever had to endure the grim fate Leningrad endured for nearly thirty months. Although some supply lines were maintained across Lake Ladoga (and on the ice in the winter), starvation nevertheless claimed the lives of more than six hundred thousand in Leningrad.[42] Harrison Salisbury, who won a Pulitzer Prize for his reporting from the Soviet Union in the years after World War II, recounted the heartbreakingly poignant story of a girl who survived the siege: how she described the strongest residents making daily rounds of apartments, taking stock of the living and carrying away the dead in sleds; her evening census to see if her friends were still living; and the realization that two, "sitting so quietly, would never move again—dead of cold and hunger in the huddled circle of the living."[43]

Stalingrad. The Volga is as revered by Russians as the Mississippi is by Americans. But, alas, the East European Plain, stretching to the Volga and beyond, is as inviting to invaders as the Atlantic is forbidding. So, when the Wehrmacht stood on the Volga at Stalingrad, it was an existential moment like none other before or since for the Russian people.

Flowing from its headwaters northwest of Moscow to the Caspian Sea, the Volga, more than any other natural feature, defines the heartland of European Russia. It was bad enough for the Wehrmacht, headed east, to cross the Don, as it did in July 1942. Then, shortly before midnight on August 16, "a panzer unit radioed that it had penetrated the northern suburbs of Stalingrad and had reached the river that flows on to the Caspian. The Germans were on the Volga."[44]

The Battle of Stalingrad has its place in history because, on November 19, generals Georgy Zhukov and Alexander Vasilevsky launched a successful counteroffensive, a massive pincer movement, from north and south of the city. By the time it was over, more than ninety thousand Germans were taken captive, including twenty-three generals. "The Stalingrad pit," as Brian Moynahan puts it, "had consumed a crack army, mangled the Luftwaffe, broken the morale of the satellite Italians, Rumanians and Hungarians and destroyed any realistic German hopes of knocking out the Red army with a final blow."[45] Both the Soviet Union and communism had survived. They were now headed for Berlin and global power.

The Unfathomable Sum: The Dead and the Physical Destruction

One cannot understand why the Cold War's immediate origins and its historical antecedents still resonate in the collective consciousness of the Russian people without reckoning with the astonishing human and material cost of World War II in the East.

World War II was the first war in history in which the military strategies of at least some of the belligerent nations included the mass killing of noncombatant civilians. (This includes not least the military strategies of the United States and United Kingdom. In March 1945, the first US firebombing of Tokyo, under the command of General Curtis LeMay, killed an estimated hundred thousand Japanese—the highest death toll of any air raid to that point in the war.[46]) Because the fog of war never quite clears, reckonings of the numbers of civilian and military deaths in World War II are, and always will be, unavoidably imprecise. But credible authors have made convincing estimates.

Civilians. The number of Soviet civilians killed is credibly estimated to have been at least seven million. The number of US civilians killed on the US mainland: six—Elsie Mitchell and five children from a Sunday school class, killed on Gearhart Mountain in Oregon while on a church picnic. They died on May 5, 1945, three months before the end of the war and long after the final outcome of the Pacific war had become inevitable. The weapon: a crude balloon bomb—ten meters in diameter, made of paper and paste—launched from Japan in the hope that the jet stream would carry it to the western United States.[47] That fatal balloon bomb, the only successful one of thousands launched from Japan, may have crossed paths, outbound from Japan, with any one of hundreds of B-29 bombers that were incinerating major Japanese cities in the final phase of the war in the Pacific.

Perhaps the first thing to remember about the Soviet civilians who died in the Great Patriotic War is that they died from starvation and the rigors of flight, as well as from bombs, artillery, and one-on-one killings. Of some 7 million[48] Soviet civilians who were killed in the war and the occupation, about 4.2 million were starved by the German occupiers.[49] Among the Soviet republics, Russia fared comparatively well. The Wehrmacht didn't make it past the Volga, whereas Ukraine and Belorussia were totally engulfed in the war in the East. The result is that, as estimated by the scholar of Russian politics Richard Sakwa, the Germans killed about one in twenty-five Russians, about one in ten Ukrainians and—astonishingly—about one in five Belarusians.[50]

Military. As is doubtless the case with reckonings of civilian deaths, estimation of the number of Soviet military deaths in the Great Patriotic War was aided by the opening of archives after the dissolution of the Soviet Union. In 2007, the Russian government's figure for Soviet military losses in the war was 8.86 million.[51] The Red Army lost 4.5 million men—killed or taken prisoner—in the first six months of the war.[52] The victory at Stalingrad came at the expense of more military deaths—just under a half-million—than the military death toll for all of World War II for US forces.[53] The death rate for Red Army soldiers in German prison camps was 57.5 percent.[54]

Let us pause briefly, then, to survey the numbers, as numbing as they are. Relatively recent and credible estimates for the total Soviet military and civilian death toll in the war in the East range from twenty to twenty-seven million.[55] The twenty-seven million figure has assumed at least semiofficial status and has been cited by Putin.[56] For the entire duration of the war in the East, using the Russian government's 2007 estimate of Soviet military dead, the death toll came to more than six thousand a day.

The numerical odds are at least as startling as the raw numbers: four-fifths of Soviet boys born in 1922 were dead by 1945.[57] The numbers cannot begin to tell the entire story. Anatoly Yakovlevich, who fought all the way to Berlin after being drafted in 1943, lost his father, six brothers, and six uncles. Two surviving uncles lost a leg and an eye, respectively, while Anatoly was twice wounded.[58]

The Legacy

In August 1945, General Dwight Eisenhower flew with Marshal Zhukov from Berlin to Moscow in Eisenhower's personal military transport. The weather was clear and the airplane flew low, so the generals could survey the landscape as they traversed the East European Plain. Eisenhower wrote, "I did not see a house standing between the western borders of the country and the area around Moscow."[59] Counting occupied Russia, Ukraine, and Belorussia, the landscape of unrelieved devastation and human destitution encompassed an area about two-thirds the size of the United States east of the Mississippi.

In the countryside, the devastation was complete. As recorded by Marshal V. D. Sokolovskiy, "In the Soviet Union alone, over 70,000 towns and villages and 1,710 cities were completely or partially destroyed and burned."[60] Russian food output had fallen by two-thirds.[61] In thousands of villages in the occupied regions, women, children, and old men had been reduced to a primitive level of subsistence in which there were two choices: be all but completely self-sufficient for the necessities of life, or die, a reality movingly described in the second chapter of Mikhail S. Gorbachev's memoir.[62]

As the international affairs scholar Gerard Toal succinctly puts it, "The Soviet victory over Nazism is a sacred memory of collective suffering before the glory of victory."[63] Victory Day (9 May) remains the country's most important national holiday, not least for the sacrifice and ongoing demographic consequences felt across the Soviet empire. Aside from the other ways in which the Great Patriotic War has such enormous and enduring significance in Russian popular consciousness, it plays a powerful morally didactic role, as can be seen in the public squares of Russian cities and towns on Victory Day.

Postwar demographics. The age pyramids, as the demographers call them, tell the tale. A comparison of the 1941 and 1946 pyramids is telling.

Few able-bodied young Russian men were near home between 1942 and the middle of 1945. More than thirty-four million men were drafted by all the Soviet services.[64] And in 1946, young fathers (and husbands) were still in short supply in Russia because so many millions of the young men never came home at all. In the immediate postwar years, there were about twenty million more women than men in the Soviet Union as a whole. Consequently, it was not until 1956 that the Soviet population finally reached the 1941 level of two hundred million.

The demographic effect of the absence of young fathers during and after the war—a huge disparity in the male-female ratio—was compounded by the vast destruction of national wealth and the sheer dislocation of millions of families. The birthrate plummeted, but the millions of Russian children who were not born (but *would* have been born if normal

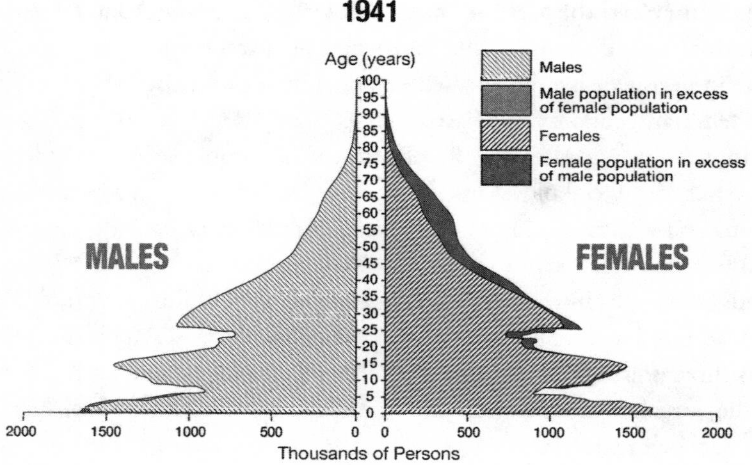

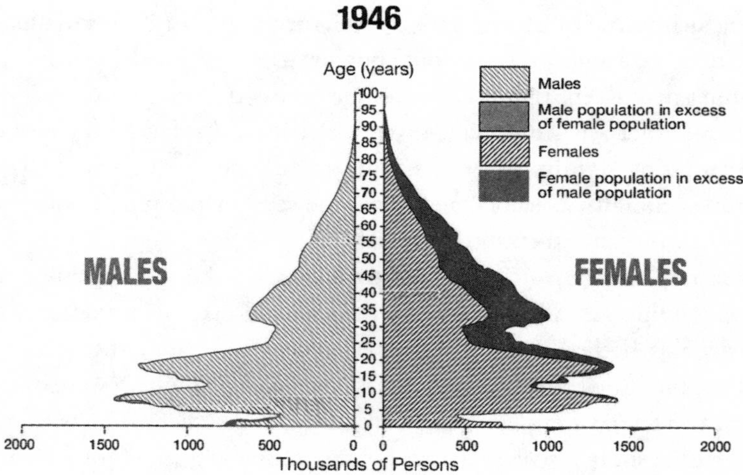

Figure 1. Age and gender composition of the Russian Soviet Federative Socialist Republic in 1941 and 1946. The vertical axis is age. The horizontal axis is population (for each age group), in thousands. Males on the left; females on the right. The darker shading on the right side of the graph indicates female population, by age group, in excess of the male population. The 1941 graph shows two declines in the birthrate, coinciding with the upheavals of the Bolshevik Revolution and the Great Terror of the Stalin era. The 1941 graph is broadest, as one would expect, at the base: barring cataclysmic events, the infant and toddler age groups will outnumber the other age groups. Data source: *The Great Patriotic War: Anniversary Statistical Collection* (Moscow: Federal-State Statistics Service–Rosstat, 2015).

demographic trends had prevailed) in the postwar years are not, of course, counted among the war dead. Even so, the absence of those who were not born at all has arguably had as much effect on Russian society and the Russian economy as the loss of the tens of millions of soldiers and civilians who were killed in the war. Consequently, the base of the age pyramid for 1946 shows demographic effects of the war that reverberated in Russian society (to say nothing of the economy) for decades.

After the war, the horrendous human cost of the war in the East gave the Russians what Catherine Merridale aptly calls "a certain moral leverage."[65] This cannot but have been in the mix at Yalta and Potsdam—especially at Potsdam where, by the time the conference was over, Marshal Stalin was at the table with a US president who had been in office for about fourteen weeks and a British prime minister who had been in office for eight days.

The Geopolitics of the War. Germany did not lose the war at Stalingrad. But after Stalingrad and its summer sequel, the battle of Kursk, the Germans no longer had a war they could win. Thus, though the Cold War began with the rhetorical exchange between Stalin and Churchill in the winter of 1946, East-West tectonic stresses began to build as early as the winter of 1943, in the wake of that epochal Russian victory. Once it became plain that Germany could not win the war, it became quite possible—if not inevitable—that a divergence of strategic objectives would begin to take root in the Grand Alliance. As historian David Kennedy put it, Stalingrad "rewrote the . . . fundamental strategic equation."[66]

Kursk, as Marshal Zhukov recorded in his memoirs, "was to be the last significant German offensive of the war. Thereafter it was retreat all the way back to Berlin."[67] Generalplan Ost—the Nazi vision of a vast eastern empire built on the bones of millions of starved Slavs—was shattered. The Germans were fighting to save themselves. In terms of strategic significance (leaving aside their sheer scale and appalling human cost), Stalingrad and Kursk simply had no parallels on the western front. After Stalingrad and Kursk, it was obvious in western capitals that in future decades it would take more than the hedgerows of France to keep the mechanized Red Army away from the English Channel. Unsurprisingly, after Stalingrad and Kursk, long-range thinkers in Washington and London stopped worrying about how weak the Red Army was and started worrying about how *strong* the Red Army was.

Chapter 1

The Second Front

The story of the second front is a stark reminder of how two different perspectives on a geopolitical problem—the view from the East versus the view from the West—can yield radically differing historical narratives that persist in the current century.

Russian historians tend to tread lightly on the fact that, thanks to the Molotov-Ribbentrop pact, Russia sat out the first two years of the war. Western historians tend to tread lightly on the fact that the cross-channel invasion, the need for which was obvious by the end of 1941, was not launched for more than a year after the tide had turned in the East. In Russia, to this day, the Great Patriotic War narrative is colored, and in some ways propelled in a certain direction, by what the Russians thought then and think now was an unconscionable delay—expedient at best and malevolent at worst—in opening up the second front in France.

Both the Russian version and the Western version can be supported with historical facts. Allowing for the practical realities confronting all the Allies in 1942, the debate really boils down to the question of whether the cross-channel invasion could have and should have been mounted in mid-1943 rather than a year later, after millions more Soviet troops bled on the soil of Ukraine, Poland, Belorussia, Romania, and the Baltics. For the Western Allies, an unsuccessful cross-channel invasion would have been an unimaginable catastrophe. The case can be convincingly made that an invasion before the spring of 1944 would have carried with it the enormous risk of just that catastrophic outcome. The desperate evacuation of the British Expeditionary Force and French troops from the beaches at Dunkirk in the spring of 1940 was, by this reckoning, but a small-scale dress rehearsal for the disaster of an ill-timed cross-channel invasion.

The Soviets, of course, had no reason to talk publicly about a cross-channel invasion until after Barbarossa was launched in June 1941. But once the Wehrmacht was streaming east, Stalin hastened to raise the issue of the second front. On July 18, just short of a month after hundreds of divisions from Germany and its cobelligerents poured into the Soviet Union, Stalin wrote to Churchill, offering military advice along with some good-natured political counsel. He argued for the prompt opening of a second front because, among other reasons, "the establishment of the front just mentioned would be popular with the British Army, as well as with the whole population of Southern England."[68] Churchill offered little comfort to Stalin, responding two days later that "from the first day of the German attack upon Russia we have examined the possibilities of attacking Occupied France and the Low Countries. The Chiefs of Staff do not see any way of doing anything on a scale likely to be of the slightest use to you."[69] So much for that.

Even as early as 1942, Stalin had cause—thanks to Franklin D. Roosevelt—for getting a bit testy about the second front. Roosevelt had invited Molotov to Washington, DC, in May 1942, for, as the White House put it, "a friendly exchange of views between the President and his advisers on the one hand and Mr. Molotov and his party on the other."[70] Molotov's visit began on May 29, culminating in a June 11 communiqué that included the following passage *specifically* approved by Roosevelt, to the great consternation (and notwithstanding the advice) of Army chief of staff George C. Marshall: "In the course of the conversations full understanding was reached with regard to the urgent tasks of creating a second front in Europe in 1942."[71] Molotov quickly returned to Moscow with the good news about the second front. The Soviet press, taking its cue from a speech by Molotov to the Supreme Soviet on June 18, "promptly spread the word throughout the country that Allied landings in the west were near."[72]

Informed by advice from a source as impeccable as General Marshall, Roosevelt could not have believed in June 1942 that a second front in Europe was feasible that year. Molotov and Stalin didn't believe it, either. Felix Chuev, Molotov's scribe for the work that amounted to his memoirs, recorded that Molotov and Stalin "were perfectly aware that the United States and Britain could not successfully launch a second front in Western Europe in 1942 or in 1943 for that matter."[73] Stalin was no fool. He knew that an unkept promise from the president of the United States might be useful later.

A bit of historiography is enlightening on the question of whether Russians were inclined, after the war, to forget about the delay of the cross-channel invasion. Marshal Zhukov, writing in the late 1960s, was no more gentle than Stalin had been in 1942: "According to Eisenhower, [the western Allies] could not open a second front in 1942–1943 allegedly because they were not prepared for this major combined strategic operation. That was certainly far from the truth. They could open a second front in 1943, but they wittingly did not hurry to do so, waiting for our troops to inflict greater damage on Germany's armed forces and, consequently, to become more exhausted."[74] Lest there be any notion that the passage of time has softened hard feelings, Zhukov's account of the Western Allies' motives in waiting until 1944 to launch the cross-channel invasion still has currency in Russia.

The Western Allies had several options available after the Axis powers surrendered in North Africa in May 1943. After the dust settled there, General Marshall, the chairman of the US Joint Chiefs of Staff, turned to serious advocacy of a cross-channel invasion of France, but the British were having none of it. Still bitter in their mouths was the taste of the desperate evacuation at Dunkirk in 1940 and the disastrous landing at Dieppe in 1942, to say nothing of the fall of Singapore, highly inconvenient stirrings of nationalism in India, and the British surrender at Tobruk, all also in 1942. True, the Nazis stood just across the channel—on a clear day, Nazi officers could easily see the white cliffs of Dover. Even so, and despite the fact that the *Kriegsmarine's* cruisers *Gneisenau* and *Scharnhorst* had insolently forced the Strait of Dover in broad daylight in February 1942, the British felt reasonably safe. Hitler's abandonment of Operation Sea Lion—Germany's cross-channel invasion—in the fall of 1940 was but a recognition that the Third Reich was not prepared to attempt what no one had successfully attempted since 1066: to invade England. The British Isles were not in immediate peril, so why hurry? Also of concern to Churchill and his British constituents was the fact that there was an empire to protect. Churchill was well aware that the empire could be lost even if the war was, by some standards, won. Control of Gibraltar and the Suez Canal meant much more in London than in Washington. And Churchill was keenly aware that, in any event, the empire would need some shoring up after the war.

By late 1943, it was, of course, obvious to the leadership of all the Allies that a cross-channel invasion would have to be launched, if launched at all, not later than the spring of 1944. If it were much later than that, the Red Army would be running the wharves at Le Havre and pouring the wine in Caen. Thus, as recorded by Zhukov, it was in an April 1944 meeting with the Soviet Supreme Command that Stalin observed: "In June the Allies intend to finally conduct a major landing operation in

France. Our allies are in a hurry," Stalin smiled. "They are afraid that we will rout Nazi Germany without them."[75]

On D-Day, June 6, 1944, Germany had 193 divisions on the eastern front and in southeastern Europe, compared with twenty-eight in Italy, eighteen in Norway and Denmark, and fifty-nine in France and the Low Countries. Although the Wehrmacht could still field almost two thousand tanks and other armored vehicles in northwestern Europe, almost two-thirds of Nazi combat strength remained committed to the fight in the East.[76] The war in Europe was over eleven months later.

The delay of the cross-channel invasion invites—and by some standards compels—a geopolitical interpretation. For politicians, generals, and admirals in the West, the question was, What degree of risk of failure was acceptable? Overlaying that politico-military question were geopolitical questions of enormous magnitude. The delay until mid-1944 made it possible for US arms manufacturers to produce a much larger arsenal of aircraft, armored vehicles, and other weapons than would have been possible for an invasion in 1943. Conversely, by mid-1944, the Luftwaffe was not, and could not be, a major factor in Hitler's response to the Normandy invasion. Stalin freely acknowledged that the cross-channel invasion was superbly planned and executed. But in 1945 and in the first decades of the twenty-first century, most Russians would maintain that there is more to the story than that. President Truman acknowledged as much when he wrote in his memoirs (published ten years after the war) that "the Russians, though fighting for their own survival, had saved us many lives in the war against the Germans."[77]

Peace

On April 12, 1945, the day Roosevelt died, the Berlin Philharmonic gave its final concert at the Philharmonic Hall. The hall was unheated. The electricity was unreliable. The howitzers of Zhukov's First Belarusian Front stood on the Oder, almost within earshot of the concert hall. Fittingly, the program concluded with the finale from Richard Wagner's *Götterdämmerung* (Twilight of the Gods).[78] Reportedly, members of the Hitler Youth offered cyanide tablets to the concertgoers as they left Philharmonic Hall.[79] Apocalypse had arrived. It was a scene that not even

Figure 2. The Hammer and Sickle flies over the Reichstag.

Cecil B. DeMille could have matched. This performance stood in stark contrast to the emotionally overpowering premiere of Sergei Prokofiev's Fifth Symphony at the Moscow Conservatory, a bare three months before the April performance of *Götterdämmerung*. Prokofiev personally conducted the orchestra. The performance was delayed by the sound of cannon fire. But "the salvos that delayed the performance came from Soviet cannons, paying tribute to the Red Army soldiers crossing the Vistula on their victory march toward soon-to-be-defeated Germany. Peace was near, only four months away."[80] Germany, largely landlocked and virtually friendless, had been exposed since the late nineteenth century to the prospect, if not the probability, of catastrophic two-front wars. Hitler had made it happen for the second time.

Peace did not come quickly, or without immense cost in blood and treasure, even after it became clear that the Germans could not win. But as the Allies closed in from east and west in the spring of 1945, the conventional wisdom in Berlin was that optimists were learning English and pessimists were learning Russian.[81] Although some on the Russian general staff were concerned that the Western Allies would take Berlin and receive the German surrender there, General Eisenhower, in keeping with assurances he had given to his Russian counterparts, held the Western forces back.

Although historical accounts differ as to which Red Army troops had the honor, on May 2, the Soviet flag was raised over the Reichstag. It is fair to say, as historian Stephen Kotkin puts it, this was for Russia "the pivot of the twentieth century."[82]

Chapter 2

The Geopolitics of the Peace, 1945–1952

War is God's way of teaching Americans geography.
—attributed to Ambrose Bierce

As the war drew to a close, centrifugal forces within the Grand Alliance could no longer be ignored. As a witch's brew of geopolitics and domestic politics came to the fore, involving Russian, American, British, and even German elements, among others, considerations of military comradeship within the alliance no longer sufficed to defer the hard geopolitical questions that had lain mostly beneath the surface, suppressed for the sake of the war effort, since 1939. To take but one example, the issue of the location of the Polish-German border was no longer just a matter of conjecture and posturing as the Red Army pushed west across the Vistula. It was obvious (as early as the Tehran conference in late 1943, if not before) that the Polish-German border as fixed in the Treaty of Versailles of 1919 would move west—but how far west? The issue was debated but left undecided at the Yalta conference in February 1945. The issue was decided, at least as a de facto proposition, at the Potsdam conference in July and August of 1945.

Nearly everything Stalin said and did in wartime and postwar conferences can be attributed to his desire to reduce to an absolute minimum the likelihood that the USSR could ever again be penetrated from the west as deeply as it had been in 1941 (to say nothing, in the case of Russia, of 1812 and 1918).

Before we expand on that subject, a concept that has always had currency in the Kremlin, but which is scarcely mentioned in the West, must be addressed.

A Brief Digression: Encirclement

For the Soviet Union and for Russia (both before and after the Soviet Union), a good working definition of encirclement, as an element of geostrategic doctrine and domestic political discourse, is that it is "the fear *of*, the anxiety *about* one's own nation being ringed in systematically, in the manner of a conspiracy planned and executed by foreign enemies."[1] Regardless of whether encirclement is a legitimate concern of Russian leaders in the twenty-first century, there is no room for doubt that encirclement animated the discussion from the Soviet side when the postwar world order was debated in 1945. The first thing to remember about encirclement is that its two variations, though interrelated, are nevertheless distinct.

The less important variation of encirclement, at least for present purposes, is the communist concept of capitalist encirclement (*kapitalisticheskoe okruzhenie*). It was a convenient element of communist doctrine because it provided a useful pretext for the strengthening of the Soviet state—not the withering away of the state as posited by Marxian doctrine. The problem was that, according to Stalin, "as long as the capitalist encirclement exists there will continue to be present among us wreckers, spies, saboteurs and murderers."[2] Consequently, in 1947, *Izvestia* quoted Stalin as saying that "the state will continue to exist under communism unless capitalist encirclement is eliminated and replaced by Communist encirclement."[3] Only then, Stalin said, would the state wither away. This, then, was the *domestic political* concept of encirclement. But more important for present purposes was (and is) the geostrategic concept of encirclement as understood by Stalin in 1945 and by Russian leaders ever since.

As for *geostrategic encirclement*, the combined effect of history and geographic (and topographic) realities was that, by the spring of 1945, the Soviet Union had, within living memory (and several times over), gained, lost, and then redeemed in blood huge swaths of its sovereign territory. Thus, Stalin came by his abhorrence of encirclement honestly.

Because Kremlin rulers had for centuries been obsessed with the fear of encirclement, they had for centuries pushed back against encircling powers. Even a skeptic such as Alfred Vagts (a German historian who emigrated to the United States and accepted a position at the Institute for Advanced Study at Princeton University), exploring the reasons for what he called the Russian "encirclement complex," allowed that "the contemplation of a country's situation from a geopolitical, diplomatic, military point of view might at least partly justify a serious, objectively speaking legitimate, concern with encirclement."[4] In 1945, Stalin had new reasons to give vent to his abhorrence of encirclement as one of the main drivers of postwar Soviet words and actions.

Yalta and Potsdam

Everyone imposes his own system as far as his army can reach. It cannot be otherwise.

—Marshal Stalin, speaking to Yugoslav communist leaders in April 1945

I take this with some reservation.

—Ambassador W. Averell Harriman, commenting to President Roosevelt on Molotov's statement that the Soviet Union was willing to have a strong, independent Poland

It is tempting, and arguably accurate as a historical matter, to say that Stalin's pronouncement quoted above suffices as a complete explanation of why the conferences at Yalta and Potsdam in 1945 ended as they did and led, as they did, to the geopolitical structure that prevailed in Europe for forty-five years. It is not much (if any) more complicated than that. But the details are, of course, more complicated. The details deserve attention because "Yalta" (or, more to the point, the "sellout at Yalta") became a political rallying cry in the United States for decades after the war. Yalta and Potsdam tell us much about why the Cold War unfolded as it did.

It may be helpful to start with a brief visit to the end of the Yalta story—"Yalta" being the pejorative political term for the combined results of the Yalta and Potsdam conferences in February and July 1945.

The end of the story is that Yalta is to blame for the extension of Russian hegemony far west of the boundaries of the USSR, all of which is, according to the most charitable of the critics, attributable to the fact that the United States was represented by a dying man in those negotiations.[5] Thus, Yalta, as a political rallying cry in the United States, is now in its eighth decade, synonymous with Western weakness at the bargaining table at which the postwar fate of hundreds of millions of people was sealed. But notwithstanding decades of recriminations about Yalta, the real question is: Did Yalta *avoidably* set the stage for the division of Europe into two geopolitical spheres? More broadly, did Yalta *avoidably* set the stage for the Cold War? This is where the realpolitik of 1945 clashes with Cold War rhetoric.

Now for the beginning of the Yalta story. Looking back from February of 1945, when Churchill and Roosevelt came to the table, hosted by Stalin at the Livadia Palace on the south coast of Crimea, a good beginning point is the Red Army's costly but crushing victories over the Wehrmacht at Stalingrad in February 1943 and at Kursk that July. In the wake of those victories (ten months before the cross-channel invasion and eighteen months before the Yalta conference), Major General J. H. Burns addressed an evaluation of the strategic situation to Harry Hopkins, Roosevelt's alter ego. Burns's conclusion: "Russia's post-war position in Europe will be a dominant one. With Germany crushed, there is no power in Europe to oppose her tremendous military forces."[6] Soon after Burns penned his memo, Stanley K. Hornbeck, advisor on political relations to Secretary of State Cordell Hull, explained the matter in geopolitical terms, commenting that "the Soviet Government has as one of its paramount political objectives the creation of well-disposed and ideologically sympathetic governments in nearby areas."[7] That was true of the Soviet Union in the 1940s, and is, to put it mildly, true of Russia under Putin. That has also been true of the United States since at least as far back as the administration of President James Monroe.

In the meantime, in 1943, there was a war to fight. Concern for the postwar geopolitical lineup was not yet dominant within the councils of the US government. It was provident, for that reason, that W. Averell Harriman was from October 1943 to January 1946 the US ambassador to the Soviet Union. Harriman, whose career in public service spanned parts of five decades, first set foot in Russia in 1899 as a seven-year-old boy.[8] (He was the son of railroad and steamship magnate E. H. Harriman.) As a confirmed capitalist (his career in public service having substantially overlapped with his career as an investment banker), Harriman dealt effectively in both business matters and public affairs with a succession of Soviet leaders who felt more at ease dealing with a true capitalist than with borderline socialists who might be tempted to pander to the Bolsheviks by professing sympathy with their cause.[9]

Because of his age, his breeding in the eastern aristocracy, and his distinguished career in business and in public service, Harriman had, to an unusual degree for an ambassador, direct access to President Roosevelt. In early November 1943, about a month before the Tehran conference (the first of the wartime conferences to be attended by all three of the leaders of the Grand Alliance), Harriman sought to dispel any notion that Stalin and Molotov would sit still for anything other than a compliant postwar regime in Poland. As for Molotov's claim that the Kremlin was "willing to have a strong independent Poland, giving expression to whatever social and political system the Polish people wanted," Harriman's response, expressed with his typical understatement, was that "I take this with some reservation."[10] To Harriman, a more reliable indication of the Kremlin's intent was Molotov's statement that the Russians "would take unilateral action in respect to [the border countries] in the establishment of relations satisfactory to themselves." That was a concise statement of the Russian prescription for relations with Eastern Europe for the next five decades—and again in the first two decades of the twenty-first century.

The need for another conference of the Big Three was obvious by late 1944, with the forces of the Grand Alliance closing in on the Reich from east and west. Stalin knew he would be dealing from a position of strength in the end-of-war talks. He had the largest army in the world. Most of that army was in Central Europe, headed west. He had no reason to doubt that when the shooting stopped, the Red Army would control much of Germany and Austria, to say nothing of Poland, Czechoslovakia, Hungary, the Baltics, and the Balkans. Of at least equal importance, if the use of force (or a credible threat of force) were to become necessary to bring about a final resolution of what country controlled what lands and peoples after the collapse of the Reich, the only political will that really mattered on the Soviet side was that of Marshal Stalin and the

Politburo. That advantage was as well known to Churchill and Roosevelt as it was to Stalin.

Because he did not want the advantages of strategic depth ever again to be demonstrated on Eastern Slav lands, Stalin's paramount objective was to extend the Soviet Union's glacis as far west as possible. This would be a protective belt *west* of the historic *Rus*. The United States had the Atlantic Ocean. Stalin, having no ocean to the west, needed land.

But there was a counterpoint to all of this. Stalin was aware that, among the Western powers, the United States would finish the war in the strongest position. He knew that US development of an atomic bomb was at an advanced stage and that development of a Russian bomb was still years away. He knew that the United States was invulnerable to attack by ground forces. L. D. Wilgress, Canada's ambassador to the Soviet Union, reported to the Canadian prime minister, the iconic W. L. Mackenzie King, that the Soviet government "fear[ed] the possibility of future clashes with the North American colossus if the latter becomes embroiled in any of the countries bordering on the Soviet Union."[11]

What later became the great power standoff was also presaged with remarkable clarity in the months before Yalta by George Kennan, the newly appointed US chargé d'affaires in Moscow. He put it quite simply: the Russians "will be confident that they can arrange the affairs of Eastern Europe to their own liking without great difficulty, and they will not be inclined to go far out of their way either for the Poles or for us."[12]

By late 1944, a fair approximation of the issues to be faced at the end of the war could quite readily be discerned. In October 1944, Churchill, his foreign secretary Anthony Eden, US Ambassador Averell Harriman and their military advisors met in Moscow with Stalin and Molotov. Churchill, Stalin, and their conferees (but not Harriman, in this session) had a meeting at the Kremlin late in the evening of October 9. The record of that meeting has Churchill counseling Stalin "not to use the phrase 'dividing into spheres,' because the Americans might be shocked."[13] This tellingly foreshadowed the Yalta conference and its aftermath, because there is no room for doubt that Stalin had his sphere in mind—essentially, Europe east of the Red Army's westernmost encampment—and Churchill had his: the British Empire, which was not yet (at least not obviously) a historical relic. Churchill and Stalin then embarked on a tour d'horizon of central Europe and the Balkans, exchanging their views as to who should hold sway in Poland, Greece, Romania, Hungary, Yugoslavia, Bulgaria, Turkey, and Italy. Churchill and Stalin agreed on an apportionment of influence in the Balkans, where two of the tectonic plates of human civilization meet and sometimes grind against each other. But, in some ways, US sensibilities were taken into account at this mid-October meeting: Churchill said, "Britain would like the Soviet Union to soft-pedal the Communists in Italy and not to stir them up." His concern was not so much for the Italians as such. The prime minister allowed that "the Italians were in a miserable condition. He did not think much of them as a people, but they had a good many votes in New York State."[14] In this, Churchill was correct. Eight days later, in another late-night session with Churchill at the Kremlin, Stalin observed (surely with a twinkle in his eye) that "the Poles deserved to get territory on their Western borders. They had suffered much for over a century."[15]

After it became obvious that the leaders of the Grand Alliance had to meet again before the end of the war, Stalin wisely insisted that the conference take place in Russia—Crimea, to be exact. The trip to Yalta was not an easy one for Churchill and the ailing Roosevelt. After Churchill and Roosevelt had a preparatory conference from January 30–February 2, 1945, in Malta, they proceeded by air (at no small risk to themselves from possible attack over the Balkans by what was left of the Luftwaffe) to the Crimea. Yalta was accessible by air, but Stalin arranged for the two Western leaders to land at a location eighty miles from Yalta, requiring them to embark on a long drive over rough roads to Yalta in vehicles furnished by the Soviet government and driven by Russian drivers. From Stalin's perspective, there was good reason for the two Western leaders to take that long drive: At a cost of well over a million lives, Crimea had been overrun and reclaimed twice during the war, leaving a devastated wasteland, strewn with wreckage and rubble.[16] That devastation provided a vivid predicate for Stalin's demands in Eastern Europe, as well as a reminder that three quarters of all German losses had been on the eastern front.[17]

Three Nations, Three Perspectives, Going into Yalta

The US Perspective. In many ways, the US position going into the Yalta conference was the least complicated. Unlike the Soviet Union, the

United States had not been physically devastated by the war. Unlike Great Britain, the United States had not been drained dry financially by the war. President Roosevelt had just won his fourth term in office, so presidential politics were not involved. But in the Northeast and the industrial Midwest, voters with personal or familial roots in Eastern Europe were plentiful enough to be a potent force in congressional elections. Aside from that, the main "political" consideration for the US delegation at Yalta lay in the fact that the American public was tired of war; it wanted the troops to come home from Europe as soon as the job was done, and it wanted to finish off Japan with no more American blood spilled than necessary.

The US delegation was intent on arriving at definitive arrangements for postwar Germany, but demonstrably less so for Poland. Nevertheless, as a matter of domestic US politics, the issue of Poland's postwar status was significant. As Churchill (who was an astute observer of US politics) put it: "The large community of Poles in the United States anxiously awaited a settlement between the three Great Powers."[18] Indeed, at least as far back as the great waves of European immigration to the United States that began in the late nineteenth century, the polyethnic makeup of the American population had influenced US politics—at first on a local level and increasingly in national politics, as the new immigrants and their American-born children found their political footing. As Paula Stern puts it in her meticulously researched and documented study of the intersection of US domestic politics and foreign policy: "Two centuries of American diplomatic history yield numerous cases of politicians' (elected officials') concern for immigrants and their half-sisters—religious, racial, and ethnic groups—shaping what America did in the rest of the world."[19] Tears are shed at naturalization ceremonies in the United States in which immigrants become US citizens. The tears are shed in happiness but also in remembrance of the homeland and the loved ones left behind.

As for the US war with Japan, the Soviet-Japanese Neutrality Pact of April 1941, which Americans always viewed as a Russian attempt to cause Japan to shift its attention to American interests in the Pacific region, was still in force (it was not denounced by the Soviets until April 1945). Thus, at Yalta, the Americans wanted assurances from the Russians that they would go after Japanese forces on the Asian mainland as soon as the Red Army could transfer troops from Europe.

The British Perspective. At Yalta, Great Britain's interest in Poland had slightly different origins than did the American interest. As Churchill put it, "Great Britain had no material interest of any kind in Poland. Honour was the sole reason why we had drawn the sword to help Poland against Hitler's brutal onslaught, and we could never accept any settlement which did not leave her free, independent, and sovereign."[20]

The provisional government based in Lublin, Poland, was established in the summer of 1944 as a Committee of National Liberation, Moscow's cat's-paw for the administration of liberated Poland.[21] The Lublin government enjoyed the favor of the Kremlin, which extended recognition to that regime in January 1945, without consultation with the British or American governments. The British, of course, wanted democratic processes to determine who would govern. And, on the subject of democratic processes, Churchill was keenly aware that the British voters would go to the polls in a general election soon after the end of the war. (General elections had been suspended in favor of a wartime coalition government for the duration of the war.)

The Soviet Perspective. For the Russians, the issues on the table at Yalta about how the war would end were of a piece with the issues as to how Eastern Europe would look for decades to come. Soviet professors N. V. Sivachev and N. N. Yakovlev were good communists, good writers, and competent historians. They wrote, with only slight oversimplification, that as far as the Russians were concerned, "Roosevelt and Churchill came [to Yalta] to ask the USSR to straighten out the complex situation on their fronts in Europe and Asia."[22]

As a practical matter, Stalin had as much control as he wanted or needed over how the war in Europe would end. By the time the three Allied leaders got to Yalta, the Red Army had crossed the Oder in hot pursuit of the Wehrmacht. Russian soldiers stood thirty-five miles from Berlin, but the armies of the Western Allies had not yet reached the Rhine. The Soviet armed forces consisted of more than eleven million men (and women),[23] the vast majority of whom were in the Red Army. They had pushed past the rubble that was Warsaw in January. There could be no doubt that, though there were thousands of lives still to be lost, the Red Army had the wherewithal to push to Berlin— or for that matter to whatever distance west of Berlin Stalin thought expedient. Nor could there have been any doubt that Stalin knew what he wanted postwar Poland to look like—and who would be in charge in Warsaw. It would not be Polish patriots.

It was also true that, as Stalin came to the table at Yalta, he, along with millions of Russians forty years old and older, could recall invasions by the armed forces of Germany, Japan, Italy, France, Great Britain, the United States, Greece, Croatia, Finland, Hungary, Romania, Slovakia, and Spain.

The Seven-Day Conference and Its Outcome

The conference began on February 4, 1945, and ended seven days later, after eight plenary sessions. The American delegation included President Roosevelt, Secretary of State Edward R. Stettinius, Roosevelt's Chief of Staff admiral William D. Leahy, Ambassador Harriman, and Harry Hopkins (who, as a practical matter, had more influence over US strategy than the recently appointed Secretary Stettinius), as well as senior military leaders. Also in the American delegation was Alger Hiss, a political officer in the State Department, whose role at Yalta helped communist hunters get traction in the postwar era. Roosevelt's interpreter at Yalta (as at Tehran) was Charles E. Bohlen, who was, in his own right, a leading Russia expert. (Eight years later, in the opening months of the Eisenhower administration, Bohlen's very presence at Yalta would become a cause célèbre when his nomination to serve as US ambassador to Moscow was debated in the Senate.)

It is arguably unfair to attach overriding significance to any single statement by an Allied leader at the conference table in the Livadia Palace. But Churchill was justified in describing as "momentous" Roosevelt's pronouncement at the first plenary session (as Churchill summarized it): "The United States would take all reasonable steps to preserve peace, but not at the expense of keeping a large army in Europe, three thousand miles away from home. The American occupation would therefore be limited to two years."[24] Although Roosevelt's statement "terrified Churchill as much as it pleased Stalin,"[25] history does not record the look on Stalin's face when he heard Roosevelt say that. Perhaps no reaction was visible on Stalin's face—after all, he knew how to play his cards and had already heard Roosevelt say, at the Tehran conference in November 1943, that if there were a future threat to peace on the Continent, "the United States would send only ships and planes."[26] Of course, actual experience in the postwar years did not match up with Roosevelt's statement of US intent. But no one at the table could know that, in nine weeks, Harry S. Truman (who was not at Yalta) would be president of the United States or that as president he would have the personal resolve and political courage to convince Congress and the American people that isolationism, even in peacetime, was no longer an option for the United States.

Poland dominated the agenda, but issues as to postwar arrangements in Germany, allocation of votes in the United Nations, and the final chapter of the war in the Pacific were also before the three leaders. Two of those matters were, all things considered, not terribly complicated. As for Japan, Stalin agreed that the Soviet Union would enter the war against Japan by invading Manchuria approximately three months after the end of the war in Europe. As for the United Nations, Roosevelt agreed that Ukraine and Belorussia could each have votes in the United Nations (interestingly enough, to offset voting rights for Canada and India, presumably as vassal states of the United Kingdom).[27]

But Poland was a sticking point. Stalin chose not to force the issue by telling Churchill and Roosevelt that true independence for Poland was a nonstarter. Instead, two days into the conference, Ambassador (later Soviet foreign minister) Gromyko recorded Stalin's assurances to the Western leaders that, to avoid being once again a corridor for invasion of the USSR, "Poland must be strong. That is why the Soviet Union is interested in the creation of a strong, free and independent Poland."[28] Roosevelt promptly responded to this assurance with a letter to Stalin in which the president insisted on prompt free elections in Poland. He concluded: "I know this is completely consistent with your desire to see a new free and democratic Poland emerge from the welter of this war."[29] History does not record whether Roosevelt thought Stalin would be moved by the president's professed belief in Stalin's good intentions for the Polish people.

Three days later, on February 9, the three leaders again discussed the issue of Polish elections. Two aspects of the election problem were foremost in Roosevelt's mind. First, there was ample reason, based on the Soviet Union's history with elections, to apprehend that words on paper calling for free elections might, a short time later, take on a different meaning for the Russians than for the Americans and the British.

Second, as Bohlen recorded in the minutes, Roosevelt "felt it was very important for him in the United States that there be some gesture made for the six million Poles there indicating that the United States was in some way involved with the question of freedom of elections."[30]

As for how "free" (i.e., free of Soviet influence) the free elections should be, Roosevelt was unequivocal: "I want this election in Poland to be the first one beyond question. It should be like Caesar's wife. I did not know her, but they said she was pure." Stalin's response was a bit more enigmatic: "They said that about her but in fact she had her sins."[31]

The joint communiqué issued by the three leaders at the end of the conference did, of course, explicitly address Poland: explicitly but with no specifics. On Poland, the communiqué began as follows: "We came to the Crimea Conference resolved to settle our differences about Poland. We discussed fully all aspects of the question. We reaffirm our common desire to see established a strong, free, independent and democratic Poland."[32]

After reading *that* introduction to the section of the document addressing the original casus belli justifying British entry into World War II, a skeptical reader could have been forgiven for declining to read any more of the document. The strongest statement the communiqué had to offer about the Soviet-sponsored Lublin government was that "the Provisional Government which is now functioning in Poland should therefore be reorganized on a broader democratic basis with the inclusion of democratic leaders from Poland itself and from Poles abroad." The fact is that the product of Yalta was nothing more than an agreement to agree, which, as any lawyer will attest, is no agreement at all—and can, in some situations, be worse than no agreement because one side or the other may have been lulled into a false sense that something meaningful has, in fact, been agreed to. It was left to Molotov and Harriman (both identified by name in the communiqué) to meet later, ostensibly for the purpose of working out the details, but in fact for the purpose of finding out whether anything meaningful had been accomplished at Yalta.

Molotov, uneasy with the US proposal for the Declaration on Liberated Europe, sought and got reassurance from Stalin at Yalta. He told Stalin, "This is going too far!" Stalin replied, "Don't worry. Work it out. We can deal with it in our own way later. The point is the correlation of forces."[33] How true—then and now. The details never got worked out, at least in any way that led to free elections.

In his memoirs, George Kennan, who served Harriman as an aide and interpreter in the ministerial-level negotiations in the spring of 1945, minced no words about the Yalta communiqué and the ill-fated negotiations that followed. Writing two decades after the events, Kennan recalled that the language about "free and unfettered elections" for Poland "struck me as the shabbiest sort of equivocation, certainly not calculated to pull the wool over the eyes of the Western public but bound to have this effect."[34]

Roosevelt Didn't Go Straight Home from Yalta

Roosevelt returned to Washington, DC, from Yalta by way of Egypt. The presidential airplane, The Sacred Cow, proceeded from the Crimea to the Suez Canal Zone. Once there, Roosevelt was ensconced aboard the heavy cruiser USS *Quincy*. But this was not a rest stop. The *Quincy* was soon joined in the Great Bitter Lake by another US ship, on which there was embarked another distinguished passenger—King Abdul Aziz bin Abdul Rahman al Saud, the founder and reigning monarch of the Kingdom of Saudi Arabia. This was no mere social call, and King Saud came prepared—with cooks, slaves, an astrologer, and a fortune-teller. Serious business was at hand, as indicated by the fact that the king had never before met with a foreign head of state. Two subjects dominated the president's several days of discussions with the king: Palestine and petroleum.

As for Palestine, the Bitter Lake discussions were decidedly unsatisfying for both of the conferees, but petroleum was a different story. The war had demonstrated more clearly than ever that oil was not just an economic asset. As the German and Japanese experience in the war amply demonstrated, secure access to abundant petroleum reserves was an indispensable strategic asset. Toward the end of the war, the Red Army overran well over a thousand Wehrmacht tanks that had run out of gas.[35]

The oil-related discussions on the *Quincy* went better than the talks about Palestine. In a straight-up oil-for-security deal, Roosevelt offered military security to Saudi Arabia. The United States got access to abundant (and, all things considered, strategically located) petroleum reserves. Two weeks after the Bitter Lake conference, Saudi Arabia declared war on Germany and Japan. In early August, the United States and the Arab kingdom signed an agreement under which the Americans would build an airfield at Dhahran.

All in all, it is fair to say that the enduring symbiotic relationship between the United States and Saudi Arabia—one of history's most enduring marriages of convenience—is a prime example of the fact that, with careful maintenance, an alliance based on shared interests can be made to last, even where the allies have almost no shared values. And it would not be much of an overstatement, if overstatement at all, to say that Roosevelt's February 1945 tête-à-tête with Ibn Saud may have had nearly as much to do with world events in the decades that followed as anything that was negotiated at Yalta.

Enter Harry S. Truman

President Roosevelt did not live to find out whether the lofty language of the Yalta declaration was illusory. Franklin Delano Roosevelt, the only president within the memory of tens of millions of Americans, died of a stroke at Warm Springs, Georgia, on April 12, 1945.

Although President Roosevelt had been unwell for a long time, his constitutional successor, Vice President Harry S. Truman, had been—to an astonishing degree—left out of the momentous inner councils (to say nothing of international conferences) as the end of the war drew near. In his eighty-two days as vice president, Truman had not been admitted to Roosevelt's inner circle and was not aware, either directly or via briefings, of some of Roosevelt's most sensitive initiatives.[36] In those eighty-two days, Truman met with President Roosevelt on official business only twice.[37] He had not been told about the atomic bomb.[38] (Stalin, whose excellent espionage services had kept him abreast of developments in the Manhattan Project, could have brought Truman up to date.) It is doubtful that the new president knew much more about the status of the East-West confrontation over the future of Eastern Europe than he could have gleaned from the newspapers. To say no more, President Truman lacked significant experience in foreign affairs. The sum total of his experience abroad was his tour in France as a captain in the field artillery in World War I. Truman had no love for the Germans. On November 11, 1918, the day the World War I armistice took effect, Captain Truman wrote to his wife that "it is a shame we can't go in and devastate Germany." Having been notified that hostilities would end at 11:00 a.m. on that day, Truman, by his own account, "fired 164 rounds at him [the Germans] before he quit this morning anyway."[39]

It would be difficult to conceive of a more critical and complex juncture for an abrupt transfer of presidential power than April 1945, and this was a transfer to a man who had had "one of the strangest career trajectories in the history of American politics."[40] The full story of this historic transition has been well told by Truman himself in his two-volume memoir.[41] The new president obviously had to get up to speed quickly because, in the spring of 1945, events were occurring almost daily, which, in any other year, would have been included in the year's top-ten news stories.

Guileful diplomacy was not in Truman's repertoire. He did not have a college degree, but he had taken a few law courses at night in the 1920s. That, combined with his solid middle-class values and first-hand knowledge of the horrors of war, may be what caused him to treat international negotiations as a serious business which for him meant there could be no substitute for men keeping their word. Another factor was that Truman, though lacking a formal liberal education, was a serious student of history. The depth and breadth of his personal readings in world history put him in a good position to digest—quickly—the import of the briefings and memos that came his way in his first weeks as president. Dean Acheson, whose formal education was as patrician as Truman's was plebian, was "awed" by Truman's grasp of history.[42]

Truman's words and actions in matters of international relations revealed a distaste for the duplicity and equivocation that have always been and always will be endemic in international diplomacy. Roosevelt thought, rightly or wrongly, that an element of calculated ambiguity could be useful in international negotiations. But, as Daniel Yergin puts it, the new president "tended to see clearly defined contests between right and wrong, black and white."[43] In his postwar memoir, Churchill described Truman as "a man of exceptional character and ability," having "simple and direct methods of speech, and a great deal of self-confidence and resolution."[44] Aside from that, he had—and needed—a tremendous capacity for work. In many ways, Truman may well have been the most underestimated American politician of the twentieth century.

It was obvious at the outset of Truman's presidency that the situation with the Russians, with respect to Eastern Europe in general, and Poland in particular, was not going well. On April 20, barely a week after Truman succeeded to the presidency, Ambassador Harriman briefed the new president on the Russian situation as he saw it. Harriman, who, by the spring of 1945, had had by far more person-to-person contact with Stalin and Molotov than any other American official, did not mince words. He told the president that he believed that the Soviets, while pursuing a policy of cooperation with the United States and Great Britain, would also seek "the extension of Soviet control over neighboring states through unilateral action" and that this would amount to an "extension of the Soviet system with secret police, extinction of freedom of speech, etc."[45]

The next day, Harriman—not given to rash pronouncements—was sure enough of his assessment of the situation to observe at a meeting of the secretary of state's staff committee that "Russian plans for establishing satellite states are a threat to the world and to us. The excuse offered that they must guard against a future German menace is only a cover for other plans." To this, "Mr. Grew [Undersecretary of State Joseph C. Grew] asked if Soviet Government were not establishing more than spheres of influence and if it were not taking complete charge in satellite countries. Mr. Harriman said that this was true."[46]

Immediately after Harriman gave these assessments, the position of the Soviet-supported government in Warsaw was cemented by the signing of the Treaty on Friendship, Mutual Assistance, and Postwar Cooperation between the Soviet Union and Poland. Stalin's announcement of the signing of the treaty concluded with his plea for the future of Poland: "May free, independent, democratic Poland live and prosper!"[47] With those words, it began to sink in with the US foreign policy establishment that at Yalta Roosevelt and Churchill had been had.[48]

To step back for just a moment, it should be borne in mind that this was the month, April 1945, that Stalin said, "Everyone imposes his own system as far as his army can reach. It cannot be otherwise."[49] This was a few weeks after Stalin reassured Molotov that "the point is the correlation of forces."[50] The tone was set toward the end of April when Truman met Molotov at the White House. The conversation did not go well. In characteristic unvarnished terms, Truman told the foreign minister that the United States expected the Soviet government to live up to the Yalta Declaration. Molotov: "I have never been talked to like that in my life." Truman: "Carry out your agreements and you won't get talked to like that."[51]

Now that we are two weeks into Truman's presidency, it is necessary to pause to reflect on the fact that more had changed than just the occupant of the White House. The political context had changed even though the party in power had not.

For reasons that were all too obvious, it had been understood by all that, regardless of how long Roosevelt might live, the 1944 election would be his last. That same principle did not apply to Truman, who was eligible to run for the presidency in 1948. In the run-up to the 1948 presidential election, Truman made some historic decisions that he would never have made if political considerations had been a decisive factor. But political considerations still could not be ignored because Truman had inherited a *foreign policy establishment.*

The Democratic Party had been in power since 1932. Almost all the senior military and diplomatic leaders in office at the beginning of the Truman presidency had held high appointive positions since before the war. Many of the senior civilian appointees were as sensitive to purely political considerations as presidents typically are. The Democratic foreign policy establishment in 1945 believed deeply in the internationalist policies of the Roosevelt administration. The senior leaders, too, were aware that the 1948 elections (to say nothing of the 1946 midterm elections) were on the horizon and that the tradition of wartime unity would no longer inhibit criticism and second-guessing, let alone outright pandering and demagoguery. John Foster Dulles, the grandson and nephew of US secretaries of state, had wide recognition as the leader of the Republican Party's shadow foreign policy establishment, and it was clear that the winning of a war and the negotiation of the peace would not give the Democrats a free pass in their handling of foreign affairs, least of all in their dealings with the Russians. Consequently, as the US relationship with the Soviet Union progressed from wartime comradeship to manageable tension to bitter recrimination in the first few months of 1945, it was unavoidable that political considerations would come into play in the administration's deliberations on foreign-policy issues. This was especially true of Poland, the ancestral homeland of millions of American voters. Truman's foreign policy advisors were convinced that continuation of Democratic control after the 1946 and 1948 elections would, at a minimum, slow what they feared would be the resurgence of the isolationism which nearly led President Roosevelt to despair in the years before Pearl Harbor.

On to Potsdam

In late May and early June, Harriman, Hopkins, and Bohlen met several times in Moscow with Stalin and Molotov in an attempt to break the impasse on the political future of Poland.[52] The talks succeeded only in removing any doubt as to Stalin's intentions with respect to Poland. The Allies had agreed at Yalta that another conference would be needed after Germany's surrender. The (July 17 to August 2, 1945) conference at Potsdam, an elegant Berlin suburb that had gotten through the war relatively unscathed, was that conference. It was the last of the conferences of the leaders of the Grand Alliance. A few days before the conference ended, the vote count in the British elections made it clear that Churchill had been unceremoniously ousted. The new prime minister, Clement Atlee (who had been at the conference from the start, as deputy prime minister in the wartime coalition government), took over for the British delegation. Stalin, having been in power since 1922, was at that point the only national leader at the table who had been in office longer than fourteen weeks. And he knew what it took to make a deal—or at least to leave his counterparts thinking that *they* had made a deal. Of the six major belligerents in World War II (Germany, Japan, Italy, the Soviet Union, Great Britain, and the United States), the Soviet Union was the only one which had, at some point in the twelve years before the Potsdam conference, entered into an alliance or a nonaggression pact with every one of the other five.

Truman, for his part, arrived at Potsdam in good political standing. When he arrived in Europe (for the first time since he had been there as a soldier in 1918), his approval rating stood at 87 percent in a Gallup poll—a higher approval rating than Roosevelt had ever attained.[53]

In theory, one of the main objectives of the Potsdam conference was to reach agreement on actual implementation of the broad principles the great powers had proclaimed six months earlier at the conclusion of the Yalta conference. But East-West relations had, of course, taken a severe turn for the worse in the intervening months. It is possible to imagine some of the more optimistic participants at Potsdam going into the conference thinking—hoping—that perhaps the problem was one of "interpretation" of the Yalta agreements. At Potsdam, the most effective aid to interpretation of the lofty language of the Yalta declarations would have been an updated map of Central and Eastern Europe—reflecting that the Red Army controlled most of the lands inhabited by the hundreds of millions of people whose futures were most directly at stake. For the foreseeable future, nothing would be happening in Poland over the objection of the Kremlin.

Thus, Potsdam brought into high relief that the wartime alliance between the United States and Russia had shallow roots and was essentially transactional. And, in Truman's short time as president, he had become convinced that there was no need to go to Potsdam with the intent of deepening those roots. Truman's experience in dealing with Molotov (directly) and Stalin (indirectly) after succeeding to the presidency convinced him that as a practical matter the alliance, having been born of necessity, had lasted scarcely longer than the necessity.

The agenda of issues that were, as a practical matter, mandatory at Potsdam was fairly short, but some of those matters were complex, such as: Poland's western border, German reparations and disposition of the German industrial base, governance of occupied Germany, war-crimes prosecutions, and getting the Red Army into China to help defeat Japan. Some subjects, compelling now (and, without doubt, morally compelling at the time), got short shrift. The three leaders never mentioned the Holocaust or the future of what remained of Europe's Jewish population.[54] But Stalin did have the pleasure at Potsdam of carving up Berlin less than four years after the Wehrmacht had stood within sight of the Kremlin towers.

The relevance of Yalta and Potsdam lies in their geopolitical and domestic political implications for the ensuing four and a half decades of what soon came to be called the Cold War. Many of those who were at Yalta and Potsdam, including, of course, many present in the second and third echelons of their national delegations, continued to be deeply involved in national security affairs in their home countries for decades after the war. The conferences and their immediate postwar consequences had an enduring effect on the attitudes and convictions of the participants and the publics they served in the decades that followed.

As heard and recorded by Churchill, Stalin set the tone for the Soviet delegation in a way which must have left the Western delegations wondering where they (or maybe Stalin) had been for the last five and a half months: "Stalin said that in all the countries liberated by the Red Army the Russian policy was to see a strong, independent, sovereign State. He was against Sovietisation of any of those countries. They would have free elections, and all except Fascist parties would participate."[55]

Of course, Churchill and Truman could easily agree with that proposition. But by the time they got to Potsdam, they had precious little reason to entertain any notion that Stalin meant it. Stalin's objective at Yalta, at Potsdam, and in the early phases of the postwar period, was to secure permanent freedom of action (including, most importantly, military freedom of action) for the Soviet Union in the lands controlled by the Soviet Union at the end of the war. All notions of political theory—including Marxian theory—must be subordinated to the imperative of the survival at any cost of the Soviet state as a rock-solid geopolitical edifice, never again vulnerable to attack from the west.

The Bomb

There was one minidrama at Potsdam that produced lasting memories for all who participated in it. That was Truman's disclosure to Stalin that the United States had just successfully tested an atomic bomb.

The US-British-Canadian effort to harness nuclear energy in the form of an atomic bomb got started in the United States with President Roosevelt's order, in June 1942, creating the Manhattan Project. After the US bomb was successfully tested at the Trinity Site in New Mexico early in the morning on July 16, 1945, Truman's military staff at Potsdam informed him (and Churchill) of that development. The timing was provident. The conference had just gotten started. On July 24, without calling it an atomic bomb, Truman, with Churchill present, quietly told Stalin that the United States had developed a new weapon of enormous destructive power. By Molotov's account: "It seemed to me that [Truman] wanted to shock us."[56] Shocked or not, "Stalin took the news calmly, showing no emotion."[57] As recorded by Zhukov: "On returning to his quarters after this meeting Stalin in my presence told Molotov about his conversation with Truman." Molotov: "They are trying to bid up." Stalin laughed: "Let them. I'll have to talk it over with Kurchatov today and get him to speed things up."[58]

Speed things up he did. As told by the highly respected Soviet diplomat Anatoly Dobrynin (about whom more later), Stalin, in short order, remedied a reported lack of electrical power to support development of the Soviet atomic bomb. "Power was simply switched off in several large, populated areas—except for their factories—and diverted to the atomic project."[59]

Of course, the obliteration of Hiroshima and Nagasaki on August 6 and 9 closed any gaps in Russian knowledge about what the United States was capable of doing with the bomb. But one reason Stalin was so impassive when Truman told him about the bomb was that he already had a wealth of information at his disposal about the Manhattan Project and its technological accomplishments. In early September, a month after the bombing of Hiroshima and Nagasaki, Igor Sergeivich Gouzenko, a disillusioned cipher clerk posted to the Soviet embassy in Ottawa, defected (in lieu of being transferred back to Moscow with his wife and son), taking with him a trove of secret documents revealing the extent of the Soviet espionage program in the United States, Great Britain, and Canada. Gouzenko's defection had ramifications beyond the realm of espionage and counterespionage. As Clark Clifford put it, his revelations about "Soviet espionage in the U.S. spurred the right wing" in its anticommunist zeal in the late 1940s and beyond.[60] The significance of Gouzenko's defection lay as much in its timing as in the content of the papers he took with him. This was five months before Stalin's Election Speech at the Bolshoi Theater and six months before Churchill's Iron Curtain speech. There was still at least a glimmer of hope in some Western councils that there might be a salvageable relationship with the Russians. After all, though they did not have the bomb, they had the largest army in the world, and Stalin's writ ran from the Bering Strait to the River Elbe.

The Russian network in the United States included the British physicist Klaus Fuchs, who worked in the Theoretical Division at Los Alamos, David Greenglass (Oak Ridge and Los Alamos), and the husband-and-wife team of Julius and Ethel Rosenberg. Fuchs was convicted and imprisoned in 1950, also in the United Kingdom. Greenglass, a key witness against the Rosenbergs, was convicted and imprisoned in 1951 in New York. The Rosenbergs were tried and convicted in New York in 1951 and executed in 1953.

Yalta and Potsdam: The Geopolitical Result

Not since Count Andrey Kirillovich Razumovsky spoke for Russia at the Congress of Vienna had Russia done as well at the negotiating table as it did at Yalta and Potsdam. The formula for success was not at all complicated, and it was the same in 1945 as it was in 1815: march your army into the heart of Europe and then sit down at the bargaining table to talk about what happens next. This postbellum status was concisely described by George Kennan in 1960: the end result of the advance of the Red Army into central Europe in the final phase of the war was "the quasi-permanent advancement of the effective boundaries of Moscow's political and military authority to the very center of Europe."[61]

The lands and peoples most directly and deeply affected by the issues in play at Yalta and Potsdam were lands and peoples that were firmly in Stalin's grip. Charles Bohlen, a first-hand witness to all of this history, put it succinctly: "The Red Army gave Stalin the power he needed to carry out his wishes, regardless of his promises at Yalta. Stalin held all the cards and played them well."[62] Although it is certainly easy to be judgmental about the ways the Soviets *actually used* the power they had in Eastern Europe after the war, that Stalin *did* have all the cards and *did* play them well is not a matter that compels or even necessarily invites moral judgment.

Bearing in mind that the Eastern European nations were the ancestral homelands of millions of Americans, it was inevitable that mere reference to Yalta became a potent rhetorical tool in US politics for decades after the war. In 1998, fifty-three years after the Yalta conferees adjourned, a US senator—Joseph R. Biden Jr.—would declare on the floor of the US Senate that it was time to erase a line: "The line I am talking about erasing is Yalta" (see the Conclusion). The crux of the matter was that no one could have traveled home from Potsdam entertaining any notion other than the obvious conclusion that Yalta and Potsdam had opened the door to the establishment of postwar spheres of influence. Thus, the most stunning and—for more than half a century—enduring geopolitical result of World War II was that in Europe, beginning in the spring of 1945, communism was no longer quarantined. Communism now reigned from the East China Sea to a few miles east of Frankfurt am Main. Although at horrific cost, Stalin had, in less than a decade, gained control of more lands than Peter I, Catherine II, and Alexander I had accumulated in over a century.[63]

As for US domestic politics, Yalta fed deep resentment among Americans of Eastern European extraction—especially Polish Americans. This went far to cement a broad anticommunist consensus during the Cold War years.[64] Yalta thus set the stage for the convergence of ethnic politics and pure anticommunist ideology. This was a potent combination because it gave the Republican Party a previously unavailable tool with which to appeal to those whose ethnic sensibilities were most affected—Americans of Eastern European descent, including millions of voters who had traditionally been reliable members of the Democratic Party's coalition of southerners and northern city dwellers.

Geopolitically, with the extension of the glacis by the addition of Bulgaria, Czechoslovakia, Hungary, Poland, and Romania, the likelihood of having to defend the Soviet Union on Soviet soil, to say nothing of having to defend *Russia* on *Russian* soil, became vanishingly small. In 1921, M. A. Demangeon, a professor at the Sorbonne, concluded that, as a result of the Great War, Europe would soon become "a little cape on the continent of Asia."[65] The professor's geopolitical prediction was only a little premature. It came true, courtesy of the Red Army, in 1945. In terms of access to ice-free southern Baltic ports, the Soviet Union went from seventy-five miles of Baltic coast before 1939 to nearly a thousand miles after the war was over. With hindsight, it can safely be said that the notion that Stalin would have countenanced any postwar outcome other than that which eventuated from victory on May 9, 1945, is entirely fanciful. The idea that he could have been somehow compelled, at and after the 1945 conferences, to accept a result that would have cabined Soviet influence within the borders of the Soviet Union was politically convenient in the 1950s, but, again, it was entirely fanciful. Twelve years after Yalta and Potsdam (and a few days after the USSR launched Sputnik), Stalin's successor, Nikita S. Khrushchev, concisely summarized the value of the USSR's glacis: "Hitler used to boast that he could march to the Urals but . . . the Soviet Union and its allies could stop [West German] Chancellor Adenauer at his borders."[66]

The larger question is why anyone would have dreamed that the Soviet leadership would have settled for anything less than hegemony in Eastern Europe. In the West, Stalin is generally regarded as having been an absolute dictator who never had any need to take ordinary political considerations into account. But the truth is more complicated. To be sure, Stalin had much more political running room than any of his counterparts in the West. He was no doubt accustomed to, and probably a bit amused by, servile praise from his colleagues. But even though Stalin had no need to be constantly looking over his shoulder at the Politburo (unlike his successors in the Kremlin), Stalin's tyranny was not, strictly speaking, a one-man tyranny.

As early as the fall of 1942, Harriman and Churchill had concluded, after several hours of frustrating discussions with Stalin in a meeting in the Kremlin, that "Stalin's fellow commissars in the Politburo possessed more power than the West commonly supposed."[67] The fact is that there can be no easy summation of Stalin's actual relationship with the Politburo[68] (or the State Committee of Defense, which was formed on June 30, 1941, and functioned as a war cabinet that included Molotov, Georgy Malenkov, and Lavrenti Beria as members). It is doubtless true that the Politburo's sway over Stalin, such as it was, depended on the issue at hand. It is also true, of course, that in the postwar years, as in the 1930s, Stalin had the prerogative of having his deputies who had fallen out of favor tried for treason and shot, as Alexey Kuznetsov and Nikolai Voznesensky found out. But if ever there was a threesome that might well make even the most entrenched dictator think twice about giving away Eastern Europe, it would be Molotov, Malenkov, and Beria.

What can fairly be said, then, is that Stalin was not totally free—and, on some issues, perhaps not nearly free—of political constraints. The reality was that once the Kremlin's control was extended as far west as the German (to say nothing of the Polish) heartland, no Soviet leader could relinquish the geopolitical security inherent in that control.[69] Stalin's success at Yalta and Potsdam is entirely consistent with Harriman's coldly objective estimation of Stalin as a geopolitician. Recognizing that others would be hard put to see any redeeming qualities in Stalin, Harriman found it necessary to give the marshal his due.

> I saw the other side as well—his high intelligence, that fantastic grasp of detail, his shrewdness and the surprising human sensitivity that he was capable of showing, at least in the war years. I found him better informed than Roosevelt, more realistic than Churchill, in some ways the most effective of the war leaders. At the same time, he was, of course, a murderous tyrant. I must confess that for me Stalin remains the most inscrutable and contradictory character I have known—and leave the final judgment to history.[70]

Letting go of Eastern Europe might well have been the *only* thing that might have resulted in a putsch, but even Stalin could not have felt that he had the leeway to put Kremlin control of Eastern Europe seriously at risk.

In sum, it cannot accurately be said that, at Yalta, Roosevelt and Churchill gave away Eastern Europe. They didn't have it to give it away. Stalin had it, and he wasn't about to give it up. A postwar order in Europe that would have prevented Stalin from "impos[ing] his own system as far as his army can reach" would have required the Western Allies to fight, and win, another war. And this war would have been against a country that, for the first time ever, did not have a real military rival on the Eurasian land mass.[71]

In terms of popular consciousness in the United States, the lines had been drawn. An article published in *Harper's Magazine* in August 1946 set the tone: "Real safety, as the Politburo sees it, can lie in only one direction: a strong Red Army and 'friendly' puppet governments in every border state—plus constant efforts to prevent the Western nations from forming any kind of association which might someday be turned into an alliance against the Soviet Union."[72] No member of the Politburo would have argued with that estimate of the situation. No one in the Kremlin would argue with those words now.

The War Is Over

On August 6, 1945, as Truman journeyed home from Potsdam aboard the cruiser *Augusta*, Hiroshima was flattened by Little Boy, the first of the two atomic bombs. Two days later, the Soviet Union declared war on Japan, and the Red Army marched into Manchuria. On August 10, one day after the second bomb, Fat Man, was detonated over Nagasaki, Japan announced its intent to surrender. On August 14, the terms of surrender were agreed on. The war was over. The land rush continued. In the Far East, US and Soviet commanders agreed that Japanese forces south of the thirty-eighth parallel in Korea would surrender to American forces and those north of that line would surrender to the Red Army.

Save for the communists' humiliation in the Hungarian election in 1945, more than half a century would pass before any country solely controlled by the Red Army in the spring of 1945 would have a government chosen in free and fair elections. It takes nothing away from Roosevelt or Churchill, or from the sacrifices of the millions of troops who fought under the flags of the Western Allies, to observe that Stalin did not triumph at Yalta and Potsdam because of his own cunning, because of Roosevelt's frailty, or because of anyone's gullibility. Stalin prevailed in 1945 because those Hitler regarded as *Untermenschen*—tens of millions of them—had succeeded at unimaginable cost in breaking the back of the Wehrmacht.[73]

From the standpoint of geopolitical realism, it was inevitable that relations between the United States and the Soviet Union would revert quickly to their longstanding prewar state of hostility in 1945. The two nations were allies in the first place only because the common enemy—Nazi Germany—had presented a compelling case for a US-Soviet alliance. But how that hostility would play out on the world stage was yet to be determined. The beginning point was known, even though the end state could not have been known: the most stunning geopolitical result of the war was that, beginning in the spring of 1945, communism was no longer quarantined.

Chapter 3

Truman and Kennan

The Beginning of Containment and the End of Isolationism

At war's end, Western leaders knew what they *hoped* would happen throughout the European peninsula, from the Curzon line—now defining Poland's eastern frontier—to the English Channel. They knew what the Yalta and Potsdam documents said in black letters on white paper. Nevertheless, given their experience in the months after the two 1945 conferences, they cannot have had any real confidence that what they *hoped* would happen in Eastern Europe would actually unfold in what they realized would be an extraordinarily momentous era. Western leaders also realized, of course, that *hope* was not a strategy. They knew by summer's end in 1945 that there was little prospect for the continuation in any workable sense of the alignment of great powers that had brought their nations to victory in World War II. They needed a policy lodestar to guide them through these uncharted waters. That policy was not developed and implemented by any one person. But it is fair to say that the predominant intellectual vision for the policies ultimately implemented by the United States in dealing with the challenges presented by the Soviet Union in Eastern Europe came from one man, George F. Kennan, and his writings in 1946 and 1947.

Enter George Frost Kennan

A good beginning point for grasping the impact of the writings of George Kennan in 1946 and 1947 is an understanding of the cascade of postwar events that provided the context for those writings.

February 9, 1946	Stalin delivered his Election Speech, prompting a request to Ambassador Harriman, which he delegated to Kennan, to provide an evaluation of relations between the United States and the Soviet Union.
February 22, 1946	Kennan fulfilled Washington's request by sending what became known as the Long Telegram to the secretary of state.
March 5, 1946	Churchill delivered his Iron Curtain speech.
September 27, 1946	Ambassador Nikolai V. Novikov sent a telegram providing his (actually, Molotov's) analysis of the status and direction of East-West relations.
July 1947	Kennan's X Article is published in *Foreign Affairs.*

The collective effect of Stalin's Election Speech, Kennan's Long Telegram, and Churchill's Iron Curtain speech, all within thirty days of one another, was to make it plain to decision-makers on both sides of the divide that the East and the West were headed for an era of confrontation. It was equally obvious that, unless war intervened to bring it to an early end, it would be a long era of tense confrontation. As for the possibility of another war, it is noteworthy that the Election Speech marked a return by Stalin to explicit articulation of communist doctrine—a frame of reference Stalin had not used in discussing East-West relations since before Hitler launched Operation Barbarossa. Any notion of "peaceful coexistence," a doctrine articulated at length by Chairman Nikita Khrushchev almost exactly ten years after Stalin and Churchill made their speeches, was precluded by Stalin's insistence that war was all but inevitable. The only thing that was obvious was that in 1946 the East and the West had not seen the last of the momentous events of the decade of the 1940s.

When he gave his Iron Curtain speech in Fulton, Missouri, in early March, Churchill was, of course, no longer the prime minister, having been turned out of office eight months before. But he was still regarded as one of the greatest—perhaps *the* greatest—statesmen of the twentieth century. When he delivered the speech, he was well aware of Stalin's Election Speech. And President Truman, having read a copy of Churchill's speech as they rode the presidential train to Missouri, told Churchill that the speech would "do nothing but good."[1] The Russian view, as articulated by Sivachev and Yakovlev, that the Iron Curtain speech was "to some extent a joint affair of Churchill's and Truman's" is not wide of the mark.[2]

Churchill's beginning point was the fact—from which he never flinched—that Britain had gone to war in 1939 because Poland was being crushed by an army acting on orders from a dictator. He was painfully aware that after Britain had lost nearly four hundred thousand lives and been beggared economically, Poland in 1946 remained in the grip of an army acting on orders from a dictator, albeit a different one this time. It grated on Churchill, more than any other British subject, that "from Stettin in the Baltic to Trieste in the Adriatic, an iron curtain has descended across the Continent."[3]

The timing of the Iron Curtain speech was perfect. Kennan's Long Telegram had arrived in Washington, DC, from Moscow two weeks earlier. Churchill's speech received front-page coverage in the United States, making "iron curtain" a permanent part of the American political lexicon. Marshal Stalin was not pleased. As disclosed in an interview with *Pravda*, Stalin's take on the speech was that "beyond all question Mr. Churchill's aim is a war aim, a summons to war against the USSR."[4] Less than a week after Churchill's speech, Stalin, in an uncharacteristic argument, played a race card of sorts, asserting that Churchill and his American friends "resembled Hitler by holding a 'racial theory' that those who spoke the English language 'should rule over the remaining nations of the world.'"[5] Of course, Stalin's problem was not racial. It was geopolitical. On this, at least, Zbigniew Brzezinski and Nikita Khrushchev agreed. As Brzezinski wrote, "To the Soviets, Churchill's speech, calling in effect for an Anglo-American alliance, revived old notions of capitalist encirclement and seemed to fit established presumptions concerning capitalist hostility."[6] Per Khrushchev: Churchill "call[ed] for the capitalist countries of the world to encircle the Soviet Union."[7]

This, then, was the context in which George Frost Kennan expounded on the USSR, Russians, and the Kremlin's ideology and intentions in 1946 and 1947. The rhetorical markers of the Cold War had been laid down; that was the easy part. But rhetoric is not policy, let alone implementation of policy. Kennan was only too happy to fill the policy vacuum.

Kennan, who was born in 1904 and died in 2005 at the age of 101, was the son of a Milwaukee lawyer. His mother died when he was a few months old. Though his childhood was not idyllic, his father and stepmother did see to it that he got a good education. His undergraduate days at Princeton University were one of the defining experiences of his life. After his initial training in the Foreign Service—straight out of Princeton—Kennan was posted to the consular service in Geneva. Before the United States entered World War II, Kennan had had postings to Geneva, Hamburg, Berlin (to study Russian, as well as Russian history and culture), Riga, Moscow, Prague, and back to Berlin, where he was interned for several months after the United States entered World War II. A bit of the flavor of Kennan's early experience in the Foreign Service can be discerned from his description of his commute to work while posted to the American legation in Riga in 1932: "The sleigh in which I am sometimes driven to the office in winter—a one-passenger open-air affair, in which the fur-coated passenger sits behind and below the massive figure of the bundled coachman on the box—is right out of Tolstoy."[8]

Kennan's progress to his status as America's foremost Sovietologist was aided immeasurably by the fact that he accompanied Ambassador William C. Bullitt to Moscow in 1933 after Roosevelt established diplomatic relations with the Soviet Union. Kennan, by then fluent in Russian and having served his country well as an observer of all things Russian from Riga, was assigned to serve as second secretary in the new embassy in Moscow. There, by his account, he served until mid-1937, outlasting Bullitt at the embassy.[9]

By the time Kennan returned to the Moscow embassy in July 1944, as minister-counselor (second in command under Harriman), Kennan had gained a deep knowledge of Russian history and culture—as well as a love for the Russian people as an ethnos, which was reflected in his writings both personal and public. His expressions of his feelings for and about the Russian people could border on the mystical. In a 1944 diary entry in which he recorded his observation of two Russian women working in a potato field outside wartime Moscow, he wrote thus: "The women had broad faces, brown muscular arms, and the powerful maternal thighs of the female Slav."[10] Kennan understood better than any Western scholar or diplomat that behind the *Soviet* façade there was a *Russian* populace and that, for reasons going back a thousand years, the two should never be equated. Kennan's deep affection for the Russian people was matched only by his loathing for the Soviet government.

Though he was a visionary, possessing a powerful intellect, Kennan was not, by nature, a leader. While he was in the Foreign Service, his politics were generally moderate. To be sure, he had an embedded ideology, but he was not an ideologue, either to the left or to the right. He was not free of various sorts of ethnic bias, but, with the arguable exception of his affinity for Slavic peoples, his ethnic biases did not noticeably affect his performance of his official duties, divorced, as those duties were, from domestic policy issues.

The Long Telegram

Washington wanted to know what to make of Stalin's Election Speech. The State Department wanted "an interpretive analysis of what we may expect in the way of future implementation of" the election speeches of Stalin and his associates.[11] Harriman (though not without his own understanding of the thinking of the Kremlin leadership) was content to let Kennan, then the deputy chief of mission, do the writing.

Kennan leapt at the opportunity.[12] He said later: "Here was a case where nothing but the whole truth would do. They had asked for it. Now, by God, they would have it."[13] Kennan, forty-two years old and undaunted by the fact that he was sick in bed, started dictating. More than five thousand words later, the missive that became known as the Long Telegram was dispatched from Moscow to Washington on February 22, 1946. Kennan's analysis was far-ranging, drawing on the totality of his understanding of Russia, Russians, and the Soviet system. No cable in the history of the Foreign Service has had a greater impact on American foreign policy.[14]

The Long Telegram was written in a style and tone that was—unlike most embassy dispatches—sure to capture and hold the attention of US policy-makers. The document[15] should be read in its entirety. But especially relevant for present purposes are Kennan's descriptions of the Kremlin's postwar outlook, his description of the Soviet Union's goals, and his prescriptions for US policy.

Kennan on the Soviet Outlook

Kennan began with his summary of the "Basic Features of Post War Soviet Outlook, as Put Forward by Official Propaganda Machine." His rendering of the existing Soviet ideology included, first, the proposition that "[the] USSR still lives in antagonistic 'capitalist encirclement' with which in the long run there can be no permanent peaceful coexistence." After articulating that and other discouraging aspects of the Kremlin's outlook, Kennan was careful to differentiate, as he always did, between the Soviet leadership and the Russian people, describing them as "by and large, friendly to outside world, eager for experience of it, eager to measure against it talents they are conscious of possessing, eager above all to live in peace and enjoy fruits of their own labor." Although Kennan consistently refused to impute the qualities of the Soviet government to the Russian people, the reverse is not true. Drawing on hundreds of years of Russian history, he freely imputed the qualities of the Russian people to the Soviet government: "At [the] bottom of Kremlin's neurotic view of world affairs is traditional and instinctive Russian sense of insecurity." All of this led to one observation relevant to the security of Western nations: communist doctrine, 1940s-style, "provides justification for that increase of military and police power of [the] Russian state, for that isolation of Russian population from outside world, and for that fluid and constant pressure to extend limits of Russian police power which are together the natural and instinctive urges of Russian rulers." In other words, communist doctrine rationalized both the police state in which the Soviet citizens lived their lives and the state-mandated channeling of resources to build up military strength.

American policy-makers would be reading these lines in the Long Telegram mindful of the contrast between the Soviet state as it existed from 1922 to 1939 and the Soviet state as it existed in 1946. Although the USSR provided US politicians much to work with in their political rhetoric during the interwar period, there had been no room for a credible suggestion that the Soviet Union was a military peer of the United States. But Western perceptions of Russian military weakness evaporated, at the latest, when the smoke cleared at Stalingrad. To US policy-makers who were keenly aware that American taxpayers anticipated a peace dividend, the thought that the Kremlin leadership was free to devote resources to the military with little regard for the wants and needs of the average Soviet citizen would be doubly alarming.

Kennan on Soviet Intentions

Kennan did not equivocate in his rendering of Soviet goals. His comments on Soviet intentions were bold and self-assured—more so than were his policy prescriptions, as will be seen. US decision-makers who read the Long Telegram were likely influenced more by Kennan's pungent description of Soviet intent than they were by any other section of his treatise. As he saw it, "Where individual governments stand in path of Soviet purposes[,] pressure will be brought for their removal from office." As for the United States as a geopolitical adversary,

> we have here a political force committed fanatically to the belief that with US there can be no permanent *modus vivendi*[;] that it is desirable and necessary that the internal harmony of our society be disrupted, our traditional way of life be destroyed, [and] the international authority of our state be broken, if Soviet power is to be secure. . . . [Soviet power is] [i]mpervious to logic of reason, and it is highly sensitive to logic of force. For this reason it can easily withdraw—and usually does when strong resistance is encountered at any point. Thus, if the adversary has sufficient force and makes clear his readiness to use it, he rarely has to do so.

No US politician or commentator, residing anywhere in the broad middle ground between the extremes of American politics, would have taken issue with the basic thrust of these pronouncements as credible, actionable descriptions of Russian goals and the nature of the Kremlin regime in the postwar period. Momentous events were to follow, many of which were traceable to belief by politicians and policy-makers in the reliability of Kennan's estimate.

Kennan's Conclusions

The Long Telegram was long on analysis of Soviet thinking and short on specific policy prescriptions. But, in a passage which was echoed in many of his later writings, Kennan made one thing clear: "We must have courage and self-confidence to cling to our own methods and conceptions of human society. After [all], the greatest danger that can befall us in coping with this problem of Soviet communism, is that we shall allow ourselves to become like those with whom we are coping."

Although the Long Telegram was widely distributed among US policy-makers, it would give Kennan both too much credit and too much blame to say that this telegram was a cause of East-West confrontation. That confrontation already existed and was intensifying almost by the day. Rather, the East-West confrontation was *explained* by Kennan in the telegram, and explained in a way that had much to do with the development of the US response to the confrontation that was already in full swing.

That in February 1946, Kennan did not elaborate at length on the approach that later became known as the containment doctrine is made more noteworthy by the fact that seven months later, and nearly a year before Kennan expounded containment in detail in what came to be known as the X Article, Nikolai V. Novikov, then the Soviet ambassador to the United States, wrote his own long telegram.[16]

The Novikov Telegram

In the fall of 1946, Molotov wanted for Kremlin consumption only a written analysis of US intentions in the postwar world. His scribe was ambassador (to the US) Nikolai Vasilyevich Novikov. Molotov wanted the memorandum quickly, and he took great interest in its content as Novikov worked on it—to the point of revising it himself.[17] The Novikov Telegram did not see the light of day outside the Soviet Union until it was released at an international conference on the Cold War in 1990.[18]

The Novikov Telegram had to get started by getting a few basics out of the way. The United States had "a desire for world domination," to be realized in part by "the creation of a system of naval and air bases from the US, an arms race, and the creation of newer and newer weapons." The overarching goal was "American world domination." But the most remarkable passage in the Novikov Telegram was its description of what the United States was doing at that time to advance its interests in the world—an analysis that was on all fours with what Kennan prescribed ten months later in the X Article. Specifically, it argued that (1) US policy is "directed at limiting or dislodging the influence of the Soviet Union from neighboring countries"; (2) the United States supports "reactionary forces with the purpose of creating obstacles to the process of democratization [i.e., Communization] of" countries neighboring the USSR; and (3) US policy "is intended to weaken and overthrow the democratic [i.e., Soviet-controlled] governments in power [in countries bordering the USSR], which are friendly toward the USSR."[19]

Cleansed of ideological froth, Novikov's words could hardly have been a more accurate description of the aspirations of US policy-makers for the outcome of the ideological and geopolitical competition between the East and the West in the postwar era. In fact, the third point ("weaken[ing]" and "overthrow[ing]" Soviet-controlled governments) went Kennan one better: it foreshadowed the "rollback" policy—actually, never much more than a political slogan—that came into US political debate as the 1952 presidential elections drew near. These mutual perceptions of the United States and the Soviet Union in 1946 had much to do with the fact that, in the ensuing forty-five years, the Cold War would exact a considerable price in lives and treasure. The combined writings of Kennan and Novikov foreshadowed Arthur Schlesinger Jr.'s apt description, nearly five decades later, of the Cold War mindsets of the two great powers: "Each superpower undertook for what it honestly saw as defensive reasons actions that the other honestly saw as unacceptably threatening and requiring stern countermeasures."[20]

Kennan's X Article

Seldom has a single document propelled a career in the way the Long Telegram propelled Kennan's career as a Foreign Service Officer. In early 1947, he was appointed by Secretary of State George C. Marshall to serve as the first director of the State Department's policy planning staff. James V. Forrestal, who served as the secretary of the navy during the last year of World War II and then as the first secretary of defense beginning in 1947, took a back seat to no one in the intensity of his focus on the Soviet threat. His correspondence with Kennan led him to ask Kennan to comment on a paper on communism that Forrestal had sent to Kennan.[21] The resulting private memorandum from Kennan to Forrestal (in late January 1947) became the X Article. Kennan regarded this invitation to communicate thoughts in writing to a man at the pinnacle of the US defense establishment as an opportunity to fire a fresh salvo. After all, nearly a year had passed since he had decided with the Long Telegram, that "now, by God, they would have it."

The X Article was published in the July 1947 issue of *Foreign Affairs*.[22] Given Kennan's position at the top of the policy apparatus at the Department of State, the usual disclaimer, to the effect that the article does not necessarily represent the official view of the US government, would have been completely ineffectual. The author of the *Foreign Affairs* article—titled "The Sources of Soviet Conduct"—was shown simply to be: X. What began as a private response to a private request became one of the seminal documents influencing US Cold War policy. As Paul Nitze would later write, it "provided the overall rationale for the policy that would guide US foreign policy for the next generation."[23]

Kennan's core proposition, which in turn became the essential premise of his—and soon to be America's—containment doctrine, was a concept no more complicated than the concept of time—time combined with a constant readiness to adapt to constantly evolving challenges and circumstances. Although Kennan will never be regarded as an expert on the collective American psyche (au contraire), he was well aware of one innate American trait: impatience. Consequently, he thought it necessary to explain that "the Kremlin is under no ideological compulsion to accomplish its purposes in a hurry." Moreover, "the Kremlin has no compunction about retreating in the face of superior force."[24]

Having expounded on the importance of patience and adaptability in the Soviet scheme of things, Kennan expressed the concept of containment as the natural response: "In these circumstances it is clear that the main element of any United States policy toward the Soviet Union must be that of a long-term, patient but firm and vigilant containment of Russian expansive tendencies." This containment should consist of "the adroit and vigilant application of counter-force at a series of constantly shifting geographical and political points, corresponding to the shifts and maneuvers of Soviet policy, but which cannot be charmed or talked out of existence."[25] Kennan concluded that the likely result of successful implementation of a doctrine of containment would be "either the break-up or the gradual mellowing of Soviet power."[26]

It was widely assumed, and soon widely known, that Kennan was the author of the X Article. Although published anonymously, the article had obviously been written by a powerful writer who had vast knowledge of Russia and Russians, had deeply held convictions, and was considered by the editors of *Foreign Affairs* to be a respectable voice on the increasingly fraught subject of relations with the Soviet Union. Major excerpts from the X Article were published in the popular press, such as *Life* and *Reader's Digest*.

The fact of Kennan's authorship, taken together with the dissemination of major portions of the text in the popular press, had greater significance in light of Kennan's concluding declaration. In that passage, Kennan was the first member of the US foreign policy establishment to state publicly (albeit anonymously) that the obligations implicit in implementation of his proposed approach to the challenges presented by the Soviet Union are "responsibilities of moral and political leadership that history plainly intended [the American people] to bear."[27] Kennan's work in 1946 and 1947 profoundly influenced American foreign policy for more than four decades, encompassing the tenures of eight US presidents. His name was forever linked to the policy of containment.

The Long Telegram and the X Article were not intended to be political documents. Just as he was not, by nature, a leader, Kennan made no attempt at competence as a politician. But the telegram and the article were not without their political implications in the United States.[28] The beginning point for assessing the political implications of the telegram and the article is to note, as Kennan would have wanted us to note, that he articulated a middle path: His basic premise was that though war with Russia would be unacceptable, acquiescence or passivity in the face of Russian expansionism would be equally unacceptable. Containment was plainly a middle path. But the concept of containment did have a certain elasticity; there were elements for both hawks and doves to like. As for the hawks, Kennan noted five decades later that "I seem to have aroused a strain of emotional and self-righteous anti-Sovietism that in later years I will wish I had not aroused."[29] Quite true. Kennan had made it plain that war-related concessions to the Bolsheviks who ruled Russia were—at long last—no longer necessary. That was enough to spin the compasses of many US politicians, especially those on the right. For the doves, one of the implications of containment doctrine, as articulated by Kennan, was that a failure of traditional bilateral diplomacy need not lead to war.

In the Long Telegram and the X Article, Kennan did not specify what *means* would be required to achieve containment and its ultimate objective of the demise of the Soviet Union. Diplomacy, of course. But what, if anything, beyond diplomacy was required to cause the Kremlin to accede to "the logic of force"? What will be the implements for "the adroit and vigilant application of counterforce"? Nor did Kennan speculate as to how long it would take for all of this to unfold, though, as has been seen, it is unmistakable that Kennan was arguing for what has come to be called in various contexts the long game. Because of his deep conviction that the Soviet regime could not last, he wanted, as much as anything else, for America's long game to be longer than the Kremlin's long game. In terms of the virtues of patience, Kennan also had great confidence in the Russian people. He put it thus in a September 1944 memorandum to Ambassador Harriman: "The strength of the Kremlin lies largely in the fact that it knows how to wait. But the strength of the Russian people lies in the fact that they know how to wait longer."[30]

Finally, in the third decade of the twenty-first century, it is worth noting—carefully—that in the X Article (as is the case with the Long Telegram), Kennan did not at any point attribute to the Russian *people* the odious characteristics and intentions that he attributed to the Soviet regime. A few years after he wrote the X Article, Kennan expressed, in a single passage, both his affection for the Russian people and the importance of patience: "Give them time; let them be Russians; let them work out their internal problems in their own manner. The ways by which peoples advance toward dignity and enlightenment in government are things that constitute the deepest and most intimate processes of national life. There is nothing less understandable to foreigners, nothing in which foreign influence can do less good."[31]

A Brief Digression: Kennan on Kennan

Before we turn to the impact of Kennan's work on US policy, Kennan himself would want us to take note of what he said later in life about the doctrine he fathered in the 1940s—and about how that doctrine was implemented. Kennan spent the first half of his life marshaling the knowledge and experience which, along with his intellectual brilliance, enabled him to be the author of containment. He spent much of the second half of his long life explaining what he really meant. He did so for decades in writings and in speeches.

Kennan came to detest the East-West strategic arms race and the wider military build-up that accompanied it. As early as 1957, in his Reith lectures on the BBC,[32] Kennan made it plain that he did not conceive of NATO in the same way that the leaders of NATO's member nations conceived of NATO. And it is fair to say that his writings later in life became more polemical and less analytical. He argued in 1985 that his concept of containment consisted of "restoring economic health and political self-confidence to the peoples of Western Europe and Japan in order that they may be resistant to local Communist pressures."[33] But in 1946 and 1947, Kennan drew no distinction between diplomatic and military measures as instruments of containment. The irony is that Kennan could quite plausibly have taken credit for the fact that containment—*because of* its combination of robust diplomatic *and* military components—was ultimately a successful geopolitical strategy. He never really explained how the peaceful tools of containment (economic assistance, cultural exchanges, propaganda, covert operations, and diplomacy) could have succeeded without military power and the political will to use it looming in the background.

Chapter 4

Geopolitical Realignment Becomes a Reality

A Tale of Two Nations and Their Leaders

It was within a matter of weeks that Harry S. Truman graduated from his status as a Missouri-based politician to his role as a key player in some of the most momentous geopolitical events in the history of the United States. A nearly forgotten quirk of history looms large here. Henry Wallace had been Roosevelt's vice president during his third term, ending in January 1945. But Roosevelt chose Truman, rather than Wallace, as his running mate in the 1944 election. After the war, Wallace had an unmistakable inclination to find moral equivalence between the United States and the USSR, and a correspondingly strong disinclination to find fault with Soviet geopolitical ambitions. Roosevelt's jettisoning of Wallace in favor of Truman in the run-up to the 1944 election may well have been the most consequential, if unsung, political judgment call made by a US president in the twentieth century.

Although he was elected president only once, Truman served nearly eight years in that office, from April 12, 1945, until Eisenhower was inaugurated in January 1953. Measured by their long-term impact on the course of events at home and abroad, Truman's eight years in office were in the same league as the eight years beginning in 1783 or the eight years encompassing the American Civil War and its aftermath.

Chapter 4

In terms of Cold War events, 1946 was a year Churchill might have called "the Gathering Storm" if he had not used that phrase to describe the interwar years. If one treats Stalin's Election Speech in February and Churchill's Iron Curtain speech in March as the opening rhetorical shots, the Cold War began in 1946. But in terms of the usual markers of Cold War history—things such as summit meetings, missiles and bombs being tested, and major legislation—1946 was a deceptively quiescent year in the Cold War. The quiescence was deceptive because 1946 saw the first tangible steps in the sequence leading to the implementation of the Truman Doctrine and the policy of containment.[1] The leaders of the erstwhile Grand Alliance, now finding themselves on opposing sides of a geopolitical divide, were not taking a time out. They were jockeying for position, and the positions they took had much to do with the positions their successors would take in the ensuing decades.

Events in 1946 gave Truman and Stalin the opportunity to take the measure of each other. On that score, Truman knew quite a bit about Stalin, but Stalin knew little about Truman, to whom he had referred as a "gentleman shopkeeper."[2] Although Molotov had sent a long report to Stalin after the stormy encounter between Molotov and Truman in Washington, DC, in April 1945, Molotov's report of his conversation with Truman provided no hint of Truman's pugnacity or of the acrimonious end of the meeting at the White House.[3] As for learning about Truman by studying history, Stalin would have had to read a history of Jackson County, Missouri, to find out much about Truman's career before his sudden ascent from presiding judge of Jackson County to US senator in 1935. Stalin was, by disposition, unwilling to simply assume that Truman had the kind of personal resolve it would take to push back against the USSR when it really mattered. Truman and Stalin would each know more about the other by the end of 1946.

A letter dated January 5, 1946, written in longhand and personally read by Truman to his secretary of state, James F. Byrnes, helps set the stage. Byrnes, who had served as a US senator and an associate justice of the Supreme Court, never overcame (and never fully concealed) his disappointment that Roosevelt had chosen Truman, rather than himself, to be his running mate in 1944—which would have made Byrnes the president on April 12, 1945. In December 1945, Byrnes returned from a very unproductive conference of foreign ministers in Moscow. He made the mistake of signing a joint communiqué at the end of the Moscow conference without first reporting to Truman. Worse yet, Byrnes had requested airtime on the major US radio networks with the intent of reporting to the entire nation before seeing Truman to report on the conference.[4] Truman was not pleased. He called Byrnes to his office on January 5, 1946, and read the letter to him. The important point for present purposes is not that Byrnes was in trouble, but that the letter tells us much about Truman's attitude toward the Russians (and his frustration with the fait accompli with which he, as a new president, had been confronted at Potsdam). Truman's estimate of East-West relations, as expressed in his own handwriting to his secretary of state, was uncomplicated: "Unless Russia is faced with an iron fist and strong language another war is in the making. Only one language do they understand—'How many divisions have you?' . . . I'm tired [of] babying the Soviets."[5]

As Truman looked ahead in early 1946, he had good reason to understand that, in terms of geopolitics, the second half of the 1940s might not be any easier than the first. Prospects for free elections in Eastern Europe were dim. Conditions in Western Europe were ripe for communist subversion, and the situation in Turkey and Greece was worse yet. Truman doubtless recalled that, in June 1945, Stalin had stipulated that the settlement in Europe must include lands in eastern Turkey which had been ceded by the USSR in 1921, as well as Soviet bases in the Black Sea Straits.[6]

Then there was Iran. During the war, Iran had been jointly controlled by the Red Army (in the north) and the British (in the south), mainly for the purpose of keeping the Germans away from Iranian petroleum reserves and refining capacity, and to provide an overland route for shipping Lend-Lease aid to the USSR. In January 1942, after Iran was securely in Soviet and British control, those allies agreed with the newly installed Shah Mohammad Reza that they would withdraw from Iran not more than six months after the cessation of hostilities. This commitment was reaffirmed at the Tehran conference of the great powers in late 1943. In September 1945, at the London Conference of Foreign Ministers, Molotov and Bevin agreed that the six-month commitment meant that the British and Soviet troops would be out of Iran by March 2, 1946. The March date came and went, but US intelligence reported to Truman that the Red Army was still in Iran, blocking roads and moving toward Tehran.[7]

On March 6, George Kennan, then the US chargé d'affaires in Moscow, delivered a strong diplomatic note to the Kremlin, reminding the Soviets of their repeated commitments to withdraw and calling for immediate withdrawal "to promote the international confidence which is necessary for peaceful progress among the peoples of all nations."[8] It probably didn't help at all that this note was delivered by Kennan one day after Churchill delivered the Iron Curtain speech. Later in March, Truman instructed Byrnes to send "a blunt message to Premier Stalin."[9] On March 24, the Kremlin announced that the troops would leave Iran, and they eventually did.

This sequence left room for concluding that Truman had backed Stalin down. There may well be some truth to that, but the whole truth is more complicated. There were two things about Iran which were important to Stalin: Iran bordered the USSR (via the Turkmen SSR), and it had a lot of oil. As for the proximity factor, Kremlin leaders had for a very long time regarded northern Iran as territory within their sphere of influence.[10] As for the second factor, it may seem counterintuitive that Russia, oil-rich as it now is, would have been keenly interested in gaining oil reserves in 1946 (after Hitler could no longer covet them). Nevertheless, as Daniel Yergin writes, "In fact, Stalin was interested in Iranian oil. Soviet oil production in 1945 was only 60 percent of that of 1941. The country had desperately mobilized a range of substitutes during the war—from oil imports from the United States to charcoal-burning engines for its trucks."[11] Aside from that, Stalin probably shared with oil barons around the world the conviction that, if your future depends on oil (as has been the case for Russian leaders for several decades), you can never control enough reserves. The net result of the US and Soviet diplomatic wooing of Iran in February and March was that Iran lodged a protest in the United Nations about the continued presence of the Soviet troops. Molotov saw that this was not going to end well. The Soviet troops got out of Iran.

Before looking at the remaining challenges of 1946 and 1947, it is necessary to pause long enough to understand where President Truman stood politically as an unelected president in his first year in office. He was the president of the United States and ex officio the foremost leader in the free world, yet he had never in his own right received a single vote from a single voter outside the state of Missouri. The 1946 midterm elections were coming. As Truman looked ahead to that election season, he could safely speculate that the American electorate in 1946 was likely as restless as the British electorate had been when, less than a year earlier, British voters unsentimentally sacked Churchill. The Democrats had controlled the House of Representatives since 1931 and the Senate and the presidency since 1933. Those years of economic depression and war left the Democratic Party at risk of being held answerable for a tremendous accumulation of voter grievances.

Perhaps because he was himself a common man in so many ways, Truman understood very well what the common man (and woman) wanted more than anything else in 1946: a return to the peace and prosperity that the people of the United States had not truly enjoyed in nearly fifteen years. Truman's biggest political challenge lay in the fact that Americans, tired of having their lives controlled by events beyond their shores, were ready to turn inward. The United States had spent billions of dollars on the war, but Americans were now ready to spend some money on themselves. Yet Truman found himself contending with strikes, meat shortages and inevitable postwar inflation.[12] Consequently, the 1946 midterm election and, soon after that, the run-up to the presidential election in 1948 forced Truman to confront the reality that there was going to be a serious divergence between what he knew America wanted and what he firmly believed America needed. Worse yet, politically, international issues afoot in the fall of 1946 were not of the sort that would automatically trigger a groundswell of patriotic support. To the average voter, they were more likely to be wearying, if not irritating, rather than inspiring. Truman doubtless found it frustrating that the confrontation over Soviet troops in Iran had no sooner calmed down than the confrontation over the Turkish Straits leapt into the headlines.

Ultimately, the Straits crisis did not produce the outcome the Russians wanted. But, inconveniently for Truman, the crisis came to a head in the fall of 1946, when Truman would certainly have preferred to be concentrating on domestic issues for the benefit of the voters going to the polls in November. Equally inconveniently, it was not clear until long after 1946 that Stalin would gain nothing by raising the issue in the first place. But the Straits crisis was in the political mix as the 1946 elections approached. At its height in the fall of 1946, the crisis proved to be a watershed event in the evolution of American policy toward the Soviet Union. It had enduring consequences.

Some context is necessary. Churchill put it quite well when he wrote that Russia was "like a giant with his nostrils pinched by the narrow exits from the Baltic and the Black Sea," a geographic fact of surpassing significance to this day.[13] Stalin was following in the footsteps of the Romanovs in his desire for guaranteed, unimpeded warm-water access from Russian Black Sea ports—Sevastopol in the Crimea foremost among them—to the Mediterranean Sea and thence to the oceans of the world.

At the end of the war, Russia looked to the south across the Black Sea and saw in Turkey a nation that had remained officially neutral during the war (until February 1945, well after it had become obvious that the Third Reich was finished). Worse yet, Turkey had allowed Hitler's *Kriegsmarine* to transit the straits, giving Germany essentially unimpeded access to the Black Sea. Russia had won, Germany had lost, and Turkey had emerged from the war substantially unscathed, clinging tenaciously to the control of the straits that it enjoyed under the terms of the Montreux Convention of 1936. This did not sit well with Stalin, for reasons which are easily understood if one looks at a map or reads even a little Russian history.

Stalin wanted joint control of the straits, secured by a Soviet military presence there. He wanted transit rights to be determined by Black Sea powers—to the exclusion of the United States. This was a nonstarter for Truman. Even without a physical military presence in Turkey, Russia could, of course, close the straits without much more than a wave of Stalin's hand. Truman saw no need to strengthen an already strong Russian position at one of the most critical maritime chokepoints in the world. The Black Sea would not on Truman's watch become a Soviet lake.

On August 15, 1946, Truman's diplomatic and military advisors presented their assessment that "the only thing which will deter the Russians [from a military move against Turkey] will be the conviction that the United States is prepared, if necessary, to meet aggression with force of arms."[14] The Truman administration had no problem with guaranteed Russian transit rights, but the president said he was prepared to pursue "to the end" the US policy opposing a Russian military presence in the straits. Dean Acheson, who came to have a very high regard for Truman, wanted to make sure the president was aware of where this might go. In response to Acheson's inquiry as to whether he recognized that this might lead to war, Truman responded that "we might as well find out whether the Russians were bent on world conquest now as in five or ten years."[15]

After the policy memorandum was approved by the president on August 15, Acheson wasted no time before publicly announcing that the United States "had determined to stand firm against any Russian military expansion into the Turkish-controlled Dardanelles."[16] Turkey's rejection of Russia's demands now had the backing of the United States, which makes it unsurprising that on October 26 Turkey's delegate to the United Nations felt that he could reiterate "his country's determination not to be intimidated by Soviet demands for bases on the Dardanelles."[17]

The diplomatic confrontation quickly faded—and disappeared completely after Stalin died in 1953. The only thing that changed was that the naval task force that Truman sent to the Mediterranean to show that he meant business became, in 1948, the US Sixth Fleet, based at Naples. The permanent US peacetime naval presence in the Mediterranean replaced that of Britain's Royal Navy. Truman had had a taste of containment. Three essential elements of containment doctrine had come together: the intellectual foundation provided by Kennan, the strategic competence provided by Acheson, and the political will provided by Truman. Thus it would be for the remainder of Truman's presidency.

Truman surely wished to his dying day that his domestic political fortunes in 1946 could have been as good as his geopolitical fortunes. The domestic issues dominating the headlines—soaring meat prices and strikes by major labor unions, to cite only two—were damaging to the Democratic incumbents who had controlled the federal government for so many years. The international issues were, if nothing else, irritating. And it didn't help that Truman had to go so far as to deny, a few weeks before the election, an assertion by his ardent leftist secretary of commerce, Henry Wallace (Roosevelt's vice president from 1941 to January 1945), that there was now "a 'school of military thinking' [that] 'advocated a preventive war,' an attack on Russia now before Russia has atomic bombs."[18] (Truman promptly fired Wallace.) In the face of unrelenting Republican attacks, Truman's approval rating in the last Gallup poll before the election fell to an abysmal 33 percent. Some Democratic candidates went so far as to play recordings of Roosevelt speeches in the hope of improving their odds.[19] Politically, Truman had almost become toxic.

The result in November was that for the Republicans, as for Josef Stalin, 1946 was a very good election year. The historic landslide cost the Democrats fifty-four seats in the House and eleven seats in the Senate—putting control of both chambers in Republican hands for the first time since 1932. The shock of the election and the prospect of divided government were such that Senator J. William Fulbright—a Democrat—went so far as to propose that the president appoint a Republican secretary of state and then resign the presidency, only to be succeeded by that appointee.[20] Truman was unimpressed. Even *Pravda* weighed in, opining that Truman's party had lost because it "did not support 'a comparatively progressive program' and borrowed most of its election promises from the Republicans."[21]

At year's end in 1946, Stalin's political prestige had never been higher; Truman's had never been lower.

The 1946 Election: Faces in the Crowd

The 1946 elections also marked the public debut of two men from whom more—much more—would be heard later: Joseph R. McCarthy and Richard M. Nixon. McCarthy was elected to the Senate from Wisconsin. His successful campaign rested, as did many others that year, on his war record. His demagogic brand of anticommunism, so prominent only a few years later, played no role in his campaign. Nixon, a navy veteran, was elected to the House of Representatives from southern California. Nixon succeeded in putting a "leftist taint" on his Democratic opponent, Jerry Voorhis (the incumbent).[22] Against charges by Nixon supporters that, as a congressman, he voted in favor of the "'party line' of Moscow,"[23] Voorhis found it necessary to insist that he was not "pro-Russian" on issues relating to "world peace."[24]

The February Surprise

On the first day of 1947, a natural occasion for reflection, Truman could look back on a year of geopolitical success. If, on that day, he could have known about the challenges that lay ahead, he would have reflected also on the powers reserved to the legislative branch—which is to say, denied to the executive branch—under Article I of the United States Constitution. The year just ended was one of executive-branch success. In terms of major initiatives, the executive powers of the president under Article II of the Constitution were all that Truman needed in 1946. The next two years would be decidedly different. From the American side, the next two years of the history of the Cold War would be written jointly by the Democratic president and a Republican-controlled Congress. The exercise of Article II executive power, alone, would no longer suffice. Since 1933, foreign policy issues had essentially been resolved by debates *within* the Democratic Party, pitting competing factions within that party against one another, with the Republicans, essentially, as bystanders. The imperative of working across the aisle to address geopolitical challenges was a new experience for virtually everyone in Congress and the administration.

On February 21, 1947, in a formal but confidential diplomatic note, the British ambassador informed the United States, quite simply, that Great Britain could no longer afford to supply aid to Greece—then embroiled in a communist-inspired insurgency—and that British assistance would stop no later than April 1.[25] Acheson's advice was that "the capitulation of Greece to Soviet domination through lack of adequate support from the U.S. and Great Britain might eventually result in the loss of the whole Near and Middle East and northern Africa."[26] Truman agreed. He could not abide, as he later put it, "the loss of Greece and the extension of the iron curtain across the eastern Mediterranean."[27]

The British had assumed principal responsibility for reconstruction aid to Greece at the end of the war. But Great Britain, beggared by two wars, lacked the human capital or the financial resources—and perhaps even the will—to resume its role as power broker in Europe. It was not necessary for the British ambassador's note to say as much, but his note effectively announced the end of Pax Britannica. Britain was spent, financially and in spirit.

Truman and the State Department quickly formulated a proposal for $400 million in aid for Greece and Turkey. But the funds had to be appropriated by Congress. There were two problems: the money and the policy. There was also the distinct possibility that, regardless of the merits with respect to the money or the policy, partisan politics would color the debate in the Republican Congress. The Republicans, looking ahead to 1948, had no reason to go out of their way to make a Democratic president—let alone one who could hardly have been regarded as a leader in international affairs before the spring of 1945—look like a serious player on the world stage.

The money—huge though that sum was in 1947—was probably the easier part of the problem. The policy question was whether the United States would turn away from its long and deeply entrenched tradition of peacetime isolationism. Truman acknowledged in his memoirs that as he prepared to make his case to Congress he "could never quite forget the strong hold which isolationism had gained over our country after World War I."[28] Actually, isolationism had had a strong hold on the United States for more than 150 years.

Isolationism

From its earliest days, the United States was interested in international commerce but not military alliances, to say nothing of aid—financial or otherwise—to nations half a world away. The new nation sought commercial power but almost invariably avoided global power politics.

In his farewell address, President George Washington set the tone, emphasizing the need to "steer clear of permanent alliances with any portion of the foreign world."[29] Less than five years after Washington gave his advice, President Thomas Jefferson, in his first inaugural address, put it even more succinctly, counseling "peace, commerce, and honest friendship with all nations, entangling alliances with none."[30] Tocqueville summed it up quite well in 1835: "The policy of the Americans toward the rest of the world is simple. One might almost say that no one needs them, nor do they need anyone."[31]

Isolationism prevailed for 150 years after Washington gave the new nation his cautionary advice. In August of 1941, four months before Pearl Harbor, the House of Representatives voted to extend the military draft for one year. The vote was 203 to 202. After German U-boats torpedoed two US destroyers in October 1941, killing 111, the House of Representatives could muster no more than a 212 to 194 vote to amend the Neutrality Act to permit the arming of US merchant ships, illustrating what might be called the background level of isolationism in the United States.

So it was that, in early 1947, Truman was confronted with challenges—political and geopolitical—as grave as those faced by virtually any other US president. At the beginning of the year, he had been the president for less than two years and was still smarting from the disastrous 1946 midterm elections. When confronted with the news about the precarious situation in Greece and Turkey, he knew that unprecedented action was needed and that the United States was the only nation in a position to take that action.

Truman's actions in the first three months of 1947 bespeak a man who gave no thought to doing anything other than that which he knew in his heart was the right thing for his country and the wider world. But he was also well aware that politics was in the mix—the response that was needed in the eastern Mediterranean far exceeded anything that could be implemented with executive power alone. Isolationism was an especially deeply rooted tradition for the Republican Party, now in control of Congress. Regardless of what might be the right thing to do, as an abstract moral and policy proposition, Truman and his advisors knew that it would not be enough for the president to go before Congress and the nation simply as an advocate for freedom (at the expense of US taxpayers) for a small country thousands of miles away. Truman had to find something to neutralize isolationism. He found it. Truman prevailed in the spring of 1947 because the threat was not just a threat to freedom; it was a *communist* threat to freedom. With the benefit of shrewd advice from several quarters, Truman delivered a message—perhaps wrapped in a rawer form of anticommunism than he and some of his advisors would have preferred—that the isolationists in Congress, the commentariat, and the public at large could not ignore.

Anticommunism was nothing new in American politics in 1947. But, more or less by common consent, anticommunism as a political cause had lain dormant during the war years. That ended with the end of the war—and, as we have seen, those for whom anticommunism was a political casus belli had plenty of material to work with beginning with Yalta in early 1945. The rhetorical raw material was readily at hand.

One of the most prominent players in resurgent postwar anticommunism was the House Un-American Activities Committee (HUAC), the role of which was to investigate and expose disloyal or subversive Americans, especially those suspected of being communists or having communist sympathies. In 1947, HUAC made national headlines by launching an investigation into alleged communist infiltration into the US film industry. The postwar Red Scare was in full swing. Although, as a conceptual matter, there was not complete congruence between the domestic communist threat and the challenges posed by international communism (far from it), Truman understood quite well that this was not the time to explain to the American people that there were some significant differences between the two.

Truman, having been fully informed of the gravity and urgency of the crises in Greece and Turkey, had the good judgment to bring key Republicans into the conversation before he went to Congress. The proposal he had in mind was distinguished by its cost to the taxpayers and, of at least equal importance, by the fact that it marked a historic turn in American foreign policy.

On the Republican side, Senator Arthur Vandenberg, of Michigan, was the chairman of the Senate Foreign Relations Committee, having assumed that coveted office after the Republican landslide in the fall of 1946. Truman's proposal would get nowhere without his support. Truman succeeded in getting both his support and his political advice. His advice: "Mr. President, the only way you are ever going to get this is to make a speech that will scare the hell out of the country."[32]

Truman delivered his address to a joint session of Congress on March 12. The speech was as strong as was politically necessary. When the speech was in draft form, Charles Bohlen, an American patriot and East-West diplomat of the first order, thought "there was a little too much flamboyant anticommunism in the speech."[33] From a diplomatic perspective, Bohlen may well have been correct. But, of necessity, domestic politics trumped diplomacy. In the speech as delivered from the rostrum of the House of Representatives, the "scare" recommended by Senator Vandenberg came in equal parts from the *nature* of the threat (the impending demise of Greece and Turkey as free nations) and the *source* of the threat. In Greece, it was the "terrorist activities of several thousand armed men, led by Communists." Truman described the ultimate ramifications of the communist threat in stark binary terms:

> At the present moment in world history nearly every nation must choose between alternative ways of life. The choice is too often not a free one.
>
> One way of life is based upon the will of the majority, and is distinguished by free institutions, representative government, free elections, guarantees of individual liberty, freedom of speech and religion, and freedom from political oppression.
>
> The second way of life is based upon the will of a minority forcibly imposed upon the majority. It relies upon terror and oppression, a controlled press and radio; fixed elections, and the suppression of personal freedoms.

On this premise, the president articulated what soon came to be known as the Truman Doctrine: "I believe that it must be the policy of the United States to support free peoples who are resisting attempted subjugation by armed minorities or by outside pressures. I believe that we must assist free peoples to work out their own destinies in their own way."

The "immediate and resolute" action the president requested was the appropriation of $400 million for aid to Greece and Turkey. "Should we fail to aid Greece and Turkey in this fateful hour, the effect will be far reaching to the West as well as to the East."[34]

Of course, as the president, Truman was perfectly free on his own to proclaim the doctrine as a matter of foreign policy. Getting the money for Greece and Turkey was another matter: legislation was required. It was provident for Truman that those legislators whose isolationist tendencies would have put them among the least likely to vote for hundreds of million dollars in aid for two small countries on the other side of the world were, with almost complete congruence, the legislators most likely to come to attention when told that this threat was a *communist* threat.

With Eastern Europe firmly in the Kremlin's grip in and after 1945, there was ample reason to be concerned about the communist brand of totalitarianism. But Truman was not, by nature, a red-baiter, as would become clear later in his presidency. Clark Clifford, one of Truman's most trusted counselors, put it well when he wrote that as far as Truman was concerned, "communism was a threat *to* America, but not a threat *in* America."[35] Nonetheless, given the tenor of the times in the spring of 1947, and given the legislative challenge confronting Truman as the chief advocate of a $400 million aid package for Greece and Turkey, it is not by chance that Truman signed an executive order creating an employee loyalty program less than two weeks after his March 12 address. He needed to remove any doubt as to his anticommunist bona fides. (An early 1948 opinion poll indicated 67 percent approval for banning communists from civil service employment.[36]) Of equal importance, he needed to demonstrate to all who might wonder about the depth and breadth of his anticommunism that he was as willing to take as strong action domestically as he obviously was internationally.

The employee loyalty program, as embodied in Executive Order 9835,[37] mandated a loyalty investigation of every applicant for employment in the executive branch, as well as every one of some two million incumbent employees. As a general proposition, Truman had no problem with ridding the government of communists. But we now know enough about him, from his memoirs and otherwise, to understand that he must have swallowed hard before he put his signature on a document directing the creation of a "loyalty board"[38] in each federal agency for the purpose of adjudicating the loyalty of incumbent employees of the executive branch. But with the employee loyalty program girding his right flank, Truman and his congressional allies were now in a position to press for enactment of the Greece-Turkey aid package.

A Movement Reborn

By 1947, the public perception of the communist threat was grounded in events, not abstract theories. The threat was real and it was Russian: the *communist* threat was, first and last, a *Russian* threat. That reality of the 1940s still has an impact on the attitudes of Americans across the political spectrum. And on the issue of loyalty and the related task of ridding the government of communists, an intellectually honest analysis of the issue must recognize that by the late 1940s communism was not some abstract collection of Marxist notions, fair game for dialectical debate but not much else. To the contrary, by 1947, communism was, unmistakably, the proprietary ideology—and intended export—of the Soviet Union. It was, thus, reasonable to wonder whether, with the Cold War in full swing, a card-carrying communist employed in a sensitive position in the executive branch of the US government would find it difficult to act solely in the interest of the United States in any matters that might affect the interests of the Soviet Union. In short, in 1947, anticommunism was not just a preoccupation for right-wing extremists. With varying degrees of intensity, attitudes across the political spectrum—save for the far-left end—evolved to equate anticommunism with Americanism.

Executive Order 9835 itself was an unmistakable sign that change was in the air. For federal employment, any form of political screening for employment in the civil service had been expressly prohibited for nearly six decades before World War II. Civil Service Rule I, adopted in 1884, stated: "No question in any form or application in any examination shall be so framed as to elicit information concerning the political or religious opinions or affiliations of any applicant, nor shall any inquiry be made concerning such opinions or affiliations, and all disclosures thereof shall be discountenanced."[39] By the spring of 1947, it was plain that Civil Service Rule I, or rules of similar import, would not stand in the way of ridding the government of communists. Where communists were concerned, Rule I was a quaint relic of late nineteenth-century reform politics.

Press coverage of Truman's employee loyalty program was favorable. A day after Truman signed the order, and under the headline "President Orders Inquiry on Disloyal Jobholders; Communists First Target," the *New York Times* duly reported that "Communists and Communist sympathizers would be the first targets of the President's prescribed loyalty standards."

In early April, with the Greece-Turkey legislation still pending, Truman had to tread a fine line. He had no stomach for pandering to the most fervent of the red-baiters, but he needed a lot of Republican votes from the Republican-controlled Congress. With refreshing candor, garnished with a generous pinch of common sense, Truman addressed the topic at his April 3, 1947, press conference—the 101st press conference of his presidency: "I am not worried about the Communist Party taking over the Government of the United States, but I am against a person, whose loyalty is not to the Government of the United States, holding a Government job. They are entirely different things. I am not worried about this country ever going Communist. We have too much sense for that."[40]

By the end of July, Congress had appropriated $11 million to implement the employee loyalty program, including $7.4 million for the FBI.[41] Once the loyalty program was in place, three thousand federal employees either gave up their jobs or were discharged from their civil service employment under a cloud of suspicion.

So it was, in late April 1947: Truman's momentous speech had been made, the loyalty program was in place, and the situation in the eastern Mediterranean was not getting any better, but isolationism was still a formidable force in American politics. Passage of the Greece-Turkey aid bill was not assured. Republicans remained torn between isolationism and anticommunism, with concern about the cost of Truman's proposal threatening to be the tie breaker. The aid package had been the subject of a spirited debate on the floor of the House on March 28, just a week after Truman enacted the loyalty program and just over two weeks after Truman's address to Congress.

Viewed through the prism of decades of American anticommunism, the debate revealed some fascinating philosophical alignments. For many Republicans, isolationism prevailed over the brand of anticommunism that was embodied in the pending aid proposal—this despite the fact that they would yield to no one in terms of ardent domestic anticommunism. In contrast, Democratic Congressman (and later Speaker of the House) John McCormack of Massachusetts argued at length in favor of the aid package, contending that it would be "unwise for our country to remain inactive and by default allow nation after nation to be taken over by a vigorous communistic minority to be followed by the people's being subjected to ruthless force and then ultimately to be taken within the orbit—I will say this frankly—within the orbit of the Soviet Union."[42] As the next decade would amply demonstrate, the Democrats were, at times, less ardent in their anticommunism than the Republicans, especially when the Democrats perceived a threat to fundamental civil liberties. But, in the spring of 1947, postwar anticommunism was still in a fairly nascent stage; the political crosscurrents could be a bit confusing. This was, in a sense, a manifestation of the mixed inclinations of the public in general. In early 1947, 60 percent of the US population was generally critical of the Soviet Union, but more than 70 percent opposed a "get tough with Russia" policy.[43]

After the congressional debates were over and the matter was put to a vote, Truman's brand of anticommunism prevailed. In late April 1947, the Senate voted overwhelmingly in favor of the aid package: 67 to 23. The House did the same, by a margin of almost three to one, in early May. As Isaacson and Thomas put it: "Both liberals and Republicans were trapped: neither could afford to appear soft on Communism."[44] By the spring of 1947, anticommunism was unquestionably becoming, once again, a potent force in US politics. Congress appropriated $400 million—an enormous sum by 1947 standards—for the purpose of combating communist influence in Greece and Turkey. Isolationism was dead.

Within a year after the aid package was enacted (and possibly sooner than that), Stalin washed his hands of any notion of aiding the insurgents who were fighting in Greece. In February 1948, Stalin and Molotov were having a wide-ranging conference (and complaint session) in the Kremlin with the prime minister of Bulgaria (Georgi Dimitrov) and the deputy prime minister of Yugoslavia (Edvard Kardelj). The conversation, as recorded by Milovan Djilas, turned to "the uprising in Greece." Kardelj had the misfortune of suggesting to Stalin that the Greek uprising might succeed "if serious political and military errors are not made." Stalin promptly set the deputy prime minister straight: "No, they have no prospect of success at all. What do you think, that Great Britain and the United States—the United States, the most powerful state in the world—will permit you to break their line of communication in the Mediterranean Sea! Nonsense. And we have no navy. The uprising in Greece must be stopped, and as quickly as possible."[45] The uprising was stopped. There is little doubt that, if the rebels had succeeded, Greece would have fallen into the Soviet orbit.[46] And the story of the ensuing forty-four years would likely have been vastly different.

Chapter 5

Two Years That Set the Stage for the Next Four Decades

Harry S. Truman had reason to be satisfied with himself after he signed the Greece-Turkey aid package into law. Working with a cadre of dedicated and superbly competent diplomatic and military officers (more about that later), Truman had brought about a sea change in US foreign policy. But satisfied though he surely was at midyear 1947, Truman remained keenly aware of the political rout the voters had handed him just a few months before. He was charged with leading the free world in some of the most momentous times the nation had seen since the Civil War. He was also keenly aware that his lease on the White House was up for renewal, or not, as those voters might see fit, in November 1948. He also knew that Western Europe was a shambles, economically and in spirit. Western Europe was ripe for communist influence. Both sides knew that it was not just the future of Western Europe that was at stake. Though Western Europe was to be the venue for the unfolding geopolitical confrontation, Truman needed no tutoring to understand that the consequences of the struggle would come to rest far beyond that subcontinent.

So it was that, with Truman's approval, Secretary of State George C. Marshall proposed what came to be known as the Marshall Plan in an address at Harvard University on June 5, 1947. Having met with Stalin in April 1947, Marshall (the newly appointed secretary of state) had concluded that Stalin was "biding his time, waiting for conditions to worsen in Western Europe, and hoping to capitalize on the deterioration."[1]

Marshall needed to convey both the need and the urgency of the need in his Harvard address. He succeeded. It helped, of course, that Marshall was by then well established as a leader whose competence, loyalty, and dedication were beyond question. To listen to the speech is to understand that Marshall was no orator.[2] But in eleven minutes, Marshall publicly laid the groundwork for one of the most consequential legislative and geopolitical initiatives of the postwar era.

At the heart of the speech was Marshall's proposal that the war-torn nations of Europe should devise a plan for their recovery and that the United States would provide economic assistance to make the plan work. That overarching objective could be plainly stated. But other considerations were at work, as can be seen if we annotate one important passage from Marshall's speech:

> It is logical that the United States should do whatever it is able to do to assist in the return of normal economic health in the world, without which there can be no political stability [*In other words: Without this aid, there is no assurance that we can quell communist-instigated political unrest and minimize the possibility of communist success at the ballot box.*] and no assured peace. Our policy is directed not against any country or doctrine but against hunger, poverty, desperation and chaos. [*Although this plan is politically dead if Russia chooses to participate in it, we also have no need to overtly pick a fight with the Kremlin.*] Its purpose should be the revival of a working economy in the world so as to permit the emergence of political and social conditions in which free [*e.g., noncommunist*] institutions can exist. Such assistance, I am convinced, must not be on a piece-meal basis as various crises develop. [*We cannot sit back and let the Russians decide where they will next cause trouble.*] Any assistance that this Government may render in the future should provide a cure rather than a mere palliative. [*Brace yourselves. This is going to be expensive.*] Any government that is willing to assist in the task of recovery will find full cooperation, I am sure, on the part of the United States Government. Any government which maneuvers to block the recovery of other countries cannot expect help from us. [*If the Russians foment unrest in the free countries of Europe, we may start talking about repayment of Lend-Lease debt.*] Furthermore,

> governments, political parties or groups which seek to perpetuate human misery in order to profit therefrom politically or otherwise will encounter the opposition of the United States. [*We mean to prevent a repeat of the postwar experiences in Iran, Greece, and Turkey.*][3]

Marshall's proposal did not exclude the Soviet Union and the Eastern European nations from participation in the recovery program. That was intentional. Russia and its satellites would be put to a choice. And here is where the timing gets interesting.

Ernest Bevin, the British Foreign Minister, and Georges Bidault, Bevin's French counterpart, wasted no time meeting in Paris to discuss Marshall's Harvard proposal. They met on June 17 and soon announced that Europe should move forward with Marshall's proposal regardless of whether the Soviet Union chose to participate. To get some clarity on that issue, Bevin and Bidault were joined by Soviet Foreign Minister Molotov—and a staff of eighty[4]—on June 27. Within four days, it was clear that Molotov was having none of a plan which might weaken Russian control of Eastern Europe. He left the conference on July 2. The Soviets then made sure that the Czechs, the Poles, and the Hungarians understood that Moscow expected them to have nothing to do with the Marshall Plan.

Molotov left the Paris conference for all the right reasons—from his perspective. In fact, there was never any real reason to believe that Russia would participate—or allow its satellites to participate—in an aid program funded and controlled (at least de facto) by the United States. The US planners who crafted the plan were well aware of that, but they made a strategic judgment that it would be bad form to expressly exclude the Soviet bloc. There was a certain element of risk here for the administration: Prospects for congressional approval of the Marshall Plan—highly uncertain until the spring of 1948—would have dimmed significantly if the Russians had been genuinely interested in it. The open invitation to the USSR was both a ploy and a gamble. The gamble paid off. As the Soviets told their children in an August 1947 issue of *Pionerskaya Pravda* (a children's newspaper): "The 'Marshall Plan' was simply a cunning way of subjecting all Europe to American capital."[5]

In the fall of 1947, what *was* unsettled was the prospect for congressional approval of an economic rescue plan of the magnitude proposed by Marshall. The Republican-controlled Congress was heavily populated with members who had never voted for a foreign aid bill and quite understandably believed that any new postwar spending should be devoted to domestic programs for the benefit of the returned service members and their families. Truman's March speech had been sufficient to get Congress to spend hundreds of millions of dollars to alleviate an unquestionably urgent need in the eastern Mediterranean, but now we were talking about billions, not millions, for a cause that did not quite so obviously demand US aid in the interest of national security. Truman needed a way to give the American people a fresh reminder of the urgency of the communist threat to stability in Western Europe. Stalin provided it. The *New York Times* was not given to screaming headlines, but its October 6, 1947, headline and the subheads were a bit of an exception:

REDS OF 9 NATIONS REVIVE COMINTERN
TO FIGHT U.S. "IMPERIALIST HEGEMONY";
2 STALIN AIDES ATTEND SECRET MEETING
Sources in Washington Expect Deterioration
in Soviet Relations
New Information Bureau Will Seek
to Unify Strategy of Reds[6]

Cominform (Communist Information Bureau), a rebranding of the prewar Comintern (Communist International), was formally founded at a multinational meeting of Communist Party delegates on October 5. Four days after he had left Paris in June, Molotov had called for the establishment of Cominform.[7] Although Cominform was not in every respect a replication of Comintern (which had been dissolved in May 1943), it was close enough. In terms of the legislative prospects of the Marshall Plan, the founding of Cominform was a gift to Truman.

At home in the United States, the receptiveness of the general public to the Marshall Plan went hand in hand with a resurgence of domestic anticommunist activity. Evan Thomas very cogently observes that the members of the House Un-American Activities Committee "tended to be blowhards or worse."[8] But sometimes even blowhards can perform a useful function, even if unwittingly. In the fall of 1947, HUAC had in hand a report asserting that more than five hundred writers in the US motion-picture industry "either belong to the Communist Party or follow the party line to the letter."[9] Beginning in October 1947, "a parade of screen personalities regaled the [HUAC] investigators with tales of Communist influence in the industry."[10] (Not the least of the witnesses in the HUAC hearings was a young actor—and former New Deal liberal—named Ronald Reagan.) Anticommunism was now getting a full head of steam. The showboating of the HUAC members probably did not appeal to Truman, but, in their own way, they were helping to get the American public ready to spend billions of dollars to stem the tide of communism. There was not much pushback against rhetoric that conflated the domestic communist threat—such as it was—with the challenge presented by the Kremlin's European adventures. HUAC's anticommunism was aimed at the domestic movement; the administration was content to focus on Russia's threat to Western Europe.

Truman called for Congress to "proceed as rapidly as possible in order that the [Marshall Plan] may become effective by April 1, 1948."[11] Truman missed that date by only two days. Though Truman and Marshall were off to a good start, prospects for enactment of the plan would improve if something were to happen that would shore up a sense of national unity, overriding the usual temptations of partisan politics.

Once again, the interplay between East and West came to the rescue. The existence of a vestigial, more or less democratic government in Czechoslovakia was an irritant to the Kremlin. That government was a potential source of outright resistance to all-embracing control from Moscow. This would never do. In February 1948, with Soviet troops camped on the border, Stalin approved a plan by Czechoslovak communists to seize power in Prague. As described by Truman in his memoir: "On February 25, 1948, however, democratic Czechoslovakia, for the second time in less than nine years, fell under the heel of totalitarianism."[12]

The Marshall Plan did not languish in Congress much longer. Three weeks after the communist coup in Prague, and one year plus three days after he addressed a joint session of Congress to seek aid for Greece and Turkey, Truman again addressed a joint session. The Czech coup had only heightened the sense of urgency with which Truman addressed the assembled legislators. In this election year, he now had a concrete basis for a plea for national unity and bipartisan resolve.

In this address to Congress (and the nation) on March 17, 1948, Truman spoke in more somber tones than he had a year previously, reiterating his case for swift enactment of the Marshall Plan. But there was more. Making his case against the backdrop of "the tragic death of the Republic of Czechoslovakia," which he said "has sent a shock throughout the civilized world," Truman told Congress that "measures for economic rehabilitation alone are not enough." There must be "some measure of protection against internal and external aggression."[13] In this speech to a nation that wanted to think of almost anything other than war and military matters, Truman delivered a full-throated call for legislation to reinstate the military draft, the authority for which had lapsed after the war. The political context was remarkable by any standard: a politically vulnerable president asked a legislature controlled by the opposing party to enact a peacetime draft a few months before the first postwar presidential election.

Truman needed a healthy measure of bipartisanship in an inherently partisan year. For that reason, the leadership, to say nothing of the integrity, of Senator Arthur Vandenberg, the Michigan Republican, must again be mentioned. Vandenberg's evolution in the sphere of foreign relations was, in large measure, the nation's evolution. The geopolitics of the war, followed by what was obviously a perilous peace, convinced Vandenberg that his—and the nation's—historical isolationism could no longer be an option, even in peacetime, for the United States.

The most notable waypoint in Vandenberg's journey to internationalism was a historic speech—as much an address to the nation as to his fellow senators—on the Senate floor in January 1945, more than two years before his relinquishment of isolationism would be put to its severest tests. Vandenberg made his case, with soaring rhetoric, for America's new role in the world: "There are critical moments in the life of every nation which call for the straightest, plainest and the most courageous thinking of which we are capable. We confront such a moment now."[14] Vandenberg's floor speech, perhaps the most influential internationalist speech ever made on the Senate floor,[15] was all the more notable for having been made three weeks *before* the start of the Yalta conference.

Vandenberg understood where Stalin was headed. Even so, he could hardly have foreseen what a thoroughgoing commitment to internationalism would require in the next three years.

Bipartisanship carried the day, and did so in a way that is all the more remarkable from the perspective of twenty-first century congressional dysfunction. Truman had the support of a conservative Republican leader, despite his political pedigree and despite that Vandenberg had his own presidential aspirations. The Marshall Plan was passed by the Senate in mid-March 1948, by a vote of 69 to 17 and by the House on April 2 by a vote of 329 to 74. (Richard M. Nixon, then a back-bench Republican House member, was one of the first House Republicans to declare his support for the Marshall Plan.) Truman promptly signed it into law. No less an authority than Charles Bohlen has recorded that two predominant factors helped assure passage of the Marshall Plan: "the indefatigable work of Senator Vandenberg" and "the Communist coup in Czechoslovakia."[16] The very idea of the United States as leader of the free world could now get traction on both sides of the political divide, albeit perhaps on the basis of slightly differing motives on the two sides. For the Republicans especially, the ideological catnip was that the Soviet threat was a *communist* threat. The unity resulting from this convergence of the two parties in an otherwise fractious political environment was of surpassing importance. Over four years, Marshall Plan aid, which in all its forms totaled more than $13 billion, was devoted to the reconstruction of devastated European economies. Of equal importance, the Marshall Plan established the concept of foreign aid as an instrument of US foreign policy.

It may well be that, for the general population of the United States, the enactment of the Marshall Plan gave rise to at least a vague, and vaguely reassuring, sense that Western Europe, and East-West relations, were headed toward a general state of equilibrium. That was not to be. The cascade of events continued at an accelerating pace. Attitudes on both sides were hardening, as was obvious from a whirlwind of momentous events in June 1948. They all had lasting significance. But perhaps of greater significance is that June 1948 did not end with Russia and the Western allies at war. June 1948 saw events and decisions that had much to do with the development of the rules of Cold War engagement that prevailed for four decades.

The Vandenberg Resolution

The events of the first five months of 1948 made it plain to decision-makers in the Truman administration and in Congress that the increasing pressure from the East might necessitate something more than economic aid to Western Europe. Western Europe needed security—and a *sense* of security—beyond that which US dollars alone could provide. In May, Truman, on the recommendation of Secretary of State Marshall, approved a draft of what became known as the Vandenberg Resolution. For Congress, the administration, and the American public, the resolution provided the beginning point for what became the North Atlantic Treaty Organization. The resolution affirmed the policy of the United States to pursue "progressive development of regional and other collective arrangements for individual and collective self-defense in accordance with the purposes, principles, and provisions of the [UN] Charter."[17]

Senator Vandenberg's sponsorship of this resolution established beyond question that his advocacy of collective security in his landmark speech in January 1945, had not been idle talk. But now there was a new wrinkle. In 1945 Vandenberg, supportive of the then-nascent UN organization, had focused on "collective security" in the form of "a vital international organization in which all of us shall honorably participate." But, to put it mildly, "all of us" were not on the same page vis-à-vis the persistent pressure from the East. Soviet use of the veto in the Security Council in the first years of the United Nations had demonstrated beyond question that, with respect to East-West conflicts, the United Nations would not be much more than a debating society. Meaningful *collective* security agreements aimed at countering the Soviet threat had to be consistent with the UN Charter while permitting collective response even when (because of a veto in the Security Council) the United Nations failed to act.

On the subject of regional or other collective-security arrangements and their viability under international law, Vandenberg knew whereof he spoke. At the San Francisco conference in the spring of 1945, the senator, as a member of the US delegation, successfully supported the adoption of Article 51 of the UN Charter, which made it clear that the United Nations did not have a monopoly on collective military action: "Nothing in the present Charter shall impair the inherent right of individual or collective self-defence if an armed attack occurs against a Member of the United Nations, until the Security Council has taken measures necessary to maintain international peace and security."[18]

Under this charter provision, three words, "collective self-defence," provided the legal gateway to the formation of the regional collective security organizations—separate from the United Nations—of the postwar era. It is, thus, not a historical accident that the eighth decade of the existence of the United Nations is also the eighth decade of the existence of the NATO alliance. The Vandenberg Resolution was passed by the Senate on June 11, by a vote of 64 to 4. On the same day (although there is no evidence that there was a specific cause-and-effect relationship), the Soviets initiated a two-day stoppage of rail traffic between Berlin and the West. In one day, the groundwork for the founding of NATO had been laid, and the West got the first taste of the Berlin Blockade.

With the benefit of hindsight, it is fair to say, also, that that June day marked a turning point in the postwar era because it unmistakably reaffirmed bipartisanship as the touchstone of US foreign policy in general, and in the Cold War in particular. That bipartisanship remains important to preserve the understanding among allies, potential allies, and coalition partners, that they do not have to guess whether they need to curry favor with Democrats or with Republicans in order to stand in good stead with the United States.

Blockade

The June cascade of events continued—and accelerated, almost as if encouraged by the arrival of summer weather. The Soviets had been attempting to impose an eastern-zone currency on all of Berlin. This did not sit well with the officers responsible for the economic viability of the western zones. The Soviet-issued reichsmarks—called wallpaper marks by Berliners—were neither conducive to stable economic activity nor free from manipulation. In anticipation of the need for a more reliable currency, the US authorities had laid in a large supply of freshly printed new bills: the deutschmark. The conversion to the deutschmark for western Germany and the western-controlled sectors of Berlin was announced by the military authorities of the Western allies on June 18. The battle of the two currencies was, as a practical matter, a battle for Berlin.[19] Of equal significance, this was all a precursor to the establishment of a separate West German government, a fact of which the Soviets were well aware. They had had enough. On the evening of the eighteenth, the Soviets began the process of blocking all road traffic between Berlin and the West, which prompted the Western allies to block all movement of goods by railroad between East Germany and the Western zone.

Three days later, on the twenty-first, the Western allies started the Berlin airlift, which was answered by the Soviets on the twenty-fourth with the cutoff of all electricity, coal, food, and other supplies flowing into Berlin and the blocking of all rail and barge traffic in and out of Berlin. Logistically, Berlin was now an island accessible only by air. Truman directed that every available plane be pressed into service.[20] Aside from transports, sixty long-range US Air Force bombers were quickly deployed from the United States to British bases, and thirty B-29s were deployed to bases in Western Germany. The American bombers were weapons in a war of nerves. B-29s were the planes that dropped the atomic bombs on Japan. Undisclosed in June 1948 was that the B-29s deployed to Germany had not been modified to carry atomic bombs.[21]

The conversion to the deutschmark, followed by the blockade and the airlift, removed all doubt: there was no future for East-West cooperation in Germany. Diplomatic efforts to end the blockade fell short. But the real problem was not the new allied-sponsored currency in Berlin. The real problem was what the Kremlin clearly—and correctly—saw as the steady progression of events toward separate statehood for the Western zones of Germany. Stopping that trend was surpassingly important to the Kremlin leadership. That was true both because of the history that had been written and the blood that had been spilled, and because of the obvious prospect of decades of East-West struggle.

It is worth pausing here to reflect on the fact that this cascade of events in the late spring and early summer of 1948 did not result in war. Stalin and Truman both had their advisors, of course, but the gravity of the events of June 1948 can only lead to the conclusion that there were times during that month when both of them must have felt very much alone. Truman had shown extraordinary political courage in this first postwar presidential election year, and had successfully exerted his influence on the Republicans on Capitol Hill. The question now hanging in the air was whether Truman, having shown that he had some persuasive power with Republicans, had any persuasive power with Stalin and the Politburo. For his part, Stalin needed no reminder that his was a war-torn country, still picking itself up from the utter devastation of the Great Patriotic War. But he also knew that if any objective was worth fighting for now, it was the objective of ensuring that Germany, having been defeated at colossal cost to his nation and its people, would not and could not rise again to pose a threat from the west.

It is perhaps provident that among their advisors, Truman had Marshall and Stalin had Molotov. Marshall, now Truman's secretary of state, had been chief of staff of the army from shortly after Pearl Harbor through the end of the war. Regrettably, Marshall never published a memoir. (He was not the kind of man who would have exaggerated his role in his memoir.) Marshall's counsel was highly influential with Truman, especially when, as in June 1948, military, diplomatic, political, and psychological issues were swept up into a single vortex. Stalin, of course, had his own inner circle, not the least of whom was the redoubtable Molotov. The old Bolshevik could not have forgotten his first conversation with Truman in the White House in April 1945, two weeks into Truman's presidency, when Truman had found it necessary or at least expedient to dispense with all diplomatic niceties.

As for the constellation of military forces in June 1948, both Truman and Stalin knew that the Soviet Army, if ordered to march west, could get to the Rhine in a weekend, and not even a long weekend. Under Secretary of State (and future secretary of defense) Robert Lovett was heard to say, perhaps with only slight exaggeration, that "all the Russians need to reach the Rhine is shoes."[22] After getting to the Rhine, it might well be slower going, but the mismatch in terms of raw numbers of available troops on either side of the Iron Curtain was stark. Russian troops stood seven hundred miles closer to the Atlantic Ocean than they had in 1939. A Russian push west would have been a bloody campaign, but it has never been persuasively suggested that the conventional forces of the Western Allies could have gone toe to toe on short notice with the Soviet Army in the early postwar years. What Stalin did not know is whether, with the arrival of the Soviet Army on the Rhine, the third atomic bomb ever to be deployed as a weapon of war would be detonated over Russian soil. Molotov's belief, at least as he later described it, was that "the bombs dropped on Japan were not aimed at Japan but rather at the Soviet Union," the message being: "You don't have an atomic bomb and we do, and this is what the consequences will be like if you make the wrong move."[23] In terms of American attitudes in the four years between August 1945 and the first Soviet detonation of an atomic bomb in 1949, Molotov may have had a point. Even an ex-governor of Pennsylvania would proclaim in 1946 that we should drop the bomb on the Russians "while we have it and before they get it."[24] As far as Stalin was concerned (and it is quite plausible that this is what he actually thought), atomic bombs were meant to frighten those with weak nerves (see chapter 7). So troops did not march, the bomb did not get dropped, and war did not result. The two sides were testing each other with measures short of war.

The testing continued. And, of course, it would continue for decades. But, on those June days in 1948, leaders in East and West were thinking in terms of hours and days, not decades. On June 24, three days after the airlift had begun and six days after the Soviets blocked road traffic to and from Berlin, Truman signed into law the legislation he had requested to reinstitute military conscription—the draft. The nonpartisan approach of the Republican congressional leadership in reinstituting the draft is vividly illustrated by the fact the twenty-fourth was also the day that, in Philadelphia, the Republican National Convention nominated Thomas E. Dewey to be the Republican candidate to run to unseat Truman in November. To close that day out, the Soviets completed the blockage of all rail and barge traffic into and out of Berlin. The Berlin blockade was now fully in place. A Gallup poll in July reported that "80 percent of respondents favored staying in Berlin even if it meant war."[25]

We now know that the world did not spin out of control in late June 1948. But no one at that time could have known for sure that it would not. Truman and Stalin were thus put to the test. They were, unquestionably, men of firm resolve. The question was whether that resolve was mindless resolve or resolve tempered with a sense of history and some semblance of geopolitical judgment. Berlin could not be abandoned to the Russians: not in a world that valued freedom, and not if containment of communist expansionism meant anything, not in an election year.

For both sides, the lesson of late June 1948—always implicit in geopolitical affairs but more sharply in focus than ever before—was that from any rung on the escalatory ladder, one could go up to the next rung, back down to a lower rung, or stand pat. In either direction there was risk. But moving to the next higher rung would inevitably present a heightened risk of triggering an uncontrollable sequence of events. The solution was the airlift—half a rung, if you will, up the escalatory ladder. Washington was content with the airlift because it was a middle path, calculated to avoid both war and the ignominy of surrender.[26] Stalin's measured response was to keep the blockade in place without shooting the unarmed transports out of the air over the Soviet zone. Truman and Stalin had chosen not to play with fire; war had been avoided, for now. Another page had been written in the book of rules of engagement—very much a work in progress in the summer of 1948.

More than two million tons of supplies (sometimes more than eight thousand tons in a single day) were airlifted to Berlin by the time the airlift ended in September 1949, four months after Soviets lifted the blockade.

Alger Hiss and Whittaker Chambers: The 1948 Campaign Gets a Bit More Complicated

With the Marshall Plan in place, the military draft reinstated, and the Berlin airlift up and running, Truman had ample reason to conclude, as the 1948 election campaign heated up, that he and his party were no longer vulnerable to attack from right-wing anticommunists. Even so, the last thing Truman needed was for the nation to be told that an ardent communist had been at the table at Yalta—already a symbol of surrender to the Kremlin—as a member of Roosevelt's delegation.[27] The Democrats could be portrayed as the lineal political descendants of the US delegation at Yalta even though many of those who were with Roosevelt at Yalta had moved on. So it was that in early August a long-simmering anticommunist story burst on to the front pages of newspapers across the nation. In testimony before HUAC, Whittaker Chambers, a distinguished *Time* magazine writer and editor, told the committee under oath that Alger Hiss, a senior political counselor in the State Department from 1939 to 1946, had been an active member of a communist cell, the mission of which was "the Communist infiltration of the American Government."[28] Hiss had been in the US delegation at the Dumbarton

Oaks conference that crafted the preliminary plan for the United Nations and had served as the secretary-general at the first meeting of the United Nations in San Francisco. Worse yet, Chambers testified that even though he had told the State Department about Hiss's communist activities "'almost exactly nine years ago' (two days after Hitler and Stalin signed their pact), nothing had been done about it."[29] Truman dismissed this story as a "red herring" designed to distract public attention away from the fact that the Republicans in Congress were not doing enough to curb inflation.[30]

Two days after Chambers gave his explosive testimony, Hiss—a Harvard-educated pillar of the eastern establishment—appeared before the same committee to testify. He told the committee under oath that he had never had anything to do with the Communist Party and had never, to the best of his knowledge, had a friend who was a communist.[31] For good measure, he added that he had never heard of Whittaker Chambers before 1947. Either Hiss or Chambers was lying under oath. Any lawyer worth his salt could recognize that this had all the makings of a perjury prosecution. Richard Nixon was such a lawyer. The future president promptly called for a perjury prosecution, leaving it to the Department of Justice to determine who should be put in the dock.[32]

As it turned out, Hiss was the one who was indicted, in part on the basis of five strips of microfilm that Chambers had hidden in a hollowed-out pumpkin on his farm in Maryland "so Communists would not find them."[33] Representative Richard Nixon went to the farm with Chambers (and a reporter for the *New York Herald-Tribune*), where Chambers duly handed the films over after removing them from the pumpkin in the pumpkin patch behind the farmhouse.[34] Nixon immediately announced that he "would bring the films [to Washington, DC] himself."[35] Hiss was indicted in December 1948 and was convicted by a jury of two counts of perjury in January 1950. The Hiss case was a no-win situation for Truman and Democrats on the left end of the spectrum who had sought to minimize the domestic communist threat.[36] For Truman, standing for election in November 1948 (thus, effectively asking the voters to ratify his succession to the presidency), it was no doubt helpful that the sensational revelations from August did not ripen into a formal prosecution until after the election. It may be a stretch to say that the trial and conviction of Hiss before the election, rather than fourteen months after, would have made a significant difference. But the Hiss case was just the sort of thing the Democrats did not need as the 1948 election approached.

The 1948 Election

The Democrats, having held the White House since the 1932 election, were on the defensive in 1948. In terms of presidential politics, Truman and the Democrats could be held accountable by the voters for sixteen years of depression and war, as well as a peace that was beginning to look like no peace at all. It was unusual in US presidential politics for a candidate to make foreign policy a major component of his campaign. But 1948 was not a typical presidential election year. Foreign policy was prominent in Truman's 1948 campaign, which was all the more unusual because the fall campaigns revealed no overarching foreign policy disagreements between the two major party presidential candidates.

Truman's strategy for the 1948 campaign was mapped out a full year before the election in a forty-three page memorandum that has rightly been called "one of the great dissertations on the art of politics."[37] The "Memorandum for the President"[38] was signed by Clark Clifford, then a bright, politically savvy Washington lawyer (with Missouri roots) who had served as special counsel to the president and would, decades later, serve as secretary of defense.[39] As relevant here, the memorandum is noteworthy for one thing it got wrong and for its focus at the intersection of geopolitics and U.S ethnic politics—what we would now call identity politics.

What the Clifford memorandum got wrong was its prediction that bipartisanship in foreign affairs would be a lost cause. He wrote, "*The foreign policy issues of the 1948 campaign will be our relations with the USSR and the Administration's handling of foreign reconstruction and relief* [emphasis in original]. The probability that the foreign affairs of the United States will remain on a basis of 'bi-partisan cooperation' is unfortunately remote."[40]

In terms of the United States versus communism, the Republican rhetoric in the 1948 campaign was noticeably feeble; the substantive differences between the two parties were even less noticeable. The Republican candidate, Thomas E. Dewey of New York, had compiled a varied career as Wall Street lawyer, crusading prosecutor, and governor of New York. In the time-honored tradition of former prosecutors running for higher office, Dewey reverted to prosecutorial mode. He did try to sound the alarm about the internal and external communist threat, but Truman had not given him much to work with. Dewey criticized the administration's "tragic concessions in many areas of the world,"[41] thus seeking, in essence, to cast the shadow of Yalta on Truman, who had been vice president for two weeks when the Yalta conference was convened (and was going about his business about ten time zones west of Crimea when the Yalta conferees sat down). As a right-wing rallying cry, Yalta lasted for decades, but the issue got very little traction in the 1948 presidential election. Outright demagoguery would have to await the early 1950s. This was an election year that saw the Marshall Plan enacted by an overwhelming bipartisan vote. In terms of both substance and campaign rhetoric, Clifford needn't have been so pessimistic about the prospects for bipartisanship on foreign policy.

On the subject of ethnic politics, the Clifford memorandum focused on groups Clifford put under the headings of "The Negro," "The Jew," "The Catholic," and "The Italian." In terms of foreign policy, Jews and Catholics warranted special attention. As for Jews, Clifford noted that the "Jewish vote, insofar as it can be thought of as a bloc, is important only in New York."[42] And, in 1948, New York had (by a considerable margin) more electoral votes than any other state. Clifford opined that "today the Jewish bloc is interested primarily in Palestine and will continue to be an uncertain quantity right up to the time of the election." Truman's main problem in New York was, of course, that Dewey was from New York and had been a popular governor of that state. As it turned out, Truman lost New York by less than 1 percent of the vote. As for "The Catholic," Clifford came right to the point: "The Catholic vote is traditionally Democratic. The controlling element in this group today from a political standpoint is the distrust and fear of Communism."[43] Despite Dewey's advantage in his home state of New York, the overall election results were fairly close in the northeastern and midwestern states with substantial Catholic populations.

As the 1948 campaign entered its final phase, the *New York Times* was impressed with Dewey, as was Radio Moscow. In an English-language broadcast delivered six days before the election and reported in the *New*

York Times, Radio Moscow "conceded the Presidential election to Gov. Thomas E. Dewey, although it still thinks Henry A. Wallace is the best candidate."[44] Wallace, who had served in various capacities under Roosevelt (including as vice president for one term), was the nominee of the far-left Progressive Party, and was endorsed by the Communist Party of the United States in the election. For its part, the *New York Times* endorsed Dewey and, like Radio Moscow, unequivocally predicted that he would win the election by a wide margin.[45]

The predictions were no better in 1948 than they were in 2016. Truman prevailed by more than two million votes and defeated Dewey by a margin of 303 to 189 in the Electoral College.[46] In the eighteen presidential elections since 1948 (through 2020), no incumbent presidential candidate who was down by as much as ten points in the polls at the time of his nominating convention (as was the case with Truman) has won the election. In the Senate, the Democrats gained nine seats, divesting the Republicans of the control they had enjoyed for only two of the preceding sixteen years. But the significance of the election for present purposes is twofold: First, the Soviets knew, on the morning after the election, that Truman and his resolute opposition to communist expansion were not going to just go away. Second, having just defeated a silkstocking lawyer from the eastern establishment in the election, Truman chose one to serve as his secretary of state. Dean Acheson returned to the State Department in January 1949, after a brief resumption of his private law practice. As undersecretary of state from just after the Potsdam conference until the middle of 1947, Acheson had earned Truman's complete confidence. He had been instrumental in formulating the Greece-Turkey aid package and the Marshall Plan. Although Acheson's patrician family background had little resemblance to Truman's, their personalities—particularly their inclinations to draw bright lines on questions of right and wrong—had much in common.

As Truman's secretary of state, George C. Marshall had been nothing if not a statesman. As undersecretary in the service of Marshall, Acheson provided indispensable support to Marshall's statesmanship. But the early postwar years had had their effect on Acheson; he would become Truman's relentless Cold Warrior. The first major product of the Truman-Acheson partnership was the North Atlantic Treaty, creating NATO, signed in Washington on April 4, 1949, less than three months after Acheson was sworn in as secretary of state. As Truman recorded in his memoir: "There would have been no NATO without Dean Acheson."[47]

NATO

The stars had to be aligned just right in 1949 (or in any other year since George Washington admonished his compatriots to "steer clear of permanent alliances with any portion of the foreign world") for the United States to enter into its first peacetime military alliance with a European nation. From the US perspective, NATO was born at the intersection of domestic politics, geopolitics, international law, and US constitutional law. For most if not all of the original European members of NATO, the story is simpler: It is not much of an oversimplification, if oversimplification at all, to say that for them NATO was born at the intersection of military destitution and acute anxiety about Soviet intentions. Europe had seen three major wars in seven decades, beginning with the Franco-Prussian War in 1870–71. For Western Europeans, security was as important as freedom. In NATO, they sought an assurance that they would have both.

Truman's unvarnished brand of anticommunism gained momentum with his stunning victory in November. The table was now set for the birth of a US-led alliance to confront the Soviet threat.

NATO Article 5 and UN Charter Article 51

Certain questions are as relevant now as they were in 1949: as to what NATO can and cannot lawfully do, and as to what the individual members of the NATO alliance are themselves obligated to do as signatories to the North Atlantic Treaty.

As of the spring of 1949, the ink had been dry on the UN Charter for just under four years. Recall that, at the San Francisco conference in the spring of 1945, Senator Arthur Vandenberg, as a member of the US delegation, had successfully advocated the adoption of Article 51, to assure that the UN Charter would not impair (in the language of Article 51) "the inherent right of individual or collective self-defence."

Vandenberg and his colleagues in the US delegation recognized that if the UN charter was going to give the Kremlin a veto in the Security Council, the Western nations could not bargain away their right to enter into other arrangements for "collective self-defence." But the origins and extent of the *right* of collective action (by NATO) and the *obligation* of a NATO member to commit its armed forces to that collective action deserve attention.

Three documents, each making specific reference to Article 51, are relevant here: (1) the Inter-American Treaty of Reciprocal Assistance (Rio Pact, signed on September 2, 1947); (2) the Brussels Treaty (signed on March 17, 1948); and (3) the North Atlantic Treaty (signed on April 4, 1949, creating the NATO alliance). The Kremlin insisted, in the spring of 1949, that the NATO alliance violated the UN Charter from the very beginning.

The obligation of one signatory nation to provide military assistance to a signatory which has been attacked was made noticeably more specific in the Brussels Treaty than it was in the Rio Pact. The Brussels Treaty (signed by France, the Netherlands, Belgium, Luxembourg, and the United Kingdom) was unequivocal. It declared, in mandatory language, that the signatory nations will afford the party that has been attacked "all the military and other aid and assistance in their power."

In terms of commitment to use military forces, Article 5 of the North Atlantic Treaty pales in comparison to the corresponding article of the Brussels Treaty. In plain terms, a NATO signatory is obliged only to take "such action as it deems necessary," which *may* include the use of armed force, to "restore and maintain the security of the North Atlantic area." Moreover, under Article 11, a NATO signatory is obliged to take action only in accordance with its "constitutional processes," which, in the United States, raises a morass of issues as to the allocation of war-making powers as between the president and Congress. There is a reason for the demonstrable weakness of the language of Article 5: the United States was unwilling to sign anything stronger.

In the formal negotiations for the North Atlantic Treaty in late 1948 and early 1949, it became clear that there would be no quick consensus on the precise terms of the collective defense commitment. As Acheson put it in his memoir, "The Europeans were naturally the most fervent advocates of strong and unequivocal commitments for aid in case of

Table 1. Three Treaties: Three Expressions of the Obligation to Commit Military Forces (emphasis added in each instance)

Rio Pact, Article 3 (1947): The High Contracting Parties agree that an armed attack by any State against an American State shall be considered as an attack against all the American States and, consequently, *each one of the said Contracting Parties undertakes to assist in meeting the attack* in the exercise of the inherent right of individual or collective self-defense recognized by Article 51 of the Charter of the United Nations.	**Brussels Treaty, Article IV** (1948): If any of the High Contracting Parties should be the object of an armed attack in Europe, *the other High Contracting Parties will, in accordance with the provisions of Article 51 of the Charter of the United Nations, afford the Party so attacked all the military and other aid and assistance in their power.*
North Atlantic Treaty (1949): Article 5: The Parties agree that an armed attack against one or more of them in Europe or North America shall be considered an attack against them all and consequently they agree that, if such an armed attack occurs, each of them, in exercise of the right of individual or collective self-defence recognised by Article 51 of the Charter of the United Nations, *will assist the Party or Parties so attacked by taking forthwith, individually and in concert with the other Parties, such action as it deems necessary, including the use of armed force, to restore and maintain the security of the North Atlantic area.* Article 11: This Treaty shall be ratified and its provisions carried out by the Parties *in accordance with their respective constitutional processes.*	

Note: An official NATO translation into Russian is available at *NATO/OTAN*, last updated December 9, 2008, https://www.nato.int/cps/en/natohq/official_texts_17120.htm?selectedLocale=ru.

attack. The British characteristically wished an opportunity to appraise an emergency before plunging in, and the Americans and Canadians were most wary of what came to be known as automatic involvement."[48] In short, Acheson had to have a treaty he could sell to the US Senate.

The last round of negotiations in March—during which Article 5 was weakened to its final form—led to the signing of the treaty in Washington on April 4, 1949, by the twelve founding nations.[49] The Canadian delegation proposed the version of Article 5 that met with the approval of all twelve nations. Article 5 was not as strong as the European nations wanted, but it was as strong a commitment as the Canadians and Americans would agree to. The Canadians also successfully advanced the version of Article 11—providing for commitment of armed forces only in accordance with the constitutional processes of a signatory nation—that was unanimously approved.

Acheson and Vandenberg then set themselves to the task of convincing the constitutionally required two-thirds of the US Senate that the North Atlantic Treaty served the security interests of the American people. The Senate Committee on Foreign Relations began its hearings on ratification in late April. For some of the senators and observers, the tone was probably set by retired US Supreme Court Associate Justice Owen J. Roberts, appearing on behalf of the newly formed Atlantic Union Committee. He described the opponents of the treaty as "well-meaning but impractical pacifists, pseudo liberals, rabid isolationists, and, of course, the Communist Party, with its assorted fronts."[50]

The legality of the NATO treaty received almost no attention during the ratification process. What *did* receive attention was the question of just what the United States would be obligated to do under Article 5 in the event of an attack on a signatory nation. Good lawyer that he was, Acheson forthrightly addressed the issue of Article 5 obligations in the Senate hearings. In terms of the obligations that would devolve upon the United States in the event of an armed attack on a member of the alliance, Acheson reassured the senators that an attack on another signatory did not automatically mean the United States would be war and that any decision to go to war "would, of course, be taken in accordance with our constitutional procedures. . . . That action might or might not include the use of armed force."[51]

Opponents of the treaty thought the argument that Article 5 imposed no obligation to use military force was, as a practical matter, just a bit too simplistic. Senator Forrest C. Donnell of Missouri, an ardent opponent of the treaty, asked Justice Roberts what the US obligation would be if half a million troops "were to be sent into Norway by Russia for armed attack." He asked whether the United States would be in compliance with the treaty if US authorities simply said, "All we have to do is take such action as we deem necessary. We think that just sending over 10 gallons of coal oil would be sufficient." Justice Roberts agreed unequivocally that

that would not be a sufficient response under Article 5. Echoing Acheson's statement at the outset of the hearing, Donnell made his point: "We would be obligated to do what you and I consider reasonably and honestly and genuinely necessary; namely, to take the reasonable steps toward repelling that attack, and treating in effect and in fact the attack against that other nation as an attack against ourselves."[52]

In short, the opponents of the treaty thought that, as a practical matter, the freedom to fight, or not, under the weak language of Article 5, was illusory. Plainly, the closely negotiated language of the treaty does not eliminate the requirement that any use of US armed forces must be permissible under US law, nor does Article 5 eliminate the possibility that the United States, "in accordance" with its "constitutional processes," might decide not to respond by committing US armed forces. But the treaty opponents had a point: as a practical matter, at least in the context of political will as it existed in the United States in 1949, the NATO treaty obligated the United States to take up arms against the USSR in the event of an armed attack by the Soviets against a signatory nation.

After ten days of debate in the Senate, the proponents of the treaty carried the day with a ratification vote in late July. The vote was 82 to 13. On the Republican side, future secretary of state John Foster Dulles (who, by a quirk of political fate, served as a US senator from New York for four months in 1949) supported the treaty and voted for it. The case for ratification in the Senate was, in all probability, bolstered by the fact that the Berlin blockade had been imposed by the Soviets and lifted in May 1949. The blockade was defeated because a resolute response from the Western allies demonstrated that continuation of the blockade was pointless. This experience was as eye-opening for US decision-makers as it was for their counterparts in the Kremlin. The case for collective security was more obvious than ever in 1949. As Jonathan House puts it, "It is difficult to imagine how a formal alliance could have come about without the shared experience and urgency of the Berlin Airlift."[53]

One other thing became apparent from the imposition of the blockade, the launch of the airlift and the lifting of the blockade. In each instance, the contending parties were not as aggressive as they could have been. This illustrates what David Holloway called "the importance of limits. Soviet awareness of limits was evident in the Berlin crisis of

1948."[54] From the US perspective, as Bohlen put it, "We had prevailed without forcing a war."[55] Because the contending powers, East and West, had no stomach for another war, each side made moves that were much more carefully calibrated than, say, Hitler's Operation Barbarossa. If the *modus* of the Cold War was going to be typified by carefully calibrated moves informed by judicious assessments of risks and benefits within the overall framework of East and West strengths and weaknesses (including military strength and the political will to use it), then it made sense for leaders in the NATO signatory nations to skew that framework as much as reasonably possible in favor of the West. The emerging rules of engagement would reward unity and resolve, which was what NATO was all about.

The treaty came into force with the requisite number of ratifications in August 1949. It had been a long two years since the enactment of aid to Greece and Turkey in the spring of 1947. Beginning with aid to Greece and Turkey, it could be said that containment was US *policy*. With the ratification of the North Atlantic Treaty, containment was US *law*.

One thing should be as evident now as it was in 1949: If NATO has a deterrent effect on would-be aggressors, that deterrent effect is rooted in the political will of the signatory nations and their leaders, not in the watered-down language of Article 5. That Article is a deterrent only if it means what Truman, Vandenberg, and Acheson hoped it meant. The sea change in the attitude of the US population (and US leaders) in the early postwar years was unmistakable. Millions of Americans had thought the United States could and should avoid being dragged into the first two world wars. But, with the signing of the North Atlantic Treaty, millions of Americans understood that if there was another war in Europe, the United States would be in the thick of it. Active—and expensive—deterrence, which lay at the core of containment doctrine, now commanded the support of most Americans and their leaders.

Putin's brutal attack on Ukraine, while he turned a revanchist eye toward Poland and the Baltics, makes it more important than ever to recognize that the deterrent value of NATO depends on whether the NATO nations and their leaders have the political will to make Article 5 mean at least a little more than what it literally says. NATO's first secretary-general, Hastings Ismay, famously said that the purpose of NATO was "to keep the Americans in, the Russians out, and the Germans down."[56]

Words on paper are not what determine whether Article 5 will "keep the Russians out." Article 5 is all about credibility. Even if the undertaking expressed in Article 5 obligated the signatory nations to commit "all the military and other aid and assistance in their power" (Article IV, Brussels Treaty), NATO Article 5 would still be all about credibility. There are few things more evanescent than credibility.

The three months before the North Atlantic Treaty came into force in August 1949 had seen the lifting of the Berlin blockade and the promulgation of the Basic Law (*Grundgesetz*) for West Germany—soon to be the Federal Republic of Germany—with the approval of the Western occupying powers. A reckoning of the East-West situation looked good from the US perspective: US resolve to protect the western sectors in Berlin had been demonstrated, aid was flowing to Europe under the Marshall Plan, and the communist insurgency in Greece had failed. There was cause to be a bit smug on August 24 when the final instrument of ratification of the North Atlantic Treaty was officially deposited in Washington. The cause for smugness did not last long.

On July 1, 1949, the US estimate (concurred with by the CIA, the military leadership, and the Atomic Energy Commission) of the date by which the USSR might be expected to produce an atomic bomb "was mid-1950," with mid-1953 estimated to be "the most probable date."[57] In September 1949, a US Air Force reconnaissance aircraft, on a routine patrol off the coast of Alaska, collected from the prevailing westerly wind a sample of airborne dust found to have an abnormally high level of radioactivity. The dust was from Semipalatinsk, on the barren steppes of Kazakhstan. To the amazement of all of those in the West who were expected to have a good understanding of these things, the Russian bomb had been detonated in a successful test on August 29, five days after NATO came into existence. The American nuclear monopoly was at an end, barely four years after Hiroshima.

Chapter 6

A Reflection on US Leadership in the 1940s and Early 1950s

We are now in a period where there are mediocre men everywhere. People have opinions but no knowledge, and leaders are made in the image of the masses. Democracy is tolerable because no other system is.

—Dean Acheson, in 1971

Henry Kissinger wrote that "destiny was surely profligate in the talent it bestowed on America in the immediate postwar period."[1] He was right. A reasonable historical observer cannot but notice the exceptional qualities that distinguished many of the leaders who saw the United States through World War II and the first years of the Cold War. As Cold War historian Louis Halle put it, in the postwar era no less than during the war, "the future of the world depended on extraordinary and commanding statesmanship by the American Government."[2] The focus here is not on all the larger-than-life personalities, of which there were more than a few. The focus, rather, is on those whose character, stature, competence, and selfless patriotism were such as to put them as statesmen in a class by themselves. In the United States of the twenty-first century, this is not a pointless inquiry.

What names come to mind? For present purposes, it will suffice to name presidents including Roosevelt, Truman, and Eisenhower; cabinet secretaries, among them Henry L. Stimson, Henry Morgenthau Jr., Robert A. Lovett, James Forrestal, George C. Marshall, and Dean Acheson; a geopolitical strategist on the order of George F. Kennan; and the diplomats W. Averell Harriman, John J. McCloy, and Charles Bohlen. They all had their faults, some of which were not trivial. But it is hard to look at this array of leaders without wondering what accounts for the palpable differences between them and many, if not most, of their twenty-first century counterparts.

To take but one example of a gathering of individuals of this ilk assembled to address a geopolitical challenge, consider the meeting Truman had in the Oval Office with some of his most trusted advisors on August 15, 1946. They were gathered to discuss the US response to the Soviet proposal for joint control of the Turkish Straits. The advisors who sat in "a crescent around two sides of the President's desk," as Acheson put it,[3] included Eisenhower (the chief of staff of the army), Acheson (speaking for himself and Secretary of State George C. Marshall), James Forrestal (secretary of the navy), and fleet admirals William D. Leahy and Chester W. Nimitz. From the perspective of the first quarter of the twenty-first century, it has, at least arguably, been decades since a cadre of advisors of that collective stature gathered around the president's desk, or, for that matter, around any other desk in Washington.

Collectively, the paramount responsibilities of the leaders we briefly consider here were to bring their country successfully through the war, protect America from foreign threats, and see to it that the postwar era did not become a prewar era. They succeeded. This group, which includes the celebrated "Wise Men,"[4] is worth a look, because this is no small matter. Louis Sell, a distinguished historian and diplomat, put the matter quite well in 2016. Referring to the caliber of US leadership in the early years of the Cold War, he wrote,

> The absence of leaders of this stature on both sides of the Atlantic only emphasizes the importance of their role at the beginning of the conflict and the need for similar qualities of leadership if the United States and other democratic nations are to find the way to overcome emerging new global challenges, some of which have their origins in the failure of U.S. and Western leaders to deal effectively with the consequences of the end of the Cold War.[5]

It is not enough to examine these men[6] individually or to look superficially at what made them succeed. The more salient question is, What did they have in common that made them step up to serve their nation with such competence, dedication, and fidelity? A related but more difficult question is whether there are differences between the current era versus the time in which these men lived and served so well that make it less likely now that individuals like these will be produced by our society and step forward to serve. On this, some obvious possibilities come to mind, but these pages do not presume to provide an answer.

The good news is that the leaders singled out here did not all come from privileged backgrounds. Forrestal, the first US secretary of defense, came from a humble Irish immigrant family. McCloy, who would come to personify the eastern establishment, was born into a family of decidedly modest means, a condition that deteriorated after McCloy's father died when McCloy was five years old. Eisenhower, born in a house next to the railroad tracks in Dennison, Texas, was the son of a railroad mechanic and creamery worker. And, of course, Truman himself was born into a Missouri farm family that lacked the means to send him to a four-year college.

By contrast, others in this group, including Acheson, Harriman, Bohlen, Morgenthau, Lovett, and Stimson, enjoyed, from birth, the perquisites of family wealth, or at least notable prosperity. For them, eastern preparatory schools and easy entry into Harvard and Yale universities were the norm.

One common thread within the group we scrutinize here is their entry into public service relatively early in life. Some, such as Harriman, moved smoothly between public service and private endeavors. Stimson takes the prize in that category, having served, amazingly enough, as secretary of war from 1911 to 1913 (under President Taft, a Republican), secretary of state from 1929 to 1933, and again as secretary of war from 1940 to 1945, with a stint as governor general of the Philippines and in a combat unit in the US Army Field Artillery—in World War I, *after* he had already served as secretary of war—mixed in.

Also relevant is that these leaders lived and worked in extraordinarily eventful times early in their adult lives. They were born in the window of time that saw them as young men during World War I, maturing during the crises of the interwar period, and called upon for leadership during World War II and the early years of the Cold War. Their ability to render superb public service in and after World War II was, without doubt, enhanced by the experience most of them had in World War I, in the military or as civilians in public service. Reaching maturity during the interwar period, they witnessed first-hand the consequences of the power vacuum that resulted from the destruction of the old order in World War I. It seems likely, then, that their experiences in the turbulent interwar period contributed to their ability to bring mature judgment to bear on momentous occasions, and perhaps even contributed to their inclination toward public service. (The military experience most of these leaders had in common leads quite easily to the conclusion that it is neither surprising nor coincidental that in the 2018 and 2020 US elections, female candidates with military—including combat—experience fared exceptionally well.)

Thus, auspicious timing and, for many of these postwar leaders, at least a modicum of family wealth, were in the mix. But, rich or poor, they all had a sense of obligation that pushed them in the direction of public service. Yet this cannot be called *noblesse oblige*, because not all of them were *noblesse* by birth. Rich or poor, they had the benefit of nurturing parents who cared very much about education. Rich or poor, they had the capacity for competent public service and the character required to achieve greatness. Those who had the benefit of elite origins tended toward the practice of law or investment banking. Those with more plebian roots were more likely to get started by direct entry into the military, or local politics, than to get their start in law or banking.

For those who were lawyers, the contrast between those of the first half of the twentieth century and those of later generations is telling. John McCloy was asked, during the 1980 presidential campaign waged by Ronald Reagan and Jimmy Carter, to suggest the name of a Wall Street lawyer from the Stimson-Acheson-McCloy tradition, wise in international affairs, who might make a good secretary of state. McCloy's response: "You won't find one. Those lawyers don't exist anymore. They're all too busy making money."[7] It is also worth noting that the talent pool for senior leadership in the federal government was significantly enhanced by the fact that Republicans were willing—and welcome—to serve in Democratic administrations, and vice versa. McCloy, a Republican who was appointed to several high posts by Roosevelt and Truman, is an excellent example of that.

A necessary but not sufficient common thread among those addressed here is that, as Isaacson and Thomas put it, "they did not need to grope for a sense of values."[8] There are those who would say that, regardless of what their personal values might have been, these leaders were—wittingly or otherwise—the architects of an American imperium and that they consequently deserve something less than unreserved admiration. But they had nothing of the sort in mind, nothing that grandiose. More to the point here, they were among the best that their country had to offer. Their character, stature, sheer competence, and selfless patriotism cannot but leave one to wonder what it will take to end the unmistakable trend toward (to pick the most charitable word for it) mediocrity that so plainly and consistently characterizes much of US executive and legislative leadership at the highest levels in recent decades. Hand in hand with that mediocrity is the general public's tacit acceptance of it, a trend nearly as disturbing as the mediocrity itself.

If the prerequisites for leadership of the kind discussed here are, indeed, character, stature, competence, and selfless patriotism, the question immediately arises: Why, in the twenty-first century, have US leaders at the national level so often lacked one or more (sometimes, at least three) of those qualities? I will venture to provide one piece of that puzzle and leave it to the reader to provide the remaining pieces. The decline of civics education in our lower schools, combined with increasing emphasis on narrow specialization in higher education, has produced waves of young adults who, though intelligent and equipped with knowledge in some specialized field, are intellectually vacuous. The result, ironic in the information age, is a shrunken pool of citizens available for public service (and, for that matter, to vote) who are thoroughly inculcated in the habits—and work—of citizenship. Dwight D. Eisenhower warned about this more than seven decades ago, on the occasion of his installation as president of Columbia University: "From the school at the crossroads to a university as great as Columbia, general education for citizenship must be the common and first purpose of them all."[9]

The result of a deficit in "general education for citizenship" is that intelligent but intellectually vacuous people sometimes eventually make it to high-executive or legislative offices, having been put there by voters who themselves are not well grounded in the civic knowledge and accompanying civic virtues that were taken for granted in earlier generations. Those deficits alone can very effectively undermine character, stature, and competence. Worse yet, they can engender a putrescent form of patriotism in both leaders and followers, as America and the world saw on January 6, 2021, when—to the everlasting embarrassment of the United States—a violent mob overran the United States Capitol. Those who would suggest that a lack of civic education was not one of the proximate causes of the January 6 riot should bear in mind that ignorance is demagoguery's best friend. Education in the basic values and fundamental democratic norms of the United States is our first line of defense against a multitude of social pathologies. Retired Associate Justice Sandra Day O'Connor puts it quite well:

> In over half the states in the union, civics education is not required. The only reason we have public school education in America is because in the early days of the country, our leaders thought we had to teach our young generation about citizenship. . . . [T]hat obligation never ends. If we don't take every generation of young people and make sure they understand that they are an essential part of government, we won't survive. We don't teach our own kids. It's insane.[10]

The supply of superbly qualified men and women willing and available, when called, to sit in "a crescent around two sides of the President's desk" (let alone behind that desk) is not what it once was.

Chapter 7

The Russian Bomb

The story of the development of the Russian bomb tells us much about Russian thinking—then and now.

The successful Soviet atomic-bomb test on August 29, 1949, shattered the sense of self-assurance America had enjoyed during its four years as the world's only nuclear power.[1] The "comfortable assumption," as Bohlen put it, had been "that it would be several years before the Soviet Union could explode a nuclear device."[2] Major General Leslie Groves, the director of the Manhattan Project, had gone so far as to estimate, in December 1945, that because of limited uranium resources (which was, in fact, a problem for the Soviets) and "rudimentary technology," Soviet scientists would be incapable of producing an atomic bomb for as long as twenty years.[3]

In November of 1941, with the very existence of the USSR hanging in the balance, Stalin was not interested in scientific research that did not promise a near-term payoff. He dismissed, as a "provocation," intelligence reports suggesting the existence of a US-British project to develop the bomb.[4] But attention to nuclear physics, at least on an academic level, continued. In 1942, a young nuclear physicist, Georgy Flerov, suspecting that the West had embarked on the development of an atomic bomb, succeeded in getting Stalin interested. The result was the adoption, by the State Defense Committee, of a resolution creating a new framework for Soviet atomic-energy research. It is surely no coincidence that the resolution was adopted in February 1943, after the tide was turned in the East at Stalingrad. The Soviet leadership now had enough breathing room to think more than a few months ahead.

With the benefit of the charter from the State Defense Committee, Igor Vasilyevich Kurchatov, an exceptionally talented young nuclear physicist, assembled a team of scientists and engineers to get busy on the design and manufacture of the atomic bomb. After Hiroshima and Nagasaki, the whole world knew that nuclear theory had become reality. But when Kurchatov got started in 1943, he knew only that the bomb was theoretically possible. Like every other nuclear physicist in the world, he could not know for sure that the theory would work in practice. He did have one advantage. Klaus Fuchs, a German physicist (and communist) who was a key nuclear researcher in the Manhattan Project, provided a steady flow of nuclear secrets to the Soviet Union during and after the war. The bomb-making secrets Fuchs gave to the Soviets did not land in the laps of uncomprehending third-rate scientists. Kurchatov and his team made good use of the intelligence. The best estimate is that Fuchs saved the Soviets one to two years in the development of the Russian bomb.[5] Nonetheless, for the Soviets, massive research, development, and construction challenges still lay ahead.

After Truman's sotto voce disclosure to Stalin at Potsdam, and especially after the bombs were dropped on Japan, the pace of the Russian effort quickened dramatically, aided immeasurably by Stalin's willingness to do whatever it took to end the reign of the United States as the sole proprietor of the atomic bomb. As for supervision of the scientists, engineers, and hundreds of thousands of laborers who worked on the Soviet nuclear project, Stalin took no chances. He chose a fellow Georgian, Lavrenti Beria, the head of the NKVD, to take charge of the nuclear project. Beria was neither a scientist nor an engineer. But, as historian Stephen Kotkin puts it, he was a "supremely skilled and murderous organizer."[6] He knew how to motivate people.

In ordering the acceleration of development of the bomb, Stalin was primarily concerned—perhaps the right word would be irritated—with the fact the American bomb was now on the board as a pawn to be played by the West in the geopolitical chess game. From 1943 on, Stalin had no real reason—given his proven willingness to take disproportionate losses if need be—to worry about the ability of his ground forces to take care of business on the European continent. But the end of World War II confronted Stalin and the Politburo with a new geopolitical reality: the elimination of German and Japanese military power meant that the new *locus* of the major opposing power was separated from the Eurasian land mass by two oceans. Never before had the Russians needed the ability to defeat an enemy by means other than massive deployment of tanks, troops, and artillery on the ground from domestic bases.

So it was that, in October 1946, Stalin did not hesitate to simply say no (apparently feeling no need to offer any further explanation) when asked by Hugh Baillie, president of the United Press, whether Russia had "developed its own atomic bomb or any similar weapon," an acknowledgment that made the front page of the *New York Times*.[7] A month before that, Stalin had told the Moscow correspondent of the *Sunday Times of London* that "I do not believe the atomic bomb to be as serious a force as certain politicians are inclined to regard it. Atomic bombs are intended for intimidating weak nerves, but they cannot decide the outcome of war since atomic bombs are by no means sufficient for this purpose."[8] This low estimate of the utility of the bomb in bringing a war to a successful conclusion may well have reflected Stalin's actual belief, a belief that had its echoes in Soviet military doctrine in the ensuing decades. Stalin was, to put it mildly, annoyed by the very existence of a weapon, in the exclusive control of the other side, that was more useful in peace than in war. Writing in 1976, George Kennan cogently summarized the matter as Stalin likely saw it: "The nuclear weapon could destroy people; it could not occupy territory, police it, or organize it politically. He [Stalin] sanctioned its development, yes—because others were doing so, because he did not want to be without it, because he was well aware of the importance of the shadows it could cast over international events by the mere fact of its inclusion in a country's overt national arsenal."[9] The marshal detested the bomb as a tool of coercive diplomacy more than he feared it as a weapon of war.

On the European continent, Stalin could not ignore (as Ambassador Novikov put it in his September 1946 telegram), "the siting of American strategic bases in regions from which it is possible to launch strikes on Soviet territory."[10] The Americans had the bomb and the Russians didn't; the USSR was within range of American bombers while the continental United States was beyond the reach of Russian bombers.

This, then, was the backdrop for Stalin's sense of urgency—but not panic—in 1945. As for the urgency, Stalin's scientific advisors, wisely setting themselves up to give the dictator a pleasant surprise, advised him that it would take five years to produce a bomb.[11] With the benefit of Stalin's resolve to get his own bomb, Beria and Kurchatov had essentially unlimited access to the resources necessary to bring that resolve to fruition.

Even though Beria and Kurchatov knew after August 1945 that their goal was attainable, that knowledge did nothing to ease the huge demand for the physical and human resources required to make the Russian bomb a reality. As has been noted (chapter 2), when informed that electric power needed for atomic-bomb research and production was in short supply, Stalin simply turned off the power to several large populated areas. Beria did have one advantage, in terms of manual labor. He had essentially unlimited access to prison labor.

THE VILLAGE OF SAROV is located in the gently rolling hills of the southern Nizhgorodskaya region, an area of surpassing bucolic beauty about 230 miles southeast of Moscow. Sarov was selected to be the Soviet counterpart of Los Alamos. Sarov, renamed Arzamas-16 from 1946 to 1991, would never be the same. The historic village was removed from publicly available maps. This was now the home of the All-Russian Scientific Research Institute of Experimental Physics, the primary design facility for Soviet atomic bombs. Andrei Sakharov would move to Arzamas-16 in 1950 to continue his work on the hydrogen bomb. Sarov remains a closed town.

Bearing in mind that the successful test of the USSR's bomb was in August 1949, it is remarkable that construction of the first reactor capable of plutonium production on the scale needed for the Soviet project did not start until March 1948; construction was not completed until June, a little more than a year before the test. As the moment of truth approached in the summer of 1949, Kurchatov and his colleagues cannot but have been just a bit tense. The criterion for recognition of those whose efforts would contribute to a successful test was simple: "Those who were to be shot in case of failure were now to become Heroes of Socialist Labor."[12]

To understand the immediate significance, in East and West, of the test in August, the chronological context is worth noticing once again. The North Atlantic Treaty was signed in early April, five months before the test. To help mark that occasion, Churchill treated a crowd of fourteen thousand, plus a national radio and television audience, to a rousing oration in the Boston Garden. Churchill's conclusion: "I must not conceal from you tonight the truth as I see it. It is certain that Europe would have been communized like Czechoslovakia and London under bombardment some time ago but for the deterrent of the atomic bomb in the hands of the United States."[13] Coverage of Churchill's speech shared the front page of the April 1 *New York Times* with news of the Kremlin's response to the impending ceremony for the signing of the North Atlantic Treaty:

Moscow Protests Atlantic Treaty as U.N. Violation
Declares "Openly Aggressive" Alliance Is Aimed
against Soviet and Satellites
Churchill Holds Atom Bomb
Saved Europe from Soviet
Our Possession of New Weapon Deterred Communists,
He Says in Boston—War "Not Inevitable," Urges Caution

Such was the temper of the times as the development of the Russian bomb moved into the final stages.

It is fitting that the Russian bomb, RDS-1, was successfully detonated on August 29, ten years almost to the day after Stalin raised a toast to Adolph Hitler's health in the Kremlin ceremonies accompanying the signing of the Molotov-Ribbentrop nonaggression pact. Stalin did not want to find himself ever again negotiating from a position of weakness. Little Boy and Fat Man ended a war. RDS-1 ended any American pretensions to geopolitical advantage on account of sole possession of the bomb.

On September 23, the news of the Soviet test was delivered calmly by Truman's press office. It was not received calmly. The heart of the press release as distributed in the press room was the laconic statement that "we have evidence that within recent weeks an atomic explosion occurred in the U.S.S.R."[14] Journalists who were present responded immediately: "There was a wild rush through the door and to the telephones in the near-by press room. One of the newsmen who sprinted out was the correspondent from TASS, the official Soviet news agency."[15] The surprise arose not so much from the mere fact that the Russians had figured out how to build a bomb as from the fact that they had built it so soon.

By the time the Sunday edition of the *Times* was on the street, Hanson W. Baldwin, the *Times's* Pulitzer Prize–winning military editor, had had an opportunity to collect his thoughts. Baldwin's editorial commentary made it official: "A new and dangerous chapter in the atomic age opened this week and the arms-aid program and Atlantic pact defense measures took on an urgent meaning as President Truman announced that henceforth we would be living in two atomic worlds."[16] As Baldwin saw it, the new problem was "to find a substitute for the atomic bomb as a deterrent to Russian aggression."[17]

The way to deter the use of a small bomb was to build a big one. As Truman recorded in his memoir, "One of the positive effects of" the Russian test was "to spur our laboratories and our great scientists to make haste on hydrogen bomb research."[18] Development of the hydrogen (thermonuclear fusion) bomb had been less urgent than the development of the fission bomb in the Manhattan Project.

For his part, Stalin ordered full-scale work on the development of the hydrogen bomb in November 1949, three months before Truman directed the development of a US hydrogen bomb.[19] And as it turned out, the first nation to successfully test a deliverable hydrogen bomb was the USSR. The fission-boosted hydrogen bomb, designed at Arzamas-16 by Andrei Sakharov and his colleagues, was successfully tested on August 12, 1953. The US military—to say nothing of senior political leadership—was astonished that the Soviets had gotten so far ahead of the Americans in the development of the hydrogen bomb. (The United States successfully detonated a hydrogen device—it could not reasonably be called a bomb—at Enewetak Atoll on November 1, 1952. It yielded the equivalent of ten million tons of TNT, 700 times greater than the fission bomb dropped on Hiroshima, but "it weighed some ten tons and took up an area the size of a small house."[20])

By year's end in 1949, there was no room for doubt that the atomic bomb was a pillar of geopolitical and defense strategy on both sides of the divide. In the United States, the bomb had become, in its own perverse way, a fiscal-management tool–a phenomenon that would continue for years to come. The cost of building more fission bombs was, all things considered, not enormous, while the cost of keeping American troops in Western Europe continued unabated. The result was that though the United States had only thirteen atomic bombs in 1947, 250 bombs were in the US arsenal in 1949. The bomb had become a relatively economical form of deterrence. As for the Russian bomb, its arrival on the geopolitical scene made it imperative for US decision-makers to spend more time focusing on Russian *capabilities* and less time engaging in airy speculation about Russian intentions. This would be highly consequential.

THIS BRINGS US to the end of the 1940s, a decade that defies easy description. It should come as no surprise that those who fought, whether on the home front or (especially) in the theaters of battle, have never, on the whole, been eager to talk about it, at least without being urged to do so for the sake of historical memory. The point so often made, at least implicitly, by those who survived the decade is that if anyone is going to speak about it, the first voices to be heard should be those of the Ivans and the Sergeys who never returned, to say nothing of their children and grandchildren who, as the age pyramid shows, have never been born. The first voices should include those whose last gasps were heard only within the walls of the Nazi death chambers. And the first voices should include those who lie forever still in the endless rows in the cemeteries of Normandy and Manila.

It is tempting to celebrate the historical memory of the triumphs in World War II, and there is nothing wrong with that. It takes nothing away from the heroes of the decade to say, against the backdrop of the unfathomable tragedies of that decade, that we can talk about the triumph of good over evil only after recognizing that "good" took a terrible beating before it prevailed over evil. Those who made those triumphs possible, having now, almost without exception, passed from the scene, would agree.

Chapter 8

NSC-68

The Militarization of Containment

Although George Kennan was the father of containment, he was neither the *proprietor* of that doctrine nor long in a position to shape its development and implementation. Others took it and ran with it, with the result that within a few years after Kennan first advocated the doctrine, he vehemently disagreed with some initiatives undertaken in its name.

Kennan stepped aside as director of policy planning at the State Department in December 1949. Acheson (who had been secretary of state since January 1949) chose Paul Nitze as Kennan's successor. Nitze took over in January 1950. This was not a routine swap of one technocrat for another from the same mold. Kennan strove, before and after the onset of the Cold War, to understand the Soviet Union in general, and the Russians in particular, from the inside out. In contrast, Nitze's strong point, as described by no less an observer than Henry Kissinger, was that he was one of the nation's "ablest theorists on national defense."[1] In the Long Telegram, Kennan had written that "at bottom of Kremlin's neurotic view of world affairs is [a] traditional and instinctive Russian sense of insecurity." As Nitze sat down with his colleagues in early 1950 to craft the national defense strategy that came to be called NSC-68, considerations such as the Kremlin's "neurotic view" may have been somewhere in the back of his mind, but purely military matters were much more influential for Nitze than they ever were for Kennan.

Unsurprisingly, Kennan and Nitze had decidedly different beliefs as to what it would take for the containment doctrine to actually *contain* the Soviet Union. George C. Marshall, as the secretary of state who appointed Kennan to serve as the first director of policy planning, had been less confrontational than his successor, Dean Acheson. Correspondingly, Kennan was less of a Cold War hardliner than his successor, Nitze. And Nitze, as the new director, did not share Kennan's interest in understanding the Russian mentality. Nitze focused more on preparing to go to war with the Soviet Union if it came to that. This is a nearly perfect example of how momentous shifts in policy can emerge from personnel changes, which, at the time, might not have seemed quite so momentous. To be sure, Acheson was well aware, when he appointed Nitze to replace Kennan as head of policy planning, that this was a move in the hawkish direction. But when Nitze took over, no one could have fully appreciated how Nitze's ideological—and, hence, policy—convictions, driven by the force of his formidable personality, would reshape diplomatic and defense policy.

The timing for Nitze's arrival as director in January 1950 was auspicious. The Russian bomb had been tested in August. By the end of 1949, the Nationalist regime had collapsed on mainland China and fled to Taiwan. At the end of January 1950, Truman ordered the acceleration of research for the hydrogen bomb and directed a special interdepartmental group of advisors to undertake a formal study of US national security policy. The product of this study was NSC-68, formally titled "A Report to the National Security Council on United States Objectives and Programs for National Security."[2] Nitze, working with his policy-planning colleagues in collaboration with representatives from the Joint Chiefs of Staff, was the principal author of the document. The overall result of the effort to craft NSC-68 was "something unprecedented: a single statement of US national security policy."[3]

Even the expansive formal title of the document fails to do justice to its broad sweep and authoritative tone. It was directly descended from the Long Telegram.[4] It serves up, in sixty-six pages, a remarkable, boldly written combination of history, ideological doctrine, economic analysis, and military strategy. More importantly for our purposes, NSC-68 formed the foundation of US military and Cold War strategy for four decades. Indeed, it is likely that, given the present state of East-West relations, some of the basic strategic postulates of NSC-68 enjoy renewed currency in the inner councils of the US national-security establishment.

NSC-68 cannot be called *only* a political document or *only* a strategic plan or *only* a military blueprint. It was all of those, but its enduring influence on US Cold War strategy cannot be grasped without some understanding of all its parts.

NSC-68: The Ideology

Nitze and his collaborators knew that implementation of their proposed national security strategy would require major changes in federal spending priorities—reallocation of resources that were much in demand for domestic programs. NSC-68 would, consequently, have been a nonstarter without a compelling ideological foundation. That foundation is laid in the first pages of the document. Even at the height of the Cold War, the typical national-security bureaucrat did not write like this:

> The Soviet Union, unlike previous aspirants to hegemony, is animated by a new fanatic faith, antithetical to our own, and seeks to impose its absolute authority over the rest of the world. Conflict has, therefore, become endemic and is waged, on the part of the Soviet Union, by violent or non-violent methods in accordance with the dictates of expediency. . . .
>
> There is a basic conflict between the idea of freedom under a government of laws, and the idea of slavery under the grim oligarchy of the Kremlin . . . The idea of freedom, moreover, is peculiarly and intolerably subversive of the idea of slavery. But the converse is not true. The implacable purpose of the slave state to eliminate the challenge of freedom has placed the two great powers at opposite poles. It is this fact which gives the present polarization of power the quality of crisis.[5]

One reason the ideological component of NSC-68 is so important is that, from one end of the document to the other, it implicitly equated Soviet military *capability* with Soviet *intent.* In 1950, during its short peacetime tenure as the dominant world power, the United States did not want any other nation, adversary or not, to equate US military capability with US intent. But Nitze and his colleagues knew that NSC-68 would be a dead letter if they failed to convince US decision-makers of one fundamental proposition: the national security of the United States demanded that Soviet military *capability* be regarded as a reasonably reliable indicator of actual Soviet military *intent*. That fundamental proposition would go nowhere if not propelled by a stark assessment of Soviet ideology.

NSC-68 on Soviet Threats and Vulnerabilities

It was also necessary to establish that Soviet ideology was not just abstract Marxist-Leninist theory. The message was that Soviet ideology represented a concrete threat to US national security: "The [Kremlin's] design, therefore, calls for the complete subversion or forcible destruction of the machinery of government and structure of society in the countries of the non-Soviet world and their replacement by an apparatus and structure subservient to and controlled from the Kremlin. To that end Soviet efforts are now directed toward the domination of the Eurasian land mass."[6] Lest anyone miss the point, Nitze and his colleagues concluded that "our free society finds itself mortally challenged by the Soviet system." The Soviet system is "implacable in its purpose to destroy ours."[7]

On the basis of their assessment of Soviet military capacity, the authors concluded that the Soviets had the military capability to (1) overrun Western Europe, (2) drive toward the oil-producing countries of the Middle East, (3) attack the British Isles as well as Atlantic and Pacific lines of communication from the air (making the United Kingdom unavailable as a base of operations for allied forces), (4) drop atomic bombs on the United States and Canada, and (5) prevent an amphibious landing to retake the European continent. As for the nuclear scorecard, NSC-68 estimated that the Soviets had "a substantial atomic stockpile," sufficient in "a strong surprise blow" to lay waste to the British Isles and to deliver "devastating attacks" on vital US and Canadian targets.[8]

In a prescient passage that foreshadowed strategic debates that would continue for decades (and is relevant in the first quarter of the twenty-first century), NSC-68 also noted the threat of "piecemeal aggression against others, counting on our unwillingness to engage in atomic war unless we are directly attacked." Thus, NSC-68, while dealing mainly with the challenges of deterring (and, if necessary, winning) a full-on war with the Russians, also recognized that there was a gamut of possibilities for conflict. The authors put it succinctly: "The shadow of Soviet force falls darkly on Western Europe and Asia and supports a policy of encroachment." One of their conclusions on this point has obvious resonance now: "The free world lacks adequate means—in the form of forces in being—to thwart such [Soviet] expansion locally. The United States will therefore be confronted more frequently with the dilemma of reacting totally to a limited extension of Soviet control or of not reacting at all (except with ineffectual protests and half measures)."[9]

NSC-68: National Goals and Prescriptions for Implementation

Goals. One of the overarching goals articulated in the document was to "change the world situation by means short of war in such a way as to frustrate the Kremlin design and hasten the decay of the Soviet system."[10] Later in the document, the authors elaborated on this general allusion to containment doctrine, but with a twist: "It was and continues to be cardinal in this [containment] policy that we possess superior overall power in ourselves or in dependable combination with other likeminded nations. One of the most important ingredients of power is military strength." Without superior military strength, "'containment'—which is in effect a policy of calculated and gradual coercion—is no more than a policy of bluff."[11]

Nitze and his colleagues also had goals for events *within* the Soviet Union. On the question of the desirability of undermining the internal order of things within the Soviet Union, they put it plainly: "We should take dynamic steps to reduce the power and influence of the Kremlin *inside the Soviet Union* and other areas under its control."[12] This was no fluke. The authors expressly endorsed (and quoted) the objectives of NSC-20/4, adopted in 1948, which had explicitly encouraged "the development among the Russian peoples of attitudes which may help to modify current Soviet behavior"[13]

Prescriptions. NSC-68, though written mostly by State Department personnel, was not—and was not intended to be—a blueprint for diplomatic strategy. On that score, it would be fair to say that the document was intended by its authors to lay out in plain terms what the United States had to do if there could be any hope that war could be avoided by diplomatic means. Thus, the core prescriptions centered on the need to build up military power and, at least implicitly, the need to credibly demonstrate the will to use it if necessary. The military prescriptions were, as a conceptual matter, uncomplicated. The United States needed "substantially increased general air, ground, and sea strength, atomic capabilities, and air and civilian defenses to deter war and to provide reasonable assurance, in the event of war, that it could survive the initial blow and go on to the eventual attainment of its objectives."[14]

Of course, none of this would come cheap. In a passage that would make many present NATO leaders smile (some sheepishly, some not), the report noted that "the military budget of the United States represents 6 to 7 percent of its gross national product (as against 13.8 percent for the Soviet Union). Our North Atlantic Treaty allies devoted 4.8 percent of their national product to military purposes in 1949."[15] As for raising the money it would take to finance a massive military buildup, the writers ventured no further than to observe that the ability of the American economy to support the buildup was limited "not so much by the ability to produce as by the decision on the proper allocation of resources to this and other purposes." In other words: Mr. President, we have reported to you, as directed, on the measures that are imperative to safeguard our nation; it is up to you to find the money and to do the politicking. Thus, Nitze recognized that the American economy, and the industrial might that was embedded in it, were strategic weapons which gave the United States an incomparable advantage on the military side of the geopolitical struggle. He did not flinch in calling upon the president to put that economic supremacy to work in the service of containment. It fell to Truman and the legislative branch to muster the political will.

NSC-68: Implementation

NSC-68 was completed by the policy planning staff on April 7, 1950, and it was promptly delivered to Truman. Although NSC-68 was not formally approved by Truman as administration policy until September

1950, it immediately—as a conceptual matter—got traction in the White House. The problem was money. The document called for a massive military buildup, the likes of which the United States had never seen in peacetime. The implications of NSC-68 for the defense budget ran to the tens of billions of dollars. As will be seen in chapter 10, Korea came to the rescue.

At base, NSC-68 was all about ideology, military strategy, economic muscle, and political will. Professors N. V. Sivachev and N. N. Yakovlev (as has been noted, good communists, good writers, and competent historians) got it exactly right when they observed that "Directive no. 68 gave a material foundation to the theoretical arguments of George Kennan (three years before it was implemented), insisting in addition on turning the economic potential of the United States into an instrument of foreign policy."[16] Nitze himself couldn't have said it better.

Chapter 9

Politics and Policy in the First Decade of the Cold War

Getting Serious about Communism

President Harry Truman may well have thought, or at least hoped, that he had laid to rest the use of anticommunism as a crude political tool when—with some private reservations—he instituted the employee loyalty program in 1947. That was not to be. Three realities combined to make a demagogic form of anticommunism a viable political tool for nearly ten more years.

First, there was just enough truth to the stories about communist infiltration into the ranks of the US government to give the issue a measure of legitimacy. In his memoirs, written at a time when he had no reason to pander to any segment of the body politic, Truman himself recognized the "new technique of infiltration and betrayal by the agents and dupes of the Communists."[1] In other words, genuine concern about communist influence in domestic institutions was not just for kooks and conspiracy theorists. Second, even politicians with untainted motives found it convenient to use anticommunism in the service of worthy proposals. Thus, "anti-Communism provided U.S. leaders with a powerful tool for mobilizing public and congressional support for policies launched for strategic reasons."[2] And third, with seemingly perfect timing, the Soviet leadership, the communist Chinese and, in their time, the North Koreans, periodically breathed new life into the cause of domestic anticommunism.

We could not have had a Cold War without ideological, cultural, and doctrinal drivers on both sides. Domestic anticommunism (not to be confused with containment, as the centerpiece of US foreign policy for more than four decades) provided an important ideological driver. And the beauty of anticommunism as an element of American ideology was that it could get traction across the entire political spectrum, save for the Far Left. Thus, at least a generalized form of anticommunism was a decidedly low-risk cause for American politicians. It was a good fit with virtually everything that would come under the heading of "American values." It is, thus, not by chance that, by 1956, at least three courts had held that a person falsely labeled a communist could recover damages for defamation.[3]

Although, in the third decade of the twenty-first century, anticommunism—demagogic or otherwise—has faded into the background as a significant motivating political force, persistent byproducts of Cold War anticommunism unquestionably remain. Those lingering by-products include, in many segments of the population, a visceral dislike and an uncritical mistrust of Russia and Russians. Mistrust has, of course, been increased by geopolitical events, as well as attempts, demonstrably originating from Russia, to interfere in the 2016 presidential election. And notwithstanding Donald Trump's flirtations with Vladimir Putin, anti-Russian sentiment had become a bipartisan phenomenon in US politics even before Putin invaded Ukraine. Related to that dislike and mistrust is the tendency, understandable but in many ways unjustified, to equate the Russian people with the incumbent governing regime. As early as 1951, Congress, with the full-throated concurrence of President Truman, differentiated between the Soviet government and the people who were subjects of that government, expressing the friendship of the American people for "the peoples of the Union of Soviet Socialist Republics."[4] (The vote in the House was 351 to 6.) Sadly, it may well be that, in terms of popular consciousness, the differentiation between the Kremlin and the people ruled from the Kremlin was more viable in the United States of the early 1950s than it is in the twenty-first century. It is, consequently, worth taking a look at how this all unfolded in the early years of the Cold War.

The first thing to remember is that although anticommunism was, by and large, dormant during World War II, it was not dead, and it had a venerable history in American politics. It was not just a secular enterprise. In the prewar era, the cause had acquired religious underpinnings from reputable clerics. In 1937, Pope Pius XI promulgated his encyclical,

Divini Redemptoris, on "Atheistic Communism." He warned of the "imminent danger" of "atheistic Communism, which aims at upsetting the social order and at undermining the very foundations of Christian civilization."[5] To say no more, the encyclical helped to remove any doubt that Americans of Eastern European extraction—a predominantly Catholic population—would find themselves well within the broad swath of the US population which had a visceral opposition to communism at home or abroad.

In the first decade after the war, trends in US popular culture, media coverage, and political discourse were mutually reinforcing. The effects of these phenomena reached their zenith in the demagogic form of anticommunism that we put under the general heading of McCarthyism.

Early Cold War Media and Popular Culture

As Oleg Barabanov put it in 2020, "Historical memory, as reflected in public opinion, is not broadly shaped by scholarly books or articles. The media and cultural spaces play the key role here in translating historical knowledge (and, occasionally, historical myths)."[6]

As for popular culture, it all began innocently enough in the US with the rerelease, in 1947, of *Ninotchka* (originally released in 1939), perhaps the most successful anticommunist movie ever made. It was probably that successful because it reduced communism to satire. On the train platform in Paris, disembarking from the train from Moscow, Nina Ivanovna Yakushova (Greta Garbo) informs her comrades: "The last mass trials were a great success. There are going to be fewer but better Russians." The Soviets were not to be outdone. At about the same time, a movie titled *The Russian Question* (1947) was released and widely distributed in the Soviet Union, portraying an American journalist who was sent to Russia to gather material for a book intended by his employer to expose the Soviet Union as a warmongering country with aggressive intentions. But the journalist was torn by a moral dilemma when, while in Russia, he came to the realization that this peaceful socialist society had no resemblance to the portrait he was told to paint.

And so it went from there, with films such as *Guilty of Treason* (1949), portraying the life and imprisonment of Josef Cardinal Mindszenty, and

The Red Menace (1949), culminating with *The Commies Are Coming, the Commies Are Coming* (1957). This is not to say, of course, that the early Cold War wave of anticommunist films actually won over the hearts and minds of the theater goers. As the *New York Times* put it, in its review of *The Red Menace:* "Pardon us for pointing—but if the Communist party in the United States is as lacking in discipline and cohesion as it is made to appear in the picture entitled 'The Red Menace,' which opened at the Mayfair on Saturday, then we need have no great anxiety about it fouling our American way of life."[7]

At a remove of seven decades, it is easy to be critical, if not also to smile, at the alarmism about domestic communist subversion that was prevalent in the first decade of the Cold War. The alarmism was fed, in part, by news from abroad, not all of which was directly generated by the Russians. Major newspapers were, of course, the messengers for much of that news, and a scan of the coverage of the activities of the "reds," as they were commonly called, leaves the impression that even at the sophisticated end of the spectrum, major news outlets didn't quite know what to make of it all. The same is true of war warnings coming from seemingly believable sources.

In early 1949, the *St. Louis Post-Dispatch* published a series of articles featuring the predictions of Grigori Tokaev, a Soviet engineer (and colonel) who had defected to the West a year earlier. Not the least of those was an article in which Tokaev warned that World War III was coming, predicting that within "at the most five years and possibly as few as three years," the Soviets would have "a practical atomic bomb upon which it has been working with furious singlemindedness since 1945."[8] (A deployable Russian bomb was successfully tested less than eight months later.) Another article, published four days before Truman's inauguration in January 1949, left no doubt about what Tokaev saw coming: "The ultimate aim of Soviet policy is the creation, by armed conflict if necessary, of a world-wide Soviet Union."[9] Heady stuff, from a former Soviet colonel.

On the sectarian side, long before the religious Right, more or less by that name, became a force in American politics, the Reverend Billy James Hargis brought the full weight of fundamentalist Christianity (at least the American version) down against "godless communism." No surprise there, even if we assume, as seems safe, that Hargis, an evangelical

Protestant, was not taking his cues from Pope Pius XI. Before Hargis's career as a clergyman ran its course, his media domain included 500 radio stations and 250 television channels.

The time is ripe to consider, again, the potency of mass media (now augmented in some pernicious ways by online social media) in shaping popular consciousness. As will be seen, the mass media of the early 1950s spared no effort in educating the American people about the perceived threat from "the Russians." There was, as a practical matter, a mutually reinforcing relationship between the media (including the mainstream press), the political classes, and "the Russians." But when the anticommunism of the early 1950s festered into the political and moral infection that came to be called McCarthyism, reliable coverage by unbiased press outlets, consumed by a broad cross section of the American public, had precisely the disinfectant effect intended by the framers of the First Amendment. It is not at all clear now that the present fragmented array of media choices available to the American public would perform the function that the mainstream media performed so well seven decades ago.

In the early 1950s, the major players in the resurgence of the brand of anticommunism that we generally put under the heading of McCarthyism were, in no particular order, demagogues such as Senator Joseph McCarthy, the politicians who acquiesced in the demagoguery until they could stand themselves no more, the few politicians who stood up to McCarthy from the beginning, the tiny handful of actual communists in the United States, the Republican strategists who saw the need to get some political traction out of the postwar situation in Eastern Europe, the press, the American legal profession, and the communist leaders in the Kremlin and elsewhere who reliably provided a new casus belli for the anticommunist movement whenever it was needed (and sometimes when it was not). Between 1950 and the end of 1954, these players collectively made an impression on American popular consciousness that remains embedded in the body politic, making a difference in US-Russian relations in the third decade of the twenty-first century.

To begin with the handful of actual communists in the United States, they were, in the main, a motley crew, and not all that diverse. Many of them were idealists, including academics and low-level bureaucrats, whose formative experiences and most indelible memories came from the depression years of the 1930s. Thus, as historian Martin Malia put it, "once [communism] had been rooted out of the labor movement, it was largely confined to intellectual circles oriented toward European cultural modernism," a fact which, as we shall see, was not lost on Joe McCarthy.[10] Conspicuously absent from the ranks of American communists were almost all urban industrial workers—the proletariat—and agrarian radicals, for whom the Granger movement and the Farmers Union were about as far left as they wanted to go. It is also accurate to say—and in fairness should be said—that the typical American communist in the early 1950s, though intellectually persuaded by communist ideology, was not drawn to actual subversive activities.[11]

With only a few communists actually in circulation in the United States, politicians and the press needed something to work with. In February 1950, with the ink barely dry on the verdict of conviction of Alger Hiss for perjury, Senator Joe McCarthy obliged.

Joe McCarthy, elected to the Senate in 1946, needed an issue on which to ride to the national fame he craved. One of the main drivers in the 1946 election had been the gratitude of the voters for the service of the candidates who served in the war and returned home to stand for election to public office. But McCarthy was smart enough to understand that he could not ride that wave forever. Three years into his first term as a senator, he found his issue. He would ride to fame—and perhaps to the national ticket in 1952—by persuading the nation that it was imperiled by the infiltration of communist subversives into the US government.

It would be a serious mistake to write McCarthy off simply as a loser who figured out a way to be a winner for a few years. In terms of any personal quality that would make us admire a public servant, he was certainly a loser, but that is far from the whole story. He was roundly disliked by his senate colleagues in both parties. He fared no better in the eyes of the working press, as witness that a poll of Washington correspondents rated him the worst senator. He got elected, in part, by grossly exaggerating his war record. When speaking in public, especially in front of cameras, he was seemingly oblivious to the distinction between that which he actually believed and that which he merely found it convenient to say. As a ruthless, amoral opportunist, he passed up few opportunities to preen, as he did when he appeared on February 9, 1950, as the guest speaker before more than 275 men and women at the Lincoln Day dinner meeting of a Republican women's club in Wheeling, West Virginia.

Early in his speech, he made it clear that "we are engaged in a final, all-out battle between communistic atheism and Christianity." Turning to Dean Acheson's State Department, McCarthy focused on "the bright young men who are born with silver spoons in their mouths," the ones with "the finest homes, the finest college education, and the finest jobs in government we can give." Having identified the enemy within, as he called it, he drove home his case against the State Department (and the government in general) with the accusation that launched him into the public eye for the next five years: "I have in my hand 57 cases of individuals who would appear to be either card-carrying members or certainly loyal to the Communist party, but who nevertheless are still helping to shape our foreign policy."[12]

McCarthy had gotten himself into the national headlines,[13] where he would remain until his dénouement in December 1954. He would test the moral strength and political courage of American leaders in ways that could scarcely have been anticipated–even by McCarthy himself–on that February night in Wheeling. As the Joe McCarthy story entered its last chapter, in January 1954, Whittaker Chambers wrote some prescient words: "Senator McCarthy will one day make some irreparable blunder which will play directly into the hands of our common enemy and discredit the whole anti-Communist effort for a long while to come."[14] Prescient indeed.

The Joe McCarthy story is the story of a man who, while wielding the authority of the United States Senate, conjoined his mendacity, his demagoguery, and his willingness to trample the truth, to write one of the most shameful chapters in the history of American politics. McCarthy acquired unquestionably formidable political power while bringing almost nothing to the table as the holder of high elected office *other than* that mendacity, demagoguery, and willingness to trample the truth. This story is also interwoven with other strands of American politics (more benign but no less important), with the press, courageous politicians, and cowardly politicians all playing their roles.

On March 30, 1950, a few weeks after McCarthy's Wheeling speech, Truman held his 221st press conference, on the naval base at Key West. Inevitably, the subject of Joe McCarthy came up. The president had an unvarnished response to a question about the Wisconsin senator: "I think the greatest asset the Kremlin has is Senator McCarthy."[15] Some context is necessary. Since the 1948 elections, the Democrats had enjoyed a 54 to 42 seat majority in the Senate, but 1950 was an election year. When Truman held his Key West press conference, Korea had not yet been invaded, but China and Eastern Europe had been lost to the communists, the Soviet Army stood on the Elbe, and the Alger Hiss case had given the Republicans just enough of a purchase on the facts to enable them to sound the alarm credibly about domestic communist subversion. Truman's worries were not just in the realm of foreign policy. He sensed in McCarthy's feral brand of anticommunism an emerging political issue that could give the Democrats problems in the 1950 elections. In this, Truman was correct. The temper of the times in 1950 is not easy to replicate in words now, but Pulitzer Prize–winning journalist William S. White said it well at the time: "An issue of immeasurable size, of unknown intensity and of unknowable hardiness has now entered American political life. It is the issue of 'communism,' real or alleged, in the Government of the United States. . . . [C]ommunism as a national issue has arrived as a bitterly ubiquitous presence in the greatest and strongest anti-Communist country in the world."[16]

And, it must be remembered, McCarthy accomplished all of that while his party was in the minority in the Senate. He was not (yet) in a position to chair a committee or select its counsel. Working with nothing much more than his ability to level sensational charges, McCarthy had created the atmosphere described so well by William White. The possibility that McCarthy might find himself in the Senate majority after the 1950 elections was (to put it mildly) unsettling to the Democrats, which makes this a good place to look at what the possibilities really were in that election year.

The end of the war had ushered in an entirely new era of competitive national politics. Both of the first two (and four of the first six) postwar elections saw a change in control of both houses of Congress. The postwar and early Cold War struggle for control of Congress was all the more remarkable when viewed in light of the experience of the two decades before the 1950 election (table 2 and figure 3).

As the 1950 election approached, what no one knew was whether the "bitterly ubiquitous presence" of what became known as McCarthyism could get enough traction with the voters to swing control of the Congress yet again. Truman had some trusted Republican allies in Congress,

Table 2. The Battle for Control of Congress in the First Decade of the Cold War

Election	Senate—96 seats	House of Representatives—435 seats
1946	Outcome: **Republicans took control** Republicans: 50 seats (+11) Democrats: 46 seats (-10)[a]	Outcome: **Republicans took control** Republicans: 246 seats (+55) Democrats: 188 seats (-54)[b]
1948	Outcome: **Democrats took control** Republicans: 42 seats (-9) Democrats: 54 seats (+9)	Outcome: **Democrats took control** Republicans: 171 seats (-75) Democrats: 263 seats (+75)[c]
1950	Outcome: **Democrats retained control** Republicans: 47 seats (+5) Democrats: 49 seats (-5)	Outcome: **Democrats retained control** Republicans: 199 seats (+28) Democrats: 235 seats (-28)[d]
1952	Outcome: **Republicans took control** Republicans: 48 seats (+1) plus Vice President Democrats: 48 seats (-1)[e]	Outcome: **Republicans took control** Republicans: 221 seats (+22) Democrats: 213 seats (-22)
1954	Outcome: **Democrats took control** Republicans: 47 seats (-2) Democrats: 48 seats (+2)[f]	Outcome: **Democrats took control** Republicans: 203 seats (-18) Democrats: 232 seats (+19)
1956	Outcome: **Democrats retained control** Republicans: 47 seats (no change) Democrats: 49 seats (no change)[g]	Outcome: **Democrats retained control** Republicans: 201 seats (-2) Democrats: 234 seats (+2)

Note: Due to seats held by members of third parties, Democratic and Republican seats in the House do not in all instances total 435.

[a]Progressive Party lost one seat.

[b]American Labor Party retained one seat; Progressive Party lost its only seat.

[c]American Labor Party retained one seat.

[d]American Labor Party lost one seat; Independent candidate won one seat.

[e]Includes Wayne Morse of Oregon, who was elected as a Republican in 1950 but declared himself an Independent during the 1952 election and caucused with the Democrats.

[f]Senator Morse of Oregon retained his seat and continued to caucus with the Democrats.

[g]Independent Wayne Morse had joined the Democratic Party in early 1955.

Arthur Vandenberg not the least among them. But he needed some help in capturing the moral high ground. He got that help from a senator from Maine, Margaret Chase Smith—a Republican. Truman was fortunate to have gotten that help in June of 1950 because, from his perspective, the political situation only grew more precarious as the election approached.

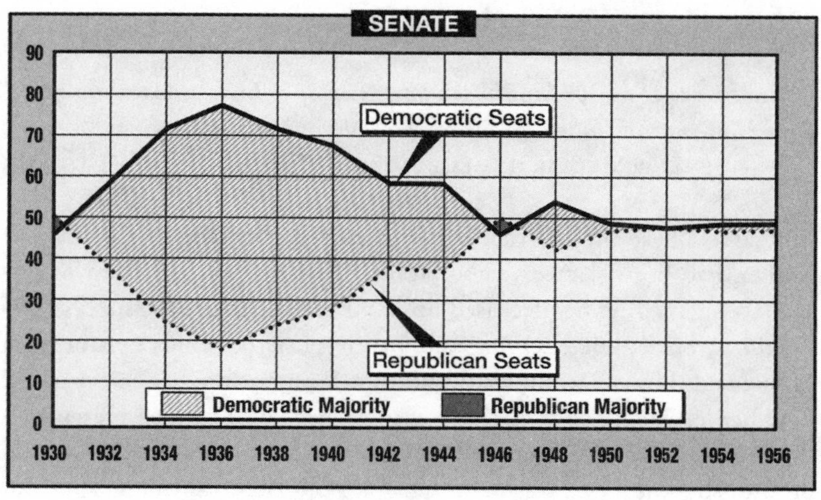

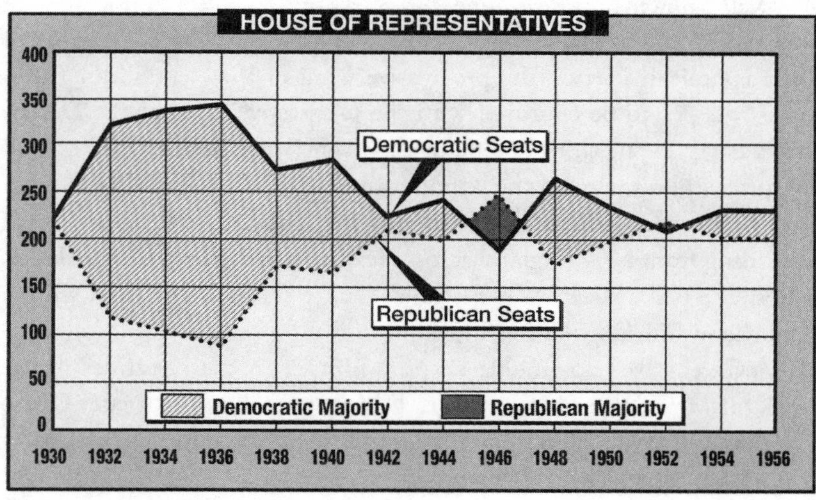

Figure 3. Congressional Elections, 1930–1956

Chapter 9

A Republican Pushes Back

I do not want to see the Republican party ride to political victory on the Four Horsemen of Calumny—fear, ignorance, bigotry, and smear.
—Senator Margaret Chase Smith

Margaret Chase Smith, the daughter of a barber and a shoe-factory worker, had been elected to the House of Representatives from Maine in 1940, succeeding her deceased husband in that office. She successfully sought an open Senate seat in 1948, making her the junior senator from Maine and the only woman in the Senate. Long before her career ended with her loss in the 1972 election, she had become a revered presence in the Senate, enjoying a deep well of respect on both sides of the aisle. But in 1950, she was still a freshman senator, popular in her home state but not well known outside Maine and Washington, DC. Politically, she was comfortably situated within what was then the progressive wing of the Republican Party. (The progressive wing of the Republican Party, c. 1950, is not to be confused with the progressive wing of the Democratic Party in the third decade of the twenty-first century, or, for that matter, with *any* wing of the Republican Party.) She shared that orientation with scores of Republicans serving in Congress from a wide swath extending from New England across New York and into the Great Lakes states. She had a steely New England Yankee sense of right and wrong. And she was plainspoken.

McCarthy had no trouble keeping himself in the headlines in the weeks after his Wheeling speech in February. By June, Margaret Chase Smith could stand it no more. She took the Senate floor on the first of June, with Joseph McCarthy looking on from his seat in the chamber: "I speak as a Republican. I speak as a woman. I speak as a United States Senator. I speak as an American."[17] Early on in her fifteen-minute speech, she lamented, without mentioning McCarthy by name, that the Senate had been "debased to the level of a forum of hate and character assassination sheltered by the shield of congressional immunity." She acknowledged that "there have been enough proved cases," including the Hiss case, "to cause Nation-wide distrust and strong suspicion that there may be something to the unproved, sensational accusations."

She then moved to the intersection of partisan politics and morality: "The Nation sorely needs a Republican victory. But I do not want to see the Republican party ride to political victory on the Four Horsemen of Calumny—fear, ignorance, bigotry, and smear." "As an American," she was "shocked at the way Republicans and Democrats alike are playing directly into the Communist design of 'confuse, divide and conquer.'" She concluded by offering what she called a Declaration of Conscience, concurred with by six other Republican senators, concisely summarizing her speech.

McCarthy sat wordless, his face drained of color, three feet behind the Maine Senator.[18] Although she had expected him to respond, he got up and silently left the chamber. The junior senator from Maine had given Truman the gift of some moral high ground.

With the onset of the Korean War barely three weeks after Margaret Chase Smith made her speech, opposition to McCarthy's demagoguery got a bit more difficult. What Martin Malia aptly termed "anti-anti-communism" was, as the 1950 election approached, politically hazardous.[19] (McCarthy later succeeded, albeit unintentionally, in making "anti-anti-communism" socially acceptable in polite company, but not in 1950.) Other complications, smaller but perhaps no less irritating to Truman, intervened as well. In early September, Major General Orvil Anderson, the commandant of the Air War College, elaborated to a reporter on what he had, in more discreet settings, advocated as preventive war. As quoted in the *New York Times*: "Give me the order to do it and I can break up Russia's five A-bomb nests in a week. And when I went up to Christ—I think I could explain to Him that I had saved civilization."[20] Such was the temper of the times as the election approached.

Although the 1950 election was an off-year contest, it was in some ways a defining moment in US politics. The nation would find out whether the issue of domestic communism still had legs. A US senate race in California would provide the clearest test of the potency of anticommunism in electoral politics. This was the contest between two California members of the House of Representatives—Helen Gahagan Douglas and Richard Milhous Nixon—for an open Senate seat. Again, some context is necessary.

Chapter 9

The McCarran Internal Security Act and Korea

Anticommunist legislation was catnip for communist-hunting legislators, in part because an argument could usually be made with a straight face that legislation of *some* sort was justified, even if the immediacy of the domestic threat was not obvious to everyone. That was true when Senator Patrick McCarran, a Nevada Democrat, proposed what became known as the McCarran Internal Security Act of 1950—a proposition that bedeviled Truman in the run-up to the 1950 election. As enacted, the McCarran Act (1) created the Subversive Activities Control Board, (2) required registration of communist organizations (with disclosure of membership and finances), (3) prohibited the employment of communists in the federal government or at defense facilities, (4) provided for preventive detention of suspected disloyal or subversive persons in times of national emergency, and (5) authorized the exclusion or deportation of communists and other subversives.

By mid-September, the legislation had cleared the House (354 to 20) and the Senate (70 to 7), triggering a veto—with a blistering veto message—from Truman. Accompanied by a personally signed letter to every member of Congress, Truman's veto message took issue with the constitutionality, necessity, and practicality of the legislation. (As for constitutionality, Truman was substantially correct. In three decisions in the 1960s, the Supreme Court held several sections of the act unconstitutional.) Given the overwhelming votes for enactment, Truman understood quite well that the math of a veto override was against him. The override vote was 286 to 48 in the House and 57 to 10 in the Senate. The political ramifications of the legislation were brought into high relief by the fact that the override in the Senate was supported by about half of the Democrats (26 out of 54) but by about three-quarters of the Republicans (31 out of 42).

The Subversive Activities Control Board was promptly installed, in an elaborate swearing-in ceremony. The *Daily Worker*, the house organ of the Communist Party USA, took a dim view of all of this. On the eve of the first hearings to be held by the SACB, *Daily Worker* columnist Elizabeth Gurley Flynn opined that the hearings would "open up the most disgusting parade of every stoolpigeon, undercover FBI agent, informer, renegade and turncoat that money can buy to do their master's bidding."[21]

In some of its initial actions to enforce the McCarran Act, the State Department canceled all visas for entry into the United States, pending review to make certain "that applicants for, or holders of, visas are not now and never have been members of the Communist, Nazi or Fascist parties."[22] Consequently, the renowned conductor Victor de Sabata, visiting from the La Scala Orchestra of Milan, was diverted to Ellis Island, there to remain until his politics could be vetted. Meanwhile, in other action consistent with the tone set by enactment of the McCarran Act, the University of California Regents voted to dismiss fifty-one professors (including numerous war veterans) who refused to sign contractual affirmations of their nonmembership in the Communist Party, leading to a ten-minute protest speech by an economics professor to a classroom full of his students. But the editorial page of the *San Francisco Examiner*, flagship of the Hearst newspaper chain (and an ardent supporter of the affirmation requirement), gave the professor a break, allowing that "[the professor], of course, is not a Communist. He is merely a confused professor."[23]

With the war raging on the Korean Peninsula, opponents of loyalty oaths were fighting a losing battle. Thirty-one University of California employees ultimately refused, as a matter of principle, to sign the contractual affirmation, though none of them was ever identified as a communist. One communist was discovered on the university payroll. She was a dance-rehearsal pianist at UCLA. She was summarily fired.

Not to be outdone, the American Bar Association capped off its annual meeting by adopting resolutions "urging that all members of the bar take loyalty oaths, and that a special committee be named to analyze Communist techniques and advise lawyers how to cope with subversive activities."[24] Lest there be any doubt as to the bar association's ideological target, the resolution specifically made it clear that, aside from communist party membership, adherence to "Marxism-Leninism" was also politically incorrect in the ranks of the American legal profession.[25] (The effect such a stricture would have on the composition of the membership of the present-day American Bar Association is unknown.)

With "anti-anti-communism" becoming more awkward by the day as the 1950 election approached, the Chinese intervention in the Korean war—which prolonged the fighting for nearly three more years—came just in time to make its own contribution to the off-year campaign.

Chapter 9

Richard M. Nixon v. Helen Gahagan Douglas

Helen Gahagan Douglas was made to order for Richard Nixon as a political opponent. A New Jersey native who had attended a prestigious New York finishing school before entering Barnard College, she established herself as a successful actress before entering politics. She was elected to the House of Representatives from California in 1944, two years before Nixon was elected to the House. Her politics were not far (if at all) left of the conventional New Deal Democrat variety, garnished with an unapologetic libertarian streak that was not necessarily required of Democratic politicians (as witness Senator Patrick McCarran).

Douglas handily won the Democratic nomination for the open California Senate seat in the June 1950 primary election (as did Nixon on the Republican side). But it can fairly be argued that Douglas set herself up to lose the November 1950 general election with a speech she made four years earlier. Less than two months after Stalin's February 1946 Election Speech and less than a month after Churchill's Iron Curtain speech, Representative Helen Gahagan Douglas felt compelled to take the floor of the House to voice her heartfelt concerns in a thirty-minute speech. The first words out of her mouth: "Mr. Speaker, I think we all know that communism is no real threat to the democratic institutions of our country." The Congresswoman argued that "we do a disservice to democracy when we dismiss communism as the devil's handiwork," concluding that "the fear of communism in this country is not rational."[26]

It was just a matter of time until Douglas's words from the spring of 1946 would find their place as building blocks of the Nixon campaign four years later. In late August, quoting Douglas's "no real threat" introduction to her 1946 speech, Nixon's southern California campaign manager proclaimed (in a long essay printed in full by the *Los Angeles Times*) that Douglas had "deservedly earned the title of 'the pink lady.'"[27] She fared no better on the editorial pages than in the news pages. Two days after Douglas voted against the McCarran Internal Security Act, the *Los Angeles Times* observed that she was among "20 Representatives who voted against controlling the Commies."[28] The editorial rhetoric heated up as the campaign progressed, with the *Times* intoning a week before the election that Douglas, "though not a Communist, voted the

Communist Party line in Congress innumerable times," making her "the darling of the Hollywood parlor pinks and Reds."[29]

Even before the election-eve intervention in Korea by the Chinese, the anticommunist thread in Nixon's campaign was internationalized, with frequent references to Yalta and to what Nixon described as the "important position Alger Hiss played in the making of our foreign policy."[30] With China an active belligerent in the Korean war, Nixon assailed Douglas for staying with what he described as the State Department's policy of appeasement of communism: "I never dreamed that she would stick to it even after we were attacked."[31]

By election day, 1950, Nixon had amassed endorsements from prominent Democrats in addition to the normal array of Republican support. But, for a back-bench Republican Congressman who had risen from humble origins, the most coveted kudos came by way of the full-throated election-eve endorsement of the *Los Angeles Times,* published by the Otis Chandler family, which praised his "demonstrated ability to act on public questions intelligently, honestly and forthrightly, because of his sense of values and his sound views."[32]

It should be noted, by way of brief digression, that Nixon's gratitude for a *Los Angeles Times* endorsement did not last forever. Twenty years, eleven months, and two days after he received the endorsement, Nixon, as president of the United States, gave an unequivocal order to Attorney General John Mitchell: "We're going after the Chandlers, every one, individually, collectively, their income tax. They're starting this week. Every one of those sons of bitches."[33] For good measure, the president directed the attorney general to cause the Immigration and Naturalization Service to raid the offices of the *Times* in search of illegal immigrants.[34] Nixon's orders were not obeyed.[35]

The tone of the California Senate race was not an outlier in the 1950 elections. The mood of the country as the election approached was aptly described by the Pulitzer Prize–winning columnist James "Scotty" Reston: "There is an uneasiness in the country that material prosperity cannot obscure. . . . The Democrats, as usual, are campaigning against Herbert Hoover and the depression of 1932. The Republicans, similarly, are campaigning against Franklin D. Roosevelt (Yalta division), Dean Acheson, Alger Hiss, and socialism (which invariably is defined as 'creeping communism')."[36] The matter was put more succinctly by another commentator, in the *Atlanta Constitution*: "There is unmistakable evidence in the country today that good morals could be good politics, but the fact is that this political campaign has seen the triumph of 'McCarthyism.'"[37]

In California, Nixon defeated Douglas by more than 680,000 votes, taking 59 percent of the votes cast. Nationally, the Republicans had a good day in the November 1952, elections, even though they did not take numerical control of either house of Congress. With a net gain of five seats in the Senate, the Republicans—in league with the conservative southern Democrats—could stymie any major Democratic initiatives.

The Mainstream Media in the Run-up to the 1952 Election

Foreign affairs rarely played a prominent role in the biennial US elections between 1789 and World War II. The early Cold War elections departed from that norm. That trend continued into the 1950s, largely because two compelling themes (internationally, the Soviet threat; domestically, the communist threat) became inextricably linked. To talk about either was perforce to talk about both. Although Democrats such as Senator McCarran succeeded at times in seizing the initiative, these issues were mostly a means by which the Republicans sought, with some success, to keep the Democrats on the defensive.

To understand how all of this unfolded in 1951 and 1952, it is necessary to understand who the main players were and to understand the backdrop for the political stage on which the players performed their roles. The main players were General Dwight D. Eisenhower, Governor Adlai E. Stevenson, John Foster Dulles, and Joe McCarthy. President Truman and Senator Richard Nixon had supporting roles. Also in a supporting role were the men in the Kremlin, but they really did not have to do much in 1951 and 1952 to stimulate the national conversation in the United States about perceived external and internal threats.

Eisenhower and Stevenson were two thoroughly decent, honorable men. The story of how they found themselves in a presidential campaign that took some exceptionally nasty turns requires us, first, to look at the national scene as presented in the mainstream media.

With the Korean War already in the headlines as an example of communist aggression, there was serious concern about what the Russians might try in Western Europe. James Reston wrote, at the turn of the year, 1951, that there were "some prominent officials [in Washington] who believe that the Soviet Union will move into Western Europe this year." And there were "a few others who feel that the chances of a general war are about even, and this latter group is arguing that the current pace of industrial and manpower mobilization should be doubled."[38] Reston was not the only one writing about the distinct possibility of war with the Soviets.

Collier's magazine, widely circulated and decidedly in the mainstream of US print media, ended 1950 with a lead article—"Russia Could Take Europe in Three Weeks"—premised on the proposition that "if the Reds choose to shoot it out in the near future, they could quickly overrun the Continent. We can only hope they'll stall for two years more while we race to build up our military strength."[39] Leading off with a photo of a bemedaled Soviet tank commander, the article told readers, echoing Churchill's Iron Curtain speech, that "from Lübeck on the Baltic to Trieste on the Mediterranean, the Russians today deploy between 25 and 30 combat-trained divisions, ready for anything." As of the end of 1950, of course, West Germany had not yet joined NATO. But the *Collier's* article ventured explicitly into that geopolitical thicket. After summarizing the NATO order of battle west of the Elbe, readers were told: "It is arithmetic of this sort that makes U.S. and Allied military commanders declare almost unanimously that we must enlist the potential of West Germany if a real defense of Western Europe is not to remain illusory. . . . To the military men, the case for West German rearmament is unanswerable. Germany is the grand prize of the cold war."[40] The purpose of this was to "build a secure wall between the liberty-loving people of Western Europe and the expansion-mad men of the Kremlin."

A month later, *Collier's* moved to a more theoretical plane with a long editorial: "Why Russia Can't Be Trusted." After reprising Yalta and Russia's domination of Poland, the editorial reminded readers of Stalin's fidelity to the teachings of Lenin, particularly (citing Stalin's February 1946 Election Speech) the "Marxist line that capitalism breeds conflict, and that as long as capitalism exists wars will continue." The conclusion was that agreement with Russia "may well be possible, but only at a time when the Soviet government finds itself faced by a strength and determination as great as its own."[41]

The urgent tone of this coverage in the popular press could not have disappointed Truman. His challenge—with NSC-68 lying on his desk alongside the daily reports on the Korean War—was to find the money to fight the war he already had, and to deter the war envisioned by NSC-68 and *Collier's*. More help came from *Time* magazine in August. The August 20 issue, featuring—none too subtly—Soviet Air Force Lieutenant General Vasiliy (Dzhugashvili) Stalin on the cover, delivered the bad news ("The Reds have about 1,000 heavy bombers. . . .") and the good news (the House had just passed a $56 billion defense appropriations bill by a vote of 348 to 2).[42] *Collier's* returned to the national conversation in October 1951, with a 130-page issue devoted entirely to a hypothetical World War III with the USSR, beginning in 1952 and ending (after massive atomic bombing of targets in the United States and the Soviet Union) in 1955, complete with full-page illustrations of nuclear holocausts in Moscow and Washington. Lest the point be missed, the editors of *Collier's* pronounced that issue of the magazine to be "the most important single issue that any magazine has ever published."[43]

Dulles, McCarthy, and the Republicans

We will never know for sure whether John Foster Dulles—the son of a Presbyterian minister—was a stern moralist as a boy growing up in Watertown, New York. But he was one as an adult. That was a convenient trait to have as a Republican in the early 1950s; stern moralists had plenty to work with, domestically and internationally.

A graduate of Princeton University (1908, Phi Beta Kappa) and George Washington University Law School, Dulles was, as has been noted, the grandson of one secretary of state and the nephew of another. His experience as at least an observer of diplomacy started when he accompanied his grandfather to the Hague conference in 1907. As a successful corporate lawyer who moved into public service as a practitioner of international affairs in the 1940s, Dulles had good reason to favor bipartisanship. Notwithstanding his close association with Thomas Dewey in Dewey's unsuccessful runs for the presidency in 1944 and 1948, Dulles answered the call in the Truman administration, helping to create and shape the United Nations in the early postwar years.

Remarkably (and this speaks well of Truman and Acheson), Dulles's service as an advisor to the Truman administration did not end when *Life* magazine published, in two issues in June 1946, an elaborate dissertation by Dulles on US-Soviet relations. Recrimination about Yalta was unavoidable. Even though Dulles had been (and would again be) of service in the Truman administration, he insisted that "we bartered away to the Soviet Union the rights of weak nations, such as China and Poland, despite the Atlantic Charter." Although Dulles himself contributed to the decline of bipartisanship as the 1952 election approached, McCarthy and McCarthyism—not yet feeling any effective restraint from congressional Republicans—must once again be given their due.

On June 14, 1951, Eisenhower was both the president of Columbia University (an office he would hold until he was sworn in as president of the United States in January 1953) *and* the supreme commander of NATO forces. Consequently, though he revered his former commander and mentor, George Catlett Marshall, Eisenhower was not in an ideal position to respond when, on the floor of the Senate (and taking full advantage of congressional immunity), Joe McCarthy proclaimed in a sixty-thousand-word speech that Marshall, along with Acheson, was a party to "a great conspiracy, a conspiracy on a scale so immense as to dwarf any previous such venture in the history of man. A conspiracy of infamy so black that, when it is finally exposed, its principals shall be forever deserving of the maledictions of all honest men." The objective of the conspiracy was that "we shall be contained, frustrated and finally fall victim to Soviet intrigue from within and Russian military might from without."[44] Marshall stood accused of treason.

It is just possible that if control of the Senate had not hung in the balance, the ugly baby called McCarthyism might have been smothered in its infancy. This was to be a telling test for congressional Republicans. It was not their finest hour. By June of 1951, it was obvious that McCarthy brought to public office a truly remarkable and dangerous combination of qualities.

Devoid of empathy, McCarthy was an endlessly vain, self-absorbed narcissist and demagogue. The obverse of his constant need for admiration was his reflexive tendency to demean his rivals or, for that matter, anyone who incurred his displeasure. His disregard for long-established norms manifested itself most prominently in his penchant for self-serving use of the apparatus of government. The demoralizing effects of his demagoguery ran deep within the ranks of committed public servants, especially in the State Department. He picked his most damning "facts" out of thin air, as a confabulator who cared far more about the impact of his words than about their truth.

His June 14 speech established for all time that there was no person whose reputation he would not seek to blacken if he thought it politically advantageous to do so. When McCarthy accused Marshall of treason, it had been just over a year since Margaret Chase Smith had taken the Senate floor to denounce McCarthy's demagoguery. A year on, her views still had precious little support on the Republican side.

The 1952 Campaign

It is fitting that, as the 1952 election approached, Eisenhower had gone on record as an outspoken supporter of education in the fundamental obligations of citizenship. In 1952, he had to decide whether, as one of the foremost leaders of his generation, he had an obligation to seek the presidency. Once he became the nominee, he was required to weigh political reality and his moral sensibilities in the balance as he decided just how far he could and would go with the demagoguery of Joe McCarthy.

For Eisenhower, the first—and in some ways easiest—dilemma was whether to seek the office. He made his decision in the spring of 1952, and formally relinquished his command of NATO forces in a ceremony at NATO's military headquarters in Rocquencourt, France, on May 30. By that time, his supporters had already rounded up substantial support by way of pledged delegates for the Republican convention in July. Senator Robert Taft was also seeking the nomination.

Eisenhower ran because he could not abide Taft's indifference, if not outright hostility, to US involvement in the defense of its European allies. In 1951, Taft had promised to cut US defense spending in half, arguing that Truman's proposal—by way of implementation of NSC-68—to enlarge the US Army would have dire economic consequences. It is safe to say that Eisenhower and Taft, though both Republicans, were from decidedly different political gene pools on all but the most theoretical issues of national security. But like any good general, Eisenhower understood the need to protect his flanks. He protected his right flank by choosing as his running mate Richard Nixon, who, conveniently, was both an internationalist and a relentless pursuer of internal subversives.[45]

Dulles was the principal author of the foreign policy plank of the platform adopted by the Republicans at their July convention in Chicago. Yalta, of course, was an irresistible target. The platform promised that Republican leadership would "repudiate all commitments contained in secret understandings such as those of Yalta which aid Communist enslavements." Republican control of foreign policy would "mark the end of the negative, futile and immoral policy of 'containment' which abandons countless human beings to a despotism and godless terrorism, which in turn enables the rulers to forge the captives into a weapon for our destruction."[46] This, in a word, was Dulles's call for "rollback." Merely to contain communism was negative, futile, and immoral. The platform was silent as to just how the communist advance to the Elbe (and some points west) would be rolled back.

For the Republicans, the problem of figuring out how to roll back communism could wait; the problem of Joe McCarthy could not. At the express invitation of the Republican National Committee, McCarthy was permitted to speak at the Republican convention in July. The invitation may on some level have been a defensible concession to a powerful senator; nevertheless, this was a little over a year after McCarthy had accused Marshall, then the sitting secretary of defense (and Eisenhower's mentor), of treason. McCarthy's warning to the delegates: "The same men who delivered nearly half of the world to Communist Russia are still in control in Washington and Moscow . . . the same men are doing your planning."[47] If there had been any doubts in Eisenhower's mind, he could now be certain that this was going to be a long campaign.

The basic themes of the Eisenhower-Nixon campaign were uncomplicated: "Ike barnstorms in Iowa, hitting corruption, Communism and Korea."[48] With a war in Korea and the Democrats answerable for twenty years in the White House, Eisenhower and Nixon had a lot to work with. By the time the campaign got started in earnest (this was the era in which general-election campaigns did not really get rolling until Labor Day), Eisenhower probably thought he had found a way to thread the needle of

McCarthy and McCarthyism. McCarthy, having been elected to the Senate from Wisconsin in 1946, was up for re-election. The outcome of the national election, in terms of control of the Senate, was going to be close. Aside from that, Ike also needed to carry the state of Wisconsin, which the Republican presidential nominee had carried only once since 1932. By the end of August, Eisenhower thought he had found the formula, which he articulated at a press conference. He would not campaign for McCarthy, but, with control of the Senate hanging in the balance, he would back any Republican running for election to that body.

To drive home his support of Marshall, Eisenhower, as reported by W. H. Lawrence of the *New York Times*, "rose from his chair at a press conference and walked into the center of the room to defend vehemently the patriotism and selfless service of his old chief, General of the Army George C. Marshall, whom Senator McCarthy had in effect called a 'traitor.' 'There was nothing of disloyalty in General Marshall's soul.'" Thus, Ike's support of McCarthy was "as much a matter of form as practical politics would permit."[49]

Eisenhower could only wish that it would be that easy. In early October, as Eisenhower's campaign train headed from Illinois into Wisconsin, McCarthy showed up—uninvited—on the train. Ike told McCarthy that he intended to denounce communism *and* defend General Marshall in his speech that night.[50] McCarthy prevailed on Eisenhower to remove the passage defending Marshall from his Wisconsin speech. As reported by Lawrence: "While he significantly failed to demonstrate any great enthusiasm at having Senator McCarthy on his special campaign train, General Eisenhower did bow to the Wisconsin senator's urging and eliminate from his Milwaukee speech tonight a defense of his old friend and chief."[51] Addressing the crowd in Milwaukee, Eisenhower went no further than to say, without naming names, that the "right to challenge a man's judgment carries with it no automatic right to question his honor."[52]

Eisenhower *did* carry Wisconsin, and McCarthy *was* re-elected. (Eisenhower got 61 percent of the Wisconsin vote; McCarthy 54 percent.) As it turned out, though Eisenhower could have been elected without Wisconsin, the Republicans could not have controlled the Senate without McCarthy.

Meanwhile, the Eisenhower campaign itself needed some "containment." As the campaign warmed up, Eisenhower's foreign policy reference points were (1) attacks on the Truman-Acheson policy of mere containment of the USSR, (2) repudiation of Yalta, and (3) cultivation of the support of voters of Eastern European heritage. By mid-August, Eisenhower had made it clear that, though "mere containment" was unacceptable, his policy was one of "obtaining *by peaceful means* freedom for the peoples now behind the Iron Curtain in both Europe and Asia."[53] And, of course, it did not take a political science professor to notice that Eisenhower's insistence on restoration of the freedom of Poland, Czechoslovakia, and China might, as reported by the *New York Times,* "have a substantial effect on the not insubstantial nationality vote in the United States."[54] But later in the month, Dulles made some people nervous. Predicting that "liberation vs. containment would be one of the big issues of the campaign," he advocated Eastern European resistance movements to foment discontent, slowdowns, and industrial sabotage. Uprisings "could be supplied and integrated via air drops and other communications from private organizations." Dulles's central proposition as secretary of state-in-waiting was that the "'containment' policy of President Truman and Secretary of State Dean Acheson must be abandoned."[55] To this, former Ambassador Averell Harriman responded that Eisenhower's "liberation policy had spread fear of war in Europe."[56] Eisenhower, needing to calm the nervousness, promptly got Dulles on the telephone to let him know that liberation was to be accomplished "by all peaceful means."[57]

In the final weeks of the campaign, the message was refined: War, Yalta and mere containment are bad. Rollback by peaceful means is good; votes from Americans of Eastern European extraction are even better. In observance of Pulaski Day, Eisenhower's message was: "It is my great privilege to send fervent greetings to American citizens of Polish descent, in this anniversary of the death of their great Polish patriot, [Revolutionary War] Gen. Casimir Pulaski."[58] In the same message, Eisenhower called for formal repudiation of the Yalta agreement and pledged to "work continually, yet peacefully, until the courageous patriots of Poland are again masters of their own destiny."[59] Nixon, hewing to the rhetorical role typically assigned to vice-presidential candidates, labeled Stevenson "Adlai the Appeaser," and a graduate of "Dean Acheson's Cowardly College of Communist Containment."[60]

So it was that Eisenhower's 1952 campaign drew to a close. Eisenhower carried thirty-nine states (including all the northeastern, Great

Lakes, and midwestern states) to Stevenson's nine (essentially the "solid south," plus Kentucky and West Virginia). Notably, at least in a twenty-first-century context, Eisenhower was endorsed for president by the *New York Times*, though the *Times* allowed that the campaign, a contest between "two eminent and distinguished men of high integrity," had been "one of the most emotional and abusive campaigns of recent years."[61] The *Times* also endorsed repudiation of the Yalta agreements in toto.[62]

As Gerard Toal writes, US foreign policy during the Cold War "was driven more by cultural axiom induced by domestic politics than by strategic calculation."[63] A comparison of the rhetoric of "rollback" with foreign policy as executed in the decade of the 1950s suggests that, for the most part, "cultural axiom induced by domestic politics" had more to do with the *rhetoric* of US foreign policy than with foreign policy as actually practiced, at least vis-à-vis the Soviet Union. The Eisenhower campaign's rhetoric of liberation, with the trappings of resistance, sabotage, and airdrops, would be tested with the East German uprising in 1953, at Dien Bien Phu in 1954, and in Hungary and the Polish city of Poznań in 1956. Not a thing was rolled back in Eastern Europe, but the rhetoric of rollback helped roll the Democrats back after twenty years in the White House.

For his part, Truman summed up the results and prospects for containment in his farewell address to the nation on January 15, 1953. His extraordinarily prescient words testified to his faith in the policies he implemented beginning on that April day in 1945: "There will have to come a time of change in the Soviet world. Nobody can say for sure when that is going to be, or exactly how it will come about, whether by revolution, or trouble in the satellite states, or by a change inside the Kremlin. Whether the Communist rulers shift their policies of their own free will–or whether the change comes about in some other way–I have not a doubt in the world that a change will occur."[64]

1953: Change of Control in the White House, the Senate, and the Kremlin

Senate Republicans, newly in control by the narrowest of margins, quickly got organized in January 1953. Joe McCarthy became the new chairman of the Senate Permanent Subcommittee on Investigations. He promptly appointed his chief counsel: a twenty-five-year-old New York attorney named Roy Cohn. Cohn was nothing if not tenacious. "'Brash kid' was one of the more genteel descriptions his opponents had for him in his early days at the bar."[65] (After being indicted three times and acquitted three times in the 1960s on charges of fraud, blackmail, and perjury, Cohn would acquire a new client at a New York nightclub in 1973: Donald J. Trump, then a young real estate developer. Cohn was disbarred in 1986, on charges of "dishonesty, fraud, deceit and misrepresentation."[66] Mr. Trump was one of Cohn's character witnesses.[67])

Scores of books have been written about the McCarthy era, especially in its 1953–54 phase. There is no need to retell that story in full here. Our focus now is on the intersection of domestic politics and foreign policy in the early years of the Cold War. McCarthy, McCarthyism, and the ultimate disgrace of Senator Joseph R. McCarthy are woven into that narrative. And, in the third decade of the twenty-first century, there is once again something to be gained by looking at this mid-twentieth-century saga of abasement of high public office.

On January 27, 1953, six days into his tenure as secretary of state, John Foster Dulles set the stage for the foreign policy of the new administration in a nationally broadcast address. Dulles had no good words for communists or communism, domestic or foreign, but he managed to get through his long speech without calling for repudiation of Yalta or a rollback of communism. Indeed, in his Senate confirmation hearing earlier in January, Dulles had the good sense (and startling candor) to acknowledge that the language he had written into the Republican platform in July "was appropriate only to a campaign season and was 'not the language I would pick or want to use today.'"[68] This relatively trifling instance of what we now call "confirmation conversion" implicitly reaffirmed the indisputable truism that, as one sits before a Senate committee considering confirmation of one's nomination, it is far more important to be regarded as noncontroversial than to have virtually any conceivable positive trait.

As for the Russians, Dulles affirmed in his January 27 address that "we have enemies who are plotting our destruction. These enemies are the Russian communists and their allies in other countries." "The Communist Party in this country is part of a gigantic conspiracy designed to overthrow our Government by violence." Internationally, Dulles insisted that one of the main objectives of the USSR was *encirclement*: "At the present time, the Soviet communists are carrying out a policy which they call encirclement. That means they want to get control of the different areas around them and around us so they will keep growing in strength and we're more and more cut off and isolated." Once the encirclement of the United States is completed, Russia will "be ready for what Stalin has called the decisive blow against us with the odds overwhelmingly in their favor."[69]

It may well be that Dulles did not mention Yalta in his January address because the administration was about to nominate none other than Charles Bohlen to serve as the new ambassador to the Soviet Union. The good news about Bohlen was that he was, by any measure, eminently qualified for service as the US envoy to the Soviet Union. He was also a career Foreign Service Officer, rather than an outright political appointee, a fact that doubtless helped the new administration get off to a good start with the State Department's career officers who naturally wondered what life would be like in the first Republican administration in twenty years. The bad news was that Bohlen had literally sat at Roosevelt's elbow at the Yalta conference. Bohlen and his supporters maintained that he was there essentially as Roosevelt's interpreter. His detractors were having none of this; Bohlen was a Yalta conspirator.

The best way to get an understanding of the piquancy of the story of the struggle leading to the confirmation of Charles E. "Chip" Bohlen to serve as the new Republican president's ambassador to the USSR is to go to the end of the story first. After a nasty floor debate, the appointment was confirmed by a 74 to 13 vote. But eleven of the thirteen votes against Bohlen were from *Republican* senators. Thirty-nine Democrats, but only thirty-four Republicans, voted to confirm. The main contestants in the confirmation battle were Eisenhower, Dulles, Bohlen, and McCarthy. McCarthy lost, but he survived to fight another day.

The confirmation fight did include some vague—and never substantiated—inuendoes suggesting Bohlen was a security risk, but the main rallying cry for the opponents came down to one word: Yalta. The narrative that Roosevelt, with the benefit of the counsel of Charles Bohlen, had acquiesced in the Russian occupation of Eastern Europe, had a life of its own.[70] The debate was also infused with newfound uncertainty about the direction of US-Soviet relations. Bohlen testified before the Senate

Foreign Relations Committee on March 2. As he did so, Stalin was on his deathbed, having suffered a massive cerebral hemorrhage on March 1. He died on March 5 (resulting, among other things, in "free borscht in celebration of Stalin's death" at a restaurant in Washington[71]). Although Bohlen was superbly qualified to help guide relations with the Kremlin through a new era of uncertainty, Stalin's death was—as a purely tactical matter—an unwelcome complication for proponents of confirmation.

Bohlen made a good enough impression on the Foreign Relations Committee to clear that committee on a vote of 15 to 0, even though he acknowledged in his committee testimony that he had been an advisor (as well as an interpreter) at Yalta. For that reason, as he put it in his memoir, he "could not act like a village idiot" when questioned by the committee.[72] Bohlen, an urbane, well-educated, and handsome man, did have the ability to impress. For Senate confirmation, Bohlen would need all the charm he could muster, as well as some friends in high places. On the day after Bohlen gave his committee testimony, the *New York Times* reported that "Charles E. Bohlen, President Eisenhower's choice for Ambassador to Russia, made it plain today to senators holding his confirmation in their hands that he never would join in Republican condemnations of the wartime Yalta agreement."[73] This was all Joe McCarthy needed; confirmation by the full Senate was not going to be a cakewalk. And this brings us to an important part of the backstory.

The professionalization of front-line diplomacy got started in the United States in 1924, with the enactment of legislation creating the United States Foreign Service. After clearing an extraordinarily stringent selection process, successful applicants to the foreign service become commissioned Foreign Service Officers, members of a select cadre of career diplomats possessing exceptional expertise and an unwavering commitment to serving the interests of the United States. Bohlen, having entered the Foreign Service in 1929, was in the first generation of career diplomats in the professionalized foreign service. He was assigned to serve on the staff of the US embassy in Moscow when diplomatic relations with the Soviet Union were established in 1934. Among the heady experiences of his career was his encounter with a German diplomat who told Bohlen about the secret protocols annexed to the Molotov-Ribbentrop pact on the day after that bargain was struck by Stalin and Hitler in August 1939.

Bohlen would later write that, with McCarthy's entry into the fray, "the career officers in the Foreign Service were watching to see if, like Kennan, I would be shunted aside because I had carried out my duties under another administration."[74] McCarthy attacked, but Eisenhower and Dulles resolutely defended. This was to be a much-needed victory for the professionals in the Foreign Service.

The decorous tone of Bohlen's hearing with the Foreign Relations Committee did not carry over to the debate on the Senate floor. For McCarthy, this fight was an extension of the fall campaign against "the treason of Yalta."[75] McCarthy charged that Bohlen had "helped abandon millions of people to the Soviet tyrants at Tehran, Yalta and Potsdam."[76] As always, any mention of Yalta invited a dive into ethnic politics. That aspect of the matter was articulated by Styles Bridges, Republican of New Hampshire: "To approve Bohlen as Ambassador to the Soviet Union, after his brazen defense of Yalta is a slap across the face of every anti-Communist Pole or citizen of Polish descent in the world. This includes the great majority of Poles inside Poland, millions of exiles, and several million of our own fellow citizens."[77]

Eisenhower weighed in when it mattered most. At his press conference on the eve of the Senate vote on confirmation, he told the reporters that Bohlen "was the best qualified man to be Ambassador to the Soviet Union and expressed sadness at the attacks being made on Mr. Bohlen's nomination from within the President's own party."[78] With the 74 to 13 vote to confirm the Bohlen nomination the next day, Eisenhower had prevailed in a fight he could not have afforded to lose. And this, importantly, was at a time—in the wake of Stalin's death—when no one really knew where US-Soviet relations were headed.

For Dulles, the lift in the morale of the Foreign Service was a priceless gift.[79] This was as much a watershed day for the fledgling Eisenhower administration as it was in the career of Charles E. Bohlen. On the train ride to Milwaukee in the heat of the 1952 campaign, Eisenhower had temporized with McCarthyism. Between the spring of 1953 and the end of 1954, McCarthy would learn that Eisenhower would temporize no more. Bohlen and his wife, Avis, left for Moscow on April 4, 1953. (All of this was doubtless impressive to their twelve-year-old daughter who, by the way, would herself become a career diplomat.)

The events of the last two years of the McCarthy era still have effects on popular consciousness in the third decade of the twentieth century. This is a study of how rank demagoguery was overcome by resilient institutions, a free press, and a soupçon of courage, all with a little help from a folksy Boston lawyer.

Getting Serious about McCarthy

There were essentially three chapters to the McCarthy story in 1953 and 1954. He started out in January 1953 as the new chairman of the Permanent Subcommittee on Investigations—armed with subpoena power and the authority to hire staff as he saw fit. Not satisfied with the competence of the FBI and an assortment of other security agencies, he used his committee position to continue his hunt for communists in the US government, particularly in the army. Next, his sordid rhetoric and tactics led to the historic Army-McCarthy hearings in the spring of 1954. Finally, with the record of McCarthy's malevolence laid bare before the American people, the Senate summoned the courage to pass a resolution of censure by an overwhelming margin in December of 1954.

As these three final chapters of McCarthy's political career played out, his support on the Republican side of the Senate gradually eroded. On that score, and as demagogues will do, he proved to be his own worst enemy. As for the White House, Eisenhower detested McCarthy and his tactics. Eisenhower ultimately played a powerful role in bringing McCarthy down, but Ike's involvement in bringing about McCarthy's demise as a force in public life—although active—was mostly behind the scenes. Once again, some context is necessary.

As Cabell Phillips, a veteran Washington correspondent put it, McCarthy had "scraped the raw nerve of the nation's anxiety and turned it into a neurosis." Worse yet, wrote Phillips, McCarthy "made cowards of all but a handful of his fellow Senators."[80] The failure of the Henry Wallace presidential campaign in 1948 and the success of the unions in combating communist influence in their ranks essentially eliminated communism as a force in the public domain. That left communism as the covert "enemy within." McCarthy could get traction in pursuing covert communism because the raw nerve described by Phillips was real. It had been made real by the proven disloyalty of David Greenglass and Julius and Ethel Rosenberg, with the perjury of Alger Hiss thrown in for good measure.

The great advantage McCarthy enjoyed in hunting for the "enemy within" is that he could define the threat as needed to serve his purposes and could then hurl accusations while wearing the cloak of congressional immunity to avoid accountability for his defamation of blameless Americans. Giants of American history such as General George Catlett Marshall could withstand McCarthy's calumny without breaking a sweat or missing a paycheck. But the tragedy of 1953-style McCarthyism is that McCarthy and Cohn had no compunction about ruining the lives of little people, such as Doris Walters Powell, a civilian clerk in the army quartermaster's office in New York. She was in a position, as McCarthy put it, to "know the amount of hams et cetera going to Alaska."[81] She had once worked as a secretary for the *People's Daily* in Harlem. Her boss had been a communist. He had her attend lectures, "I think it was on Negro history."[82] When she repeatedly—and, under all the circumstances, credibly—testified that she had not, to her knowledge, been a member of the Communist Party, Roy Cohn would step in to assure Doris Powell that "we have other witnesses who are coming in here to testify. If you don't tell the truth here, we will send the case to the Department of Justice. You can be indicted for perjury. There is a jail penalty attached to it."[83] McCarthy labeled Doris Powell "a 100 percent Communist."[84] His treatment of Powell was a prime example of his techniques for intimidating witnesses and getting himself into the headlines. Doris Walters Powell lost her job.

McCarthy's irreversible slide to oblivion began in the spring of 1954, on March 9, to be exact. McCarthy ran up against a free press, a lawyer who was confident of the justness of his client's cause, and more stirrings of courage from his Republican colleagues in the Senate.

As for Republicans in the Senate, Ralph Flanders of Vermont joined the small cadre of those who could no longer remain silent. Forsaking the genteel tenor of most speeches on the Senate floor, Flanders made it plain that his angst was both political and moral. On the political side, the Vermont senator offered up a beautifully turned phrase, appropriate in so many situations, then and now: "Is [McCarthy] a hidden satellite of the Democratic Party, to which he is furnishing so much material for quiet mirth?" Flanders answered his own question: "It does not seem that the Republican label can be stuck on very tightly, when, by intention or through ignorance he is doing his best to shatter the party whose label he wears." [85] Well said.

As entertaining as Flanders's floor speech undoubtedly was, the real blow was struck that evening on CBS television. If Edward R. Murrow—already legendary in 1954 because of his dramatic wartime broadcasts from London—had been a lawyer, he would have been a successful one. In his March 9 episode of *See It Now*, Murrow impaled McCarthy on his own words, as good trial lawyers (and journalists) have always done. Using a montage of footage from McCarthy's committee hearings, Murrow portrayed a relentless demagogue. Murrow took a nationwide audience of television viewers on a guided tour of McCarthy's committee speeches and committee hearings. To be sure, the program, which was broadcast live, included some pointed commentary by Murrow. But the devastating effect of the presentation rested on the film clips portraying McCarthy in his element, utterly enthralled with himself as a bully and purveyor of half-truths.

Murrow's presentation was made more dramatic by the fact that he—broadcasting live except for the film clips—was able to quote from the speech Senator Flanders had given earlier that day on the Senate floor. Murrow left no doubt as to the conclusions to be drawn.

> We will not be driven by fear into an age of unreason, if we dig deep in our history and our doctrine, and remember that we are not descended from fearful men—not from men who feared to write, to speak, to associate and to defend causes that were, for the moment, unpopular. This is no time for men who oppose Senator McCarthy's methods to keep silent, or for those who approve. We can deny our heritage and our history, but we cannot escape responsibility for the result. There is no way for a citizen of a republic to abdicate his responsibilities. As a nation we have come into our full inheritance at a tender age. We proclaim ourselves, as indeed we are, the defenders of freedom, wherever it continues to exist in the world, but we cannot defend freedom abroad by deserting it at home.[86]

Given the vernacular of the time, Murrow may be forgiven for his observation that we are not descended from fearful men. Still, it would have been a nice touch for Murrow to have mentioned that the first "man" who had not feared to speak had been Senator Margaret Chase Smith.

The Murrow presentation was the beginning of the end for McCarthy. Comments to CBS ran fifteen to one in favor of the show.[87] At his press conference on the day after the Flanders speech and the *See It Now* presentation, Eisenhower made it a trifecta. Deviating from his usual unwillingness to discuss personalities, he praised Flanders for his service to the party and the nation.[88] The second week of March 1954 was not a good week for the junior senator from Wisconsin.

McCarthy's bitterest—and politically fatal—encounter with the army grew out of the army's refusal to give special treatment to David Schine, a draftee (and an unpaid consultant on McCarthy's subcommittee) with whom Cohn had an exceptionally close personal relationship. Of course, McCarthy had been hounding the army and people associated with it since his 1951 defamation of George Marshall. But when the army would not do Cohn's bidding by giving cushy assignments to Private Schine, Cohn persuaded McCarthy to teach the army a lesson. This, with a five-star general in the White House.

If Private Schine could not be assigned to New York so he could look for "evidence of pro-Communist leanings" in textbooks at the United States Military Academy, Cohn vowed to "wreck the Army."[89] This and similar charges were leveled by the army in a thirty-four-page report sent by the army to every member of McCarthy's subcommittee two days after Murrow's *See It Now* broadcast. The army's charges triggered the Army-McCarthy hearings, the last stop on the road to the Senate's censure debate in the fall of 1954. The hearings got started on April 22. The purpose was to air the army's allegations and McCarthy's response, all so that the matter could be resolved in the court of public opinion. The hearings—thirty-six days in all—were a signal event in the civic life of the United States in the 1950s.

The nationally televised hearings were not conducted as a formal trial, but the committee, McCarthy, and the army all had their counsel. By the time the hearings were over, the American public would see the best and the worst of the American legal profession. The army needed outside counsel. It needed a trial lawyer of the highest caliber the American legal profession could offer, and that is what it got in Joseph Nye Welch of the Boston firm of Hale and Dorr. Although this will probably never be provable with certainty from the historical record, David Nichols makes a persuasive case that Thomas Dewey, then in his third term as governor of New York, recruited Welch, and that Dewey undertook that recruiting chore at Eisenhower's behest.[90] The American public's perception of the integrity of the US Army as an apolitical military organization was at stake. The "trial" of the army's charges of gross misconduct against McCarthy was as important to Eisenhower as if he himself had been on trial.

In assembling his team for the hearings, Welch made one decision, surely difficult at the time, that later provided the fulcrum for what can fairly be called the most dramatic ten minutes in the history of hearings in the US Senate. Fred Fisher, a young lawyer at Hale and Dorr, was a member of the Young Republicans League in 1954.[91] But his personal political journey had been circuitous. Though now a card-carrying Republican practicing law with—to put it mildly—an establishment law firm, Fisher had been a member of the National Lawyers Guild while at Harvard University. In 1950, the Guild had been labeled the "the legal bulwark of the Communist Party" by the House Committee on Un-American Activities.[92] Fisher had resigned from the Guild in 1950, but Welch, as he assembled his team for the Army-McCarthy hearings, was under no illusions as to the mileage McCarthy and Cohn could get out of that former association by a member of the army's legal team. Fred Fisher, having forthrightly disclosed to Welch his previous association with the Guild, would have to return to Boston.

Predictions were, as the hearings got started, that the nationally televised proceedings might last two weeks. The thirty-six days of hearings ended on June 17. The hearings had little of the solemnity and calm of a courtroom. As Welch would write a few weeks after the hearings ended: "The first sight of the hearing room was a shock to a lawyer used to the traditionally ordered interiors of courtrooms. It was utter confusion. Photographers leaped up and down to get pictures. Messengers crawled beneath chairs. The cameras turned to follow the action."[93] The hearings were knocked out of the headlines only by such momentous events as the Supreme Court's unanimous decision, in mid-May, declaring that racial segregation in public schools violated the US Constitution.

The central issue was whether McCarthy and Cohn had tried to put undue pressure on the army to get preferential treatment for Cohn's good friend David Schine, via an unremitting campaign of extortionate threats and intimidation. The subcommittee was empowered only to investigate and render a report. It could adjudicate nothing. (The closest thing to an adjudication was the Senate's censure vote in December.)

At the end of May, Eisenhower helped lay the groundwork for the climax of the hearings. He returned to Columbia University, where he had been president, to give an address at a dinner celebrating Columbia's bicentennial. One of Eisenhower's purposes was to set the tone for the public's evaluation of the revelations at the Army-McCarthy hearings as those hearings reached their climax. He spoke, of course, of the value of education and the evils of communism. But McCarthyism, without mentioning McCarthy, was his main target:

> Whenever, and for whatever alleged reason, people attempt to crush ideas, to mask their convictions, to view every neighbor as a possible enemy, to seek some kind of divining rod by which to test for conformity, a free society is in danger. . . . [I]f we allow ourselves to be persuaded that every individual, or party, that takes issue with our own convictions is necessarily wicked or treasonous–then indeed we are approaching the end of freedom's road.[94]

Eisenhower had once again laid down his marker. And, at this point in the Army-McCarthy hearings, a discerning observer could probably conclude that the proceedings were unlikely to end well for McCarthy. Still, McCarthy's grip on public discourse in the realm of anticommunism was such that, for most elected officials (Eisenhower included), an anti-McCarthy speech would have to be leavened by an anticommunist speech, and the sooner the better. Thus, two days after his Columbia speech, Eisenhower conspicuously reinforced his anticommunist credentials, announcing that his administration had obtained convictions of forty-one communist party leaders, indicted twenty more in pending cases, added sixty-two organizations to the official list of subversive groups, and deported eighty-four alien subversives. As the president put it, the surveillance of communists "is being done quietly and relentlessly, and those who best know its effectiveness are the Communists themselves."[95]

Although the Army-McCarthy hearings didn't end until June 17, the end came, in the eyes of the public, on June 9. Although McCarthy had repeatedly claimed to have a list of 133 communists he said were employed at US defense plants, he had been cagey about letting anyone have that list. McCarthy had also, of course, pursued alleged communists in the army, most notably at Fort Monmouth, New Jersey. On June 2, while cross-examining Cohn, Welch got Cohn to acknowledge the urgency of turning over to the FBI the names of the subversives in the defense plants.[96] Cohn (and McCarthy) would soon regret Cohn's agreement to that commonsense proposition. On June 9, Welch, resuming his cross-examination of Cohn, got Cohn to acknowledge that "when we learn of a Communist or a spy anywhere," we "want them out as fast as possible."[97]

McCarthy, watching this questioning (not as a member of the subcommittee, but in essence in the dock as the defendant), could see the trap closing. It would take, at most, only one more ill-considered answer by Cohn for McCarthy to be backed into a corner with no plausible excuse for refusing to give his purported list of 133 communists to the FBI, "by sundown," as Welch liked to put it. Welch pressed; Cohn squirmed. McCarthy was compelled to intervene to change the subject. It was time to play the Fred Fisher card. McCarthy had confided to his lawyer, Edward Bennett Williams, that he had "planned to drop this [Fred Fisher] grenade at the appropriate moment."[98] That moment had arrived.

> [McCarthy:] In view of Mr. Welch's request that the information be given once we know of anyone who might be performing any work for the Communist Party, I think we should tell him that he has in his law firm a young man named Fisher whom he recommended, incidentally, to do work on this committee, who has been for a number of years, a member of an organization which was named, oh, years and years ago, as the legal bulwark of the Communist Party, an organization which always swings to the defense of anyone who dares to expose communists.[99]

McCarthy's suggestion that Fisher's former affiliation might be new information for Welch was, of course, pure fiction. In April, nearly two months before this famous exchange, the *New York Times* had reported that Welch had relieved Fisher of service on the army's legal team "because of his admitted previous membership in the National Lawyers Guild, which has been listed [by the attorney general] as a Communist-front organization."[100]

If there had been any doubt that the Army-McCarthy hearings marked the beginning of the end of McCarthy's political career, Welch's rejoinder to McCarthy removed that doubt.

> [Welch:] Until this moment, Senator, I think I never really gauged your cruelty or your recklessness.
>
> So, Senator, I asked him [Fisher] to go back to Boston. Little did I dream you could be so reckless and so cruel as to do an injury to that lad. It is true he is still with Hale & Dorr. It is true that he will continue to be with Hale & Dorr. It is, I regret to say, equally true that I fear he shall always bear a scar needlessly inflicted by you. If it were in my power to forgive you for your reckless cruelty, I will do so. I like to think I'm a gentleman, but your forgiveness will have to come from someone other than me. . . .
>
> Let us not assassinate this lad further, Senator. You have done enough. Have you no sense of decency, sir, at long last? Have you no sense of decency?[101]

Whereupon "the crowded hearing room burst into applause."[102] There is no better illustration than this of the power that mere words can have in a democracy. It is no exaggeration to say that those last twenty words from the Boston lawyer representing the United States Army changed the course of not only McCarthy's political career but also of McCarthyism and his curdled brand of anticommunism.

McCarthy maintained to the end, after thirty-two witnesses had testified, that he still had the names of 130 communists who had infiltrated defense plants. But he steadfastly refused to produce the list.[103] Generals are not famous for their affection for lawyers, but Eisenhower invited Joseph Welch to visit him at the White House on the day after the hearings ended. Welch accepted the invitation. By the end of July, Cohn had mailed in his resignation from his employment with the Senate, the slightly wizened face of Boston lawyer Joe Welch graced the cover of *Life* magazine, and a motion to censure McCarthy had been filed in the

Senate. But Radio Moscow apparently did not see the Army-McCarthy proceedings as a politically fatal setback for McCarthy. As quoted by the *New York Times*, the Soviet radio outlet told its listeners on July 29 that McCarthy and his followers "propose to take over Congress this year and the whole of the country in two years' time."[104] This was, after all, an election year.

The Army-McCarthy subcommittee released its majority and minority reports at the end of August. Both the subcommittee majority (Republicans) and the minority (Democrats) were critical of McCarthy. The differences were only in degree. But, amid the onrushing events of late summer 1954, the reports were not much more than footnotes to history. By the time the reports were released, the censure motion had been pending before the Senate for more than a month. This would be the main event.

By late summer, 1954, it was obvious in Washington—mainly because it was obvious nationwide—that the time was nigh to do something definitive, something with a sense of finality, about Joe McCarthy. But it would not be easy. With or without Joe McCarthy as a viable force in national politics, this *was* an election year, there *were* communists in the United States of America, and no one could say that the government was free of communist subversion. It is, then, no coincidence that the push toward censure in the fall was preceded by one of the more remarkable, if ineffectual, legislative initiatives of the mid-twentieth century.

Protecting the Right Flank in an Election Year

This amendment would make the Communist Party, its membership, and its apparatus illegal. It would make membership in the Communist Party subject to criminal penalties.[105]

—Senator Hubert H. Humphrey, on the floor of the Senate, August 12, 1954

Senator Hubert Humphrey of Minnesota, a liberal icon who had been National Chairman of Americans for Democratic Action in 1950, stood for re-election in 1954. He wanted no more headlines like the August 5 headline in the *Minneapolis Star*: "Bjornson [Humphrey's general election opponent] Hits Humphrey as Leftist Leader."[106] As Humphrey put it on the Senate floor a week later: "I am tired of reading headlines about being a leftist."[107] Though Humphrey's seat was considered to be fairly safe (and it did prove to be safe), he was taking no chances. His proposal to criminalize mere membership in the Communist Party, joined in by Senator John F. Kennedy,[108] was not a tactical "poison pill," designed to kill a pending legislative proposal. As Humphrey made clear on the Senate floor and later in the campaign, he wanted it to be a federal felony, punishable by imprisonment for up to five years, simply to be a member of the Communist Party.[109]

Interestingly enough, Humphrey's proposal to criminalize mere membership was unsuccessful, with much of the opposition coming from Senate Republicans (as well as the administration[110]), who maintained that this outright ban would hamper the administration's ongoing efforts to combat communism under other laws already on the books. A watered-down proposal—enacted with no committee hearings in either house—was sent to the president on August 19. That legislation, the Communist Control Act of 1954, cleared the House by a vote of 265 to 2 and the Senate by 79 to 0. Congress adjourned; its members headed home to campaign.

Eisenhower signed the Communist Control Act of 1954 into law on August 24. A lot had happened since President Truman, in vetoing the McCarran Internal Security Act in 1950, had condemned that legislation because it made "a mockery of the Bill of Rights and of our claims to stand for freedom in the world."[111] The 1954 act declared that the Communist Party was "an instrumentality of a conspiracy to overthrow the Government of the United States." Although not making membership as such a crime, the act outlawed the Communist Party and required anyone knowingly becoming or remaining a member of the party to register under the McCarran Internal Security Act. For good measure, it listed thirteen factors a jury could consider in determining whether an accused person (presumably accused of failure to register under the McCarran Act) was a member of the party.[112]

But by Humphrey's account, the bill as enacted was "not as strong a blow as [he] would have liked to strike."[113] The Communist Control Act of 1954 remains on the books and looks pretty strong. Strong enough, that is, that there is no reported case of a successful prosecution under the 1954 act. Key provisions of the act were declared unconstitutional in 1973 by a federal district court.[114] The government did not appeal that decision, but the statute technically remains on the books. Ironically, the only substantive effect the 1954 act has had is that, in 1956, the Supreme Court held that the 1954 legislation, taken together with the other federal legislation dealing with communism and communists, made it clear that Congress had precluded any attempts by state legislatures to enact sedition laws dealing with communists.[115]

By the time the 1954 legislation was sent to the president in August, every senator knew there would likely be an up or down vote on whether to censure McCarthy. The censure resolution was in the hands of a select committee. The committee rendered its report on September 27, unanimously recommending that McCarthy be censured for his behavior as a US Senator. As described in *Time* soon after the report was released, the report "was a scathing indictment of McCarthyism, condemning the Wisconsin senator for disregarding the principles of democracy, good government, fair play and decency."[116] There was just one problem. This was an election year; control of the closely divided Senate was up for grabs. Thirty-eight of the ninety-six seats would be on the ballot in November. In late September, the Senate majority leader, Republican William Knowland of California, announced that the full Senate would not consider censure until after the election. But that offered little comfort to those senators who were standing for re-election and understood all too well that they could probably not avoid taking a stand on censure before election day. Nevertheless, with enactment of the Communist Control Act of 1954, support for censure was now less politically hazardous. The senators had bought some insurance against being labeled "anti-anti-communist."

The End of the Road for Joe McCarthy

The 1954 election did not go well for the Senate Republicans. Their loss of two seats shifted control of the Senate to the Democrats—the fourth shift of control in the last five Senate elections. (This shift of control was more permanent; the Democrats would have a Senate majority until 1981.) As of election day, 1954, very few Republican senators had sharply criticized McCarthy.

Despite the Republican losses and the resultant impending shift of control of the Senate, there was work to do in the few remaining weeks of Republican control. The Senate convened for consideration of the select committee's report recommending censure on November 8, six days after the election. The debate continued on and off until December 2, but the outcome was never seriously in doubt.

During the debates, McCarthy was not the only senator to raise the rallying cry of Yalta, but he left no doubt that, nearly ten years after the "sellout at Yalta," the issue still had legs: "Who, in the light of the small membership of the Communist Party, would have supposed that an American President could be persuaded to turn over the fruits of a victorious war to international communism and to condemn with one stroke of his pen literally millions of Europeans and Asians to Soviet domination? Yet at Yalta, through the efforts of Alger Hiss, and perhaps others we know not of, Franklin Roosevelt was persuaded to do this."[117]

The final vote subjecting McCarthy to the moral condemnation of the Senate came on December 2, 1954.[118] The vote was 67 to 22. Censure was supported by all forty-four Democrats present for the vote (plus one Independent). The Republicans were evenly split at twenty-two votes each way. It had been more than three years since McCarthy had proclaimed George C. Marshall to be a party to a "conspiracy of infamy so black that, when it is finally exposed, its principals shall be forever deserving of the maledictions of all honest men." For nearly two years as subcommittee chairman, McCarthy had used the perquisites of that office to torment little people while doing essentially nothing to actually eliminate subversives from the halls of government. Short of treason or outright corruption, one wonders what it would have taken to get something approaching a unanimous vote by US senators to censure a fellow senator who had desecrated fundamental American values as thoroughly as McCarthy had done.

Although McCarthy himself was no longer a political force, the influence of McCarthyism was still not extinct, even as the votes were recorded. Senator John F. Kennedy, absent for medical reasons on the day the vote was taken, could have announced his position on censure by "pairing" himself with a senator holding an opposing view, as permitted by Senate rules. Kennedy's failure to take a position was no accident. He later explained to Arthur M. Schlesinger Jr., as recounted by Schlesinger himself in *A Thousand Days*: "Hell, half my voters in Massachusetts look on McCarthy as a hero."[119]

In late April 1957, McCarthy, in his eleventh year as a US senator, was admitted to the Bethesda Naval Hospital for treatment of what his soon-to-be widow said was a knee problem. On May 2, he died of liver failure. In August, Wisconsin voters chose a Harvard and Yale-educated Democrat as McCarthy's successor in the Senate.

McCarthyism and Anticommunism—A Brief Retrospective

To call the phenomenon of McCarthyism by that name gives Senator Joseph McCarthy a bit too much credit. The political and social pathology underlying McCarthyism took root before McCarthy gained prominence in 1950 and remained, in various forms, after his censure and death. Thus, as Kennan says in his memoir, "it is a pity that his name came to be given to this episode in American political life. It deserved a wider and less restrictive designation."[120] "McCarthyism" connotes a political phenomenon, but that was not all there was to it. Again, Kennan puts it quite well, insisting that the "cultural and spiritual" implications, "while more difficult to define, were no less disturbing. For the political intolerance was accompanied by a comparable one in other fields: a rousing antiintellectualism, a mistrust of thought, a suspicion of education, a suspicion of the effect of foreign contacts and foreign influences on the individual personality, a demand for uniformity within the framework of a cheap provincial chauvinism."[121] Kennan's portrayal might have been slightly overwrought, but not by much.

Chapter 10

From Korea to Khrushchev and the Thaw

The Korean War was the West's first experience with the implementation of containment doctrine in Asia. We see what can happen when a nation fights a war that is not existentially necessary for that nation to win. As for Khrushchev, we see that for all his crudeness and bluster he had a shrewdness and a desire for peace that made it possible to lay some of the early groundwork for ending the Cold War.

Korea: Causes and Consequences

On September 2, 1945, on the deck of the USS *Missouri*, the Japanese empire came to its ignominious end, or least got a new emperor in the person of General Douglas MacArthur. With that, Japan no longer owned Korea. But with the USSR having (less than a month before) joined the United States as an ally against Japan, the postwar disposition of the Korean Peninsula was not a simple matter.

Japan had wrested the Korean Peninsula away from China in 1895 and succeeded, in the Russo-Japanese War of 1904–5, in keeping Korea from becoming an outpost of the Russian Empire. With MacArthur's arrival in Tokyo in 1945, Korea, to the great relief of Koreans, would no longer be a Japanese dominion. Leaving no uncertainty as to the Kremlin's intentions, Soviet forces invaded the Korean Peninsula from Manchuria on August 9, 1945, the day the atomic bomb was dropped on Nagasaki, one day after the USSR declared war on Japan, and three days after the bomb was dropped on Hiroshima. Consequently, pending political unification of the peninsula, the United States and the USSR had the Korean Peninsula in their military custody. The temporary line of demarcation between the occupying powers was drawn at the thirty-eighth parallel. The Japanese north of that line surrendered to the Soviet Army; south of that line to the US Army. This, of course, was an arrangement, thoroughly understandable at the time, that would have consequences for decades to come. Soviet interest in Korea was nothing new. Writing in 1948, British journalist Paul Winterton observed that "the Russians had always intended, if they could, to obtain exclusive control of the whole peninsula."[1]

We focus here on the causes and consequences of the Korean War, giving attention to what happened *during* that war only as necessary to understand what happened before and, especially, after.

At dawn on June 25, 1950, the Korean People's Army—seven infantry divisions supported with 150 Russian-made T-34 tanks—launched its assault south across the thirty-eighth parallel. Much of the story of Soviet involvement in the Korean War is told by a trove of documents—some from the Presidential Archive in Moscow and some released directly by Russian President Boris Yeltsin—that became available after the dissolution of the USSR. The declassified and translated source materials ended the need for speculation about the Kremlin's role. No more than a short visit is needed here:

In a March 18, 1950, message to North Korean leader Kim Il Sung, Stalin assured Kim that "I have received your proposal of 9 March about the delivery to you of arms, ammunition and technical equipment for the people's army of Korea. The Soviet government has decided also to satisfy fully this request of yours."[2]

Stalin was only too happy to urge the Chinese to commit ground troops while the Soviets would, if possible, provide some air support. On July 5, Stalin instructed his ambassador in Beijing to inform Chinese foreign minister Zhou Enlai that "we consider it correct to concentrate immediately 9 Chinese divisions on the Chinese-Korean border for volunteer actions in North Korea in case the enemy crosses the 38th parallel. We will try to provide air cover for these units."[3]

When US major general John Church was asked on July 1, 1950, "what would happen if the Russians came to the Northerners' aid," he answered: "If the Russkies come down, we'll fight the Russkies."[4] As indicated by Stalin's July 5 message to Zhou Enlai, General Church needn't have worried about Russian ground forces. As for the wisdom of starting a war on the Korean Peninsula in the first place, Stalin, although not initially enthusiastic, was emboldened by the success of the communists in China (freeing up troops to go south if they were needed) and, more generally, by the negative trend in East-West relations, exemplified by the formation of NATO less than a year before he effectively gave the green light to Kim Il Sung.

Militarily, South Korea was ripe for the picking. American forces, save for a small advisory element, had been withdrawn in 1949. Khrushchev recalled that Kim Il Sung predicted to Stalin that the invasion would trigger a people's uprising in South Korea, ensuring a short war.[5] At the outbreak of the war, South Korea was no match for the North, but the initial successes of the Korean Peoples' Army were not due to cooperation from the populace in the South. The north had an overwhelming advantage in troops and armaments, due in no small part to the fact that Stalin had supplied the arms and ammunition requested by Kim. The net effect of all this was that Seoul was overrun within four days after the assault began. Interestingly enough, Andrei Gromyko, who would become the Soviet foreign minister in 1957, recorded in his memoir that "one of the worst examples of US aggressiveness in international affairs was the Korean war."[6]

Korea in the Security Council

Just before midnight on June 27, 1950, the Security Council adopted—with Jacob Malik not present to cast the Soviet veto—an emergency resolution recommending that "the Members of the United Nations furnish such assistance to the Republic of Korea as may be necessary to repel the armed attack and to restore international peace and security in the area."[7] In late August, Stalin asserted (in a message to be delivered to the president of Czechoslovakia) that Malik's absence was a strategic ploy. By this telling, Stalin had laid a trap, with the result, as Stalin put it in August, that "America became entangled in a military intervention in Korea and is now squandering its military prestige and moral authority."[8] Gromyko, who was a deputy foreign minister at the time, claimed in his memoir that he had specifically warned Stalin about the consequences of withholding the Soviet veto and that Stalin specifically overruled him.[9] Regardless of which version—Stalin's or Gromyko's—is correct, what matters is that that the resolution adopted for lack of a Soviet veto led to the creation of the first collective-security force of the Cold War. More than a dozen nations would send armed forces to Korea under the UN flag.

Korean War Politics: 1950 and 1952

The ebb and flow of the Korean War inevitably intersected with the domestic political forces in play in the early 1950s. By early September 1950, the UN forces had almost been driven into the sea at the southeastern tip of the peninsula. But MacArthur's spectacular success in the mid-September amphibious assault at Inchon, north of Seoul, dramatically turned the tables. Seoul was retaken by the UN forces by the end of the month. As recorded by Khrushchev, "the situation had turned catastrophic for North Korea and for Kim Il Sung."[10] This, obviously, raised the specter of China's entry into the war, but, in a meeting on Wake Island on October 15, MacArthur told Truman that the Chinese were not likely to intervene.

Another turning point was at hand. Khrushchev vividly recalled that Stalin and Zhou Enlai "agreed that China should give active support to North Korea."[11] Khrushchev's memory served him well. The trove of declassified source material released after 1991 enabled Dr. Evgueni Bajanov, of the Russian Foreign Ministry, to write, in 1995, "On 1 October 1950, Stalin came to the conclusion that China had to come to the rescue of the collapsing Kim regime."[12] Chinese help was no doubt needed. Pyongyang was in UN hands, with MacArthur on the ground there, three weeks into October. A week later, UN troops were less than a hundred miles away from the Manchurian border. There was cause for great optimism, bordering on euphoria, in some quarters. As late as November 1, five days before the 1950 election, the US ambassador to Korea told the UN Interim Committee on Korea (as reported in the

New York Times) that "he believed the fighting in that country would be over in a few days."[13] The Korean armistice would be signed exactly a thousand days later. But the pre-election news about Korea was mixed. With Chinese forces flooding in from Manchuria, the view from Korea at the end of October—also duly reported in the *New York Times*—was not nearly as optimistic: "Cheerful hopes that the war was virtually over were squelched here this evening. The belief is growing among observers here that the war will probably continue through the winter."[14] The war continued through three winters.

The net effect of the confusion about what was going on in Korea as the election approached was that the war did not overshadow the domestic issues that usually dominate in an off-year election. The confusion about the war probably helped the Democrats. In a wide-ranging survey of the political scene a week before the election, James Reston observed that the Republicans had "counted heavily on the Korean war to bring them through and again they were robbed of a major issue by the successful Inchon landings, directed by their own darling, Gen. Douglas MacArthur."[15] Those words had been overtaken by events on the ground by the time they were published, but the situation was still too muddled in the last week before the election for Korea, as an issue cutting one way or the other, to make much of a difference.

The confused Korean picture did not keep communism, in a broader sense, out of the election. It was convenient for the Republicans that communism was a hybrid issue. If the predominant threat at the moment was foreign, then the focus was on what the communists were doing abroad. Absent a foreign threat, the domestic threat was always available. This was especially true, as seen in the last chapter, in the California Senate race between Richard Nixon and Helen Gahagan Douglas. The state of that race at the end of October was that, as reported by the *New York Times*, "nowhere in the country will the outcome of the Nov. 7 election show more conclusively than in California the attractiveness, or lack of it, of the constant hammering on communism as a campaign issue."[16]

Domestic anticommunism also had a less visible, indirect effect on the national conversation leading to the 1950 election. In the series of essays published in the run-up to the election, Reston noted the "furor on various campuses about the Communist oath," as well as some of the accusations Joe McCarthy had already made (he would not give his Wheeling speech until February 1951), and "the general atmosphere of suspicion against anybody who ever said a good word for the Russians." Reston concluded that "all these things have helped bring about a marked change upon the activities of the so-called intellectual Left. They are much more cautious in their public statements and even in their private conversations with visiting reporters."[17] This, to be sure, was a subjective observation from a writer who, though politically moderate, was sympathetic to what he called the "intellectual Left." But it was telling. Even though McCarthyism by that name did not yet exist, Reston's observation made it clear that the field was fertile for McCarthy to take exploitation of the issue of domestic communism to a whole new level. After the votes were counted in 1950, the Democrats kept control of the Senate–though just barely—and stayed in charge in the House even though they lost twenty-two seats in that body. The 1950 election was, as has been noted, the only one of the first five postwar elections that did not result in a change of control of both houses of Congress.

The situation on the ground in Korea continued to deteriorate after the election. In the north, fighters from the Soviet air force—with Soviet markings eliminated—joined the fray, which dramatically increased aircraft and air-crew losses on the UN side. The Soviet MiG-15 interceptors were faster than anything the UN forces could put up against them. Worse yet, in bombing runs in "MiG alley," in the northwest region of North Korea, the US bombers were constrained to attack bridges across the Yalu by making their runs *parallel* to the river and *perpendicular* to the bridges, lest they intrude on Chinese airspace.[18]

By the end of November, the communist forces had broken through the UN front and were advancing on Pyongyang. UN forces were in full retreat. In a press conference on November 30, Truman threatened to use the atomic bomb if that was what it took to win the war. Neither of those things happened—the bomb was never used and the war was never won—so that episode is notable mostly for the near-record speed with which the White House walked back Truman's threat. In his press conference, Truman had been asked whether the use of "all necessary steps" (as he had put it) to deal with the increasingly dire military situation would "include the atomic bomb." Response: "That would include every weapon we have." When asked whether the use of the bomb would have to be cleared with the United Nations, Truman said, "The military commander in the field [i.e., MacArthur] would have charge of the use of the weapons, as always." Before the day was over, the president's press secretary issued a formal statement making it clear that "only the President can authorize the use of the atom bomb, and no such authorization has been given."[19]

By March 1951, talk of a decisive military victory had vanished, in favor of speculation about a political and geopolitical compromise. The reason for the change of heart was obvious: The massive Chinese communist commitment to the war made it plain that this war was not going to be "won," in the conventional sense, without an equally massive military commitment from the allies on the UN side.

The public speculation about a mushy compromise in Korea set in motion the final sequence of events leading to Truman's famous sacking of MacArthur in mid-April. MacArthur could not accept the notion that a war could be fought, and ended, without being won. At the end of March, the opposing forces were arrayed along a line that was remarkably close to the thirty-eighth parallel, where this had all begun. Five months earlier, UN forces had stood on the Yalu, more than 250 miles to the north, looking across the river at communist China. But now, in March, none other than Secretary of Defense George C. Marshall told the world in a press conference that the question of a sweep across the parallel into the region held by communist forces is "a matter for political consideration."[20] This was a formulation of the line between military strategy and political strategy that would bedevil US military and civilian leaders for decades to come. History does not record whether it grated on Marshall to say that retaking territory so recently held by UN forces was now a political question, but the open clash between MacArthur and his civilian superiors in Washington made his dismissal inevitable.

With China in the war and the troops bogged down not far from where it all started, the war became an exercise in risk management for Truman—the risk to be managed being the risk of major escalation by China on the Korean Peninsula, or, indeed, of a geographically (and geopolitically) wider war. Truce talks began in July. The war settled into a long, bloody stalemate, with combat operations grinding ever more slowly. This was fine with Stalin. In June, he had advised Mao Zedong by telegram that "the war in Korea should not be speeded up, since a drawn-out war, in the first place, gives the possibility to the Chinese troops to study contemporary warfare on the field of battle and in the second place shakes up the Truman regime in America and harms the military prestige of the Anglo-American troops."[21]

The story of the Korean War in the 1952 presidential election is less complicated than the 1950 story. The Democrats' annual Jefferson-Jackson Day celebration in the National Guard armory in Washington, DC, at the end of March 1952, was "a gay social gathering as well as a political rally with the male Democrats decked out in dinner jackets, women wearing their prettiest long party dresses."[22] When it was his turn to address the crowd of 5,300, Truman stunned the nation with his announcement that he would not run for re-election. Truman recorded in his memoir that he had made the decision not to run in April of 1950 and had recorded his thoughts in a memorandum that he "locked away" (and from which he quoted in his memoir).[23] Truman's account of when and why he made his decision is believable. Although he had been elected to the presidency only once, he would hold that office a few weeks shy of two full terms—two of the most momentous terms in the history of the presidency.[24] As of the first of April 1952, the Democratic field was wide open.

As for the Republicans, Eisenhower relinquished his post as supreme commander of NATO forces in May 1952. He was still the president of Columbia University, so, even with his departure from NATO headquarters, he had to be somewhat coy about his political plans. Nobody was fooled. Eisenhower and Nixon came out of the July convention as the leaders of a party hungry for its first presidential victory in twenty years. As for the situation on the ground in Korea, there was precious little difference between July 1951 and July 1952, save for the lives lost in a year of stalemate. Eisenhower's acceptance speech at the convention was silent on Korea, but the Republican platform was not: "By their [the Truman administration's] hampering orders they produced stalemates and ignominious bartering with our enemies, and they offer no hope of victory."[25] That line could have been written by MacArthur himself.

The war did not become a dominant issue in the 1952 campaign until Eisenhower said five words in a speech in Detroit on October 24: "I shall go to Korea." Although acknowledging that he could not end the war by "any imminent, exact date," he pledged to bring the war to "an early and honorable end."[26] The next day, Adlai Stevenson, Eisenhower's opponent, had a ready and reasonably plausible response to Eisenhower's dramatic pledge to go to Korea to end the war: "The General has announced his intention to go to Korea. But the root of the Korean problem does not lie in Korea–it lies in Moscow." For good measure, and to guard his right flank, Stevenson also pledged that "if I find any Communist or fellow travelers or Soviet agents or dupes in our Federal Government, I will root them out promptly and ruthlessly."[27] Five weeks after this exchange between the two candidates, President-Elect Eisenhower was in Korea. Of course, as president-elect, Eisenhower could do nothing in Korea other than ask questions and make innocuous remarks. His most notable comment was that a "definite victory" would be out of reach without "enlarging the war."[28] He had no intention of "enlarging the war." There would be no "definite victory."

It does no disservice to President Harry S. Truman to observe that, with the inauguration of Dwight D. Eisenhower in January and the death of Josef V. Stalin in March, ending the war in Korea became a more urgent priority both in Washington and in Moscow. Armistice negotiations, in which one of the main sticking points had been the communists' insistence on the repatriation—forcibly, if necessary—of North Korean and Chinese prisoners of war held in the south, finally led to the signing of an armistice agreement at Panmunjom on July 27, 1953. There was, and is, of course, no political settlement. The armistice essentially left the north and south divided by a narrow demilitarized zone snaking across the thirty-eighth parallel, matching the then-existing front from the Yellow Sea to the Sea of Japan. That jagged line was, at best, only slightly less arbitrary than the straight line that had been agreed to in 1945.

Korean War: The Consequences

As witness that the voters ejected the party in control of both houses of Congress in four of the first five postwar elections, the Democrats and Republicans ran neck and neck at the polls in the first decade of the Cold War. The partisan divide manifested itself mostly on domestic issues. Even on domestic issues, the partisan divide in that first decade cannot be equated with the toxic polarization of the opening decades of the twenty-first century. As for international affairs, it is not much of an exaggeration, if exaggeration at all, to say that whenever an external catalyst was needed, in those early years of the Cold War, for the purpose of forging a national consensus, the Kremlin could be relied on to provide it. The Korean War was no exception. The consequences of the Korean War in terms of the preparedness of the United States—and, more broadly, the West—to contend with the Soviet bloc can be placed under two headings: (1) the general US military buildup, and (2) the transformation of NATO from its original status as an essentially aspirational military alliance into a new role as the host entity for a viable fighting force under a unified command.

Military Buildup. The doctrinal foundation for a massive military buildup was in place when the Korean People's Army invaded South Korea in June 1950. That doctrinal foundation was NSC-68, which had been sitting on the president's desk since April, awaiting his approval of its budgetary and program recommendations. On September 30, Truman, with the concurrence of the National Security Council, adopted NSC-68 "as a statement of policy to be followed over the next four or five years," with "implementing programs [to] be put into effect as rapidly as feasible, with the understanding that the specific nature and estimated costs of these programs will be decided as they are more firmly developed."[29] This, it will be noticed, was pretty feeble bureaucratese. That all changed when communist China entered the war, triggering a radical change in the Truman administration's plans for implementation of NSC-68. As Dean Acheson put it, "Korea saved us."[30] The costly buildup of armaments had originally been slated to continue through mid-1954. In late 1950, with Chinese communists in the thick of it in Korea, Truman concluded that the United States had underestimated the threat posed by the Soviet Union and China. He ordered that the buildup envisioned by NSC-68 be completed by mid-1952.[31]

China's willingness to put massive numbers of troops on the ground in Korea represented a quantum leap in the geopolitical stakes, giving Truman the leverage he needed to implement NSC-68—expensive though that would be—without delay. The record of a National Security Council meeting in late November reveals the president's thinking: "If the Chinese threat evaporates, the President questions that you could go through with a $45 billion program."[32] From 1950 to 1951, Truman succeeded in quadrupling the defense budget and doubling the size of the armed forces. This created a new baseline for military spending—and the resultant arms buildup—for the next four decades. In constant dollars, there would be peaks (as during the Vietnam War and again during the Reagan administration) and valleys, but the valleys now had a new, dramatically higher floor.

Transformation of NATO. In December 1950, the North Atlantic Treaty had been in force for nearly a year and a half. The Berlin blockade had provided the impetus for the creation of the alliance on paper. But NATO had no military structure and no unified command until the North Atlantic Treaty powers agreed, in December 1950 (as refugees were streaming south to get out of Seoul before Chinese troops arrived), to create an integrated armed force under a unified command. The commander would be General Dwight D. Eisenhower. His headquarters were established in Rocquencourt, west of Paris. The unanimous agreement of the foreign ministers of the NATO allies to install Eisenhower as the commander of the integrated force reflected the fact that, in Europe, Ike's credentials as a diplomat matched his reputation as a general. As Hanson Baldwin, the Pulitzer Prize–winning military editor of the *New York Times* put it on the Sunday after the NATO meeting: "If anyone can make Western European defense more than a vaguely comforting phrase in newspaper headlines, it is Eisenhower."[33]

At the same NATO meeting, the foreign ministers made it plain that the next step was the rearmament of West Germany and the integration of the revived Bundeswehr into NATO. That aspect of the matter was conveyed without equivocation in the communiqué issued by the Atlantic Council: "The Council also reached unanimous agreement regarding the part which Germany might assume in the common defence. The German participation would strengthen the defence of Europe without altering in any way the purely defensive character of the North Atlantic Treaty Organization."[34] Those pieces didn't fall into place so quickly—the Federal Republic of Germany did not join NATO until 1955, coincident with the formal ending of the American-British-French occupation of West Germany. But at the end of December 1950, for Truman and Acheson, there was no longer room for debate as to whether Germany should be integrated into the West's strategy for defending Europe from the Russians. The only question was when that would be accomplished.

Solarium and NSC-162/2

Solarium. In the spring of 1953, Eisenhower was new to the presidency but was not a neophyte in geopolitics or national security strategy. To be sure, he had never served as secretary of state or defense, but he needed no tutoring to understand what was at stake in East-West geopolitics and the related national security issues. Kennan, who was not overgenerous in his praise for the foreign policy expertise of others, wrote in his memoirs that Eisenhower was, notwithstanding some outward appearances, "a man of keen political intelligence and penetration, particularly when it came to foreign affairs."[35]

Eisenhower understood the complexity of the challenge of preserving the peace and dealing with the Russians without bankrupting the country or compromising fundamental American values. His middle-class origins constantly reminded him that there were millions of American children whose prospects would be foreshortened if they were to grow up in a nation beggared by the cost of defending itself. In a nationally broadcast speech in April 1953, three months into his presidency (and a few weeks after Stalin's death), Eisenhower proclaimed his hope that we were at a turning point in the quest for peace and security. He also lamented the prospect of "a burden of arms draining the wealth and the labor of all peoples," elaborating that "every gun that is made, every warship launched, every rocket fired signifies, in the final sense, a theft from those who hunger and are not fed, those who are cold and are not clothed. This world in arms is not spending money alone. It is spending the sweat of its laborers, the genius of its scientists, the hopes of its children. The cost of one modern heavy bomber is this: a modern brick school in more than 30 cities."[36] The heavy bomber, of course, was the B-52 Stratofortress, which first flew as a developmental aircraft in April 1952.

Eisenhower was astute enough to have many more questions than answers to the peace-security-prosperity quandary. He got his answers from what he called Project Solarium. As a result of a series of conferences he held in the White House Solarium in the spring of 1953, Eisenhower pressed more than twenty experts—including Kennan and others of similar stature, with Dulles sitting in more or less ex officio—into service to undertake an urgent and highly classified in-depth study of national security strategy.

In the correspondence leading to the start of Solarium, Kennan was listed as a retired Foreign Service Officer, political planner, and Russia expert. At the age of forty-nine, he was "retired" because, during his short stint as US ambassador to the USSR, he had been declared persona non grata due to his decidedly undiplomatic remarks about what it was like to live in Moscow. Dulles did not find a place for Kennan in the new administration, so he returned to his beloved farm and to Princeton University.

By mid-1953, when the Solarium working group was working day and night to produce its reports, the "rollback" concept (never more than a campaign slogan describing an aspirational *outcome* rather than a strategy) had receded from public discourse but had not yet been accorded a decent burial. Robert Bowie, another Solarium participant, recalled that "I think he [Eisenhower] did want to bury the rollback idea. I don't think it was ever serious. But it had been in the campaign, and it had been talked about and there had been a lot of people, particularly [in the] press, who said: 'Well, this is what's going to be different.' I think he wanted to make that clearly a thing of the past and finish it."[37]

What Eisenhower got out of Solarium was the end of talk about rollback (or so he thought) and NSC-162/2, which amounted to a new gloss on NSC-68. The key points of NSC-162/2 were: (1) the Russians must understand that the United States is willing to use the bomb to defend its NATO allies in Europe, (2) a full-on nuclear exchange is not a prerequisite to our use of nuclear weapons to counter the huge Soviet advantage in troops on the ground in Europe, and (3) the Russians must understand—lest they be tempted to launch a pre-emptive strike—that we have the capacity to withstand a first strike and retaliate massively.[38] This doctrine of first use, essentially reserving the option to use nuclear weapons as conventional armaments, came to be called the New Look. It was intended to provide "more basic security at less cost," as Dulles wrote in an April 1954 essay in *Foreign Affairs.* As for the role of the United States in contending with the USSR, Dulles stressed the importance of military power, economic strength, and national resolve in deterring and, if necessary, responding to Soviet aggression wherever and whenever it might erupt. All of this while noting some signs that Kremlin leaders may be "dimly perceiving that there are limits to their power indefinitely to suppress the human spirit."[39] Dulles had just one small problem in writing his *Foreign Affairs* essay. He had to tell the world about the new administration's overall strategy for holding back the Russians without using the word "containment," because, less than two years before, the foreign policy plank of the Republican platform—written by Dulles—had proclaimed containment to be a "negative, futile and immoral" policy that abandoned humanity to "a despotism and a godless terrorism" (see chapter 9). Dulles succeeded in avoiding the word. But the combined effect of NSC-162/2 and Dulles's exposition of administration policy in April 1954, was to codify containment as the policy of the Eisenhower administration.

Khrushchev and the Twentieth Party Congress

Khrushchev's arrival at the top. Americans tend to lose sight of the fact—or never understood it in the first place—that Soviet leadership after Stalin died (and to some degree even while he still ruled) was *collective* leadership. The preeminent body was the Politburo, which was an organ of the much larger Central Committee of the Communist Party of the Soviet Union, which had 133 members after the Twentieth Party Congress in 1956. The Central Committee, in turn, included substantial representation from party secretaries from the republics, oblasts, and other territories across the huge expanse of the USSR. (Beginning shortly before Stalin died and continuing until Brezhnev was installed as Khrushchev's successor in 1964, the Politburo was called the Presidium, but it was functionally the same as the Politburo.) The Central Committee and Politburo—organs of the Communist Party—must not be confused with the *government* of the USSR, a separate organization consisting of the military and the ponderous bureaucracies that did the day-to-day work of governing the vast nation, implementing all the while the Politburo's policy prescriptions, which were, in theory, the modern embodiment of Leninist doctrine.

When Stalin died in early March 1953, few persons in the Soviet Union understood this political and governmental structure as well as Nikita Sergeivich Khrushchev. But as Stalin lay in state in the Hall of Columns before his mid-March move to the Lenin Mausoleum in Red Square (where he would remain until 1961), there was no certainty as to where the political infighting would ultimately lead. Khrushchev, who joined the Bolsheviks in 1918, had dedicated his life to the party. Fifty-eight years old when Stalin died, Khrushchev, a native of the Kursk region in western Russia, had held party offices in both Russia and Ukraine. His third wife, Nina, whom he married in 1924, was Ukrainian.

Khrushchev's ascent in the party was steady. He became a member of the Politburo in 1939. After his service as a political commissar during the Great Patriotic War, Khrushchev served at various times as the first secretary of the Communist Party in Ukraine and as the chairman of the Ukrainian Council of Ministers. In that capacity, as *Time* reported in April 1956, he had become "absolute boss of a country three times the size of England and almost as populous." Though Khrushchev was in fact the Kremlin's viceroy in Kyiv, he managed to fit right in. "He spoke Russian with a phony Ukrainian accent, put on an embroidered Ukrainian shirt and wore a *kartuz* (workingman's cap)."[40] Though he was not a culturally refined man, he was able to ascend in the party hierarchy, as a declassified 1955 intelligence report put it, because of his "combination of dogged perseverance, ruthlessness and native shrewdness." Those are the things that mattered. Better yet, "unlike most Bolsheviks he is reputed to have a sense of humor."[41] He could also be somewhat impulsive.

The contestants for power in the spring of 1953 included Khrushchev, Georgi Malenkov, Nikolai Bulganin, Vyacheslav Molotov, and the murderous Lavrenti Beria. Malenkov was named chairman of the Council of Ministers immediately after Stalin died, but he was ultimately outflanked by Khrushchev, who became first secretary of the party in September. Khrushchev's power base had been the party, not the government, and his standing in the party enabled him eventually to gain his position of primacy in the Kremlin. Malenkov, Molotov, and Bulganin clung to power, in one office or another, until the maneuvering came to a head in 1957. But it didn't go so well for Beria. Beria once again became the head of the secret police and its large paramilitary force (then called the Ministry of Internal Affairs). But, for Beria, the good news and the bad news were the same: he knew too much and controlled too much. Khrushchev had Beria arrested on charges of treason and conspiracy in the summer of 1953. (He was arrested after spending an evening with other top Kremlin leaders at the Bolshoi Theater.) Beria stood trial before a special tribunal on December 23, 1953, was found guilty, and was shot in the head before that day was over.

Conventional wisdom would have indicated that Khrushchev's ascent to the office of first secretary would have been the final step in his climb to undisputed power. After all, Stalin had gone from 1922, when he became general secretary of the CPSU, to May 1941 (a few weeks before Barbarossa) without holding any office in the government. But it was not until the summer of 1957, *after* his denunciation of Stalin's personality cult at the Twentieth Party Congress in 1956, that Khrushchev fully consolidated his hold on power when he overcame a revolt in the Presidium by prevailing in a vote of the Central Committee. That was the end of the line (albeit without shots fired) for the "anti-party" group, including Malenkov and the old Bolshevik Molotov. Khrushchev was now fully in charge. It would be a mistake to view this as an instance of one-man rule in any sense similar to Stalin's dictatorship (or, for that matter, Putin's reign as an unchallenged autocrat). Yet, subject to truly extraordinary circumstances compelling a putsch, Nikita Khrushchev had arrived at the top.

For millions of Americans, Khrushchev was the personification of the Russian side of the Cold War. In some ways, he still is. Almost lost in the West's collective memory of this crude, blustery man is that, as Vladislav Zubok put it, his ascent "opened the way for the most productive, reformist, and moderate phase in Soviet foreign policy in years."[42] He was the last revolutionary to rule from the Kremlin.

The Gift of Crimea

Khrushchev was the prime mover—even before he had fully consolidated his power—in the transfer of Crimea from the Russian Soviet Federative Socialist Republic to the Ukrainian Soviet Socialist Republic in February 1954, a few months after he became first secretary. Though ethnically Russian, Khrushchev had a soft spot in his heart for Ukraine. One official justification for the transfer was that this was a fitting way to commemorate the three hundredth anniversary of the unification of Russia and Ukraine. With "front page fanfare," the transfer was touted as "a further strengthening of the unity and indestructible friendship of the Russian and Ukrainian peoples."[43] A more compelling reason for the transfer was that Khrushchev, a skilled politician, knew the net effect of the transfer would be to help him consolidate his position in the Soviet hierarchy. Most of the Crimean Tatars—of Turkic ethnicity—had been deported to Central Asia in 1944, making room for an influx of ethnic Russians to the peninsula, thus adding significantly to the ethnic Russian population of Ukraine. The gift of Crimea was a gift that keeps on giving, as can be discerned from Putin's denunciation of the transfer in his July 2021 historical manifesto, "On the Historical Unity of Russians and Ukrainians" (see the Conclusion).

The Twentieth Party Congress

Three important party conventions were held in 1956. The communists of the Soviet Union had theirs in Moscow in February. In the United States, the Democrats and Republicans each had theirs in August. The result was a rematch between Stevenson and Eisenhower. It takes nothing away from President Eisenhower and Governor Stevenson to acknowledge that, by far, the most momentous of the three conventions—the communists called theirs the Twentieth Party Congress—was the one in Moscow.

In 1956, Khrushchev was still fortifying his position. It was obvious that the highest echelon of Soviet leadership would be *collective* leadership, more so than had been seen in the USSR in several decades. But there still had to be a man (there was no possibility that it would be other than a man) at the top, and Khrushchev was that man. Khrushchev was a committed communist who had not gotten cynical about the possibility that Soviet society could someday reach the Marxist-Leninist promised land. He was convinced that his version of the socialist dream could not be realized unless the country was liberated from the legacy of Stalinism. As for foreign relations, by the mid-1950s, Marxian doctrine had plainly taken a back seat to more pedestrian concerns. The overriding objectives of Soviet foreign policy were to retain control of the satellite nations and to avoid war. No other foreign policy goals came close to those two.

The Congress opened in Moscow on February 14, 1956. The open proceedings ended on February 24, but Khrushchev let it be known that he would make a speech at a closed session on the twenty-fifth. Although his speech came to be known as his "secret speech," it was not, and could not possibly have been, secret for long. As described by Mikhail Gorbachev, then a young Komsomol apparatchik, the speech "caused a political and psychological shock throughout the country."[44] As the *New York Times* would describe the speech in June, after the text of the speech became available in the West: "Its bloodcurdling account of Stalin's crimes, its quotation of the piteous pleas of innocent men writing with 'two feet in the grave,' its revelation of the magnitude of Stalinist terror, all these make it one of the most dramatic documents in history."[45]

The speech did, indeed, dwell at length on the ghastly facts of Stalin's brutality—the torture, the falsification of cases, and the summary executions. As for more theoretical matters, one of the basic thrusts of the speech (also politically astute) was the proposition that Stalin's personality cult was diametrically at odds with fundamental tenets of communism as conceived by Marx and Lenin, who denounced "the cult of the individual." It always helps to be right on the facts, and, in attacking the personality cult, Khrushchev was right on the facts. (To take but one example, it is doubtful that any other leader in history had ever had his name appear 101 times on the first page of his party's newspaper. Stalin accomplished that with the November 17, 1950, issue of *Pravda*.[46]) The speech portrayed Stalin as incompetent as well as evil. On that score, Khrushchev's account of the credible warnings Stalin had received of Hitler's intent to launch his attack in June 1941 left no doubt that Khrushchev's objective was to permanently destroy Stalin's iconic status in the minds of Soviet citizens.

The speech was not a foreign policy manifesto. In fact, despite the extraordinary length of the speech, one would have to look hard to discern any forward-looking policy prescriptions, either foreign or domestic. Policy was not the purpose of the speech. Khrushchev's purpose was to make a clean break with Stalinism, and with any nostalgic attachment to Stalinism, to the end that he could position himself to chart a new course in both foreign and domestic policy. He accomplished that. The speech was consequential both in the USSR and in the West. (And, as will be seen, it is also noteworthy that the concept of "peaceful coexistence" received the party's blessing in other proceedings at the Congress.[47])

Within the Soviet Union, the actual text of the speech was not released until long after Khrushchev was gone, but, as Soviet Ambassador Oleg Troyanovski put it in an interview after he retired, the speech "was read out in various groups or party groups." Some of the communist faithful were shaken by the denunciation of Stalin. Troyanovski quoted the wife of one of his colleagues: "This is terrible. I have lived by idealising Stalin all my life, and now I hear about all these terrible things."[48] The speech, or at least the gist of it, also appeared in samizdat, the informal, underground genre of written material that would be passed from hand to hand among those who were hungry for information from sources outside of state-approved channels. The resultant changes in Soviet society were not superficial. As one Russian baby boomer recalled: "After the Twentieth Congress the police in Saratov stopped checking to see if my father was at home. In 1957 my father was fully rehabilitated. It was now possible for me to enroll in the English-language school and later in medical school. Before [the Congress] that would have been unlikely or would not have happened at all."[49] To be sure, this was not glasnost, but Khrushchev actually did get some traction in his efforts to eradicate the dark legacy of Stalinism.

In the West, the fact of the secret speech was soon known, as was some of its anti-Stalin thrust. As early as April, *Time* was able to report that "as the 20th Congress ended, Khrushchev called his famous secret meeting in which he tearfully blabbed the whole story of Stalin's mass murders, torturings and evil motives. Nikita's reasons could be deduced: if the party was going to open that one up, he was going to be the chief opener."[50] (Accounts differ as to whether there were tears.) Thanks to a Polish journalist cooperating with Shin Bet, the Israeli intelligence service, the text of the speech was in the hands of the CIA by early June. The State Department (headed by John Foster Dulles) promptly got the text from the CIA (headed by Foster's brother, Allen) and made a strategic decision to release it into the public domain, with the result that the translated text, along with commentary by James Reston, took up four full pages in the *New York Times* on June 6. Voice of America broadcast long reports on the speech in forty-three languages. John Foster Dulles—not yet ready to get cozy with Khrushchev—pronounced the speech to be "the most damning indictment of despotism ever made by a despot."[51] The full text of the speech was not officially released to the public by the Soviet government until Mikhail Gorbachev was in charge thirty-three years later.

The Thaw

Thaw is a conveniently vague term (like *détente*) for the relaxing of tensions that followed Khrushchev's arrival at the head of the table in the Kremlin. The thaw had its diplomatic, cultural, and political aspects, but it was a hit-or-miss proposition in all those spheres. To the extent that the introduction of the concept of "peaceful coexistence" between Russia and the West was a component of the thaw, it is true that coexistence did continue—for the most part—peacefully. But the easing of international tensions was spotty, and it didn't last.

For a Soviet leader even to talk about peaceful coexistence was a major development. The inevitability of war was no longer embedded in communist doctrine–at least the Soviet version of it. The prospect of "peaceful coexistence" between communism and capitalism replaced Stalin's insistence—supported by Marxist-Leninist doctrine going back decades—on the inevitability of war. In practice, peaceful coexistence meant that Soviet leaders (and their Western counterparts) at least had the good sense to avoid a nuclear holocaust. But the concept did not rule out "just" wars of national liberation or support for insurgencies, as long as that could be accomplished without direct military engagement with US or NATO forces.

Khrushchev articulated his doctrine of peaceful coexistence in an essay in *Foreign Affairs* in 1959. For context, it should be borne in mind that during the three years between the Twentieth Party Congress and the publishing of Khrushchev's essay, the USSR and the United States had successfully launched their first earth satellites, the USSR had successfully tested the first intercontinental ballistic missile (which Khrushchev had boasted the USSR was producing "like sausages"), the Hungarian revolt had been crushed, US B-52 bombers had been put on constant ground alert (to remain in that status until 1991), the United Kingdom had added the atomic bomb to its arsenal, and East-West tensions over Berlin had reached a level not seen since the blockade.

When Khrushchev wrote his *Foreign Affairs* essay, "rollback" had not been unequivocally repudiated in the public domain as US doctrine (though NSC-162/2 had effectively consigned rollback to the political history books). Khrushchev mentioned rollback several times. (For example, "the policy of 'rolling back' Communism can only poison the international atmosphere, heighten the tension between states and work in favor of the cold war.") With that out of the way, and with some obligatory bluster filtered out ("Communism will ultimately be victorious throughout the world"), Khrushchev's essay may be taken as a reliable expression of the peaceful coexistence proposition the Kremlin wanted to present to the West. Khrushchev rhetorically asked: "What, then is the policy of peaceful coexistence?" He then defined it, in one paragraph, as having three components: (1) the "repudiation of war" as a means of solving controversial issues, (2) an "obligation on the part of all states to desist from violating each other's territorial integrity and sovereignty in any form and under any pretext," and (3) the "renunciation of interference in the internal affairs of other countries with the object of altering their system of government or mode of life or for any other motives."[52] Thus defined, Khrushchev's doctrine of peaceful coexistence would take some serious beatings over the ensuing decades.

Khrushchev went on to serve as first secretary and chairman of the Council of Ministers until he experienced his own October revolution in 1964. His ouster ushered in the Brezhnev era of Soviet socialism, which is aptly described by Stephen Kotkin as "lethargically stable."[53] The Khrushchev era was neither lethargic nor particularly stable, as will be seen. But first, we should go to the other side of the East-West divide to look at how communists and communism were doing in the United States.

Chapter 11

Communism and the United States Supreme Court

The greatest danger that can befall us in coping with this problem of Soviet communism, is that we shall allow ourselves to become like those with whom we are coping.

—George F. Kennan, in the Long Telegram, February 1946

It is in the nature of American democracy that major social and political movements will inevitably generate intense controversies that must be resolved by the least democratic branch of government. These controversies tend to present extraordinarily difficult constitutional questions as to the boundaries between the powers of the three branches of the federal government—and, of equal importance, the boundaries between the powers of the states and the powers of the national government the states joined together to create more than two hundred years ago. The Cold War and communism did their part to keep the courts busy in the first two decades of the Cold War. The constitutional doctrine developed during that era is now woven into the fabric of American life.

Red Monday

On June 14, 1957 (which came to be known as Red Monday), the communists had a great day in court—in the US Supreme Court, to be exact. On that day, the court handed down four decisions in which communists or the Communist Party USA had squared off against federal or state authorities. At the end of the day, the communists were four for four. The communists would have more victories—and some defeats—in the years to follow, but it is fair to say that Red Monday was the beginning of the end for the efforts of the US government to prosecute the Communist Party out of existence.

The Communist Party USA is now in its second century, operating unmolested by the federal government.[1] It has not fared as well in the marketplace of ideas as it did in court on Red Monday. Of course, in some ways, the epic struggle between the party and federal prosecutors in the federal courts was laden with irony. The irony lay mainly in the fact that the US communists were by and large genuine civil libertarians. But by successfully invoking civil liberties enshrined in the US Constitution, they were asserting their right to advance a cause for which the "mother country" was a nation whose leaders remained in power by denying those very liberties to the hundreds of millions who lived behind the Iron Curtain.

This story, ultimately, is the story of the success of the US Constitution—and the justices who were sworn to enforce it—in safeguarding fundamental civil liberties against the forces of fear and demagoguery that dominated so much of public discourse during the Cold War. This story brought to life the closing paragraph of Kennan's Long Telegram, quoted above.

It will easily suffice for present purposes to focus on the major Smith Act decisions, beginning with *Dennis v. United States*, handed down in 1951.

Stripped to the essentials, the Smith Act,[2] which became law in 1940, made it a federal felony (1) to knowingly or willfully advocate the overthrow of the US government by force or violence, (2) to publish printed matter advocating overthrow by force or violence, with intent to cause the overthrow, or (3) to organize *or simply be a member* of any group advocating overthrow by force or violence. And, importantly, the Smith Act made it equally criminal to *conspire* to do any of those things. (The membership clause of the act differed from Senator Hubert Humphrey's unsuccessful 1954 proposal in that Humphrey's proposal would have made mere membership in the Communist Party a jailable offense *without* proof of advocacy of overthrow.)

The Smith Act, as a platform for prosecutorial and judicial decisions in the first fifteen years of the Cold War, played a significant role in shaping public attitudes toward communism and communists well into the 1960s, if not beyond. Three Smith Act decisions handed down by the US Supreme Court, viewed in the broader context of Cold War events, tell the story. As an initial matter, it is important to understand what those cases were about. Those cases were:

The court's 1951 decision in *Dennis v. United States.*[3] *Dennis* was a conspiracy case. Eugene Dennis and his co-defendants were charged with conspiring (1) to organize the Communist Party as a group of persons who teach and advocate overthrow of the US government by force and violence, and (2) to advocate the duty and necessity of violent overthrow.

The 1957 decision (one of the Red Monday decisions) in *Yates v. United States.*[4] *Yates*, like *Dennis*, was a conspiracy prosecution in which the defendants were charged with conspiracy to organize and to advocate.

The 1961 decision in *Scales v. United States.*[5] *Scales* was a prosecution under the membership clause, with no conspiracy allegations. Junius Scales was charged simply with being a member of an organization which advocated violent overthrow.

Eugene Dennis was the general secretary of the National Committee of the Communist Party USA. In 1949, after a nine-month jury trial in federal court in New York City, Dennis was convicted, along with ten other communists, of conspiring to violate the Smith Act. Dennis and his codefendants (all members of the national board of the US Communist Party) were sentenced to prison. Ten of the eleven got five-year prison terms. (The eleventh, Robert Thompson, a decorated World War II combat veteran, was sentenced to a three-year term in consideration of his heroism in the fighting in the Pacific theater. The remains of this communist repose in Arlington National Cemetery.)

The facts underlying the convictions in *Dennis* were (as described by the court) that (1) the defendants controlled an organization they transformed into the Communist Party, (2) the party had a policy "which worked for the overthrow of the Government by force and violence,"

(3) the party was "a highly disciplined organization," and (4) the literature of the party and the activities of its leaders had the goal of achieving "a successful overthrow of the existing order by force and violence." On appeal, Dennis and his codefendants challenged the constitutionality of the Smith Act, on its face and as applied to them.

In the year before the *Dennis* case was argued in the Supreme Court in December 1950, Alger Hiss had been convicted, communist troops had overrun the Korean Peninsula, and Joe McCarthy had touted his list of communist subversives in the State Department. This quite clearly was not a good environment in which to argue for a communist's constitutional right to advocate the violent overthrow of the US government. We usually recoil from the thought that judicial decisions are influenced by day-to-day headlines, but in its June 1951 decision in *Dennis*, the Supreme Court itself made current (or at least relatively recent) events relevant to the adjudication of guilt. The *Dennis* defendants argued in the Supreme Court that they could not be convicted unless, as Justice Oliver Wendell Holmes had written in *Schenck v. United States* in 1919, they had created "a clear and present danger" that their words will "bring about the substantive evils that Congress has a right to prevent."

The *Dennis* case is remarkable not so much for what the government *did* prove as it is for how little the government was *required to prove* to convict the defendants. As Justice Robert Jackson correctly pointed out in his opinion concurring with the court's decision to uphold the convictions of the defendants, the prosecutors were not obligated to prove a single overt act in furtherance of the Smith Act conspiracy charged in the indictment.[6] At the jury trial in New York in 1949, the trial judge instructed the jurors that, to convict the defendants, they had to be satisfied beyond a reasonable doubt that the defendants (1) conspired—in other words, agreed, with no overt acts required—to organize a society, group and assembly of persons[7] who advocate the overthrow or destruction of the US government by force and advocate the duty and necessity of overthrowing or destroying the government of the United States by force, (2) with the intent to incite persons to such action, and (3) all with the intent to cause the overthrow of the US government by force and violence as speedily as circumstances would permit. (Contrast this with the concept of a *present* danger.)

The judge instructed the jurors that if they found that the government had proved those elements, then "I find as a matter of law that there is sufficient danger of a substantive evil that the Congress has a right to prevent to justify the application of the [Smith Act] under the First Amendment of the Constitution." In other words, the trial judge watered down the "clear and present danger" test and then—remarkably—treated it as an issue of law for the judge to decide rather than as a question of fact for the jury. Equally remarkably, on appeal, the Supreme Court left no doubt that application of the "clear and present danger" test was a legal issue, not an issue of fact for the jury to consider: Chief Justice Fred M. Vinson wrote that "we hold that the statute may be applied where there is a 'clear and present danger' of the substantive evil which the legislature had the right to prevent. Bearing, as it does, the marks of a 'question of law,' the issue is properly one for the judge to decide." On the up-or-down issue of whether a clear and present danger existed, the court, in upholding the convictions of Dennis and his codefendants, concluded that their conspiracy to organize the Communist Party and to teach and advocate the overthrow of the government of the United States "by force and violence" as speedily as circumstances would permit was sufficient to create the necessary clear and present danger.

The clear and present danger test articulated by Justice Holmes in 1919 asks "whether the [defendants'] words used are used in such circumstances and are of such a nature as to create a clear and present danger that they will bring about the substantive evils that the United States Congress has a right to prevent." In the nature of things, the issue of whether words spoken or written by politically motivated actors present a clear and present danger of violent overthrow of the US government could be viewed as a political question (and thus not subject to adjudication in a federal court), or as a question of fact to be determined by the jury, or as a question of law to be decided by the judge. The Supreme Court's explicit characterization of the issue as a question of law recalls Alexis de Tocqueville's observation in 1835: "There is virtually no political question in the United States that does not sooner or later resolve itself into a judicial question."[8]

Interestingly enough, the court gave no explicit guidance as to the extent to which the trial court (or, for that matter, an appellate court), in determining the existence or non-existence of a clear and present danger, could consider that issue in light of the ebb and flow of current events. But it is fair to say that the existence of a clear and present danger is not a question that is answerable from law books, not even the law books to be found in the Supreme Court's magnificent law library.

Although the vote of the justices in *Dennis*—affirming the convictions of eleven communists—was six to two, the misgivings of two of the six justices in the majority were plainly apparent. Justice Felix Frankfurter was especially torn. Because of his formalist approach to the law and his respect for the constitutional separation of powers, he voted to affirm the convictions. But, as Frankfurter himself put it in his concurring opinion: "The wisdom of the assumptions underlying [the Smith Act] and prosecution is another matter." Frankfurter, a Jewish Austrian immigrant, had more reasons than most jurists to detest any form of oppression. He was uneasy. So as he crafted his long concurring opinion, he must have been delighted to read an article by George Kennan, published in the *New York Times Magazine* eight days before the decision (including Frankfurter's concurring opinion) was handed down. As Frankfurter wrote in his concurring opinion, "No one is better equipped than George F. Kennan to speak on the menace of Communism and the spirit in which we should meet it." Frankfurter was inspired to quote from Kennan's article at length. The passage quoted by Frankfurter read in part: "If our handling of the problem of Communist influence in our midst is not carefully moderated—if we permit it, that is, to become an emotional preoccupation and to blind us to the more important positive tasks before us—we can do a damage to our national purpose beyond comparison greater than anything that threatens us today from the Communist side."[9]

For his part, Justice Jackson, though acknowledging that "there was power in Congress to enact this statute," succinctly summed up his misgivings in his own concurring opinion: "Communism will not go to jail with these Communists." It took nearly one hundred pages, in five separate opinions, for the justices to explain their reasoning in *Dennis*. An astute reader, taking the long view, might well have discerned from these opinions the seeds of the ultimate demise of prosecutions of communists. That, of course, was cold comfort for the eleven board members who went to jail. Officially, the status quo on the day *Dennis* was decided was that "new Federal prosecutions of the nation's Communists were foreshadowed here . . . as a result of the Supreme Court's decision upholding conviction of eleven of the party's top leaders."[10]

Chief Justice Vinson, the author of the main opinion in *Dennis,* had been appointed to the court by Truman in 1946. Vinson's death in September 1953 cleared the way for Eisenhower's appointment of California's Republican governor, Earl Warren, as chief justice. Although we should surely be cautious about any supposition that a jurist's judicial philosophy is necessarily driven by his life experiences, it is fair to note that, in his ten years as governor of California, Warren had seen Richard Nixon's red-baiting campaigns in 1946 and 1950 and, perhaps more importantly, had served ex officio as a member of the University of California Board of Regents during the loyalty-oath controversy. Warren detested the loyalty oath (both on principle and as a practical matter) and had successfully guided the board to a workable compromise. Warren's arrival as chief justice in 1953 would make more difference than anyone could have known when he was appointed and confirmed without opposition. The jurisprudence of Earl Warren, as his Supreme Court colleagues soon discovered, differed significantly from that of Fred Vinson.[11]

As the *New York Times* had predicted, prosecutions of communists continued in the wake of the 1951 decision in *Dennis.* With the high court's decision in hand, the government launched more than a dozen Smith Act prosecutions against well over a hundred communists. Among them was Oleta Yates. She and her thirteen communist codefendants were the next Smith Act defendants to have their day in the Supreme Court. The decision in their case was handed down on Red Monday, June 17, 1957.

When *Yates* came before the court for argument in October 1956, Warren was chief justice. There were several other justices new to the court since *Dennis* had been decided. One of them was Justice John Marshall Harlan II. Harlan—as good a lawyer as any who served on the court in the twentieth century—was the namesake of his grandfather, Justice John M. Harlan, who had served on the court for more than thirty years. The younger Harlan was appointed to the court by Eisenhower in March 1955. His arrival on the high bench was significant. Like any Supreme Court justice worthy of that office, he could, by "interpreting" it, eviscerate an act of Congress when he (along with at least four of his colleagues on the court) thought necessary. He would write the majority opinion in *Yates.* The personal papers that became available after Harlan's death revealed that he had directed his law clerks to find a way to stop Smith Act prosecutions.[12]

Oleta Yates and her codefendants had been convicted in federal court in California of conspiring (1) to advocate the duty to violently overthrow the US government and (2) to organize a society of persons—the Communist Party—to advocate violent overthrow, all with the intent to cause the violent overthrow "as speedily as circumstances would permit." This last phrase, of course, reflected the watered-down version of "*present* danger" that the court adopted in *Dennis*. All fourteen defendants were sentenced to five-year prison terms by the federal court in Los Angeles.

The nonjudicial events that unfolded in the fall would not have been welcomed by a lawyer arguing for the freedom of convicted communist conspirators. It was a presidential election year—never a good time to tout the First Amendment rights of communists. Less than a month after *Yates* was argued, Soviet troops flooded into Budapest to crush a revolt in Hungary. At a diplomatic reception in Moscow, in mid-November, Nikita Khrushchev proclaimed to the Western diplomats: "We will bury you."[13] (Discussed in the next chapter.) As revolutionaries, the *Yates* defendants were, as Warren's biographer Ed Cray put it, "an unprepossessing bunch. Their lives had been divided between spasms of dialectic debate and idealistic efforts to organize labor unions in the face of police and strikebreakers." Their party organization had been penetrated so thoroughly that they joked that "without the FBI's dues, the party would have died."[14] Having made no secret of their affiliation with the Communist Party USA, they had no hope of infiltrating the government. It is undeniable that their ideology, rather than anything they had actually accomplished, was the catalyst for the prosecution.

The court's first major holding in *Yates* was that the Smith Act's prohibition of *organizing* a group advocating the violent overthrow encompassed "organizing" only in the sense of *founding* or *establishing* the organization and did not connote the "continuing process which goes on throughout the life of an organization." The defendants argued that since their original organizing activity had occurred long before they were indicted, the prosecution was barred by the three-year statute of limitations. The court agreed. But quite apart from the "organizing" charge, the defendants had also been charged with *advocating* the duty to violently overthrow the US government. The problem with that charge, as Harlan wrote, was that the "jury was never told that the Smith Act does not denounce advocacy in the sense of preaching abstractly the forcible overthrow of the Government." That required reversal of the convictions, because "the essential distinction is that those to whom the advocacy is addressed must be urged to do something, now or in the future, rather than merely to believe in something." "The advocacy must be of action and not merely abstract doctrine."[15]

The result of the *Yates* decision was that the court directed acquittal of five of the defendants and remanded the case for retrial as to the other nine. Those nine were never retried; the government dismissed the case, concluding that it could not satisfy the burden of proof that Harlan had articulated for the court. Save for the case against Junius Scales (to be discussed), the *Yates* decision effectively spelled the end of Smith Act prosecutions. More than a hundred prosecutions in six major cities came to an end.[16] The first casualty was the prosecution of seven Colorado communists who had been convicted under the Smith Act after a sixty-day trial. Their convictions were reversed by the US Court of Appeals in Denver barely two months after *Yates* was handed down.[17]

The other three Red Monday decisions were *Watkins v. United States*,[18] *Sweezy v. New Hampshire*,[19] and *Service v. Dulles*.[20] Though these three decisions were collectively as provocative as *Yates*, they need not be discussed at great length here except to note, importantly, that all four of the Red Monday decisions required the court to expound on the relationship between the judicial branch in general (and the Supreme Court in particular) and other major governmental institutions.

It was nothing new, of course, for the court to undertake to define the role of the federal courts in American society. It had done so as far back as *Marbury v. Madison* in 1803. But in its four Red Monday decisions, the court, under Chief Justice Warren, squarely confronted other institutions of state and federal government in the context of the high-stakes emotionally, politically and geopolitically fraught conflict between communism and capitalism. The court did not shrink from that challenge.

In *Watkins*, the court, rejecting the arguments of both the government and the American Bar Association, reversed the conviction of John Watkins of contempt of Congress. Testifying before the House Un-American Activities Committee, Watkins, a labor union leader, had been most willing to talk about his own activities in the Communist Party, but he refused to identify others who were no longer members of the party. He might well have succeeded in invoking his Fifth Amendment privilege against self-incrimination, but avoiding self-incrimination was not his purpose. He refused to testify in aid of the committee's effort to expose former party members just for the sake of exposing them: "I am not going to plead the fifth amendment, but I refuse to answer certain questions that I believe are outside the proper scope of your committee's activities. . . . I do not believe that any law in this country requires me to testify about persons who may in the past have been Communist Party members or otherwise engaged in Communist Party activity but who to my best knowledge and belief have long since removed themselves from the Communist movement."[21]

In a similar vein, Paul Sweezy, a professor at the University of New Hampshire and a committed Marxist, refused on First Amendment grounds to answer questions put to him by the attorney general of that state. The attorney general had been given what amounted to a roving commission by the New Hampshire legislature to conduct investigations to "find out if there were subversive persons" in New Hampshire. In Sweezy's case, the attorney general wanted to know about the content of the professor's lectures at the university and about his activities on behalf of the Independent Progressive Party in the 1948 presidential election. Much as John Watkins had done with HUAC, Sweezy declined to answer questions about his lectures and his personal political activities. This, Sweezy said, was none of the attorney general's business.

In *Watkins*, the court held that the purpose of the congressional investigation had to be reasonably ascertainable and that Watkins was not obliged to answer a question if he could not determine the relevance of the question to the committee's work. In *Sweezy*, the court held that the professor had no obligation to answer where the attorney general had "such a sweeping and uncertain mandate" that there was no way to determine whether the legislature had actually "asked the Attorney General to gather the kind of facts comprised in the subjects upon which [Sweezy] was interrogated." Chief Justice Warren—who had not forgotten the fight over the University of California loyalty oath—wrote the majority opinions in both *Watkins* (a 6 to 3 decision) and *Sweezy* (6 to 2).

The Red Monday losers, so far, were Congress and the executive branch of the US government (*Yates*), Congress in the form of the House

Un-American Activities Committee (*Watkins*), and the executive branch of the government of the State of New Hampshire (*Sweezy*). The civics lessons continued. The federal executive branch next got its comeuppance in *Service v. Dulles*, the last of the Red Monday decisions. John Stewart Service, a Foreign Service Officer, had survived six loyalty investigations between 1945 and 1951. But in late 1951, in a "post-audit" review that was not authorized by departmental regulations, a loyalty review board found "reasonable doubt" as to Service's loyalty. Service's dismissal resulted from an investigation undertaken at the instance of Joe McCarthy.[22] Service was summarily fired by Dean Acheson immediately after the board made its finding.[23] Concluding that Service could not be fired using a procedure nowhere to be found in the applicable departmental regulations, the court unanimously held that Service had been unlawfully fired.

It is fitting that the operative events in the Red Monday decisions bookended the most virulent phase of the McCarthy era. Yates was indicted, and Service was dismissed in 1951. Sweezy and Watkins were subpoenaed in 1954. (When Watkins appeared before HUAC, the Army-McCarthy hearings had been in progress on the other side of the Capitol building for a week.) By the time the Supreme Court threw a large bucket of cold water on McCarthyism on Red Monday, Joe McCarthy had been dead for forty-six days.

Red Monday: The Blowback

Red Monday generated banner headlines on Tuesday. The headlines in the *New York Times* read, in part:

> **HIGH COURT, RELEASING WATKINS,**
> **RESTRICTS CONGRESS ON PRIVACY;**
> **FREES 5 REDS IN SMITH ACT CASE**
> **Judiciary Seen as Setting Limit on Other Branches**
> **Supreme Court Declares Rights of Individuals**
> **Must Be Protected**[24]

Writing in the same Tuesday issue of the *Times*, James Reston accurately commented that "today's majority opinions were studded with passages critical of the exercise of power by the Federal Government, and strong in defense of the individual's rights." The effect of Eisenhower's three appointments to the court—Warren, William Brennan, and Harlan–was not lost on Reston: "The feeling here is that the Eisenhower appointments to the court have established a new balance in which there is a reliable majority extremely sensitive to the defense of civil liberties."[25] As might be inferred from the favorable coverage in its news pages, the *New York Times* was equally complimentary of the Red Monday decisions on the editorial page. But the *Los Angeles Times* was not so sanguine, lamenting that as "a weapon against the Communist menace, the Smith Act is currently a broken reed."[26] True enough.

For Senator Strom Thurmond of South Carolina, the Red Monday decisions proved that "the Supreme Court of the United States is a menace to the people of this country." [27] Others, though equally displeased, were more nuanced. Senator James O. Eastland, the chairman of the Senate Judiciary Committee (which he would chair for nearly twenty-three years) was especially incensed by *Yates* (Smith Act) and *Watkins* (powers of HUAC). On the floor of the Senate, the Mississippi Democrat complained that the decision in *Yates,* by construing "organize" to refer only to the original organization of the party, had rendered the statute inapplicable to any present activity "and therefore useless."[28]

Eastland was in a position to act on his umbrage. These things do take time, but, in 1962, Eastland's Judiciary Committee advanced legislation, which was enacted that year, to amend the Smith Act to provide that "organize" includes current activity as well as original organizational activity.[29] That legislation was advocated by then-Deputy Attorney General Byron R. White, a former law clerk to the late Chief Justice Vinson, who had authored the *Dennis* opinion in 1951. White informed Eastland by letter that enactment of the amendment "would be extremely valuable in future Smith Act prosecutions."[30] White's letter was dated January 31, 1962. Ten weeks later, White was a justice of the Supreme Court (although there is assuredly no reason to think that his work on this legislative matter had anything to do with his appointment by President John F. Kennedy, who had long held a high opinion of White).

The American Bar Association—at that time the self-anointed voice of the American legal profession—was no more pleased with the Red Monday decisions than was Senator Eastland. The ABA's Special Committee on Communist Tactics, Strategy, and Objectives got busy, as did the House of Delegates, the policy-making body of the association. As to the *Watkins* decision, the bar association recommended adoption of a resolution strengthening the authority of the House Un-American Activities Committee. The association's prescription in *Yates* was that legislation was necessary "to eliminate obstacles to our internal security" by overruling the Supreme Court's restrictive interpretation of the Smith Act's prohibition of "organizing." For good measure, the association recommended that persons refusing to answer questions about communist associations be barred from federal employment.[31]

The bar association also took exception to the court's decision in *Jencks v. United States*, handed down two weeks before Red Monday. In *Jencks*, a communist had been prosecuted for allegedly filing a false "noncommunist affidavit" with the National Labor Relations Board. The court held that the government must give defense counsel the written reports submitted by the government's paid informants who testified at the trial.[32] The American Bar Association was not pleased. At the ABA's annual meeting in the summer of 1957, just a few weeks after Red Monday, the special committee rendered a report specifically referring to *Jencks* as one of fifteen recent Supreme Court decisions which, as reported by the association's committee on communist tactics, "directly affected the right of the United States to protect itself from Communist subversion."[33] (The ABA has since thought better of its criticism of *Jencks*. The government's obligation to produce reports of statements by its trial witnesses is now part of the bedrock of federal criminal procedure.)

The ABA and its special committee on communism were particularly concerned about communist infiltration into the ranks of the legal profession. With the authorization of the Board of Governors of the association, the committee filed an *amicus curiae* brief with the Supreme Court of Florida asserting the "duty of the bar and of the courts to cleanse its ranks of an unfit member" who refused to answer "questions concerning his activities in the Communist Party or Communist-dominated fronts."[34] The disbarment effort was not successful.[35]

Chapter 11

Prosecuting Reds for Being Red: The Last Gasp

Julius and Ethel Rosenberg, loyal communists, were successfully prosecuted for espionage in the service of the Soviet Union. (Subsequent events—including the post–Cold War opening of Soviet archives—have substantially undermined suggestions that the Rosenbergs were wrongfully convicted.) Others, communist or not, have also been convicted of betrayal of the United States in favor of the Soviets. This brings to mind Aldrich Ames and Robert Hanssen, to name only two. But in the Smith Act prosecutions, the government's evidence consisted predominantly of proof of protected conduct—political speech—from which the government asked the jurors to *draw inferences* of intent to engage in conduct that could genuinely (and constitutionally) be treated as criminal.

The Red Monday decisions were not the last word, and the Smith Act cases were not the only arena for prosecution of communists. Scores of cases and years of litigation revolved around matters such as registration of communists with the Subversive Activities Control Board,[36] the investigatory powers of HUAC (again),[37] prohibiting communists from working at defense facilities,[38] and the denial of passports to communists.[39] But it is fair to say that the Red Monday decisions, as civics lessons to a nation from the Warren court, did much to change the tone of public discourse and to reorder prosecutorial priorities. Although those decisions ignited a firestorm of anticommunist rhetoric, they ultimately were instrumental in forcing the domestic battle with communism and its rabble of US adherents out of the courtroom and into the marketplace of ideas. Ironically, that point is made by the last two noteworthy Smith Act decisions—one upholding a conviction and one overturning. Those decisions, *Scales v. United States*[40] and *Noto v. United States*,[41] were handed down on June 5, 1961.

Scales was a 5 to 4 decision affirming the Smith Act conviction of Junius Scales. *Noto* was a unanimous decision reversing the Smith Act conviction of John Francis Noto. Justice Harlan—surely by now growing weary of Smith Act cases—wrote the dispositive opinions in both cases. Unlike *Dennis* (1951) and *Yates* (1957), *Scales* and *Noto* were prosecutions under the *membership* clause (as distinguished from the *organizing* and *advocacy* clauses) of the Smith Act. They were the first cases under the membership clause to reach the Supreme Court.

Junius Scales, the offspring of a wealthy North Carolina family, became enthralled with communism in 1939. He joined the Communist Party club at the University of North Carolina. Careful study of the literature surrounding his case suggests with reasonable clarity that, though "a misguided idealist," as the *New York Times* described him, Scales was not a "menace to our Government or to the United States as a nation."[42] His brand of communism strongly resembled the version that was later called Eurocommunism, exemplified by Enrico Berlinguer in Italy. (Eurocommunists, though resolutely anticapitalist, rejected Stalinism and willingly participated in democratic processes. They were basically social democrats, albeit at the leftmost fringe of that movement, driven by a strong undercurrent of impatience, garnished with an equally strong sense of grievance.)

Scales was indicted under the membership clause by a North Carolina grand jury in November 1954, about three weeks before Joe McCarthy's final descent into disgrace. Scales was convicted in 1955, but that conviction was summarily reversed on the authority of the *Jencks* decision—Scales had been denied access to the pretrial statements of his accusers. He was tried and convicted again in February 1958, and sentenced to six years' imprisonment. The merits of the second conviction were argued in the Supreme Court in 1959 and reargued in October of 1960, in tandem with arguments in *Noto.* (Scales was represented in all phases of the case by retired Brigadier General Telford Taylor, who had served as one of the lead prosecutors in the Nuremburg war crimes trials.)

The essence of the charge against Junius Scales was that, from 1946 to the date of the indictment in 1954, he had been an active member of a party that advocated the violent overthrow, that he was aware of that prohibited purpose, and that he had a specific intent to accomplish the violent overthrow "as speedily as circumstances would permit." At trial, the jurors were instructed that, to convict, they had to find that the government had proved all these elements beyond a reasonable doubt.

By 1961, when *Scales* was decided, it can fairly be said that McCarthyism, as a national blight, was as dead as Joe McCarthy. McCarthyism, unlike Joe McCarthy, did not die on any particular day, so, unlike Joe McCarthy, it did not have an elaborate funeral. But the demise of McCarthyism cannot be equated with the demise of anticommunism. International events such as the Berlin crisis, the Soviet nuclear buildup, and the Bay of Pigs fiasco (all to the accompaniment of Khrushchev's blustering), taken together with the remonstrances of the domestic US communists, kept communism on the front pages. Anticommunism, untainted by McCarthyism, was respectable in 1961, even if talk of a *domestic* communist threat had begun to take on a certain air of unreality. And aside from all considerations relating to foreign or domestic communism, it was unmistakable by 1961 that the Warren court had undertaken an activist course which, regardless of its merits, had become a casus belli for conservatives throughout the nation. It is fair to say, as it is put in a leading history of the federal courts, "The federal courts have a store of public confidence, something akin to deposits in a bank account, to which they deposit and on which they can draw."[43] Harlan did not want to get overdrawn. So if the membership clause of the Smith Act was fated to live or die via a 5 to 4 decision, it may not be too surprising that, as a technical matter, it survived.

Harlan's opinion for the court in *Scales* rejected the argument that the membership clause was unconstitutional. But, as a practical matter, the opinion left an impossibly narrow window for successful prosecutions under the membership clause. To drive home the stringency of its approach, the court, undertaking an extraordinarily detailed assay of the evidence presented in the district court, unanimously reversed the conviction of John Francis Noto on the same day it handed down the *Scales* decision.

In the wake of *Scales* and *Noto*, the Department of Justice dropped every remaining membership-clause case. Scales surrendered to start serving his six-year prison term in October 1961. President Kennedy commuted the sentence on Christmas Eve, 1962, with the result that Junius Scales, the only person ever jailed under the membership clause, served about fourteen months of his six-year term.

It fell to Junius Scales to bear the burden of a decision in which the Supreme Court wanted to set a nearly insuperable bar for Smith Act membership prosecutions while avoiding the opprobrium that would flow from flatly declaring the membership clause unconstitutional. Public opinion polling in 1955 revealed that communist ideas, not communist espionage or sabotage, were what Americans feared the most.[44] The vice of prosecutions under the Smith Act and the small handful of kindred enactments was that, inevitably, the vast bulk of the evidence offered to secure a jury verdict was proof of constitutionally protected speech.[45] The protected speech was used as a vessel with which to transport into the jury deliberation room the notion that the accused must have had, and must be found to have had, the specific criminal intent required by the Supreme Court. This tested our system of trial by jury to the limits.

The net effect of more than fifteen tortuous years of litigation under the Smith Act was that domestic communism was given the leeway it needed to lose—decisively—in the competition provided by the "the free trade in ideas," as Justice Holmes wrote in 1919. Although it was cold comfort for Junius Scales, *Scales* and *Noto* put opinion leaders in a position to write, as early as two days after those decisions were handed down, "The real Communist challenge is from abroad; and the sooner Americans get over the idea that we can solve the problem by persecuting the tattered remnants of American communism at home, the better able we will all be to face the really hard decisions and hard problems posed by the genuine menace of communism pushing outward from China and the Soviet Union."[46]

Chapter 12

Avoiding Armageddon

As he continued to work toward predominance in the Kremlin in 1955, Khrushchev was well aware that he needed to establish himself as a player on the international stage. Khrushchev, the former political commissar at Stalingrad and master of Ukraine, had to establish himself as a competent geostrategist. He now had no choice but to focus on the twin problems of Germany and NATO, because that was where the Soviet military and most other Russian leaders were focused.

West Germany—the Federal Republic of Germany—had become a juridical entity in 1949. As early as 1950, Acheson had begun talking about West German rearmament. In the fall of 1950, NATO had formally adopted a policy of stationing as many military forces as possible in West Germany. By 1955, it was obvious that the occupation of West Germany (as a matter of postwar legal status) was going to end. Talk of West Germany joining NATO was coming to a head. The Soviets were working hard on strategic weapons—missiles to deliver atomic bombs to targets in the continental United States—but, as always, the situation on the ground between the Vistula and the Elbe commanded at least equal attention from the Soviet leadership.

The Warsaw Pact and the Geneva Summit

Thus was the Warsaw Pact born. The treaty, formally known as the Treaty of Friendship, Cooperation, and Mutual Assistance, was signed on May 1, 1955. The Warsaw Pact nations were the USSR, Albania, Bulgaria,

Czechoslovakia, East Germany (German Democratic Republic—GDR), Hungary, Poland, and Romania. Although the pact expressly provided for a joint military command, every signatory knew the military decisions would be made in Moscow. Militarily, the Warsaw Pact had its work cut out for it. The Warsaw Pact nations had more territory to defend than the United States, Europe, and China combined. (And as it turned out, Warsaw membership was a rather dubious distinction. The Warsaw Pact is the only military alliance to have invaded *only* its own members—Hungary in 1956 and Czechoslovakia in 1968.)

As a practical matter, the formation of the Warsaw Pact in the East was not as momentous, militarily, and geopolitically, as the formation of NATO had been in the West. But if nothing else, the pact reminded the world that the USSR now effectively controlled more than a thousand miles of the Baltic coast ("from Wyborg to the very gates of Lübeck"[1]), as compared with less than seventy-five miles before World War II. The result, at least according to one contemporary commentator, was that "the Soviets have penetrated so deeply into the center of Europe that the Kremlin disdainfully likes to call the free part of Europe 'the balcony of the great Russian house.'"[2]

On May 9, eight days after the Warsaw Pact was signed, and ten years to the day after Victory Day in the Soviet Union, West Germany officially joined NATO. Although the West German Bundeswehr would not be formed until November, German rearmament, with the guns once again trained to the east, was a fait accompli.

The table was now set for national leaders, East and West, to meet face to face. This was the Geneva summit of July 1955, attended by the heads of government and foreign ministers of the USSR, the United States, the United Kingdom, and France. For the USSR, the head of government was Bulganin, accompanied by Khrushchev, appearing as a member of the Presidium of the Supreme Soviet, and the redoubtable Molotov. (This was before Molotov fell out of favor and was appointed to continue his diplomatic career as ambassador to Mongolia.)

Amazingly enough, in the run-up to the summit, Dulles was still talking about rollback. At a May 19 meeting of the National Security Council (called for the purpose of preparing for the summit conference), Dulles told his colleagues, including Eisenhower, that "he believed that we were now confronting a real opportunity in the present situation for

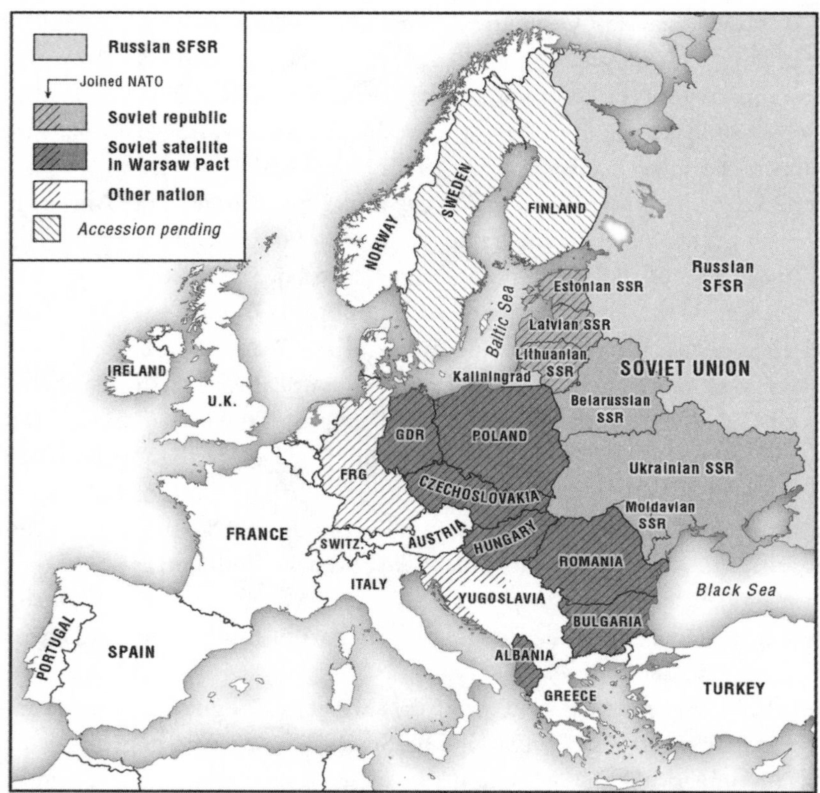

The Soviet Union's western republics and satellites, 1955. Ultimately joining NATO were the former German Democratic Republic (East Germany, on unification with the Federal Republic of Germany in 1990), Czech Republic, Hungary and Poland (1999), Bulgaria, the Baltics, Romania, Slovakia and Slovenia (2004), and Albania and Croatia (2009). The original twelve Western European and North American members formed the alliance in 1949. Greece and Turkey joined in 1952. West Germany joined in 1955. Montenegro and North Macedonia, not shown here, joined in 2017 and 2020. At the time of publication, the accession of Finland and Sweden was pending.

a rollback of Soviet power." The secretary's idea was "was to get the Russians out of the satellite states and to provide these states with a real sense of freedom."[3] To be fair, Dulles qualified his comment by suggesting that the outcome for the satellites might be a "status not unlike that of Finland." Nevertheless, his statement reflects yet another collision between ideology and reality. Of course, if Dulles had lived to be 103 years old, he would have seen (by the end of 1991) the full emancipation of the satellites, but even that was not the result of anything resembling the rollback narrative Dulles promoted during the 1952 presidential campaign.

The acid test of substantive success for the summit conference would be whether progress could be made on the intractable problem of Germany, now that the FRG and the GDR were ensconced in NATO and the Warsaw Pact. But pronouncements made by both sides on the eve of the conference left no doubt that the West would agree to no arrangement that would preclude NATO membership for a united Germany—an outcome the Kremlin said it could not abide.

The conference—the first meeting between US and Soviet leaders since Truman and Stalin met at Potsdam in 1945—lasted a week and was accompanied by great formality, with the Russian delegation enjoying recognition on an equal footing with the other three powers. The meeting produced no substantive result, in terms of Germany, disarmament, East-West trade, or anything else. One disappointment for the US delegation was Khrushchev's unequivocal rejection of Eisenhower's "Open Skies" proposal. The proposition was that the United States and the USSR would exchange maps showing the locations of their military installations and that each would allow essentially continuous reconnaissance overflights of those installations for the purpose of thwarting surprise attacks and to enable verification of compliance with the arms-control agreements each side hoped would soon be reached. Eisenhower did not go to Geneva with high hopes that Khrushchev would countenance US aerial surveillance over the USSR, but he saw nothing to lose—and perhaps a propaganda advantage to gain—by advancing the Open Skies proposal. As will be seen, Khrushchev's rejection of the Open Skies proposal caused Eisenhower and his military advisors to look for other ways to find out what was happening on the ground in the USSR.

Despite the lack of substantive results from the Geneva summit, the conference did help reduce tensions, giving leaders on both sides the opportunity to take the measure of their counterparts. The lessening of tensions led to talk of "the spirit of Geneva," which was fairly ephemeral but better than nothing. The memory of World War II was neither distant nor faint for the principal players at the table in Geneva. They all knew the next world war would be a global holocaust on an unimaginable scale. Not much more than a year later, with various combinations of the four powers seriously at odds with each other in the twin crises of the Hungarian revolt and Suez, the tensions that ratcheted down at Geneva would ratchet right back up.

Fall 1956: The Perfect Storm

As a chapter in the story of the Cold War, the 1956 presidential election differed in some noticeable ways from the first five postwar elections. The Cold War was no longer a new phenomenon, and any uncertainty about how the nations of the North American and Eurasian continents might line up along the East-West divide was long gone. The rhetoric from leaders on either side of that divide had almost become rote. At their convention in August, the Democrats again chose Adlai Stevenson to run against Eisenhower. As an incumbent, Eisenhower could credibly talk about peace and prosperity. Internationally, not much was happening until events spun out of control in Hungary and Egypt about two weeks before the election.

The story begins in Poland and then plays out in Hungary and the Sinai Peninsula. It provides another lesson in what can happen when rhetoric collides with reality in foreign policy. In October, Khrushchev and Bulganin managed to quell some serious unrest in Poland by acquiescing in the return to power of Wladyslaw Gomulka, who was a good communist and a good enough politician to win the support of both the Kremlin and the Polish populace. The Hungarians—especially Hungarian students and intellectuals—were watching. Of Magyar, not Slavic, extraction, the Hungarians had no ethnic, cultural, or linguistic affinity for their Eastern Slav overseers in the Kremlin.

By the third week in October, the situation in Hungary was progressing from street protest to open revolt. Problems had been brewing for more than a year. Premier Imre Nagy, though assuredly a communist, was just a bit too liberal for the Kremlin. On orders from Moscow, Nagy was purged as premier and from all his party positions in April 1955. Mátyás Rákosi was the nation's de facto ruler until the summer of 1956, when he, in turn, fell out of favor with the Soviet leadership, setting the stage for months of chaos at the top of the Hungarian government.

The turmoil at the top was a product of the turmoil in the streets. There was never any possibility that Dulles-style rollback could become a reality in Hungary in 1956. But, as Gerard Toal puts it, in the streets of Budapest, "the tensions between normative and pragmatic strains of U.S. geopolitical culture had tragic implications."[4] Radio Free Europe (funded by the CIA until the early 1970s) became a player.

At the urgent request of the Western powers, the UN Security Council met on October 28 to address the crisis in Hungary. In aid of the effort being pressed in the Security Council, RFE's October 28 broadcast to Hungary appealed to the Hungarians to "fight vigorously because this will have a great effect on the handling of the Hungarian question by the Security Council of the UN."[5]

Of course, in the UN, there was no possibility that the USSR would make the mistake Ambassador Malik had made in June 1950, when the Russians lost the opportunity to veto a military response to the North Korean invasion of South Korea. Consequently, UN action would mostly (if not entirely) amount to little more than an effort by the West to put the Russians and the satellite regimes they controlled on the defensive in the eyes of the rest of the world. The Western powers needed to mount a full-court press at the UN, even though the USSR would veto any meaningful action.

There was just one problem. Israeli troops, coordinating with their British and French counterparts, invaded the Sinai Peninsula on October 29. The Israelis were headed for the Suez Canal in response to the nationalization of the canal—mostly owned by the UK and France—by Egyptian President Gamal Abdel Nasser. The next day, British and French air forces were bombing Cairo, Alexandria, and Port Said. This instantly put the British and the French nose to nose with the Eisenhower administration, which was aligned with the Kremlin in vocal opposition to the fighting in the Sinai.

On the thirtieth, Britain and France vetoed US and Soviet resolutions calling for an immediate cease-fire in Egypt. The US Treasury Department moved to freeze British access to dollar-denominated accounts in the United States. The British pound sterling was under pressure, and Eisenhower wanted it to fall faster. He blocked British access to International Monetary Fund credit. Meanwhile, as the British were sinking an Egyptian frigate and bombing targets in and near the canal, and the Soviet Army held sway in Hungary, the US presidential election was a week away. Stevenson, having already charged that the US had "come dangerously close to losing, if indeed it has not lost, its leadership in the world,"[6] was not letting presidential politics stop at the water's edge. Taking advantage of the opportunity to dodge the "soft on Communism" label that had dogged the Democrats for ten years, Stevenson warned of "the long-held plans of Communist Russia to split the free world."[7]

RFE also weighed in with its broadcast to Hungary on the thirtieth, giving "detailed military instructions to the population of Hungary, this time on the techniques of anti-tank warfare."[8] Khrushchev, surely heartened by disarray in the West, was taking a hard line on Hungary. On the thirty-first, he told the Presidium that the Soviets "should not withdraw our troops from Hungary and Budapest. We should take the initiative in restoring order in Hungary. If we depart from Hungary, it will give a great boost to the Americans, English, and French—the imperialists."[9] Nagy (having returned to power as prime minister on October 24) sealed his personal doom on November 1. With Nagy at the head of the table (and with Soviet ambassador to Hungary Yuri Andropov sitting in), the Hungarian cabinet renounced the Warsaw Pact and declared Hungary's neutrality.[10] The result: on November 2, Budapest was "ringed with Soviet steel once again."[11] By the morning of the fourth, Budapest was under Soviet artillery fire; the parliament building on the left bank of the Danube was stormed by Soviet armor and infantry. Nagy and most members of his government were prisoners by the end of the day. The RFE broadcast to Hungary on that day was later found to have led "listeners to believe that military intervention by the West can be expected within a few days."[12] It never came. The revolt was crushed, with the loss of thousands of lives (including more than a few Soviet casualties, not the least of which was the crew of a Soviet IL-28 bomber shot down over Budapest).

The Hungarian revolt and the Suez crisis were effectively over by the eighth, two days after Eisenhower's overwhelming victory in the presidential election. Eisenhower won with more than 57 percent of the popular vote, amassing a 457 to 73 margin in the Electoral College. The twin crises in Egypt and Hungary enabled (and required) Eisenhower to attend to presidential business as he coasted to victory in the final days of the campaign. It is worth noting that, in the 1956 election, Eisenhower again enjoyed the endorsement of the *New York Times*. Never again, through the 2020 election, would the *Times* endorse a Republican presidential candidate. The endorsement from the *Times* was just a bit short of full-throated. On that score, the *Times* intoned that one of the "things that have not gone the way we wish they might have gone" was the nomination of Richard Nixon, for the second time, as Eisenhower's running mate. The *Times* allowed that Nixon had conducted "a more moderate and honorable campaign than he made in earlier years," but the New York paper was still concerned that Nixon's career had "certainly not revealed much evidence of deeply rooted and consistently held principles."[13] Eighteen years later, Nixon could only have hoped for such faint praise from the *Times*.

As the Hungarian revolt was coming to an end, Khrushchev made it plain to Ambassador Bohlen that "Moscow would not give up its control of the Sovietized buffer state."[14] That was the reality of the Hungarian revolt. Eisenhower understood quite well that nothing other than a US military response would alter the course of events in Hungary. Short of that, as Eisenhower's chief of staff later wrote, "Eisenhower could do little but watch the Hungarians suffer and offer them sympathy, relief and asylum."[15] A military response was never in the cards.

As for the effect of the simultaneous Suez crisis, when he was interviewed more than four decades later, Ambassador Troyanovski observed that from the Soviet perspective the Suez crisis "looked like a godsend for the Soviet Union" in diverting attention from Hungary to Suez.[16] That was doubtless true in terms of Soviet ability—always to be desired in this kind of a situation—to foment a sense of disequilibrium within the Western camp while Soviet troops were taking care of business in Hungary. As for the longer term, the brutal suppression of the Hungarian revolt eliminated any doubt in the West about the Kremlin's resolve to maintain its grip in Eastern Europe and, consequently, as to the magnitude of the challenges that lay ahead. Yes, for the USSR, there was a price to be paid in the currency of world opinion, but that price would not, in any event, have deterred the Kremlin. The glacis was far more important than that. Twelve years later, in Czechoslovakia, the Kremlin proved that it did not need the cover of an unrelated crisis—such as Suez—as a prerequisite to ruthless intervention in Eastern Europe. And, of course, in February 2022, Putin cared not a whit about world opinion or about any need for the distraction of an unrelated crisis.

In a broader political context, the Hungarian revolt and its outcome can only be called a setback for the Republicans. In May 1957, a Democrat-led study group formed by the House Foreign Affairs Committee rendered a report charging that the administration's inaction in response to the revolt "weakened the morale of the freedom fighters and emboldened the Soviets to take their ruthless action without fear of counter-measures from the free world."[17] Although acknowledging that no one expected US troops to be actually sent to Hungary, the report insisted that "the fact remains that we were without any measures or devices at our disposal to meet this crisis." Notably, the report advanced no contentions as to what the administration should have done. The net effect of all this was that, politically, the administration had the worst of both worlds: liberation of the satellites by aggressive means was a nonstarter, but containment, by that name, was unmentionable even though it was the de facto (and, since NSC-162/2, semiofficial) US policy. As nationally syndicated columnist Peter Edson put it in March 1957: "In summary, with both 'containment' and 'liberation' tabooed, U.S. policy on the Communist satellites is very much up in the air."[18]

This was not a good election cycle in which to show the voters a lack of resolve (regardless of the fairness of that charge) in comparison with obvious Soviet resolve. It would get worse. Before the 1958 elections, the Soviets would test the world's first intercontinental ballistic missile, put the world's first artificial satellite into earth orbit, and continue testing atomic bombs. In the 1958 elections, the Republicans lost forty-nine seats in the House and twelve in the Senate. The losses in the Senate included four seats in the Great Lakes states, where voters of Eastern European heritage, especially, may well have had what one postelection analysis called "a general sense of lack of leadership in both foreign and domestic affairs."[19] To be sure, an economic recession was also very much a factor in the 1956–58 election cycle, but the 1958 election also established, to the great relief of the Democrats, that the Republican Party no longer had the upper hand in domestic Cold War politics.

"We Will Bury You"

So said Khrushchev to the diplomats—including Ambassador Bohlen—assembled for a reception at Poland's embassy in Moscow on November 18, 1956, about two weeks after Soviet troops crushed the Hungarian revolt. For American defense contractors, these were probably the four most profitable words ever spoken. In the US, Khrushchev's vodka-fueled boast was promptly published nationwide. To add insult to injury (and as was also reported nationally), Khrushchev also declared that "things are going very well with us. If we believed in the existence of a God, we would thank Him for it."[20]

The story had legs. It was perfect material for Senator Barry Goldwater's speech accepting the Republican presidential nomination at the 1964 Republican convention: "I believe that the communism which boasts it will bury us will, instead, give way to the forces of freedom."[21] (This was also the convention at which Goldwater famously proclaimed that "extremism in the defense of liberty is no vice. And let me remind you also that moderation in the pursuit of justice is no virtue."[22])

Khrushchev's boast was (and still is), without doubt, better remembered in the United States than anything else he ever said. Although, given the temper of the times, it was natural for Americans to take Khrushchev's statement literally, Bohlen (who was there to hear the statement first-hand and was surely a reliable judge of these things) believed that the "bury you" statement was not a threat of lethal attack. Rather, it was Khrushchev's expression of his "confidence in prevailing over the long haul—of being present at an opponent's funeral."[23] Bohlen's assessment was undoubtedly correct. For one thing, if Khrushchev had wanted to be taken literally (with resultant effect on public perceptions of Russian intentions), he would have chosen a more public venue than a reception at the Polish embassy. Either way, it is fair to say that Khrushchev's boast was taken literally in many quarters in the United States and did nothing to ease East-West tensions.

Sputnik

In May 1946, Project RAND, then a division of Douglas Aircraft Company, produced a classified study titled "Preliminary Design of an

Experimental World-Circling Spaceship." One of RAND's conclusions: "The achievement of a satellite craft by the United States would inflame the imagination of mankind, and would probably produce repercussions in the world comparable to the explosion of the atomic bomb."[24] It could hardly have been imagined in the United States, less than a year after the end of World War II, that the inflaming of the imagination of mankind would be accomplished by the Russians.

It is easy to remember the first (and only) time I saw my father, a World War II combat veteran, with a look of profound shock on his face. It was the morning of Saturday, October 5, 1957. The morning newspaper was not the *New York Times*, but the headlines in our town's paper doubtless conveyed essentially the same message as the *Times* that morning:

> **SOVIET FIRES EARTH SATELLITE INTO SPACE;**
> **IT IS CIRCLING THE GLOBE AT 18,000 M.P.H;**
> **SPHERE TRACKED IN 4 CROSSINGS OVER U.S.**

His explanation of the situation was easily understood, even by a ten-year-old boy: "The Russians are going to be shooting at us from space." The USSR had successfully launched a 184-pound earth satellite. The high-pitched beeps its radio emitted as it orbited the earth mocked the United States from space. Sputnik-1 was a spectacular technological feat—and a stunning propaganda victory for the Russians. Paul Nitze called it "electrifying," and he was right.[25] The Russians could not have hoped for a better centerpiece for the celebration of the fortieth anniversary of the October Revolution.

Although the segment of the US population that has any recollection of the launch of Sputnik is now small (and getting smaller), the enduring impact of Sputnik-1 on politics, policy, education, and collective memory in the United States can hardly be overstated. There is still much to be learned from the story of how the world got to October 4, 1957.

How the Russians got there first. In 1903, Konstantin Tsiolkovsky, a Russian scientist, demonstrated, as a theoretical matter, that an object launched from Earth at a certain velocity could reach orbit. Tsiolkovsky died before the Germans convincingly demonstrated the military potential of rocketry in World War II, but his theoretical work was not forgotten. The story resumes at the dawn of the Cold War. The massive undertaking that led to the successful launch of Sputnik is tightly intertwined with the story of the development of the first intercontinental ballistic missile.

Put yourself in Stalin's place as he presided at a meeting of the Politburo and the Council of Ministers on March 15, 1947. This was nineteen months out from Truman's successful use of the atomic bomb, a year after Churchill's Iron Curtain speech, and three days after Truman proclaimed the Truman Doctrine in a speech to a joint session of Congress. It was obvious that the USSR's main geopolitical adversary was now the United States, a nation insulated by two oceans from Soviet ground troops. Strategic bombing had not been a priority—or even much of a capability—for the Soviets during the war. There were several reasons for this, not the least of which was that, in the late 1930s, many of those who would have urged Stalin to develop a strategic bombing capability were shot.[26] Consequently, in 1947, Soviet long-range strategic bombing capacity was essentially nil compared with that of the US Air Force. US freedom of action in Europe and the eastern Mediterranean was vastly increased, in Stalin's scheme of things, by the fact that the US homeland was out of reach. At that March 15 meeting, referring to German progress in development of two-stage rockets during the war (the Sänger Project), Stalin addressed G. A. Tokaty, the chief Soviet rocket scientist, directly: "Do you realize . . . the tremendous strategic importance of machines of this sort? They could be an effective straightjacket for that noisy shopkeeper Harry Truman. We must go ahead with it, comrades. The problem of the creation of transatlantic rockets is of extreme importance to us."[27]

In what Tokaty later described as a turning point in Soviet missile development, Stalin decreed the creation of a state commission "for the study of the problems of long range rockets."[28] As might be expected in consequence of an order from Stalin, the USSR soon had a network of research facilities, design bureaus, and manufacturing plants for the development and production of long-range missiles.

Meanwhile, in the United States, postwar enthusiasm for a long-range missile program was much more muted, which may have been understandable for a nation that could, if need be, put hundreds of B-29s over Moscow or any city in the Volga region on any given night. In testimony before the Senate Committee on Atomic Energy in early December 1945,

Dr. Vannevar Bush, director of the US Office of Scientific Research and Development, told the senators: "Let me say this: There has been a great deal said about a 3,000-mile high-angle rocket. . . . I say technically I don't think anybody in the world knows how to do such a thing, and I feel confident it will not be done for a very long period of time to come."[29]

Dr. Bush was correct. No one in the world knew how to do it. The Russians figured it out first. Their educational system had much to do with that success.

Historian Orlando Figes has written that "the Soviet system was defined by its belief in science and technology."[30] Although that observation is perhaps too generous (taking into account that there were some other, less praiseworthy, defining characteristics of the Soviet system), it remains true that the development of the educational system enjoyed a high priority throughout the Soviet era. One result of that was that a mostly illiterate nation was transformed, over a remarkably short period of time, into a mostly literate one.[31] To be sure, the advancement of science was not the only reason for the Soviet emphasis on literacy. As Zbigniew Brzezinski noted in his master's thesis in 1950, it was "the profound conviction of the communist leaders that the people must be literate in order to properly be indoctrinated."[32] But the hard sciences (enjoying somewhat greater emphasis on academic merit and correspondingly less emphasis on political correctness) unquestionably benefited from the emphasis on education in the decades before Sputnik was launched.

Being a high school student in the Soviet Union (especially Russia) in the 1950s was serious business. Many high school students survived competition, long before graduation, more rigorous than would have been required to get a US student admitted to a major US university.[33] Thus, though it was not until Mikhail Gorbachev took office that the USSR had a leader who had completed university studies, rigorous education at the secondary and university levels was not just a relic of the Tsarist era; it was a central feature of the Soviet era. Consequently, just as Kurchatov's atomic bomb project commanded the time and talent of a highly qualified cadre of scientists and engineers, the expertise necessary to jump-start the development of Stalin's "transatlantic rocket" was available to answer his urgent demand for action. In 1953, the lead Soviet design bureau began work on the rocket that would become known as the R-7 Semyorka, the world's first intercontinental ballistic missile—and the rocket that would carry Sputnik-1 into orbit.

The early warnings. Stunning though the launch of Sputnik-1 was, the world was not caught entirely by surprise. In April 1957, six months before the satellite was launched, the CIA rendered a classified assessment that the "USSR may be preparing to test an intercontinental ballistic missile (ICBM) or to launch an earth satellite within the year."[34] The only thing wrong with this assessment was the "or." The Russians were getting ready to do both.

On August 21, 1957, the Soviet Union became the first nation to successfully test an intercontinental ballistic missile, the R-7 Semyorka. Carrying a dummy hydrogen bomb, it flew more than 3,700 miles from the test site in Kazakhstan to the Kamchatka Peninsula in the Russian Far East. Of course, it was one thing to successfully test the complex new weapon and quite another to produce operationally reliable copies in quantity, deploy them to newly built bases, logistically support them, and train crews to maintain them and prepare to launch them when ordered to do so. But by late 1957, US intelligence estimates predicted that the Soviet Union would have the capacity to produce a hundred intercontinental ballistic missiles by 1960.[35] The Soviet announcement of the successful R-7 test was issued by TASS a few days after the August 21 launch: "A super-long distance intercontinental multi-stage ballistic missile was launched a few days ago. The tests of the rocket were successful." Lest anyone miss the point, the announcement was at pains to note that "the results obtained show that it is possible to direct [a] missile into any part of the world."[36]

The Russians now had the full attention of US leaders. In an article in the October 1957 issue of *Foreign Affairs*, published a few weeks after the R-7 test and shortly before Sputnik was launched, Senator (and future president) John F. Kennedy, commenting generally on the "capacity of the Russians to compete with us militarily and economically" and specifically on their development of the hydrogen bomb, wrote that "we underestimated their technological manpower in numbers and quality."[37] That assessment was accurate—and foreshadowed Kennedy's less accurate claim of a "missile gap" during the 1960 presidential campaign. In the same October 1957 issue of *Foreign Affairs*, Dulles—now well into his fifth year as secretary of state—acknowledged the reality leaders on both sides of the East-West divide now faced: "Today a general war between the great military Powers could destroy almost all human life, certainly in the northern latitudes."[38]

The Semyorka proved itself again on October 4, 1957. With Sputnik-1 aboard, it was launched from the Baikonur Cosmodrome in Kazakhstan while Khrushchev was on his way back to Moscow from a vacation in the Crimea.

The reality check. As might be expected, the stunning reality that the Russians had beaten the Americans into space triggered a gamut of immediate reactions, ranging from scoffing to political attacks to deep public introspection. Apparently for lack of anything more perceptive to say, the immediate reaction of the Chief of US Naval Research was that the satellite was "a hunk of iron thrown up, which almost anyone could do," unless it had some scientific value.[39] Nearly three weeks after the launch, Presidential Assistant Clarence Randall opined that Sputnik was "a silly bauble in the sky. I am glad that our nation was not first."[40]

Commentary from mainstream opinion leaders was a bit more insightful. Two weeks after the launch, *Life* editorialized that the Russians "are apparently ahead of us on intercontinental ballistic missiles. For years no knowledgeable U.S. scientist has had any reason to doubt that his Russian opposite number is at least his equal." On a less negative note, the editorial concluded that one of the hard realities now is "that the conflict between freedom and Communism is a long, tiresome and seesaw business in which the apparent lead can change many times."[41] Any continuing temptation to scoff at the Russians' rocketry was stilled on November 2, when Laika, a stray dog recruited from the streets of Moscow, became the first mammal to enter earth orbit, complete with instrumentation and telemetry to measure and report her vital signs. As significant as the fact of launching and supporting Laika in orbit—albeit for a short time—was that the Sputnik-2 capsule, at 1,121 pounds, was more than six times heavier than Sputnik-1.

Political pressure on the administration began to build in parallel with the diplomatic angst. With the Democrats in control of the Senate by only two seats, a lot was riding on the 1958 elections. A potent political issue was now emerging. There were congressional calls for a thorough investigation of US missile and satellite programs.[42] All of this left Eisenhower with a challenge and a corresponding opportunity. The challenge was to quell any acute sense of alarm, let alone panic, in the

US population and among US allies, while capitalizing on the urgency of the situation to get legislative action for an effective response. Eisenhower took his case to the people.

On November 13, the president, speaking to a crowd of six thousand in Oklahoma City and to a nationwide radio and television audience, addressed with equal bluntness the threat and his proposed response. As for the exact nature of the threat, there was, of course, no need for Eisenhower to spend time expounding the implications of a successful Soviet ICBM test and two satellite launches within the last three months. So (recalling Khrushchev's rhetorical gift to the US defense industry), he simply reminded his audience that we were dealing with "an expansionist regime declaring 'We will bury you.'" He cautioned that "it would be a grave error not to take this kind of threat literally." (We don't know whether he had the benefit of Bohlen's views on that.) Laying the groundwork for his most consequential proposal, Eisenhower acknowledged the Soviets' "rigorous educational system and their technological achievements," declaring that "when a Russian graduates from high school he has had five years of physics, four years of chemistry, one year of astronomy, five years of biology, ten years of mathematics and trigonometry and five years of a foreign language." Pointing out that the Soviet Union had more scientists and engineers than the United States, Eisenhower came to "the most critical problem of all. . . . We need scientists." In the next ten years, "we need them by thousands more than we are now presently planning to have."[43] As for the cost of all this, Eisenhower cautioned that the defense budget, averaging over $42 billion a year, would necessarily have to be increased to meet projected needs. Ten months after Eisenhower's Oklahoma City speech, Congress enacted and the president signed into law the National Defense Education Act.

Back on the political side, any restraint there may have been in the political blowback resulting from the Sputnik launches evaporated on December 6. In front of the press and thousands of spectators, the first US attempt to launch a satellite ended two seconds after ignition. The Vanguard rocket rose about four feet, burst into flames, and crashed into the sand at Cape Canaveral. The satellite itself, undamaged, transmitted its radio signals until chagrined technicians opened it and turned it off.

The military implications. Given the state of the art in rocketry and nuclear weapon development in 1957 and 1958, it was well understood that the science of mass destruction had progressed to the point that in one massive attack the population and productive capacity of any nation could be substantially destroyed. The problem for the United States was that, to all outward appearances, the Russians had a significant lead over the Americans in their ability to design, produce, and deploy the devastating weapons it would take to accomplish that result. No one could predict exactly when the Russians would be able to land a missile with an atomic warhead on (or reasonably near) a target in the continental United States. But it was no longer possible for anyone to ignore the reality that the Russians would frighteningly soon have that capability. On that note, in early 1958, basking in the afterglow of the two Sputnik launches, Khrushchev told the world press that the Soviet Union would be turning out missiles "like sausages on an assembly line."[44]

As for the sheer ability to put an object into orbit, the United States achieved redemption, of sorts, at the end of January 1958, with the successful launch of Explorer I from Cape Canaveral. The problem was that Explorer I weighed all of thirty-one pounds. Explorer I was followed up by a 3.25-pound Vanguard satellite in March. US scientists could speculate all day about a US advantage in sensors and instrumentation (presumably enabling a relatively small US satellite to do the scientific work of a relatively big Russian one), but for the purpose of putting a bomb on a target an ocean away, lifting power was what mattered. At nearly three thousand pounds, Sputnik-3, launched with an upgraded R-7 in mid-May 1958, was almost a hundred times heavier than Explorer I.

Apart from the obvious military potential of the R-7, one inherently destabilizing characteristic of that missile was that, as with other liquid-fueled missiles in those first generations of ICBMs, it took several hours to prepare it for launch, and it could not stand on the pad ready for launch for more than a few hours. It would be launched from pads whose locations were, because of U-2 overflights, well known to US war planners. Consequently, after it became operational, the R-7 was, as a practical matter, usable only as a first-strike weapon. The impossibility of getting the R-7 off the ground quickly enough to escape an incoming attack meant that it could not be counted on as a retaliatory strike weapon—thus increasing the incentive to launch a first strike if the weapon was going to be used at all.

The political and policy fallout. The Sputnik launches brought two policy questions to the fore: (1) how do we survive a nuclear attack on the US homeland? And (2) how do we catch up with the Russians in the development of our own scientists and engineers?

As for survival, a blue-ribbon presidential advisory committee rendered a report to the president on November 7, 1957, a month after Sputnik-1. The report recommended a "nationwide fallout shelter program to protect the civil population." The theory was that "with proper planning the post-attack environment can permit people to come out of the shelters and survive."[45] The fallout-shelter recommendation was echoed two months later in a report prepared under the direction of a young Harvard professor, Dr. Henry Kissinger.

The impact of Sputnik in the educational realm was profound. Before Sputnik, repeated legislative efforts to augment local education budgets with federal funds had failed. The main problem was fear of the federal control that always comes with federal dollars. Conservative opposition to federal funding was surmounted by legislating not just for education but also for *defense* education. This was about the ability of the United States to defend itself from the Russians. With that, the National Defense Education Act was enacted in late August 1958, one year and three days after the USSR successfully tested the R-7.[46] The vote in the Senate was 66 to 15. Originally oriented mainly toward support of education (including teacher training) in science, engineering, and modern languages, the act was amended in 1964 to open the door for federal support of education in history, civics, geography, English, and reading. It is fair to say that the NDEA changed millions of American lives for the better.

Even with the enactment of the NDEA, the pressure for improved public education continued. In mid-1959, Vice Admiral Hyman Rickover, popularly known as the father of the US nuclear-powered submarine fleet, visited the Soviet Union. Upon his return, Rickover noted that, in 1957, 1,600,000 secondary school graduates in Russia passed an examination "which only about 2 percent of American high school graduates would have been able to pass." A bit more acidly, the admiral commented that "I searched far and wide in Russia and Poland and could not find a single drum majorette. Nor did I hear of a single school where the principal was an ex-athletic coach."[47]

It may help round out our tour of post-Sputnik public discourse to consider a passage from one of George Kennan's famous Reith lectures, which were sponsored and broadcast live throughout the United Kingdom and Europe by the Home Service of the BBC in late 1957 and early 1958. In his lecture on November 10, 1957, broadcast just a few days after the launch of Sputnik-2, Kennan sought to introduce what we might call some instant historical distance into the conversation. His words were both contrarian and prescient. They are worthy of consideration now, in the seventh decade after he spoke from London:

> To my own countrymen who have often asked me where best to apply the hand to counter the Soviet threat, I have accordingly had to reply: to our American failings—to the things we are ashamed of in our own eyes: to the racial problem, to the conditions in our big cities, to the education and environment of our young people, to the growing gap between specialized knowledge and popular understanding. I imagine that similar answers could be found for the other Western countries. I would like to add that these are problems which are not going to be solved by anything we or anyone else does in the stratosphere. If solutions are to be found for them it will be right here on this familiar earth, in the dealings among men and in the moral struggles of the individual. If one had to choose between launching satellites and continuing to give attention to these more homely problems, I should say a hundred times the latter, for unless we make progress in them, no satellite will ever save us. Whether we win against the Russians is primarily a question of whether we win against ourselves.[48]

Remarkable words, spoken as millions in the West were trying to fathom the significance of those two Russian satellites circling the earth.

The U-2 Incident

Never believe anything in politics until it has been officially denied.
—Attributed to Otto von Bismarck

Victory Park is a serenely quiet place high on Sokolovaya Hill, overlooking the Volga in Saratov. In the park, a decommissioned Soviet S-75

Dvina antiaircraft missile rests on its launcher, pointing skyward at a high angle. At thirty-five feet long and more than two feet in diameter, the missile is a rather imposing sight, especially considering its mid-1950s vintage. To be sure, the missile display is secondary to the revered Great Patriotic War memorial in this park, and the missile is no match for the war memorial in its ability to render a person speechless. But the missile is on display for a reason. The reason is made plain by the sign accompanying the missile, telling the reader that, in 1960, above Sverdlovsk, an S-75 missile "shot down the American U-2 spy plane piloted by G. Powers" and that the system also distinguished itself in Vietnam, shooting down more than 150 aircraft, including B-52s.

In Russia, events such as the downing of the U-2 as it penetrated deeply into Russian territory are remembered, and the history of those events is taught. The story of the downing of CIA pilot Francis Gary Powers and his U-2 high-altitude reconnaissance aircraft on May 1, 1960, is relevant here not so much for what happened on May 1—remarkable though that was—as for the context in which those events unfolded and for the fact that the unwritten Cold War rules of engagement sufficed once again to enable Russian and American leaders to bring the matter to a peaceful conclusion. The story of the ill-fated U-2 mission can be traced to the early days of the Eisenhower administration.

It was painful for Eisenhower, as a newly elected president, to contemplate the alternative peaceful uses to which funds in the fast-growing defense budget might have been devoted. Another important variable was that Eisenhower was perhaps matched only by George C. Marshall in his understanding of the importance of getting reliable information before making high-stakes decisions about allocation of military resources. If billions of defense dollars were to be spent to counter a Russian strategic threat, Eisenhower wanted some reasonable assurance that the threat was real. He was, thus, willing to go to extraordinary lengths to find out what was really happening on the ground in the Soviet Union. So it was that, despite serious concern about the potential consequences of the loss of an aircraft over Soviet territory, Eisenhower authorized the U-2 project in 1954. He wanted, and got, a high-altitude reconnaissance aircraft that was capable of flying deep penetration missions over the Soviet Union. Now Eisenhower had to decide whether, how, and when to use the U-2.

Khrushchev's rejection of Eisenhower's Open Skies proposal at the Geneva summit in July 1955 moved the needle, even if only slightly, in favor of using the U-2 for its intended purpose. Khrushchev moved the needle even more in late April 1956, when he volunteered, while visiting the United Kingdom, that "the Soviet Union would make a guided missile with a hydrogen bomb warhead capable of hitting any target in the world."[49] So it is perhaps unsurprising that the first operational U-2 mission authorized by Eisenhower was flown in June 1956 over Poland and East Germany. Eisenhower was astonished at the high quality of the photos the mission produced. Though he was skittish about the risk of a shootdown or other mishap, the president gave the green light for overflights of the USSR. As for the risks, CIA director Allen Dulles had assured the president that there was simply no way that the pilot of a U-2, shot down flying at the extremely high operating altitude of the U-2, would survive to be interrogated by the Russians. (In other words, the risk to the Eisenhower administration was inverse to the risk to the pilot.)

The maiden flight over the Soviet Union was, fittingly, flown on July 4, 1956. Nominally, the aircraft was an asset of the CIA, not the US Air Force. The flight originated in West Germany, traversing Poland and the Belarusian SSR before heading north to Leningrad, then turning south to reconnoiter the Baltic Soviet republics on the final leg of the flight. The second flight, the next day, searched for Bison bombers and the facilities to manufacture them, audaciously overflying (and photographing) Moscow before continuing to other facilities east of Moscow.

The good news from these initial missions was that the photographic results were superb. The bad news was that the overflights had been detected. The Soviets lodged a formal protest with the State Department on July 10. The protests made it plain that the Soviet authorities had been able to accurately track the routes flown. The State Department responded, with the approval of Secretary John Foster Dulles, that no *military* plane had violated Soviet airspace. This, of course, was a technicality that only a lawyer could love. The Kremlin chose not to raise the issue publicly. Ambassador Anatoly Dobrynin would later record in his memoir (commenting on the situation as of May 1960) that although the Soviets were well aware of the overflights, they "remained silent about this intrusion because our artillery had until then been unable to shoot down one of these extraordinary planes, which flew at an altitude of more than 80,000 feet."[50] MiG-15 and MiG-17 fighters were equally unsuccessful. Photos taken by the U-2 cameras showed the Soviet fighters attempting, without success, to climb high enough to engage the American plane.

Even though one of the original arguments in favor of the U-2 missions—that the Russians would have a hard time detecting and tracking the flights—had been eliminated, the high-quality photographic product was irresistible. What the CIA was especially interested in was U-2 photography to aid estimation of the Russians' ability to put nuclear weapons on targets in the continental United States. And a "specific by-product" of the proposed missions over Soviet territory would be "terrain information from which accurate radar navigation and bombing charts" could be prepared.[51] By the middle of October 1957, Eisenhower had been shown U-2 photo images from the Kazakh SSR and Siberia. High-quality photos were also taken above the Saratov-Engels airfield and the Kapustin Yar launch complex, both in the heart of the Volga region.[52] In the "very good to know" category of intelligence gleaned from these missions (mostly flown from Turkey) was the fact that most of the launch sites for the early Soviet ICBMs were, for logistical reasons, located along the Trans-Siberian Railroad.

Needless to say, the impunity with which the Americans continued to overfly Soviet territory—including the Russian heartland—was deeply galling to Khrushchev and the Soviet defense establishment. The overflights continued, albeit with some long pauses, in 1958 and 1959, until it all came to a head in 1960.

In late 1958, Khrushchev told Senator Hubert Humphrey, while the senator was on a visit to Moscow, that the Russians had an ICBM that could put a nuclear warhead on a target nearly 8,700 miles away, all of which the senator duly relayed to the president. In the fall of 1959, a Soviet Luna-2 rocket planted a flag on the moon, a feat to which the United States could respond only by feebly admonishing the Kremlin that this accomplishment did not create any territorial rights. Within the administration, varying estimates—with varying degrees of plausibility—of Soviet missile capabilities were being bandied about. As far as Eisenhower was concerned, the United States could not hope to counter the Soviet military threat without having actionable intelligence shedding light on just what that threat amounted to. He authorized the last series of U-2 overflights of Soviet territory in the spring of 1960. The last successful mission was flown on April 9. Three shootdown attempts failed.

With a summit meeting scheduled to start in Paris in mid-May, the president wanted to avoid the provocation of an overflight shortly before the meeting. He authorized one last mission—to be flown no later than May 1. It was indeed flown on May 1, a day of celebration for communists everywhere from Moscow to Havana. As Charles Bohlen put it, flying the mission on May Day was "like spitting in a Bolshevik's eye."[53]

As planned, the flight was to be the most ambitious yet. Originating in Pakistan, and ending in Norway, it was to be a nine-hour photographic tour of Soviet military installations. The U-2, piloted by veteran U-2 pilot Francis Gary Powers, took off from Pakistan at about 6:30 a.m. local time. The flight was detected over the Tajik SSR just a few hours before the annual May Day parade was set to begin in Red Square. As Khrushchev and his comrades gathered on the platform atop the Lenin Mausoleum, they were well aware that, as they spoke, a foreign aircraft was aloft deep in Soviet territory, flying with apparent impunity. The pressure on the Soviet air-defense arm was intense as Soviet interceptors were scrambled but couldn't fly high enough to engage. To clear the air for Soviet interceptors and antiaircraft missiles, all civilian aviation was grounded across a huge swath of Soviet territory. On this, Powers's twenty-eighth mission, his luck ran out. Four and a half hours into the mission, near Sverdlovsk, 1,200 miles inside Soviet frontiers and deep inside the Russian SFSR, the U-2 was downed by an S-75 Dvina, one of a three-missile salvo fired from the Sverdlovsk battery. This would be the final penetration of Soviet territory by the U-2. Powers successfully parachuted to earth, to be greeted by curious farmers, much as Yuri Gargarin would be greeted in a field near Saratov—under much happier circumstances—less than a year later, after he rode a Semyorka into orbit. And as would be the case with Gargarin, Powers was promptly transported to Moscow.

With Powers in custody, Khrushchev played his hand shrewdly. On May 5, he publicly disclosed some of the details at a session of the Supreme Soviet, but he kept under wraps that Powers was alive and well and in the hands of Soviet authorities. Operating on the basis of their working assumption that Powers was dead, the US authorities issued a cover story—a fabrication in all material respects—which had been preapproved by Eisenhower in 1956. The cover story was issued by the National Aeronautics and Space Administration, because the U-2 was a "flying weather laborator[y]." This mission was purportedly part of "a continuing program to study gust-meteorological conditions found at high altitude." The pilot reported that he was "having oxygen difficulties over the Lake Van, Turkey area." NASA pretended to theorize that if the oxygen problem continued, the path of the aircraft would be impossible to determine, but "it is likely it would have continued along a northeasterly course" if it was on automatic pilot.[54] This, of course, would explain the presence of the U-2 hundreds of miles due east of Moscow. The story was embellished by NASA's director of public affairs, who said that "not until Mr. Khrushchev's announcement today was there any suspicion that the Soviet Union was involved."[55] For good measure, the NASA spokesman added that all U-2s had been grounded for equipment checks. Even at the time, this all smacked of a story that was told not so much because of any supposition that it would be widely believed as for the thought that the mere telling of it would shift the burden to the Soviets to prove otherwise. Khrushchev promptly proved otherwise.

On May 7, after the fabricated weather research story had received worldwide coverage, Khrushchev "jubilantly reported" the capture of Powers, adding that Powers was in custody and would be put on trial.[56] Khrushchev accurately described the route of the May 1 flight, elaborating that the camera had been removed from the wreckage, some of the film had been developed, and that the pilot was carrying 7,500 rubles, a pistol with a silencer, and a small hypodermic needle with which to inject himself with poison in the event he was captured. With the US cover story in tatters, the next chapter was written by the State Department, which promptly issued a statement—reported by James Reston to have been cleared by Eisenhower—that was as false as the original cover story but less provably so.[57] The new story told the world that the president had ordered an inquiry and that the inquiry had "established that insofar as the authorities are concerned, there was no authorization for any such flights as described by Mr. Khrushchev."[58] Unsurprisingly, that assertion provoked "considerable skepticism" in Washington, to say nothing of the rest of the world.[59] For one thing, to believe this new version, one would have to believe that the president's regular national security briefings omitted any mention of what was being revealed about

Soviet activities as shown by thousands of photos from the U-2 flights. The new statement went on to justify the flight as a legitimate national defense measure, necessitated by the Soviets' rejection of Eisenhower's "Open Skies" proposal at the 1955 Geneva summit.

This new cover story, released on May 7, lasted two days. After going to church near his farm in Gettysburg on May 8, Eisenhower decided he had had enough of the deception.[60] On May 9, the secretary of state issued a new statement disclosing, albeit obliquely, that the "aerial surveillance by unarmed civilian aircraft, normally of a peripheral character but on occasion by penetration," had taken place at the direction of the president.[61]

All of this made the Paris summit conference, which convened on May 16, a non-event. Khrushchev, having received an acknowledgment of the U-2 flights he had known about for several years, expected but did not receive an apology for the intrusions into the sovereign territory of the Soviet Union. He made his thoughts plain in a blistering forty-five-minute speech during which, as Charles Bohlen noted, "Eisenhower's bald head turned various shades of pink, a sure sign that he was using every bit of will to hold his temper."[62] Eisenhower responded briefly, denying that the U-2 flights had been undertaken with any aggressive intent and confirming that there would be no more flights over the Soviet Union. The proceedings adjourned and did not resume.

Francis Gary Powers was tried for espionage in August 1960, convicted, and sentenced to ten years' imprisonment. He was repatriated in a prisoner exchange, a year and nine months after he was shot down over Sverdlovsk. (In June 2012, Powers was posthumously awarded the Silver Star for gallantry. The Air Force chief of staff placed the medal in the hands of Powers's young grandson, Francis Gary Powers III.)

As it turned out, Khrushchev—perhaps in jest or perhaps not—took credit for helping Kennedy win the fall election in 1960. Specifically, he recounted in his memoir that by waiting until after the 1960 election to release Francis Gary Powers, "we kept Nixon from being able to claim that he could deal with the Russians; our ploy made a difference of at least half a million votes, which gave Kennedy the edge he needed."[63]

In terms of the overall objectives of the U-2 overflights, the propaganda defeat that resulted from the May 1 shootdown, to say nothing of the humiliating exposure of the fabrications that followed, may well have been substantially offset by the value of the intelligence gathered in the overflights. By way of example, the successful reconnaissance of Soviet defense facilities gave Eisenhower the intelligence he needed to slow down the procurement of liquid-fueled missiles, in favor of development of solid-fueled missiles with their distinct strategic and operational advantages. The first operational solid-fueled ICBM entered service in 1962. It was, appropriately, called the Minuteman, because it could be prepared for launch in a fraction of the time it took to prepare a liquid-fueled rocket.

Nuclear and Conventional Strategy

Much was said in the mid-1950s through the '60s about how to deter a nuclear war and about how to win one. The notion that there could, in any meaningful sense, be a real "winner" after a full-on nuclear exchange has long since been discarded both in Washington and Moscow, and the very idea of theorizing about how a nuclear exchange would play out to a successful conclusion seems ludicrous. Eisenhower suggested as much, more than six decades ago, when he ended a nuclear-war strategy session by observing: "We don't have enough bulldozers to scrape the bodies off the streets."[64] No theory for winning a nuclear war is offered here. But even on the US side, in the early years of the Cold War, national security strategists explicitly contemplated the possibility that a nuclear war might not be a short war. In a meeting of the National Security Council in November 1950, thirteen months after the USSR successfully denotated an atomic bomb, Secretary of State Dean Acheson allowed, somewhat phlegmatically, that "we must expect to lose some of our production capability in any atomic attack." His solution was "to produce a reserve of end items [military equipment and munitions] to tide us over the period of lost production due to atomic attack."[65]

Setting the stage: a melange of old and new doctrine, East and West. In the mid-1950s, the Soviet Army had 175 active divisions, far exceeding anything NATO could deploy, under a unified command or otherwise. As important as the Soviets' clear preponderance of strength in conventional forces was the fact that military planners in Moscow now had a glacis that Peter I or Catherine II could only have dreamed of. The

Russian heartland, and indeed all the western Soviet republics, could, more effectively than ever, be defended from ground forces by trading space for time. Military planners in the capitals of the Western European nations had no such luxury.

Also in the mix for East and West (but perhaps with more impact in the East) was the fact that political and military leaders had lived through the searing experiences of World War II. Consequently, the articles of faith for military strategists in Moscow were not at all complicated. The keys were conventional force strength, preparedness, the Warsaw Pact satellites' compliance with Moscow's security-related requirements, and the ability to exploit the battle-tested strategy of defense in depth. Soviet advances in nuclear weaponry and rocketry, welcome though they were in the Kremlin, would never render these fundamental elements of Soviet military doctrine obsolete. But as Khrushchev consolidated his political position in the Soviet hierarchy, he added some new dimensions to the East-West dynamic. The historical record, beginning at least as early as the July 1955 Geneva summit, plainly shows that, for all of his bluff and bluster, Khrushchev recognized that possession of nuclear weapons carried with it the obligation to manage East-West relations so as to minimize the likelihood of a nuclear holocaust. Khrushchev's challenge, in touting the virtues of peaceful coexistence in and after the mid-1950s, was that he was starting out with a doctrinal hill to climb.

At the Twentieth Party Congress, Khrushchev eased his comrades over the doctrinal hill—the Marxist prediction of war with the capitalists—by suggesting that war was not "fatalistically inevitable." Obviously, that concession to the possibility of lasting peace did not do away with the need to deter war (quite the contrary), or to fight, and win, a war if there was to be war. The concept of victory, whatever that might ultimately amount to in practical terms, still had meaning for the Kremlin leadership. In their eyes, as David Holloway writes, "War might not be inevitable, but neither was it impossible. Moreover, if it occurred, it would end in victory for socialism. The goal of military strategy, therefore, was victory in a world nuclear war."[66]

Strategic doctrine in the West: massive retaliation. Khrushchev's advocacy of peaceful coexistence at the Twentieth Party Congress in early 1956 was well known in Washington within days after the Congress ended. Nevertheless, the official view of Soviet intentions was less sanguine. A strong current of US opinion held, as the National Security Council reported to the president a month after the launch of Sputnik-1, that Soviet intentions were expansionist, and that Soviet "efforts to build military power go beyond any concepts of Soviet defense."[67] The challenge, as it was seen in Washington, was to come up with a way to deter the Russians from acting on their natural expansionist instincts. For a country (and an alliance) that had no intent to start a war with the USSR, by surprise attack or otherwise, the challenge of deterrence was to convince the Russians that US retaliation for a Soviet attack would be certain to raise the cost of Soviet aggression to a level that would be entirely unacceptable to the Kremlin. Consequently, after both the United States and the USSR had in place an operational nuclear-strike capability, one of the predominant objectives of nuclear strategy was to develop and maintain a fearsome *second*—retaliatory—strike capability. The question, in terms of strategic-deterrence doctrine, was, What do we want the Russians to think our retaliation will consist of, and what do we want them to think it will take to trigger that retaliation? Eisenhower and Dulles had some definite ideas about that.

Aside from his remarkably deep appreciation of the nonmilitary consequences of military spending, Eisenhower understood that, even within the confines of military spending, any expenditure of defense dollars on unneeded military assets (such as a weapon system designed to counter a non-existent or overstated threat) could itself degrade the ability of the United States to defend itself. Driven by the firm belief that the Cold War was going to be a very protracted struggle, the Eisenhower administration devised a defense doctrine intended to leverage defense dollars by deterring both an all-out attack and any smaller scale (Korea-style) forms of aggression the Russians might have in mind. This was the doctrine of massive retaliation. At the heart of it was the "New Look," based on the proposition that the use of nuclear weapons would not necessarily be a last resort (chapter 10).

In fiscal terms, the result of the doctrine of massive retaliation was that expenditures on conventional forces could be substantially reduced in favor of a massive buildup of nuclear weapons, to be available for first use, with the intended effect of deterring anything from a conventional assault through the Fulda Gap to an all-out nuclear exchange. And, of course, an essential component of the doctrine of massive retaliation was the administration's willingness, actually eagerness, to talk about it in public.

Almost by definition, US defense doctrine became NATO doctrine, and Eisenhower's decisive victory in the 1956 presidential election assured the continuation of his defense doctrine. The West's reservation of the prerogative of resorting to nuclear weapons in virtually any armed conflict was unequivocally reiterated in a formal communiqué from the Atlantic Council in May 1957: "The Atlantic alliance must be in a position to use all available means to meet any attack which might be launched against it."[68]

The acceptance of the doctrine of massive retaliation by European NATO allies is a testament to the credibility the United States enjoyed in the 1950s with those European partners. Implicit in European reliance on the massive-retaliation doctrine were the assumptions that (1) the United States would actually be willing to face the possibility of a full-on nuclear exchange, for the sake of preventing (or, if necessary, defeating) a conventional Soviet assault in Europe, and (2) the Kremlin's perception of US resolve would be sufficient to deter an attack. Those assumptions are at least as critical now as they were when Khrushchev was in the Kremlin. Not for nothing did NSC-162/2 state without equivocation that "our allies must be genuinely convinced that our strategy is one of collective security," and that "firm confidence in the steadiness and wisdom of U.S. leadership" was essential.[69] And, on that score, not for nothing did French President Charles de Gaulle later put to President Kennedy the question of whether the United States "was prepared to act by trading New York for Paris."[70]

Eisenhower, who had served as the supreme allied commander for the D-Day invasion, may well have been one of a tiny handful of American leaders (if, indeed, there were any other than Eisenhower) who could have engendered confidence in European capitals that the United States, insulated by an ocean from a conventional Russian assault, would actually risk a devastating nuclear attack on its homeland for the sake of deterring an attack by Soviet conventional forces in Europe. The vague language of Article 5 of the North Atlantic Treaty, obligating the United States to take only "such action as it deems necessary," was demonstrably weaker than the corresponding language of the Warsaw Pact, the Rio Pact, or the Brussels Treaty (chapter 5). With the doctrine of massive retaliation, the

United States was saying: "Trust us, we'll do what it takes to deter the Russians, or defeat them if necessary, even if we have to up the ante by putting the US heartland at risk." That trust, assuredly not compelled by the language of the North Atlantic Treaty, was the product of European confidence in the elected leaders on the other side of the Atlantic.

That trust was made all the more remarkable by the fact that the doctrine of massive retaliation potentially forfeited the benefit of escalation dominance—the ability to exert effective control over the level at which a conflict will play out. A nation which has the upper hand in an armed conflict does not *decisively* have the upper hand unless, in addition to dominating on the field of battle, it also has the ability to deter the opposing regime from attempting to turn the tide by escalating the conflict to a higher level. This requires the capacity, in terms of military assets and doctrine governing their use, to confront the enemy with costs of escalation significantly exceeding the probable benefits. An example would be an asymmetrical ability (withheld for the time being) to inflict massive civilian casualties. In Cold War terms, the consequence of yielding escalation dominance to the Kremlin in a European war would have been that the USSR could put NATO to a choice between defeat or ratcheting the violence up to a level that would put the continental United States at grave risk of a catastrophic outcome—all for the sake of saving European NATO partners.

European trust in US intentions did require some maintenance from time to time. European members of NATO were alert for anything coming out of Washington that might raise a question (especially in the Kremlin) about the reliability of the US commitment under Article 5 of the North Atlantic Treaty. This is why, in 1959, an unguarded statement by Christian Herter, Eisenhower's nominee to succeed the ailing Foster Dulles as secretary of state, had to be walked back by the State Department. At his senate confirmation hearing in April 1959, Herter testified that he could not "conceive of the President of the United States involving us in an all-out nuclear war unless the facts showed clearly that we are in danger of devastation ourselves, or that actual moves have been made toward devastating ourselves."[71] After European leaders had an opportunity to digest that snippet, the department had to do some damage control. All US embassies in NATO capitals were informed by the chief of missions in Washington (with quotations from Herter's testimony) that "we have noticed evidence of certain misgivings in Europe . . . concerning US readiness [to] use atomic weapons in defense of another NATO country if US itself is not attacked." The embassies were instructed to assure "foreign officials" that any interpretation that Herter's testimony suggested "a reservation on part of US is wholly foreign to Secretary's views and intent."[72]

This, then, is what deterrence, and, if necessary, the road map to victory, looked like in the West in the latter years of the Eisenhower administration. We will now look on the other side of the divide.

For Russia, it was (and probably still is) ultimately about control of territory. For the Russians, Cold War military strategy was the product of geography, climate, technology, and—not least—history. As for history, Russians recalled that foreign invaders, having reached Moscow in 1812 and 1941, had obliged the Russian army to march into Paris in 1814 and the Red Army to march into Berlin in 1945. In the opening decades of the Cold War, no one remembered this better than Vasiliy Danilovich Sokolovskiy, a marshal of the Soviet Union and chief of the Soviet General Staff from 1953 to 1960, who retired from the General Staff in 1970. His 1968 book, *Soviet Military Strategy*, has been authoritatively called "a military classic."[73] Echoing Marshal Zhukov's writings from the mid-1950s, Sokolovskiy wrote: "To achieve victory in a future war, it is not enough to have nuclear weapons and to have means for delivering them to a target with high accuracy; it is also necessary that the Ground Troops be able to move into regions which have been subjected to nuclear strikes."[74] To be sure, after the ICBMs with their nuclear warheads were in place on both sides, the Russians recognized that, as Soviet defense minister Rodion Malinovsky put it in a speech in the fall of 1962, a nuclear war "would be for us an exceptionally severe war." But, in the same breath, Marshal Malinovsky emphasized that "we are deeply convinced that in this war, if the imperialists thrust it upon us, the socialist camp will win and capitalism will be destroyed forever."[75]

The US assessment of Soviet doctrine—specifically, the importance of ground forces in achieving victory in a nuclear war—was the same. Writing in 1962, Dr. Raymond Garthoff, a CIA expert on Soviet doctrine and capabilities, observed that "victory, to the Soviets, requires defeating the enemy's military forces in order to seize and occupy vast areas of land—and in the final analysis only a ground force can do this. In a nuclear war this requirement may even be *greater* than in a non-nuclear one."[76] Declassified documents strongly support Garthoff's point.[77] Soviet military leaders were serious about developing the capacity to use ground forces to enter and subdue (to the extent anything might be left to subdue) territory devastated by nuclear weapons. But one major deficit in the USSR's otherwise formidable warfighting capability was the inability to occupy the United States after a thermonuclear exchange.[78] This, once again, was relevant to an assessment of the relationship—and degree of trust—between the United States and its European NATO partners. It may still be relevant, as otherworldly as that may seem. As recently as 2003, the Russian Ministry of Defense told the West that the role of ground forces in a major conflict will be to "consolidate the military success achieved [in the air, in outer space and at sea] and directly ensure the attainment of political goals."[79] To remove all doubt, the ministry concluded that "although gaining air supremacy and massive application of precision weapons are decisive in determining the outcome of armed struggle, they do not dispense with massive ground operations mounted by land forces."[80]

Mutual Assured Destruction (MAD). The doctrine of massive retaliation lasted less than ten years as US defense policy. To give Eisenhower and Dulles their due, it must be said that their doctrine served its purpose. The United States and its NATO allies were free from Soviet attack while Eisenhower was in office. But as US and Soviet scientists developed and tested hydrogen bombs with destructive power seemingly growing by orders of magnitude with each test, it became clear that it was necessary to reconsider a policy explicitly contemplating first use, let alone "massive" use, of nuclear weapons as a possible response to a less-than-existential threat.

The new reality was that nuclear physicists were hard put to tell national leaders what the limits to the destructive potential of the hydrogen bomb might be. In 1954, the Soviet atomic ministry, after evaluating the reports of a US test, reported to Khrushchev that "modern atomic practice, based on utilization of the reaction of fusion, opens a limitless potential for increasing the explosive power of the Bomb, which makes defense from this weapon virtually impossible. It is clear that the use of atomic arms on a massive scale will lead to the devastation of combatant countries." The prospect presented to Khrushchev and Malenkov was the prospect of "termination of all life on earth."[81] This, in 1954, was recognition of what, in 1961, Secretary of Defense Robert McNamara called "mutually assured destruction." McNamara and his colleagues came to the realization that East and West had clearly developed the capacity to devastate each other even *after* a first strike.[82] This reality led McNamara to recommend to Kennedy a force structure that would, "in the event of a Soviet nuclear attack," enable the United States, first, to destroy Soviet long-range nuclear forces "while, second, holding in protected reserve forces capable of destroying the Soviet urban society, if necessary, in a controlled and deliberate way."[83]

In the fall of 1961, rising East-West tensions led to the demise of an informal moratorium on nuclear-weapons testing. This culminated with the Soviet test, on October 30, 1961, of the "Tsar Bomba," the most powerful bomb ever detonated. The detonation of a bomb more than three thousand times more powerful than the bomb dropped on Hiroshima may or may not have been scientifically justified (that was a contested issue). But it is fair to say that the test marked a new high point in East-West tension in a remarkably fraught phase of the Cold War. During the year before the Soviet test, the US submarine-launched Polaris nuclear missiles had entered service, the US-backed invasion of Cuba at the Bay of Pigs had failed, and the Berlin Wall had been built, bringing tensions over Berlin to a boil.

The fully matured, mutual retaliatory-strike capability that McNamara called mutually assured destruction was, in terms of nuclear warfare logic, a new, qualitatively different kind of deterrence. It was now unmistakably clear that a full-on nuclear attack would be deterred—not by the entire panoply of nuclear weapons at the ready in the silos, bombers, and submarines, but by a nuclear force that could either be launched before being rendered inert by a first strike or survive a first strike and inflict a devastating retaliatory strike. Both the United States and the USSR had had first strike capability for several years. It was not until the 1960s that the far more stable deterrent effect of credible retaliatory strike capability was in place on both sides of the East-West divide.

The enduring dilemma resulting from the undeniable fact of mutually assured destruction is, What would happen without it? This is obviously not an idle inquiry. In the fall of 1972, Professor (and future national security advisor) Zbigniew Brzezinski pointed out what he deemed to be "the extraordinarily salutary effect of nuclear weapons." He explained that "in a more traditional setting, without the restraining effect of nuclear weapons, it is likely, given mutual hostility and occasionally very sharp provocations, that a major American-Soviet war would have occurred."[84] Of course, the disadvantage of having the nuclear arsenals, with their hoped-for deterrent effect, is that the possibility of a catastrophic miscalculation or operational blunder cannot be excluded. A declassified 1977 memorandum to Brzezinski (as national security advisor) from the secretary of defense advised Brzezinski that, with a nuclear weapon targeting plan focused on economic targets in the USSR, a US nuclear attack would kill 33 percent of the Soviet population (more than eighty-four million persons). Direct targeting of the Soviet population, rather than economic targets, was projected to result in 44 percent fatalities (about 115 million persons).[85]

Armageddon has been averted, so far.

Chapter 13

From Camelot to Saigon

The Cold War rules of engagement, well established by 1960, served both sides admirably. The rules of engagement kept improvident decisions (some of which were garnished with large measures of dishonesty, hubris, or both) from resulting in a nuclear holocaust.

The 1960 Election

When he was inaugurated in January 1961, President John F. Kennedy was the youngest president of the United States, the first one born in the twentieth century, and the first Catholic. He won the popular vote by a tiny margin over Richard M. Nixon—113,000 votes out of 68.8 million cast. The 1960 election was not, of course, the first presidential election of the Cold War. But it was the first election in which the voters had good reason to believe that the main geopolitical adversary of the United States now had the ability, on very short notice, to incinerate major US population centers. Not since the last British soldiers returned home at the end of the War of 1812 had there been any reason for serious concern about the security of the continental United States.

The run-up to the election. East-West tensions were high after the collapse of the Paris summit in May 1960. U-2 pilot Francis Gary Powers was still incarcerated east of Moscow. In the eyes of Khrushchev and the Presidium, the USSR had an edge on the United States in terms of global public opinion. As far as they were concerned, the next move was up to the Americans, but they knew that any serious diplomatic movement would have to await the outcome of the election.

On the US side, anticommunism still had two decidedly different flavors. There was strident, ideologically driven anticommunism (we could call it election-year anticommunism), which some Republicans thought might still be a good wedge issue against the Democrats. Overlapping with that, but with a somewhat different look and feel, was the broader set of geopolitical and policy issues: just what should we do, militarily and diplomatically, to hold the Soviet Union in check?

As for the strident strain of anticommunism, ironically, with McCarthy dead and McCarthyism no longer acceptable in polite circles, a cleaner (but still strident) variety of anticommunism was very much in the political mix. Symbolic gestures could touch responsive chords. In July 1959, Congress designated the third week in July "Captive Nations Week." The congressional resolution decried the "imperialistic and aggressive policies of Russian communism" that had "resulted in the creation of a vast empire which poses a dire threat to the security of the United States and of all the free peoples of the world."[1] The nations designated as Captive Nations included all the Soviet satellites in Eastern Europe and almost all the Soviet republics other than Russia. The resolution was sponsored by legislators from Illinois, Massachusetts, Michigan, and New York, all of which had (and have) substantial populations with roots in the designated Captive Nations.

A few days after the Captive Nations resolution was passed, Vice President Nixon hosted Khrushchev at the US pavilion of the American National Exhibition in Moscow (a cultural exchange resulting from the thaw). Khrushchev chose this as the venue for an attack on the Captive Nations resolution, which Nixon expertly parlayed into the famous "Kitchen Debate," bolstering his standing as one US official who could go toe to toe with Khrushchev. This set-to with Khrushchev—politically priceless—dovetailed nicely with Nixon's posture as the statesman (and presumptive 1960 Republican presidential candidate) who had, as vice president, visited nearly seventy countries. Nixon's point during the 1960 campaign was that Kennedy would be "a well intentioned, but naïve president," whereas Nixon was "a man Nikita Khrushchev and the Communists cannot mislead or delude."[2] It comes as no surprise, then, that early in the election year, Nixon staked out national security and foreign policy as the dominant issues for the 1960 campaign.[3]

For his part, Kennedy had to defend himself on two fronts—anticommunism and religion. He handled the religion question with characteristic adroitness, neutralizing the whispers about the influence the pope might have on a Catholic president. As for anticommunism, Kennedy's approach, understandable for the candidate of a party that had been out of the White House for nearly eight years, was to talk about US weaknesses, leading Republicans to accuse him of "giving aid and comfort to Communists." This obliged Kennedy to make it clear that "the enemy is the Communist system itself—implacable, insatiable, unceasing in its drive for world domination."[4]

The Russians preferred Kennedy's brand of anticommunism over Nixon's—and they acted on that preference. In the heat of the fall campaign, Averell Harriman brought his Russian experience (going back more than six decades) and contacts into the fray on Kennedy's behalf. Harriman directed a special plea to Khrushchev, "beseeching him to be equally tough on both presidential candidates, lest he help the Republicans by seeming to favor the Democrats."[5] Khrushchev went Harriman one better. He instructed the KGB station chief in Washington to "propose measures, diplomatic, propagandist" or otherwise, to help Kennedy win the election.[6] This, it should be noted, was an instance of Russian interference in a US presidential election—solicited from the American side.

Kennedy makes his national security case. As has been seen (and, from the vantage point of the third decade of the twenty-first century, oddly enough), in the Truman and Eisenhower administrations, the Democrats were the spenders on national defense and the Republicans were the penny pinchers. The Eisenhower-Dulles massive retaliation doctrine was, as much as anything else, a strategy for deterring the Russians as inexpensively as possible. This, together with the lingering embarrassment over the Soviets' Sputnik successes, gave Kennedy an opening in the 1960 campaign.

Hoping to put Nixon on the defensive, Kennedy reprised his arguments, first advanced in 1958, about a missile gap that left the United States vulnerable to Soviet attack. His missile-gap claim triggered some helpful commentary, including a column by Joseph Alsop: "In the period of the missile gap, which we have now entered, the [bomber] bases in the United States and overseas are nakedly exposed to the Kremlin's long-range and medium-range rockets."[7] In fact, there was no missile gap.[8] Some competent and highly respected historians have written that Kennedy was probably well aware that there actually was not a missile gap,[9] but like successful Democratic presidential candidates throughout the Cold War era, Kennedy found it necessary, on any military or national security issue, to protect his right flank. This was especially true, of course, when the opposing candidate was as experienced as Nixon was in getting political leverage out of the communist threat. (And it is worth noting that, at the height of the fall campaign, Khrushchev succeeded in keeping concerns about the USSR—and, specifically, the stability of Soviet leadership—on the front pages when he registered his protest of the proceedings in the UN General Assembly by removing his shoe and pounding it on the desk, "adding to the lengthening list of antics with which he has been nettling the General Assembly."[10])

A campaign preview of problems ninety miles offshore. In early 1959, Fidel Castro and his fellow revolutionaries triumphantly marched into Havana, having overthrown the dictatorship of President Fulgencio Batista. At that point, there was no particular reason to anticipate Castro's bloody post-bellum reign of terror or his wholesale expropriation of US-owned property in Cuba. In the immediate aftermath of the Cuban Revolution, Kennedy did not, by nature or as a matter of policy or political expedience, have any reason to be hostile toward the Castro regime. He went so far as to describe Castro as "part of the legacy of Bolivar," and he had been critical of Dulles's policy of support for Batista.[11] But all this was before Fidel Castro, Cuba's new revolutionary leader, made his own contribution to the 1960 campaign.

Castro had gotten off to a fast start in building his socialist paradise. On September 26, at the height of the fall campaign, and with an admiring Premier Khrushchev in the audience at the UN General Assembly, Castro ranted about the depredations of Cuba's neighbor to the north. Castro described Kennedy as "a millionaire, illiterate and ignorant." Kennedy was never again heard to liken Castro to Simón Bolivar. In a comment in his UN speech that eerily foreshadowed the disastrous Bay of Pigs invasion a year and a half later, Castro also castigated Kennedy for thinking "that socially it's possible today to carry out a guerrilla warfare in Cuba."[12] Given the then-existing triangulation between Kennedy, Nixon, and communism, Kennedy could only have been delighted at being attacked by the new leader of the country the Republicans had, by Kennedy's reckoning, lost to communism. Kennedy made the most of Castro's gift. In October, Kennedy lamented that "we have lost Cuba, 90 miles from our shores," for which his prescription was that "we must attempt to strengthen the non-Batista democratic anti-Castro forces in exile, and in Cuba itself, who offer eventual hope of overthrowing Castro."[13] (In another comment foreshadowing things to come, Kennedy augmented his complaint that "we have lost Cuba" with the observation that Cuba was only "a few minutes, as the medium-range rocket flies, from Miami." The world would reach the brink of nuclear war during the Cuban missile crisis exactly two years later.)

We have now become accustomed to interference by one sovereign state in the internal affairs of another, but Kennedy's proposal to support the overthrow of the Castro regime provoked pointed comments by both Nixon and James Reston. Nixon called Kennedy's idea "the most shockingly reckless proposal ever made in our history by a Presidential candidate during a campaign."[14] Nixon's comment can be discounted as campaign hyperbole, but Reston called Kennedy's proposal "probably his worst blunder of the campaign" and "a clear violation of the inter-American treaty prohibition against intervention in the internal affairs of the hemisphere republics."[15] (That said, in the same column, Reston observed that, with the benefit of his strong performances in the televised debates, Kennedy had "at least held his own" against Nixon and "is now riding the powerful engine of his party.")

The 1960 outcome: a new direction for national security. The last of the four televised debates of the 1960 campaign was held on October 21, long enough before the election to give Nixon the opportunity to finish the campaign on his own terms. Because Kennedy had come across in the debates as a poised, knowledgeable, and well-prepared (to say nothing of likable) candidate, Nixon knew he had to regain some ground on the issue of Kennedy's youth and inexperience.

For his part, though Eisenhower endorsed Nixon in the 1960 campaign, he generally stayed above the fray. But Nixon's relentless effort to capitalize on his eight years of experience at the highest level of the executive branch was not aided by Eisenhower's answer, at a press conference in late August, to an inquiry as to whether Nixon had come up with any ideas that had been adopted by Eisenhower as president: "If you give me a week, I might think of one. I don't remember."[16]

Kennedy's exceedingly narrow popular vote victory translated into a healthy margin in the Electoral College (303 to 219), mainly because many states went one way or the other by a small margin.

Eisenhower's farewell; Kennedy's flexible response. This brings us to another of the great paradoxes of the Cold War. To the end of his presidency, Eisenhower spoke—with credibility befitting a five-star general—of the "grave implications" of spiraling defense spending and the concomitant growth of what he called the "military-industrial complex." He lamented the influence, "economic, political, even spiritual," of "an immense military establishment," concluding that "in the councils of government, we must guard against the acquisition of unwarranted influence, whether sought or unsought, by the military-industrial complex. The potential for the disastrous rise of misplaced power exists and will persist."[17]

Kennedy thought the Eisenhower administration's massive retaliation strategy was potentially suicidal.[18] The result was the "flexible response" doctrine developed by Kennedy and his secretary of defense, Robert McNamara. The fundamental premise for flexible response was that the United States, no longer the sole power capable of launching (or, of equal importance, threatening) a devastating strategic nuclear strike, had no choice but to prepare itself to mount a carefully calibrated response to aggression at any point along the entire gamut of potential Soviet military threats.

Implementation of the flexible response doctrine required a tremendous increase in military forces, armaments, and spending by the Kennedy administration. The army grew from eleven to sixteen divisions. The navy doubled its fleet. By the mid-1960s, the air force had twenty-three tactical squadrons, up from sixteen at the end of the Eisenhower administration. The continuing build-up of the strategic nuclear arsenal matched the growth of conventional forces.

Although there were fewer than twenty thousand US military personnel actually in Vietnam when Kennedy was assassinated in November 1963, most of the conventional forces which would be needed by Kennedy's successor, Lyndon Johnson, were in place when he succeeded to the presidency on that November day.

Chapter 13

The Bay of Pigs Fiasco

The Cold War era was marked by an extraordinary series of cause-and-effect relationships among seemingly disparate events. That, of course, does not make the Cold War era unique. But whether we look at the momentous chain of events from 1946 to 1948 or at the consequences for US defense policy of Stalin's decision to foment and support the North Korean invasion of South Korea, we see that it is not unusual for the consequences of major decisions to be *both* natural and probable *and* unanticipated. So it was with the Bay of Pigs.

On April 12, 1961 (as it happens, the day Soviet air force major Yuri Gargarin became the first person to orbit the earth), President Kennedy held a press conference. He told the nation (and the world) that "there will not be under any conditions, . . . an intervention in Cuba by United States armed forces." To remove all doubt, Kennedy elaborated that he "would be opposed to mounting an offensive" against Cuba.[19] The questions, and Kennedy's answers (disingenuous at the very best), had been prompted by persistent rumors that his government might be planning to support reported efforts by Cuban exiles to infiltrate Cuba, using guerilla tactics in an effort to establish a provisional government (promptly to be recognized by the United States), all of which would lead to the overthrow of the Castro regime. The rumors were correct.

Planning for the invasion got started in the Eisenhower administration. The new president's initial theory was that it would be a CIA operation, not an overt US military mission, and that initial success in mounting the invasion would trigger a popular uprising, quickly leading to the demise of the Castro regime. In late January, a few days after Kennedy was inaugurated, CIA director Allen Dulles briefed the new president on the plan. Kennedy was, by nature, intrigued by the CIA and its capabilities. But he held back, for the time being, on giving the go-ahead to the operation.[20] Kennedy was not alone in his interest in eliminating the Castro regime. Though the new administration's anti-communism was less strident and not as purely ideological as that of the Eisenhower administration, there was a strong school of thought that the very existence of a communist regime less than a hundred miles off the coast of Florida was a menace to the United States. Thus, though Paul Nitze, a newly appointed assistant secretary of defense, was uneasy about the Bay of Pigs operation, he firmly believed, as he later put it, that in the form of the Castro regime the "Soviet Union had inserted itself in our backyard by stealth and deception." As far as Nitze was concerned, "Like a spreading cancer, [the Castro regime] should, if possible, be excised from the Americas."[21]

The new president's initial misgivings about the Cuban adventure were allayed by reports from the training camp in Guatemala and by his own firm belief in his good luck. As for the reports, the advice to Kennedy was that the leaders of the invasion force were convinced that "after they have inflicted one serious defeat upon the opposition forces, the latter will melt away from Castro, whom they have no wish to support."[22] As for the luck, Schlesinger's first-hand account, based on his service as a special assistant to Kennedy, recorded that "everyone around him thought he had the Midas touch and could not lose."[23] In mid-April, Kennedy gave his final approval to the operation. This was not the first (nor would it be the last) attempt by the United States to overthrow a communist government with which it was not at war (see chapter 1).

The small invasion fleet reached the south coast of Cuba early on the seventeenth. It immediately ran into heavy resistance. Though the landing had been preceded by a few air strikes, the Kennedy administration had modified the CIA's original plans, which had called for direct US air support for the invasion if that was necessary to enable the invasion forces to establish a beachhead. Diplomatic protests were lodged within hours of the initial assault. Consequently, for fear of revealing the extent of US involvement in the invasion, even the previously approved air support was withheld. Castro's forces crushed the invasion within days.

Dissembling about the US role in the invasion did not end with Kennedy's public statements. In a debate at the United Nations on April 17, during that very short interval before the disastrous outcome became apparent, Ambassador Adlai Stevenson—having been given incomplete if not outright false information by his State Department superiors—told his UN colleagues that "the United States has committed no aggression against Cuba and no offensive has been launched from Florida or from any other part of the United States."[24] Although the second part of Stevenson's statement was literally true (because the invasion was not launched from Florida), the first part was plainly false. The fiction that the invasion was entirely the work of a band of Cuban patriots who were dedicated to overthrowing Fidel Castro was no more successful as a cover-up than Eisenhower's attempt at deception as to the purpose of the ill-fated flight of Francis Gary Powers in the U-2 incident, a little less than a year before the Bay of Pigs debacle.

One hundred fourteen of the invaders were killed and nearly 1,200 were taken prisoner. Castro fully understood the value of the 1,200 prisoners, alive and incarcerated in a Cuban prison, so he did not have them shot (a fate which befell many others in the Cuban Revolution). In December 1962, the Bay of Pigs prisoners were ransomed by the United States for $53 million worth of food and pharmaceuticals. The first of the released prisoners arrived in Miami on December 23.

Castro's defeat of an invasion known by the entire world to have been sponsored by the United States was also a stunning propaganda victory. Irritating though that may have been to the Kennedy administration, much more significant was the fact that Khrushchev believed that the invasion—a half-baked, half-hearted adventure—gave him some valuable insights into John F. Kennedy. Half-hearted military operations were not—as witness Hungary in 1956—the way the Russians went about their business.

Khrushchev, despite some occasional shows of bravado, was not at base a reckless leader (impetuous, yes; habitually reckless, no). As recounted by former Soviet Ambassador Oleg Troyanovski, the Bay of Pigs fiasco had a major influence on Khrushchev's estimation of the new president.[25] Khrushchev was emboldened, which affected his approach to dealing with Kennedy in the Cuban missile crisis in October 1962.[26] And as will be seen, even before the Cuban missile crisis, Khrushchev's estimation of Kennedy manifested itself in Berlin.

Six decades on, some aspects of the Bay of Pigs almost defy belief. In 1961, the senior US defense and intelligence establishment—from the president on down—consisted of World War II veterans, from all the services, from all the commands within those services, and from all levels within those commands. They had seen the results of good planning and bad planning. They had seen the results of well-supported combined-arms operations and poorly supported combined-arms operations. They nevertheless undertook to plan and execute a military operation while attempting to preserve the ability to deny any involvement with it. Related to that is the fact that the Bay of Pigs fiasco illustrates what Robert

Jervis called "the costs of unsuccessful lying." Lying in wartime is one thing. During the blitz in 1940 and 1941, Churchill and his government used disinformation to save thousands of lives. But lying in peacetime, when hopes still hang on prospects for success in diplomacy, is quite another matter. As Jervis explained: "It is in a state's interest to be believed, and an important determinant of whether it will be believed in any given situation is its reputation for telling the truth and doing what it says it will do."[27] It is to Kennedy's everlasting credit that, by October 1962, he and his national security team were able to regain enough credibility to avert nuclear war.

Operation Mongoose. Humiliation at the Bay of Pigs only sharpened Kennedy's desire to rid the Western Hemisphere of the Castro regime. He pressed for new proposals for covert operations against the regime, and he brought new faces to the table. The president's brother, Robert, could summon a special kind of relentlessness when necessary. That is likely the reason the president put Attorney General Robert F. Kennedy on the team tasked with getting rid of the Cuban dictator. Kennedy the president and Kennedy the attorney general pushed hard for what we could now call a "whole of government" approach to overthrowing the Castro regime.[28] Proposals for covert operations aimed at overthrow were submitted to and coordinated by an interagency team called Special Group (Augmented), created by the president in November 1961. The "augmented" feature was the inclusion of the attorney general in the very select group. The overthrow project was called Operation Mongoose.

As witness the fact that the regime founded by Castro is in its seventh decade, Operation Mongoose did not accomplish its objective. Some of the proposals that were bandied about at high levels in the Kennedy administration were carried out; most were not. What is telling, for our purposes, is the quality and level of attention the problem of Castro's Cuba commanded as a sequel to the failed Bay of Pigs operation.

Attorney General Robert Kennedy's role in Operation Mongoose was essentially that of an overseer. From a legal standpoint, there was nothing particularly complex about the operation, nothing that could not easily have been addressed by the legal staff of the Department of Defense. The short version of that part of the story is that the execution of a scheme to use subversion and violent means to bring about the overthrow of the government of a sovereign state plainly contravened numerous norms of international law, not the least of which was the Rio Pact of 1947. Robert Kennedy was included in the Special Group (Augmented) not because his legal acumen was needed but because he was to serve as the president's personal representative to see to it that the project did not get mired in the defense and national-security bureaucracy. On that point, Lieutenant General Marshall Carter, serving as deputy director of the CIA, "privately compared [Robert] Kennedy's performances at Mongoose meetings to the gnawing of an enraged rat terrier."[29]

Plans for Operation Mongoose and its military component, Operation Northwoods, began to come together in late 1961, several months after the Bay of Pigs. But nothing on the scale of the preliminary plans submitted to the joint Chiefs of Staff was carried out, and President Kennedy suspended Operation Mongoose in mid-October 1962, when the Soviet missile bases in Cuba were discovered. Perhaps it will come as no surprise that Robert McNamara, Kennedy's secretary of defense, would later testify before a Senate committee that: "We were hysterical about Castro at the time of the Bay of Pigs and thereafter, and . . . there was pressure from [President Kennedy and the Attorney General] to do something about Castro."[30] The result of the hysteria, the committee found, was that "the effort to assassinate Castro began in 1960 and continued until 1965."[31]

Castro survived President Kennedy by fifty-three years.

Khrushchev, Kennedy, and Credibility

The broader story of Khrushchev and Kennedy is a dramatic story of credibility squandered and credibility regained. For Americans, this is of more than passing interest in the third decade of the twenty-first century. The story begins in Berlin, stays there for a while, and ends in Cuba.

Though the leaders of the satellite nations were fairly docile subjects of Soviet hegemony for a few decades, the people—especially the East Germans—who lived in those countries were among the least so. As early as the fall of 1950, the voters of East Berlin mocked the East German regime by mailing in ration-card stubs—more than 375,000 of them, representing nearly half the eligible voters—instead of voting in local elections in East Berlin.[32] Dissatisfaction in the East did not abate with the passage of time.

By the late 1950s, East Germany was hemorrhaging precious human capital to the West. The escape route was the Berlin subway, which ran freely throughout the city. The wave of emigration—3.4 million by the summer of 1961—included hundreds of thousands of young and talented Germans, including physicians, academics, teachers, and technical specialists. This was precisely the kind of talent East Germany desperately needed if it was going to have any hope of offering a way of life comparable to that which was so clearly available on the other side of the Brandenburg Gate. In Berlin, the emigration problem was aggravated by the fact that East Berliners could receive radio and television broadcasts from the West, with the result that, to a far greater extent than in the other satellite nations, the East Berliners were under no illusions as to how they fared compared with their erstwhile compatriots. For many of those left in East Germany, passive resistance to the repressive Walter Ulbricht regime was the main source of personal (if not economic) satisfaction.

For the Kremlin and the East German regime, the emigration problem reached the crisis stage by late 1959. In December 1959, the Soviet ambassador to the GDR summed up the situation for his Kremlin colleagues with classic bureaucratic understatement: "The presence in Berlin of an open and, to speak to the point, uncontrolled border between the socialist and capitalist worlds unwittingly prompts the population to make a comparison between both parts of the city, which, unfortunately, does not always turn out in favor of Democratic [East] Berlin."[33] In his seminal article, "On Peaceful Coexistence," in the October 1959 issue of *Foreign Affairs*, Khrushchev made it plain that he wanted a peace treaty that would formalize the de facto postwar borders of Germany.[34] What he didn't explicitly say, at that point, was that he wanted a juridical basis for ending western access to Berlin.

In late May 1961, Khrushchev decided to lay down his marker. He proposed, and the Presidium agreed, to pursue a separate peace treaty with the GDR. This was the first page of one of the most dramatic chapters of the Cold War. As the summer of 1961 approached, Khrushchev had the psychological upper hand. Francis Gary Powers languished in a Soviet prison. Yuri Gargarin's successful orbital flight in April had been a propaganda victory on par with the Sputnik launch in 1957. The Bay of Pigs debacle had been worse than an embarrassment, because it made Kennedy and his most trusted national security appointees look like callow amateurs, and faint-hearted ones at that. But one thing that was not obvious in the West was that Khrushchev, for his part, was also under pressure. Every leader who mattered in the USSR was a veteran of the Great Patriotic War. Among their shared life's lessons was the unshakable belief that there is no adequate substitute for geographic advantage, augmented by military power and—equally importantly—the will to use it. Consequently, Khrushchev's emphasis on peaceful coexistence did not sit well with some in the party leadership. Worse yet, unlike Stalin (and the Beria execution notwithstanding), Khrushchev was not in a position to deal with his perceived adversaries by having them shot. As Louis Halle put it, Khrushchev was, thus, a "dictator only by consent of the governing oligarchy in Moscow, [and was] in some sense on probation."[35] If he failed to deliver results, his detractors could get the upper hand.

Kennedy made the first move. He proposed a summit meeting, to be held in June, and Khrushchev readily accepted. Columnist Joseph Alsop aptly described it: Khrushchev "went to Vienna expecting to bullyrag President Kennedy into some sort of surrender at Berlin."[36] Khrushchev set the tone at the outset of the Vienna summit when he recalled, from his brief first contact with Kennedy (in 1956, when Kennedy was a US senator and Khrushchev was visiting the United States), that he (Khrushchev) had been told that Kennedy was "a young and promising man in politics."[37] One of the few things Kennedy and Khrushchev had in common was the fact that they both understood the cost of war on a very personal level, Khrushchev having lost a son and Kennedy having lost his older brother in World War II.

The agenda in Vienna may as well have consisted of only one word: Berlin. Khrushchev told Kennedy that the Soviet Union wanted to conclude a German peace treaty to bring a formal end to World War II and give legal force to the then-existing borders in Eastern Europe. Absent a multiparty treaty, Khrushchev announced his intent to sign a separate treaty with the GDR. Khrushchev set a deadline of the end of the year for the West to come to an agreement. Without an agreement, as Khrushchev put it, "the state of war will cease and all commitments stemming from Germany's surrender will become invalid. This would include all institutions, occupation rights, and access to Berlin, including the corridors."[38] Kennedy's response can fairly be regarded as marking the beginning of his recoupment of the credibility his administration had so recently lost: "If we were to accept the Soviet proposal US commitments would be regarded as a mere scrap of paper." On the same day, after lunch, Kennedy and Khrushchev met privately (with interpreters only), at Kennedy's request. Khrushchev made it clear that "the decision to sign a peace treaty is firm and irrevocable and the Soviet Union will sign it in December if the US refuses an interim agreement." Kennedy "concluded the conversation by observing that it would be a cold winter."[39] The Vienna summit was over.

Kennedy was hard on himself—probably too hard—in his evaluation of his own performance at the Vienna summit. He confided to Reston of the *New York Times* that he had been "savaged" by Khrushchev in Vienna.[40] "It was the worst thing in my life."[41] But Kennedy really could not have hoped to accomplish more in Vienna than to demonstrate that he could not be cowed into making concessions to a counterpart who thought he had the upper hand (and was under some pressure to produce results). Kennedy did demonstrate that he could not be pushed around. That, in the circumstances, was a good day's work. Another benefit, from Kennedy's standpoint, was that, as recorded by Charles Bohlen (who was in the room for Kennedy's long session with Khrushchev on June 4), "the Vienna talks conditioned the President for the crises on Berlin and Cuba that were soon to follow."[42]

US press coverage of Kennedy's performance at the Vienna summit was generally friendly, a result which was probably attributable in no small measure to the fact that the sour encounter in Vienna was vastly overshadowed by the wildly enthusiastic reception (with commensurate press coverage) accorded the radiant First Lady, Jacqueline Bouvier Kennedy, when the Kennedys stopped in Paris on their way to Vienna. And it may well be that the most astute thing Kennedy did before leaving Paris to sit across the table from Khrushchev in Vienna was to meet with the NATO council to say, quite simply, that "I want to restate again the strong commitment of my country to the defense of Western Europe."[43]

The gravity of the standoff over Berlin was serious enough that Kennedy reached out for the counsel of Dean Acheson, one of the most venerable of the Wise Men who had guided US policy in the early years of the Cold War. Acheson, a lawyer in private practice in 1961, willingly gave unvarnished advice to Kennedy. That advice, rendered in a long memorandum less than a month after the Vienna summit, went straight to the issues of national resolve and credibility: "At present, Khrushchev has demonstrated that he believes his will will prevail because the United States and its allies will not do what is necessary to stop him."[44] Acheson's diagnosis was that there had been a "decline in the effectiveness of the [nuclear] deterrent." He prescribed strong medicine. The United States must be willing, he wrote, to threaten to use—and to use—nuclear weapons. There must be "a change in Soviet appraisal of U.S. willingness to go to nuclear war," because "the problem is how to restore the credibility of the deterrent."[45] (While he was at it, Acheson recommended that the administration "should try to convince the USSR that it would and could, in the event of a Berlin crisis, stir up dissidence in East Germany and Eastern Europe."[46] Acheson thus suggested explicitly, albeit quietly, letting the Russians know what US special services might be able to accomplish with covert action.)

Acheson's recommendations were toward the hawkish end of the spectrum of advice Kennedy was receiving. Although Kennedy did not implement the full gamut of aggressive moves advocated by Acheson, the president, surely feeling about as lonely as any president has ever felt, concluded that decisive action was imperative to rectify the credibility deficit Acheson had so bluntly described. This is a study in political and geopolitical courage. Kennedy was willing to tell the nation what the stakes were and what his proposed solution would cost. And he was willing to risk nuclear war.

In a nationally televised address on July 25, 1961 (crafted with the help of Theodore Sorenson), Kennedy did not mince words: "In Berlin, as you recall, [Premier Khrushchev] intends to bring to an end, through a stroke of the pen, first our legal rights to be in West Berlin and secondly our ability to make good on our commitment to the two million free people of that city. That we cannot permit."[47] Kennedy told the nation that he would request $3.2 billion in new funding, to support 217,000 additional military service members. He ordered that "our draft calls be doubled and tripled in the coming months," and he activated reserve airlift and tactical squadrons in the air force, as well as 150,000 army reservists. Kennedy squarely addressed the possibility that the cost of the administration's response to Khrushchev's threat would lead to an unacceptable federal budget deficit: "Should an increase in taxes be needed—because of events in the next few months—to achieve [a balanced budget], or because of subsequent defense rises, those increased taxes will be requested in January." And leaving no room for doubt as to his assessment of the gravity of the situation, Kennedy introduced Americans to the concept of public nuclear fallout shelters: "Tomorrow, I am requesting of the Congress new funds for the following immediate objectives: to identify and mark space in existing structures public and private that could be used for fall-out shelters in case of attack; to stock those shelters with food, water, first-aid kits and other minimum essentials for survival."[48] A fair reading of the historical record from those tense days tells us that Kennedy genuinely believed that there was more than a negligible chance that Americans would actually need the fallout shelters.

After Kennedy's speech, Khrushchev ratcheted up the rhetoric, but Kennedy held firm on the German question. US-Soviet tensions were now higher than at any time since the blockade.[49] Here is where the unwritten norms of the Cold War rules of engagement once again came into play, perhaps saving millions of lives. In July alone, thirty thousand refugees crossed into West Berlin, intent on breathing the free air of the West even if they had to start over with only the few possessions they could carry. It was as obvious to the Kremlin as it was to the Ulbricht regime that the GDR was rapidly being hollowed out. East Germany, the critical western front of the glacis, would soon become a basket case, raising the specter of German reunification on terms favorable to the West and by definition to NATO. Although Khrushchev did not want war, the situation in Berlin was intolerable and he was under pressure to do something meaningful about it. But Kennedy had proclaimed to the nation and the world that he would not yield. The question was whether the Kremlin would believe Kennedy.

The Kremlin believed Kennedy. Khrushchev did not sign a separate treaty with the GDR and western access to Berlin was not cut off. But, to stop the hemorrhage of human capital, the Soviets and the East Germans did the one thing they believed—correctly—they could get away with. They built a wall. Construction of the Berlin Wall, complete with a "zone of death" to give East German guards a clear shot at those who might try to surmount it, began at 2:30 a.m. local time on August 13, 1961. The wall had two immediate effects. It stopped virtually all migration to the West from East Berlin. In the twenty-eight years that the wall stood between East and West Berlin, only about five thousand people managed to escape; more than 135 died in the attempt. And the wall eliminated any remaining room for ambivalence in the collective American consciousness about Soviet communism and its role in the world order.

From the Bay of Pigs low point in April to the Vienna summit to his dramatic address to the nation at the end of July, Kennedy had clearly regained a significant measure of credibility with the Kremlin. Khrushchev decided to backtrack on his threat to sign a separate treaty with the GDR by the end of the year and, treaty in hand, to evict the West from Berlin. This, quite clearly, was not the same Nikita Khrushchev who had "savaged" Kennedy in Vienna. For his part, Kennedy listened to and rejected advice that the US should tear the wall down as fast as it was being built. Taking into account the consequences the Soviets—and probably Khrushchev personally—were facing if they allowed westward emigration to continue to the point of East German collapse, there is much more than a passing chance that Kennedy avoided war by declining to knock the wall down. And it is worth noting that the resolve that could be discerned from Kennedy's late July speech was not illusory. In October, Kennedy approved (and National Security Advisor McGeorge Bundy signed) National Security Action Memorandum No. 109, which provided for a stepwise response to various degrees of Soviet or East German interference with western access to Berlin. The final escalatory step, after "selective nuclear attacks," was "General Nuclear War."[50]

The key to the peaceful resolution of the 1961 Berlin crisis was that, as Nitze would record in his memoirs, it was important for Khrushchev to realize "that maintaining our position in Berlin was more important to us than evicting us could possibly be to him."[51] And it is true, as Brzezinski wrote eleven years later, that "the Berlin crisis produced several years of acute tensions, launching in turn the massive US strategic build-up of the Kennedy years, escalating the arms race, setting in motion the U.S. counteroffensive, and postponing by almost 15 years any abatement in U.S.–Soviet hostility."[52] But the result of the 1961 standoff over Berlin was a wall, not a war.

From the nadir of the Bay of Pigs in April to the "cold winter" that started in Vienna in June, to the evaporation of Khrushchev's threat to cut off access to Berlin at the end of the year, 1961 was for Kennedy a story of credibility at least partially restored, freedom preserved, and war avoided. To be sure, the ugly wall traversing the city of Berlin squelched any sense that there was cause for celebration. But even that odious wall—as a constant reminder of communism's need to keep people from voting with their feet—had its benefits. By the end of 1962, Kennedy would need every ounce of his restored credibility.

It is, then, no accident of history that, to this day, the Russians and the Americans enjoy a parity of honors in the political geography of Berlin. In 1805, Frederick William III of Prussia, grateful for the commitment of Tsar Alexander I to throw Russian troops into a coalition against Bonaparte's France, renamed a public square in Berlin as Alexanderplatz. John F. Kennedy Platz, where Kennedy delivered his famous "Ich bin ein Berliner" speech in June 1963, four months before he was assassinated, is a few miles to the southwest.

The Cuban Missile Crisis

In geopolitics, resolve (and the perception of resolve), political will, and the willingness to take calculated risks can be at least as important as sheer military might. In the second half of the twentieth century, there was no more vivid illustration of that than the Cuban missile crisis. Two nations went to the brink and stepped back.

The Cuban missile crisis has seemingly been recounted in the memoirs of everyone who had anything to do with it, including some of the players on the Soviet side. Even President Kennedy, who did not live long enough to write his memoirs, effectively published a posthumous memoir in the form of the account authored by his brother, the attorney general, before he, too, was assassinated.[53]

In the winter and spring of 1962, Khrushchev's political situation in the Kremlin was as complicated as it had been at any time since the mid-1950s, when he was vying for power in the wake of Stalin's death. In terms of Soviet-US relations, Khrushchev's complications included the fact that, though the USSR had the biggest bomb and had detonated it the preceding October, the Soviets still lagged in their ability to execute a massive nuclear attack on the continental United States. Compounding that problem was the fact that, aside from the US advantage in long-range bombers and nuclear submarines, the United States had Jupiter medium-range missiles with nuclear warheads based in Turkey, leading to a newly heightened sense of encirclement in the Kremlin.

The US Jupiter missiles in Turkey were a special irritant. Given Russia's long history with Turkey, the mere fact of Turkey's membership in NATO (since 1952) grated on the Kremlin leadership. The presence in Turkey of missiles capable of reaching the Russian heartland (including Moscow) in a few minutes' time only added to the irritation. As Khrushchev and Defense Minister Rodion Malinovsky strolled on the beach at the Bulgarian resort of Varna in April 1962, the defense minister pointed across the Black Sea and asked the chairman why the USSR couldn't have missiles based close to the United States. Khrushchev didn't have a good answer, and he soon laid the problem before the Presidium.

On May 24, 1962, the Presidium had before it Malinovsky's proposal for deployment of five Soviet missile regiments, with fifty-four launchers, to Cuba.[54] The proposal was unanimously approved. Launched from Cuba, the Soviet missiles would be able to reach any city or military asset in the continental United States, other than those in the Pacific northwest, with accuracy far exceeding the capabilities of missiles launched over the north pole from Russia. US surveillance detected a surge in Soviet ships headed for Cuba during the summer of 1962, but the shipping, and the activity on the ground in Cuba, didn't raise alarms until the fall, when U-2 overflights of Cuba revealed the nature and scale of the project.

On October 15, U-2 photos unmistakably revealed the presence of SS-4 missile components at San Cristobal. The photographic evidence, laid on Kennedy's desk on the morning of the sixteenth, eliminated any possibility that the facilities under construction were to house antiaircraft missiles or other defensive weapons. There could be no doubt that the facilities being built were to house missiles capable of carrying nuclear warheads to most any target in the continental United States. As Khrushchev would later record, the USSR "hadn't had time to deliver all our shipments to Cuba, but we had installed enough missiles already to destroy New York, Chicago, and the other huge industrial cities, not to mention a little village like Washington."[55]

On the eighteenth, Kennedy had a previously scheduled meeting with Foreign Minister Andrei Gromyko at the White House. Disclosing nothing about the photographic evidence in hand, Kennedy listened carefully while Gromyko denied that the USSR was doing anything other than helping Cuba with its defensive capability. Without disclosing the discovery of the bases under construction (either publicly or to the Kremlin through diplomatic channels), Kennedy convened the Executive Committee of the National Security Council (ExComm) to address what was now obviously a major threat to national security. Once again, the president sought the counsel of Dean Acheson, who maintained that it was necessary under the Monroe Doctrine to put an end to the USSR's meddling in the Western Hemisphere.[56] His counsel was based on more than just nostalgia for the days when no nation would have entertained the thought of breaching the limits set by President Monroe in 1823. For Acheson, this was, again, all about credibility as an essential element of deterrence.

Khrushchev still had the psychological upper hand. The net effect of the parade of events from the Bay of Pigs in the spring of 1961 to the discovery of Soviet missiles in Cuba (October 1962) was that the Russians were on a roll. The Kremlin had ruthlessly protected *its* sphere of influence by brutally putting down the Hungarian revolt in 1956. The question facing Kennedy and his advisors in October 1962 was whether a communist nation less than a hundred miles off the Florida coast would be permitted to serve as a launch pad for Soviet nuclear weapons. Related to that, of course, was the question of whether, in 1962, the United States—led by a young and inexperienced president who had been roughed up in his only face-to-face meeting with Khrushchev—had anything comparable to the resolve the Russians had shown in 1956. The existence of a militarily weak communist dictatorship off the Florida coast was tolerable (if barely); one armed with Russian nuclear missiles was not.

The proposals discussed by ExComm ranged from immediately bombing the missile sites out of existence, to instituting a naval blockade of Cuba, to opening negotiations to remove the US missiles from Turkey in exchange for getting the Russian missiles out of Cuba. The most aggressive advice came from Air Force chief of staff Curtis LeMay (who had commanded the firebombing of Japanese cities in the spring of 1945, resulting in far more deaths than the atomic bombing of Hiroshima and Nagasaki). LeMay, who believed that the US strategic bombing capability should not be reserved for an all-out nuclear exchange with the USSR, argued that "the Russian bear has always been eager to stick his paw in Latin American waters. Now we have got him in a trap, let's take his leg off right up to his testicles. On second thoughts, let's take off his testicles, too."[57] That sort of bombast did not go unnoticed. Attorney General Robert Kennedy met secretly with Soviet Ambassador Anatoly Dobrynin—one of the most skillful diplomats appointed by any nation in the Cold War era—on October 27. As Dobrynin reported in a top-secret cable to the Foreign Ministry after that meeting, Robert Kennedy "mentioned [to Dobrynin] as if in passing that there are many unreasonable heads among the generals, who are itching for a fight."[58]

After exhaustive deliberations with ExComm, President Kennedy decided on a blockade to be enforced by the navy. As a matter of cosmetics, the blockade was to be called a quarantine—a blockade being an act of war under international law. Kennedy spoke to the nation in a televised address on October 22: "This Government, as promised, has maintained the closest surveillance of the Soviet Military buildup on the island of Cuba. Within the past week, unmistakable evidence has established the fact that a series of offensive missile sites is now in preparation on that imprisoned island. The purpose of these bases can be none other than to provide a nuclear strike capability against the Western Hemisphere."[59] Kennedy spoke of communism (specifically, "Communist missiles"), the Monroe Doctrine ("hemispheric policy") and, most important, US credibility. The missiles cannot remain in Cuba "if our courage and our commitments are ever to be trusted again by either friend or foe."

The most dramatic action Kennedy announced in his address was "a strict quarantine on all offensive military equipment under shipment to Cuba." And, directly addressing "Chairman Khrushchev," Kennedy called on Khrushchev to "move the world back from the abyss of destruction."

The naval blockade was in place the next day. US naval ships were tasked with intercepting and searching all ships bound for Cuba. There was just one problem. Soviet nuclear warheads—and forty thousand Soviet troops—were already in Cuba. They had to go. This brought Kennedy to the severest test of his credibility. In a letter to Kennedy on the twenty-sixth, Khrushchev offered in essence to pull the missiles out of Cuba in return for an assurance that the United States would not invade that island. Kennedy immediately recognized this as a proposal that could be made to work. But, in a broadcast the next morning, Radio Moscow upped the ante: the US missiles in Turkey also had to go. At this point, the Cold War rules of engagement came into play once again. Amid all of the rhetoric and posturing, there had to be a measure of trust between the two sides.

Kennedy was willing to pull the US medium-range missiles out of Turkey. The Jupiter missiles in Turkey were vulnerable and had been rendered obsolete by development of other land-based missiles, to say nothing of the fleet of nuclear submarines carrying Polaris missiles with nuclear warheads. But the president could not *publicly* commit to closing the missile bases in Turkey. In his report to the Foreign Ministry on his meeting with Robert Kennedy, Dobrynin quoted Kennedy as saying that removing the missiles from Turkey need not be an insurmountable obstacle, but (said Kennedy to Dobrynin): "The greatest difficulty for the president is the public discussion of the issue of Turkey. . . . To announce now a unilateral decision by the president of the USA to withdraw missile bases from Turkey—this would damage the entire structure of NATO and the US position as the leader of NATO."[60] Yes, the president, through his brother, was asking the USSR to do its part—on the sly—to help maintain US credibility as a NATO ally.

President Kennedy responded favorably to the proposal in Khrushchev's letter (missiles out of Cuba, no invasion, and blockade removed) while committing through back channels to take the Jupiters out of Turkey. And Khrushchev, by his own account, was looking "for a dignified way out of this conflict."[61] The deal was done. On the morning of Sunday the twenty-eighth (Washington, DC, time), Khrushchev announced, via Radio Moscow, that the missiles would be dismantled and returned to the Soviet Union. Nothing was said about removal of missiles from Turkey. Dismantling of the missile sites got started immediately. The nuclear warheads were out of Cuba by the end of November.

The US Air Force had moved an overwhelming force of fighters to bases in Florida, while the B-52 force was placed on airborne alert. More than a hundred thousand US troops had been mobilized, ready to invade Cuba if that order came. The Strategic Air Command had put intercontinental ballistic missiles on high alert. Kennedy had clearly taken huge risks. If the Soviet leader had not backed down, nuclear war would have been the likely result.[62] Indeed, Kennedy's speechwriters had prepared an address to the nation, an address he never had to deliver:

> My fellow Americans:
> With a heavy heart, and in necessary fulfillment of my oath of office, I have ordered—and the United States Air Force has now carried out—military operations, with conventional weapons only, to remove a major nuclear weapons build-up from the soil of Cuba.[63]

Although Kennedy's draft address referred to conventional weapons, there was then and is now little doubt that the action described in the draft—necessarily resulting in the deaths of Soviet troops and the destruction of Soviet strategic assets—would ultimately have led to a nuclear exchange.

Kennedy kept his side of the bargain. He ended the blockade and ordered the removal of the missiles from Turkey. It would be hard to call this a major retrenchment: the US overseas military presence was now reduced to bases in Bermuda, Canada, Canal Zone, Cuba (Guantanamo Bay), France, Greenland, Iceland, Italy (including Jupiter missiles), Japan, Libya, Morocco, the Netherlands, the Philippines, Portugal, South Korea, Spain, Taiwan, Trinidad, the United Kingdom, and West Germany.

After four years of keeping the world on edge over Berlin, Khrushchev never delivered on a single one of his ultimatums. All he had to show for it was a wall—a wall that advertised to the world the moral bankruptcy of communism. Instead, the Kremlin's adventurism, turning away from Berlin, spent itself in places such as Nicaragua, Angola, Ethiopia—and Afghanistan.

For his part, Kennedy reaped immediate gains in domestic and international prestige. In the Kremlin, the fallout from the crisis was not so good. *Time* speculated, correctly, that Khrushchev "must have rivals who would like to get his hide."[64] Having miscalculated, in his Cuban adventure, as badly as Kennedy had miscalculated in the Bay of Pigs fiasco, Khrushchev never recovered from the political and geopolitical setback of the Cuban missile crisis. He was ousted in 1964. In the end, Khrushchev, a Bolshevik, veteran of Stalingrad, and dominant figure in Soviet political life for more than a decade, got only a one-sentence obituary in *Pravda*.[65]

As Zubok and Pleshakov put it, the Cuban missile crisis "marked the watershed between the first, virulent stage of the Cold War and the second, long period of truce, when the competition between the two superpowers was constrained by a mutual fear of nuclear force."[66] The end of the "virulent stage" is attributable in no small part to the fact that John F. Kennedy had managed, inside of eighteen months, to recover enough credibility for himself and his nation to protect vital US interests while averting a nuclear holocaust.

Vietnam

Although the war in Vietnam seemingly had no end in sight, Richard Nixon was unequivocal. As reported by the *New York Times*, Nixon insisted that "the United States would seek an 'honorable peace' but would oppose outright surrender."[67] Nixon spoke those words on April 20, 1954, nineteen years before his representatives signed the papers that were sufficient, at least for the moment, to enable him to say with a straight face that the war was finally over.

These pages will not at any great length revisit the Vietnam War. That war has generated a vast literature of its own, including some of what Henry Kissinger has aptly called "cult literature."[68] But that war is relevant here because one of the pitfalls of containment theory as formulated in the first decade of the Cold War was that it presupposed that America's challenges from the communist side of the divide would be *both* unambiguously evil *and* existentially threatening. That presupposition—perhaps most dramatically expressed in NSC-68—came very naturally when the evil was personified by Stalin and the threat took the form of mechanized Soviet ground forces capable of swiftly overrunning Western Europe. But, as Americans found out in Korea, and, even more so, in Vietnam, if the evil is not quite so obvious and the threat not even close to existential, the matter can be much more complicated—and tragic.

Containment theory had its practical component (we don't want to be overrun by the Russians, but we also don't want to trigger another world war) and its ideological component (this cancer of communism must be stopped in its tracks). Thus conceived, the containment doctrine was thoroughly Eurocentric. In that context, it fit perfectly. It is easy to visualize Kennan, Acheson, and Nitze writing their cables, speeches, and memoranda while pondering a map of "the world" from the Urals to Gibraltar. This should come as no surprise. Acheson, for one (and in this he was not alone), had always thought of Asia as a distraction from Europe.[69] But in Vietnam, as Kissinger puts it, "fundamental differences between the geopolitics of Europe and Asia, together with America's interests in each, were submerged in the universalist, ideological American approach to foreign policy."[70] Although that morally grounded justification was potent enough to get us *into* Vietnam in the 1960s, it could not, ultimately, keep us there.

To be sure, the justification for the commitment of American blood and treasure to Vietnam did have one element that was, at least in theory, grounded on national security concerns. That was the domino theory, which held that if we permit communist aggression to succeed anywhere along communism's Eurasian periphery, there will be no end to the spread of that form of totalitarianism by force of arms. Truman's formulation, in the context of the Korean War, was typically blunt: "If aggression is successful in Korea, we can expect it to spread through Asia and Europe to this hemisphere. We are fighting in Korea for our own national security and survival."[71] Eisenhower preferred the domino metaphor. When asked, in 1954 (shortly before France was defeated in the battle of Dien Bien Phu), to comment on "the strategic importance of Indo-China to the free world," the president's response was that "you had a row of dominoes set up, and you knocked over the first one, and what would happen to the last one was the certainty that it would go over very quickly."[72]

Under President Kennedy, the US military presence in Vietnam grew from six hundred to sixteen thousand US personnel, serving essentially (and officially) in an advisory role. Historians and memoir writers disagree (and, in the absence of definitive archival evidence, will always disagree) as to whether Kennedy had planned to withdraw US forces from Vietnam after the 1964 election. Suffice it to say here that within nine months after Kennedy was assassinated in November 1963, President Lyndon Johnson reached the firm conviction that the only way to bring the conflict to a successful end was to demonstrate that the United

States was willing to make a massive commitment of ground combat forces to Vietnam. The hope, of course, was that the North Vietnamese, faced with a massive commitment from a global superpower, would see the light and come to the negotiating table.

As of midyear, 1964, it was not at all clear that Johnson could get congressional support for any real qualitative change in the mission of the US forces in Vietnam, let alone a massive commitment of combat troops. But then, in early August, there was some surface action (some provable and some subject to serious doubt) in the Gulf of Tonkin involving North Vietnamese patrol boats and the destroyer USS *Maddox*. The headline in the *New York Times* read "Red PT Boats Fire at U.S. Destroyer on Vietnam Duty."[73] In a message on August 5, Johnson took his case to Congress and the nation, asking for "a Resolution expressing the support of the Congress for all necessary action to protect our armed forces and to assist nations covered by the SEATO treaty."[74] Two days later, by a vote of 416 to 0 in the House and 88 to 2 in the Senate, Congress passed what came to be known as the Tonkin Gulf resolution: "Congress approves and supports the determination of the President, as Commander in Chief, to take all necessary measures to repel any armed attack against the forces of the United States and to prevent further aggression."[75]

The Tonkin Gulf resolution was the only legal foundation, if it could be called that, for the US military commitment that continued for nearly nine more years. As the war ground on, with mounting US casualties and no obvious strategy for achieving an outcome resembling "victory" as Americans had come to understand that concept, domestic US opposition to the war inexorably took root. The opposition started on the left, eventually encompassing all of the left, much of the center, and some of the right end of the political spectrum. On the left, opposition to the war could be traced to uncompromising pacifism or (for those who would eventually become neoconservatives) to disillusionment. On the right, those conservatives who saw the East-West struggle through a strongly ideological lens saw Vietnam "as a diversion from the primary struggle," as Kissinger put it.[76] By the fall of 1968, the "diversion" was exacting a toll of more than a thousand US combat deaths each month.

The breaking point, engendering broad-based opposition to the war, came in 1968, as Johnson was preparing to run for re-election. The Tet offensive was launched by the North Vietnamese army and the Viet

Cong in early 1968. Militarily, the Tet offensive was a defeat for the north, but psychologically it was a defeat for the Johnson administration. Suggestions from US military leadership that the end was in sight now rang hollow. As the north's will to stay in the fight despite enormous losses became painfully apparent, the iconic evening news anchor Walter Cronkite commented that "it seems now more certain than ever that the bloody experience of Vietnam is to end in a stalemate."[77] Johnson's reading of the situation was correct: "If I've lost Walter Cronkite, I've lost middle America."[78]

At the heart of Johnson's growing political problem was the fact that, after Tet, large segments of the US population were convinced that there was no discernible moral difference between the two opposing Vietnamese populations or their governments. This was essentially a civil war between two totalitarian regimes. US leaders, beginning with Truman, had done too good a job of selling containment, with its human and material costs, as a *moral* cause. Aside from that, the most obvious beneficiaries of containment, as originally sold to the American people, were Europeans who shared a national patrimony with the vast majority of Americans—and looked like them. That made containment, Vietnamese-style, a much harder sell. Any sense the American public may have had that the Vietnam War was a necessary war—as compared, for instance, with World War II or even Korea—was quickly dissipating.

In a stunning televised address at the end of March 1968, Johnson told the nation, "I shall not seek and I will not accept the nomination of my party as your President."[79] Johnson also announced a partial bombing halt and new peace initiatives. But peace was years away, and peace, when it came, had no resemblance to the peace envisioned by Johnson in his address to the nation.

Johnson's withdrawal paved the way for Nixon's victory over Vice President Hubert Humphrey in the 1968 presidential election. By inauguration day in January 1969, there were more than 540,000 US troops in Vietnam. Nixon promptly embarked on a policy of "Vietnamization," the implicit premise for which was that an enemy that wasn't being defeated with the help of more than a half million US troops could be defeated without them. Over the next three years, US troop strength (and casualties) in Vietnam dropped dramatically. This is where Nixon's skill at geopolitical triangulation, with the able assistance of National Security Advisor (later secretary of state) Henry Kissinger, made a difference in arriving at an exit strategy that could be presented to the American public with a straight face.

The Kremlin, quite naturally, had supported communist North Vietnam in the civil war. Although, by every human and economic measure, the war had been costly to the United States, Vietnam was a more agreeable experience for the Kremlin, which had done its part mainly by providing what amounted to Lend-Lease aid, communist-style, consisting of trucks, tanks, aircraft, missiles, and other essential arms.[80] Nixon knew the Kremlin was not going to force a peace deal on Hanoi, but he also understood that some quiet encouragement from Moscow could make a real difference in the tortuously slow peace negotiations that had been underway—fitfully and mostly in secret—since the last year of Johnson's presidency. The North Vietnamese had done a masterful job—as small nations with shrewd leaders have done many times—of playing the Chinese off against the Russians, with the result that the combined Soviet and Chinese military aid sufficed to keep the North Vietnamese and Viet Cong forces equipped and in the war to the end in 1975. The USSR and China, having come close to war in 1969, had every reason to cultivate North Vietnam as a client state.

Not for nothing, then, did Nixon, at first by way of secret trips by Kissinger and ultimately with his February 1972 trip to Beijing, initiate his famous rapprochement with China. The Shanghai communiqué, issued by Nixon and Chairman Mao Zedong in late February, brought home to the Russians the fact that there might be much to be gained, as a matter of geostrategy, from détente with the United States. And Nixon clearly did put a high value on the China card in dealing with the Russians. In April 1972, as Nixon and Kissinger were discussing strategy for a trip Kissinger was about to make to Moscow to prepare the ground for the May 1972 Moscow summit, Nixon coached Kissinger—as shown by the White House recordings that were secretly made at Nixon's direction—to tell the Russians that "the President thinks his China initiative is the most important thing he's done so far."[81] Thus, unspoken but understood by everyone at the table at the May summit in Moscow was the fact that the warming Sino-American relationship could portend nothing good for the USSR. By the same token, the Hanoi leadership could easily see that it shouldn't presume that open-ended support—from either Moscow or Beijing—would continue indefinitely.

As the 1972 presidential election approached, Nixon had no trouble fending off a challenge by Senator George McGovern, a determined pacifist. The outcome was even more lopsided—with an electoral vote of 520 to 17—than the 1964 Johnson-Goldwater election. Nixon was no doubt pleased that, on the Thursday before the election, Kissinger announced that "'peace is at hand' in Indochina and that a final agreement on a cease-fire and political arrangement could be reached in one more negotiating session with the North Vietnamese 'lasting not more than four days.'"[82] Kissinger's announcement, though well-timed for the election, was premature. The Paris Peace Accords were signed three months later, in late January 1973. The document was more of a cease-fire agreement than a peace treaty, and the cease-fire did not last long. US troops left, and American prisoners of war were freed. But communist forces remained, undaunted, in the South. The Paris Accords were an exercise in face saving, giving the administration an opportunity, for a short interval, to talk about "peace with honor."[83]

Saigon fell to the North Vietnamese army and the Viet Cong on April 30, 1975, resulting in the humiliating emergency evacuation, mostly by helicopter, of thousands of US and South Vietnamese military and civilian personnel. One of the last persons to leave the US embassy was Ambassador Graham Martin, who spent his first night as the former ambassador as a guest on a US aircraft carrier in the South China Sea.

As had been the case with the Allied intervention in Russia in 1918–1920, America had gotten itself into another conflict in which winning was far more important to the other side than it was to the United States. North Vietnam was producing draft-age males—about two hundred thousand a year—far faster than US forces could kill them.[84] North Vietnam, placing a much higher value on victory than did the United States, was willing to absorb more grievous losses than the United States was willing to inflict, and was able, in turn, to inflict on US forces more grievous losses than Americans would tolerate.

The lessons of Vietnam came at a high price, in lives lost, bodies broken, and, in some ways, a broken American spirit. The recovery took decades, and, in some ways, may not be complete. There are those who would argue that the recovery, in terms of public consciousness, should never be complete, lest we repeat the mistakes that spanned four presidential administrations. The United States had committed more than a half million of its troops to a long, bloody war without a concrete, politically and militarily realistic plan for forcing the desired outcome (assuming that the desired outcome could have been forced at all). The failure of such a plan, if one had ever existed, might have been forgivable; the lack of such a plan—or the courage to admit that no such plan was possible—was not.

Chapter 14

Stalemate and the Birth and Death of Détente

Khrushchev was abruptly overthrown by the Central Committee in October 1964. Unlike some others who had fallen out of favor, he was allowed to take his pension and to go peacefully into retirement, with a promise of the use of a dacha for the rest of his life. He was succeeded by Leonid Brezhnev as general secretary and by Alexey Kosygin as chairman of the Council of Ministers. Consistent with the official and unofficial prerogatives of his position as general secretary, it soon became apparent that Brezhnev was the man in charge in the Kremlin. Although it has been suggested that, late in his reign, Brezhnev encouraged a personality cult, it is fair to say that as personality cults go Brezhnev and Kosygin were not much competition for Stalin. The duo of Brezhnev and Kosygin was short on personality and, for that matter, not much of a cult.

Détente

Brezhnev's eighteen years in power spanned all or part of four US presidencies: those of Johnson, Nixon, Carter, and Reagan. The most consequential years of Brezhnev's engagement with US leaders were, without question, the eight years of the Nixon presidency. Brezhnev had his priorities. The glacis would be protected, regardless of what that might mean in terms of public opinion in the noncommunist world. He made that clear in August 1968, five months before the Johnson administration ended, when Soviet forces, augmented by troops from Bulgaria, East

Germany, Hungary, and Poland, invaded Czechoslovakia to put an end to the liberalization then in progress under Czech First Secretary Alexander Dubček. The TASS announcement on the day of the invasion asserted that Czech leaders had "asked the Soviet Union and other allied states to render the fraternal Czechoslovak people urgent assistance, including assistance with armed forces."[1] The airing of that palpably false narrative was, for the Kremlin, an acceptable price to pay to establish the Brezhnev Doctrine, which Brezhnev explicitly articulated in November 1968, at a meeting of the Polish Communist Party Congress.

In an Orwellian introduction to the doctrine that came to bear his name, Brezhnev declared that socialist states "emphatically oppose interference in the affairs of any states."[2] In case anyone had missed the point, Brezhnev affirmed that "the Soviet Union has done much for the real strengthening and independence of the socialist countries." (These words were spoken after Dubček had been put in handcuffs and transported to Moscow, there to learn how the independence of the socialist countries worked in practice.) Brezhnev then came to his point: If "*internal* [emphasis supplied] and external forces hostile to socialism seek to halt the development of any socialist country and restore the capitalist order," we reserve the right to intervene—militarily, if necessary.[3] Brezhnev had laid down his marker. Now, with the Nixon administration set to take office in January, the talk about détente could begin.

Especially when viewed in retrospect, détente is a fluid concept, both in terms of when it began and ended and in terms of what it amounted to as a substantive theme for one era of US-Soviet relations. Nixon, for all his faults, was probably an ideal practitioner of détente. He understood that détente and appeasement were two entirely different things. Nixon and Brezhnev were, in some ways, a good combination as the chief interlocutors of détente. Although Nixon had gotten traction as a politician in the late 1940s and early 1950s as an idealogue, his ideology (if ideology is what it actually was) did not keep him from practicing realpolitik as that art was expounded by Henry Kissinger, his national security advisor and secretary of state. Thus, as Martin Malia put it, "the high noon of détente was the Nixon-Kissinger years following the American failure in Vietnam."[4]

Brezhnev, for his part, was a good judge of when to fight and when to talk. On one level, he was, of course, a committed communist. But on another level, his thinking may not have been too far from Ambassador Troyanovski's observation that "you were supposed to believe that Communism would prevail; but this was a little like the Second Coming of Christ. You were supposed to believe in it, but very few do."[5] As for East-West relations, Brezhnev had good reasons to engage with Nixon. Soviet military spending was taking an enormous bite out of an economy that was less than half the size of the US economy (let alone the combined economies of the NATO allies). Aside from that, the Kremlin leadership still yearned for some form of recognition that the constellation of nations and coerced allegiances in Eastern Europe was not subject to question in any Western capital.

In terms of both domestic politics and geopolitics, Nixon was not in a good position to make the significant concessions that real détente would inevitably require until a Vietnam settlement appeared to be within reach. Consequently, in the hope of loosening up the North Vietnamese negotiators *and* to give the Russians something to think about, Nixon went to China in February 1972, as discussed in the last chapter. The historic China trip was followed by an intensified campaign of bombing carefully selected targets in North Vietnam. On that subject, as Kissinger prepared to embark on a trip to Moscow in April 1972, to meet with Foreign Minister Andrei Gromyko to lay the groundwork for the May summit (chapter 13), Nixon made it clear to Kissinger (as shown by the White House tapes) that "we will bomb the living bejeesus out of North Vietnam and then if anybody interferes we will threaten the nuclear weapon."[6] Kissinger did not push back on this. Au contraire. While discussing strategy for both the bombing of North Vietnam and his imminent meeting with Gromyko, Kissinger opined that "the more [bombing] we do now the better. The more reckless we appear, because after all, Mr. President, [what] we're trying to convince them of is that we are ready to go all the way. The only way we are able to convince them is to do reckless things." In turn, Nixon coached Kissinger to "give them a little bullshit to the effect that the President has great respect for Mr. Brezhnev—he's a strong man, a determined man."[7]

Thus was all put in order for Nixon's May 22–30, 1972, summit meeting in Moscow. This was détente at its zenith. Nixon and Kissinger had been working toward this day since Nixon took office in 1969. It was a productive summit, time well spent. Nixon was warmly received by the

Russian people and their officialdom, though, as the head of the KGB would observe fifteen years later, "the applause for [Nixon] would have been even warmer had he not been bombing Hanoi and Haiphong."[8]

As for substance, the SALT I Treaty, the Anti-Ballistic Missile Treaty, and the Interim Agreement on strategic offensive arms, all the culmination of long and complex negotiations, were signed in ceremonies befitting the importance of those accords. Also signed by Nixon and Brezhnev was a statement of basic principles of relations between the two nations. Although it was entirely aspirational, the document declared that "differences in ideology and in the social systems of the USA and the USSR are not obstacles to the bilateral development of normal relations based on the principles of sovereignty, equality, non-interference in internal affairs and mutual advantage."[9] This was a remarkable statement to appear over the signature of the man who, twenty-two years before, had bet his political future on his anticommunist credentials in his successful campaign against "the pink lady," Helen Gahagan Douglas. But it was precisely Nixon's anticommunist pedigree that enabled him to sign the document in an election year without having to worry about his right flank. And, as Nixon would later record, he also *privately* urged Brezhnev to "lift limitations on Jewish emigration in order to gain support for détente in the United States."[10] The fact that that subject was broached privately was noteworthy.

On May 28, before the week-long summit concluded, Nixon spoke directly to the Soviet population from Moscow in a nationally televised address that was gracious, conciliatory, and well received. This was indeed, and for more than one reason, the peak of détente. As Nixon addressed the citizens of the USSR, five operatives of Nixon's reelection campaign were preparing to break into the headquarters of the Democratic National Committee at the Watergate hotel and office building, to plant surveillance devices and photograph documents. On the night of the twenty-eighth, bugging devices were planted on the phone lines of the Democratic National Chairman and one of his assistants, a crime marking the onset of a cascade of events leading to the end of Nixon's presidency. (The burglars returned to the DNC Watergate offices on June 17. They were detected and arrested that night.) The Watergate scandal, though an entirely domestic affair, was a major event in the Cold War. Because the Moscow summit gave a powerful lift to Brezhnev's prestige at all levels of Soviet society, especially among the elites, Brezhnev—still in good health—was on the way up. Not so for Richard Nixon. Although the process would take two years, Nixon was on the way out.

Initially, and even with the counsel of an ambassador as sophisticated as Dobrynin (whose tenure in Washington ultimately spanned five presidencies), the Kremlin leadership was baffled by all the furor over Watergate. How could a man in Nixon's position become so vulnerable in his own country? But it didn't take long for the Russians to figure out that a weakened Nixon, focused on salvaging his presidency, might make some welcome concessions.[11] By the summer of 1973, Nixon needed all the help he could get if he was to salvage his presidency.

Help came in the form of a Nixon-Brezhnev summit in Washington, DC, in June 1973. The Senate Watergate committee, exploring the scandal in fine detail, obligingly recessed its hearings during the week of the summit, sparing Nixon, as Kissinger put it, "The humiliation of spreading the malfeasances of the President on the public record while Brezhnev was in the country."[12] Thus, it was not until the day Brezhnev departed for Moscow (the summit having concluded the night before) that John Dean, Nixon's former White House counsel, began his riveting testimony describing Nixon's personal participation, over a period of months, in the criminal conspiracy to cover up the Watergate burglaries.

Unsurprisingly, the 1973 summit produced nothing of geopolitical significance, the closest thing to that having been an aspirational document, signed by the two leaders, intended to accelerate the SALT II negotiations. As a matter of optics in domestic politics, the summit was a plus for Nixon. A Louis Harris poll, taken during the week of the summit, indicated that 78 percent of the population approved of the summit.[13] And, as will be seen, it was significant that the Harris poll respondents indicated, 84 to 4, that they favored an agreement "to get Russia to allow Jews to leave that country more easily."[14] Alas for Nixon, the political benefit of the June summit evaporated quickly. Nixon was in survival mode from the summer of 1973 until he resigned in lieu of impeachment in August 1974. He did pay another visit to Brezhnev in Moscow in June 1974, and that summit did result in some incremental progress on arms control (such as reducing the number of permitted anti-ballistic missile sites from two to one). But Nixon's presidency was by that time in its agonal stage.

On July 25, 1974, the Supreme Court, in a unanimous opinion written (and read from the bench) by Chief Justice Warren Burger, ruled that Nixon must turn over the secret tapes that were demanded by the Watergate special prosecutor. Thus began the final, short chapter of the Nixon presidency. Nixon was well aware that the tapes would reveal his personal participation in the criminal conspiracy. On August 5, Nixon released sixty-four tape recordings, including the "smoking gun" tape, recorded just a few days after the June burglary. On August 7, a delegation of leading Senate Republicans went to the White House to inform the president that eighty-five senators would likely vote to convict him on the obstruction of justice charge in the then-pending articles of impeachment—an estimate that, as a matter of simple arithmetic, indicated that at least twenty-five Republican senators would vote to impeach.

Beginning with the discovery of the Watergate burglaries in the summer of 1972, there had been a direct relationship between the prospects for Nixon's presidency and the prospects for détente. Meaningful progress with the Soviets—necessarily involving concessions—required the same kind of political capital that Nixon had to spend to open the door with China in early 1972, when "Watergate" was just the name of an upscale address in Washington, DC. But, as Kissinger put it, "Watergate deprived Nixon of the moral authority essential for the educational task his [détente] policy required."[15]

By some reckonings, détente did not end until the Soviet Union invaded Afghanistan in 1979. But détente, as an ongoing reciprocal process of engagement aimed at lessening tension and reducing the risk of a nuclear holocaust, effectively ended with the demise of the Nixon presidency. The Helsinki Accords, signed by the United States, the USSR and thirty-three other nations in 1975, were a post-Nixon bright spot. But the success at Helsinki stands virtually alone as an example of major détente-like progress between the end of the Nixon administration and the arrival of Reagan and Gorbachev on the scene.

All of this is not to say that détente, while it lasted, wasn't important. As Zubok puts it, détente was viewed in the Kremlin and in the West "as managed competition, as a continuation of the Cold War by less dangerous means."[16] It was a way to reciprocate caution with caution rather than responding to belligerence with belligerence. From a US perspective, the backstory is that détente was, in one important respect, all about time. Nixon and Kissinger wanted to buy time by decelerating the negative trends in the relationship. They wanted the two sides to mark time peacefully, to allow the process of internal decay to continue unabated in the Soviet Union (as Truman and Kennan had predicted), undermining its capacity to compete with the West. Whatever Nixon's preoccupations may have been, Kissinger was easily astute enough to understand that, as Kennan had written a quarter of a century before, time was on the side of the West as long as, by dint of containment, the communists were forced to stew in their own juices.

Helsinki

Kissinger continued in his dual role as national security advisor and secretary of state after Gerald Ford succeeded to the presidency in August 1974.[17] This continuity was provident for many reasons, not the least of which was that Nixon's departure and Ford's arrival in the Oval Office did not interrupt the protracted negotiations at the Conference on Security and Cooperation in Europe in Helsinki. The arduous negotiations culminated in the signing, by thirty-five nations, of the Helsinki Final Act on August 1, 1975. It is noteworthy now that the provisions of the Final Act on the inviolability of frontiers was of prime importance to the Soviet negotiators: "The participating States regard as inviolable all [of] one another's frontiers as well as the frontiers of all States in Europe and therefore they will refrain now and in the future from assaulting these frontiers." This required the signatories to "refrain from any demand for, or act of, seizure and usurpation of part or all of the territory of any participating State."[18] To the Soviets, this was hard-won "Western recognition of the post-World War II borders forcibly carved out by the Red Army."[19] When the document was signed, of course, Ukraine, including Crimea and Donbas, was a constituent republic of the Soviet Union.

What the Russians were willing to concede in return for the recognition of the sanctity of international frontiers was language broadly recognizing fundamental political and personal freedoms such as freedom to travel, family reunification, freedom of communication, and freedom of the press. The human rights provisions of the Final Act were a time bomb for the Kremlin—albeit a bomb with a long fuse.[20] The Russians have always maintained (and usually with a truculent tone) that human rights are an internal matter, immune from meddling by other nations or the international community. This mindset, ironically, contributed to the Politburo's authorization to Brezhnev to sign the Final Act, because, as recorded by Dobrynin, Gromyko assured his Politburo colleagues that "we are masters in our own house."[21] But, as Dobrynin would record, the Final Act ultimately became "a manifesto of the dissident and liberal movement, a development totally beyond the imagination of the Soviet leadership."[22] Although Gerald Ford's trip to Helsinki to sign the Final Act seemed to some at the time to be an exercise in lame symbolism, the Final Act was ultimately one of the most significant documents signed by East and West during the Cold War, not least because of its explicit provisions on human rights and its affirmation of each nation's "right to be or not to be a party to treaties of alliance."[23]

Jackson-Vanik

The townspeople asked: "Is there a proper blessing for the Tsar?"

The rabbi replied: "A blessing for the Tsar? Of course! May God bless and keep the Tsar . . . far away from us!"

—*Fiddler on the Roof*

Such was life for Jews living within the Pale of Settlement established by Empress Catherine II. Life beyond the Pale was riskier yet. A more-or-less straight line can be drawn from the life exemplified by *Fiddler's* long-suffering Tevye, in prerevolutionary Russia, to the halls of Congress in the mid-1970s.

The Jackson-Vanik Amendment to the Trade Act of 1974, denying "most favored nation" (MFN) treatment to nations that restricted the right to emigrate, was signed into law by President Ford on January 3, 1975, and remained on the books until it was repealed by the Magnitsky Act, signed by President Barack Obama in December 2012. Although the legislation did not, in terms, single out any nation, it was aimed directly at Soviet restrictions on Jewish emigration. An understanding of the Jackson-Vanik story requires an understanding of ethnic politics as practiced in the United States and the Soviet Union in the twentieth century.

Ethnic politics in the United States. In the 1970s, individuals of Anglo-Scots-Irish stock amounted to about a third of the US population. They were the largest American group, but still only a minority among other minorities.[24] Americans of Slavic (including Polish and Russian) extraction amounted to about 12.6 million; the Jewish population was estimated by the American Jewish Committee at just over six million.[25] It is worthy of note, then, that Theodore H. White, an eminent historian who had a Jewish upbringing, wrote in 1973 that "the Slavs and the Jews," among other blocs, "vote by ethnic interest beyond all other interests."[26] White's point was that "on the keyboard of [these groups'] fears and hopes, politicians have always played campaign melodies."[27] This was (and to some extent still is) a potent form of identity politics tied, as it was, to family history and inherited values.

There was nothing new about ethnic politics as practiced in the 1970s. At the Teheran Conference in 1943, thirty years before White wrote the lines quoted here, Roosevelt confided to Stalin (as recorded by Charles Bohlen, who witnessed the conversation) that he, Roosevelt, "could not publicly take part" in any arrangement to reset the borders of Poland until after the 1944 election.[28] Roosevelt explained to Stalin that "there were in the United States from six to seven million Americans of Polish extraction, and as a practical man, he did not wish to lose their vote."[29]

An essential component of the practice of ethnic politics is the fact that Jews and Americans of Eastern European descent are not scattered randomly among the fifty states. Roosevelt was as conscious eight decades ago as politicians are now that voters tracing their heritage to Eastern Europe are important segments of the populations of the swing states of the Great Lakes region.

Ethnic politics in Russia. In the Soviet Union, Jewishness was officially treated as a nationality (*natsional'nost'*) and not as a religious faith. Consequently, in the internal passports that all adult Soviet citizens were required (beginning in 1932) to have, Jews were required to list their nationality—Jewish (*Yevrei*)—just as nationalities such as Russian, Ukrainian or Armenian were required to list theirs.[30] Thus, in the USSR, a Jew could become a devout Russian Orthodox believer but he or she could never be Russian as a matter of nationality (unless he or she had a parent registered as a Russian national).[31] The nationality line—the notorious Category 5—was eliminated from internal passports in 1990. (Some ethnically-conscious people wanted the Russian government to reinstate this field in their passports, but the Constitutional Court denied their petition in 2004.)

To be a Jew in the Soviet Union in the 1970s had consequences. In 1968, fewer than 300 Jews were permitted to emigrate.[32] They had difficulty getting sensitive jobs and were subject to restrictive quotas in university admissions.[33] The treatment accorded Jews in the broader Soviet society was nourished, in part, by a persistent backdrop of antisemitism in the Soviet government—an antisemitism which was perhaps more pervasive in government than in the upper reaches of Soviet society in general. The Kremlin's attitude toward Jews was not a recent development. For decades, Jews contended with varying degrees of disfavor from the Soviet regime. Educated Jews who had fallen out of favor were derisively labeled as "cosmopolitans," or, worse yet, "rootless cosmopolitans." This was akin, in some ways, to the more recent practice of labeling opponents of the Kremlin as "extremists." As recently as the latter years of Stalin's rule, Jews had difficulties entering or staying in the professions, and a plan was in the works to deport them to Siberia.[34]

From 1969 to 1972, Jewish emigration increased more than tenfold, to nearly 30,000 in 1972. This was not just a brain drain—it was getting to be a political problem. Ideologically, emigration was betrayal.[35] In August 1972, a few weeks after the Brezhnev–Nixon summit in Moscow (in which Nixon had promised Brezhnev some trade concessions), and just as détente was gaining some momentum, the Kremlin announced that emigrants would be denied permission to leave the country unless they reimbursed the government for the cost of their higher education. In the first two months after the "diploma tax" was imposed, fewer than 400 Jews were allowed to emigrate, paying more than 1.5 million rubles for the privilege.

The Soviet emigration restrictions were tailor-made for US politics. So it was that, in the summer of 1974, a comprehensive package of trade legislation, sought by the administration for nearly two years, was at long last nearing final passage. But one major hurdle remained. Senator Henry Jackson of the state of Washington (with seventy-four senatorial cosponsors), joined by Congressman Charles Vanik of Ohio, was sponsoring an amendment to the pending trade bill which would require abolition of the emigration restrictions as a prerequisite to granting MFN trade status to the USSR. Nixon had no interest, at least at that terminal stage of his political career, in linking trade policy to Jewish emigration. Kissinger strongly agreed, as did the Kremlin. As early as the fall of 1973, Treasury Secretary (and future secretary of state) George Shultz, fresh back from a trip to Moscow, quoted the Russian leaders as saying that "if this is the way people think Jews will get out of the Soviet Union, they are mistaken."[36] Kissinger chimed in, making no bones about his concern with "this frivolous monkeying around with the domestic policy of the Soviet Union."[37]

Writing in *Foreign Affairs* nearly a year before all of this came to a head, Theodore Sorensen, who had served as special counsel to President Kennedy, accurately assessed the situation: "It would be contrary to our knowledge of the whole philosophy and experience of the U.S.S.R. to expect it to yield on this political issue as the result of our economic sanctions."[38] Sorensen's evaluation was accurate. And one other major consideration—reciprocity—was in play. Reciprocity is elegant in its simplicity as an international norm because, by definition, it leaves no room for double standards. For the Russians, the attraction of reciprocity was (and is) the fact that it gives a nation license to replicate the behavior of its counterpart, unhindered by the highly fraught considerations of morality that sometimes affect one nation's judgments about another. And regardless of moral justification, there could be no doubt that Jackson-Vanik violated any notions of parity between the USSR and the West—a parity which was, for the Kremlin, a major goal of détente.[39]

The introduction of the Jackson-Vanik amendment triggered intense behind-the-scenes efforts by the administration to resolve the Jewish emigration issue. The Kremlin tried to quell the furor in the United States by granting exemptions from the emigration restrictions on a selective and politically propitious basis, but that—predictably—only fanned the flames. In domestic US politics, Jackson-Vanik had broad support, rooted in the proposition that emigration is a fundamental human right.[40] Thus, it is unsurprising that Ambassador Dobrynin recorded that when Congressman Vanik called on him to discuss the issue, he "mentioned his Slavic origins, and said he was not predisposed against the Soviet Union. But he frankly explained his cosponsorship of the discriminatory Jackson-Vanik amendment principally by his desire to be re-elected in his Cleveland District with its many East European voters."[41]

Negotiations continued through the summer, even as Nixon's political capital was eroding by the day. Despite Nixon's Watergate problems and preoccupation, Kissinger and Gromyko were able, with quiet but intensive negotiations, to make a deal. This brings us to one of the most bizarre chapters in the history of US-Russian relations. The problem of Jewish emigration from the Soviet Union was solved—or so the main players seemed to think—by way of an exchange of letters between the US secretary of state and a US senator.

In quiet negotiations, Kissinger prevailed on Gromyko to acknowledge that forty-five thousand emigrants annually might be a tolerable figure for the Soviet side.[42] But, to Dobrynin's perception (and the historical record strongly supports this), Jackson, not satisfied with the results of Kissinger's quiet diplomacy, kept moving the goalpost.[43] Eventually, Dobrynin told President Ford in confidence that the Kremlin would allow fifty thousand Jews to leave each year—a major improvement, but the Russians wanted this understanding to be kept under wraps.[44] Kissinger tried—successfully, he thought—to satisfy Jackson's demand for something he could show the press by giving Jackson a letter, dated October 18, informing him of assurances Kissinger had received from the Soviet side that "unreasonable or unlawful impediments" to emigration would be eliminated and, specifically, that the emigration tax, which had been suspended, would remain suspended. As for numbers, Kissinger wrote only that it would be "our assumption" that the "rate of emigration from the U.S.S.R. would begin to rise promptly from the 1973 level and would continue to rise to correspond to the number of applicants."[45]

Jackson promptly released Kissinger's letter with a triumphal splash of publicity.[46] Jackson, in turn, gave Kissinger a letter outlining Jackson's interpretation of Kissinger's representations and agreeing that the deal, as interpreted by Jackson, was good enough to support adding a provision to the trade bill that would give the president the authority to grant MFN status to the Soviet Union. But Jackson added that "we would consider a benchmark—a minimum standard of initial compliance—to be the issuance of visas at the rate of 60,000 per annum."[47]

The news of this breakthrough hit the press, complete with a photo—carried on the front page of the *New York Times*—of a celebratory gathering in the Oval Office. Pictured in that group were Ford, Kissinger,

Jackson, Vanik, and New York Senator Jacob Javits. The only thing missing from the photo was anyone from the Soviet Union.

Paula Stern, whose meticulously researched book (based on her doctoral dissertation) tells this story in granular detail, commented that "Jackson, the presidential candidate, was more interested in declaring victory for the benefit of his domestic audience and less concerned about the negative consequences that such publicity might have on the arrangement with the Soviet Union." Jackson's "unblushingly immodest" portrayal of the October developments "could not have been designed to have worse diplomatic repercussions."[48] Stern's biting criticism rings true. Jackson's patriotism was beyond question. His judgment, in balancing policy goals against personal ambition, is another matter.

Later in October, while Kissinger was in Moscow laying the groundwork for a strategic-arms limitation agreement, Brezhnev reacted forcefully to the US publicity surrounding the somewhat ephemeral deal the Kremlin had made on emigration and trade.[49] The appearance that the Kremlin had bowed to pressure from Jackson was deeply offensive.

The trade bill sailed through Congress in December, clearing the Senate by a vote of 77 to 4 and a House vote of 323 to 6. As the legislation neared final passage, TASS released a letter Gromyko had handed to Kissinger on October 26, while Kissinger was in Moscow (and eight days after Jackson and Kissinger had exchanged their letters). Kissinger probably brooded about the Gromyko letter for hours on the long flight home from Moscow in October, but he never said anything about it until TASS put it in the public domain in December, nearly two months later. As might be expected, the Gromyko letter indignantly denied that the Russians had given any specific assurances about easing up on emigration in return for the MFN status (and trade credits) the Kremlin had sought, admonishing Kissinger that emigration was a matter "entirely within the internal competence of our state." Lest there be any doubt as to which way the wind was blowing, Gromyko ended his letter by telling Kissinger that the "present tendency" in emigration was down, not up.[50]

Jackson tried to put the best face on a rapidly deteriorating situation, rationalizing the Soviet protest—and disavowal of an emigration deal—as a "face saving" effort by the Kremlin that "did not mean the arrangement was falling apart."[51] Events would soon prove otherwise. For his part, Kissinger had some explaining to do. Why had he not said anything about the Gromyko letter? His answer to that question in December was that he had intended to show the letter to Jackson and Javits but "forgot."[52]

Ford signed the trade bill into law on January 3, 1975. Jackson announced his candidacy for president on February 6. The Jackson-Vanik amendment thus became the law of the land, there to remain until it was repealed by the Magnitsky Act in 2012. (Russia's MFN status was revoked in April 2022, in the wake of Putin's assault on Ukraine.) Not only did Jackson-Vanik become law without a deal with the Kremlin on emigration; it became law in a newly (and unnecessarily) toxic diplomatic environment that was almost entirely the result of choices that were made on the US side.

In November 1985, nearly eleven years after enactment of Jackson-Vanik, President Ronald Reagan dictated a memo to collect his thoughts on the eve of his first summit with General Secretary Mikhail Gorbachev. Reagan used a metaphor harkening to the days when he was a play-by-play announcer for the Chicago Cubs: "Front page stories that we are banging away at them on their human rights abuses will get us some cheers from the bleachers but it won't help those who are being abused. Indeed, it could wind up hurting them."[53] In this, Reagan had the benefit of history. Jewish emigration plummeted quickly after the Jackson-Vanik amendment to the trade legislation was enacted. By the time President Reagan took office in 1981, there was virtually no Jewish emigration.[54] By 1976, Jewish emigration was down to fourteen thousand, the lowest rate since 1971.[55] Although emigration was allowed to rise somewhat in the late 1970s, that relief came to an end after the Soviet invasion of Afghanistan. The low—fewer than nine hundred emigrants—was reached in 1984. Emigration restrictions were relaxed under Gorbachev with the result that about 1.7 million Jews have emigrated since 1989 (including nearly six hundred thousand between 1989 and 1992).

The lesson of Jackson-Vanik is not complicated. Soviet treatment of Jews who sought to exercise the fundamental human right of expatriation was reprehensible. The fact that the communist regime found it necessary to place restrictions on emigration was as embarrassing as the Berlin Wall, and for many of the same reasons. As for the obvious meddling by one nation in the internal affairs of another, the US attempt to modify Soviet emigration policy was without doubt a manifestation of the core values of the United States, as a nation Kissinger described as "the first society in history to have been explicitly created in the name of liberty."[56] But the hundreds of thousands who were denied the opportunity to seek their liberty during the last fourteen years of the existence of the Soviet Union would argue that meddling by one nation into the internal affairs of another is best attempted by way of quiet diplomacy.

Chapter 15

From the Wilderness to the Promised Land

Carter and Brezhnev to Reagan, Bush, and Gorbachev

New information from both Washington and Moscow, declassified after much of the existing post–Cold War literature was published, sheds much light on the last phase of the Cold War. And then there is *newly relevant* information shedding light on the formative years—the 1970s and '80s—in the public life of a young politician from Delaware who graduated from the New Castle County Council to the US Senate in January 1973.

Enter Joseph R. Biden Jr.

When elected to the Senate, he was the fifth-youngest senator in the history of that body. At the end of his career as a senator from Delaware, Joseph R. Biden Jr. had served longer than all but fourteen of the nearly two thousand men and women who had been members of the Senate.

During the latter part of his senatorial career, Biden served two stints (2001–3 and 2007–9) as chairman of the Foreign Relations Committee. A look at his early years on the committee is at least equally instructive. During the twelve years of the Reagan and George H. W. Bush presidencies (1981 to 1993), encompassing some of Biden's most active and productive years on the Foreign Relations Committee, the Democrats had no executive control over foreign policy. Biden never served as chairman of the committee during those years, but Claiborne Pell, the slightly eccentric Democratic senator who did serve as chairman when the Democrats controlled the Senate, was not animated by a desire to run for higher office (and, unlike his colleague from Delaware, was not particularly loquacious). The result was that, during those momentous years, Joe Biden came to the fore in many ways as a Democratic spokesman on foreign policy issues.

Rome ranked with Washington and Moscow as the locus of one of the three most significant decisions relating to the Cold War during the presidency of Jimmy Carter (January 1977 to January 1981). The Washington decision was Carter's commitment to proceed with production of the Pershing II intermediate-range ballistic missile. In Rome, the College of Cardinals elected Karol Wojtyla, the archbishop of Krakow, to the papacy. (Although the new pope—John Paul II—surely had no use for the missile, the missile and the pope had important roles in bringing about the *fin de regime* in Moscow.) And in Moscow, the Politburo decided to deploy the Soviet Army for the purpose of installing a new regime in Afghanistan.

The Pershing II story is no ordinary tale of tit for tat in the East-West arms race. In the spring of 1976, a few months before Carter was elected, Brezhnev deployed solid-fuel Soviet SS-20 intermediate-range missiles in the western region of the USSR. From there, the nuclear-armed and highly accurate SS-20 could—*without* putting any target in the United States at risk—destroy, as Nitze put it, "every military installation, airfield, port, rail junction, command center, and city in Western Europe."[1] Brezhnev's defense ministry had given him mixed advice about whether to deploy the SS-20. In the end, the decision to deploy reflected a tendency aptly described by George Kennan in a 1976 article: "They will, rather because they are Russians than because they are Communists, continue to cultivate and maintain armed forces on a scale far greater than any visible threat to their security would seem to warrant."[2]

The purpose of the SS-20 was to drive a wedge between the United States and its European NATO allies. It did this by raising the possibility that US leaders could be put to a choice as to whether to respond to a limited nuclear attack in Europe with ICBMs launched from the United

States, thereby inviting the destruction of every city in the United States for the sake of staying true to Article 5 of the North Atlantic Treaty. In the parlance of the day, the purpose of the SS-20 was to "decouple" Europe from the United States. Mikhail Gorbachev would later record that the decision to deploy SS-20 missiles had "reflected the style of the Soviet leadership at the time, decision-making fraught with grave consequences for the country."[3]

Carter's answer to the SS-20 was to sign off—with the concurrence of NATO ministers—on the continued development of the Pershing II, as well as ground-launched Tomahawk cruise missiles. The Pershing II mirrored the threat of the SS-20, while the cruise missiles upped the ante with their ability to cross into Soviet territory at a height of fifty feet above the ground—under the radar. The deployment of the US and Soviet medium-range weapons would have more than a little to do with the development of the political career—and foreign policy credentials—of Senator Joe Biden.

Pope John Paul II was the first non-Italian pope in 455 years, the first-ever Slavic pope, and the youngest in more than a century. Elected in 1978, the new pope hastened to visit his native Poland, where twelve million Poles heard his thirty-two sermons. The pope's visit was a watershed event in Poland.[4] "'How could you possibly allow the election of a citizen of a socialist country as pope?' [KGB chief and later general secretary Yuri] Andropov demanded of his unfortunate bureau chief in Warsaw."[5] Andropov's question was unanswerable. Not even the KGB controlled the College of Cardinals.

The invasion of Afghanistan triggered a US embargo on grain exports to the Soviet Union and doomed the prospects for ratification of the SALT II Treaty, which Carter and Brezhnev had signed in Vienna in June 1979. Carter, as described by Zubok, "had a curious combination of good intentions, strong ideas, vagueness in priorities, and micromanaging style."[6] That problem was aggravated by tension between realpolitik, as practiced by his national security advisor, Zbigniew Brzezinski, and the less assertive preferences of his secretary of state, Cyrus Vance. Brzezinski, the son of a Polish diplomat who had the good fortune to have been posted to Canada at the time of the Nazi invasion of Poland, had deeply rooted views on East-West relations. His 155-page master's thesis at McGill University, titled "Russo-Soviet Nationalism" (1950), demonstrated intensive study of the origins and effects of nationalism in the USSR. Brzezinski's life experiences and intellect put him in the same league as Henry Kissinger as a force in national security policy.

Enter Ronald Reagan

In mid-August 1980, as the presidential campaign was beginning to heat up, seventeen thousand workers at the Lenin Shipyard in Gdansk, Poland, went on strike under the leadership of Lech Wałęsa, demanding that Communist Party–controlled trade unions be disbanded in favor of unions controlled by the workers. This was good timing for the campaign of Ronald Reagan, running on a Republican platform pledging support for "the captive nations of Central and Eastern Europe in their hope to achieve self-determination."[7] (The platform mentioned the Soviet Union forty-four times.)

Reagan proceeded to pummel President Carter in the fall campaign, portraying him as weak and irresolute. The fulcrum for Reagan's attack was the brazen capture and continuing captivity of fifty-two American hostages in Tehran in late 1979. Reagan won the election with 50.7 percent of the vote, carrying forty-four states, resulting in an Electoral College vote of 489 to 49. (The hostages were released on January 20, 1981, minutes after Reagan's inauguration as president.)

In 1981, Reagan's first year in office, the Department of Defense reckoned the Soviet Union to have "the most powerful land army in the world."[8] The Kremlin's explanation for that would have been that the European members of NATO alone had more than a million troops under arms (not including half a million in France), augmented by US naval, air, and ground forces in place in a 180-degree arc from the North Cape to the Black Sea. Reagan made clear in his inaugural address that while he would not hesitate to negotiate with America's adversaries, he intended to negotiate from a position of strength. But first, Reagan had to have someone to *negotiate with.* The Communist Party of the Soviet Union had four general secretaries during Reagan's first five years in office. Brezhnev died in November 1982; Yuri Vladimirovich Andropov, in February 1984; and Konstantin Ustinovich Chernenko, in March 1985, to be succeeded by Mikhail Sergeievich Gorbachev.

Perhaps because of his long track record of strident anticommunist and anti-Soviet rhetoric, Reagan had some doubters from the outset of his presidency regarding his potential as a peacemaker. George Kennan, for one, in a speech at Dartmouth College in November 1981, decried the "systematic dehumanization of the leadership of another great country," concluding that the prevailing anti-Soviet rhetoric revealed "intellectual primitivism and naiveté unpardonable in a great government."[9] (And this was more than a year *before* Reagan famously called the Soviet Union an evil empire.) But by mid-1982, a few months before Brezhnev died, Reagan made it clear that his approach to relations with the Soviet Union was not as simplistic as might have been thought in some quarters. In an address to the British House of Commons in June, Reagan freely acknowledged the need to negotiate. He told the Brits that the very existence of nuclear weapons was "why negotiations on intermediate-range nuclear forces now underway in Europe and the START talks—Strategic Arms Reduction Talks—which will begin later this month, are not just critical to American or Western policy; they are critical to mankind."[10] Reagan's explicit reference to intermediate-range nuclear force (INF) negotiations was one of the early indications of his commitment to elimination of those weapons.

The main problem at that point in Reagan's presidency was that though the president was willing and able to come to the table, Brezhnev, due to his failing health, was not. Brezhnev died in November 1982. His successor, quickly selected, was Yuri Andropov. There was some thought in Western circles that despite his upbringing in the KGB (of which he had been chairman for fifteen years), Andropov might have some reformist instincts and might be willing to act on those instincts. By Ambassador Anatoly Dobrynin's estimate, Andropov's "intellectual abilities were certainly a cut above those of Brezhnev and Chernenko."[11] That intellectual ability, and any reformist tendency he may have had, would have been sorely tested if his health had permitted him to lead the country in a new direction. One fundamental problem, later addressed by Gorbachev with cataclysmic results, was that by the early 1980s, the Politburo had become as insulated from societal feedback mechanisms as any tsar had been. But Andropov's fifteen-month tenure was essentially an interregnum.

Meanwhile, the Reagan administration had to deal with some internal conflicts on national security policy. The policy differences within

Reagan's national security team were as pronounced as the Vance-Brzezinski misalignment during the Carter administration. But here we find evidence of Reagan's resolve and his willingness to follow his instincts, even if the resulting course was at odds with the advice of some career national security professionals. Reagan's willingness to follow his instincts manifested itself in the realm of arms reduction, particularly with intermediate-range nuclear forces (INF)—the SS-20 and the Pershing. Here, careers of the president from California and the senator from Delaware intersected.

The issues surrounding INF reductions had the attention of Senator Joe Biden in 1982 and 1983. He was not then the chairman of the Foreign Relations Committee; he was not even the ranking minority member. But, remarkably, he entered the INF discussion in his capacity as the chairman of the NATO Special Committee on Nuclear Weapons in Europe, a multinational committee established by the North Atlantic Assembly—the parliamentary arm of NATO—to develop policy recommendations amid intense controversy in Europe, and to a lesser extent in the US, on the whole issue of introduction of intermediate-range nuclear weapons into Western Europe.

On November 18, 1982, under the leadership of Joe Biden (then two days short of forty years old), the NATO Special Committee secured the adoption by the North Atlantic Assembly of a resolution strongly advocating the two-track strategy of proceeding with "modernisation of . . . theatre nuclear forces while seeking negotiated East-West limits on such forces."[12] Although Biden's statement to the North Atlantic Assembly in support of the resolution did not specifically mention Article 5 of the North Atlantic Treaty, he told the assembly that the central purpose of the two-track policy was to "retain a strategic link between West European-based [i.e., INF] and U.S.-based forces [i.e., long range-bombers and ICBMs] which would, in addition to its military benefits, *reassure public opinion of the continuing validity of our defensive plans and posture*." This, said Biden, was "the only practical and responsible policy."[13] In other words, Europeans—as well as Kremlin leaders—need to understand that the whole purpose of the two-track policy is to sustain the credibility of the Article 5 commitment to collective security while engaging with equal seriousness in negotiations to remove Europe from the shadow of intermediate-range nuclear weapons. It took nearly six more years (which included some cooperation and some friction between Biden and Reagan) to get an INF treaty negotiated, signed, and ratified on both sides.

In 1983, the Republicans had a four-seat majority in the Senate. The Foreign Relations Committee was chaired by Charles Percy of Illinois, who—as was traditional for that committee—generally took a bipartisan approach to committee business. Biden was a beneficiary of that bipartisanship, and it is fair to speculate that Percy and Biden probably had some interesting conversations about Reagan's rhetoric, especially after Reagan, in an address in March to a convention of the National Association of Evangelicals in Orlando, cautioned the audience not to "ignore the facts of history and the aggressive impulses of an evil empire."[14] (This was after delighting his audience with a story about the first politician ever to make it to Heaven.) Conservative evangelical Christians had been a major factor in Reagan's 1980 victory over Carter; he was not about to disappoint them with a milquetoast speech. The audience gave the president a standing ovation as the orchestra played "Onward, Christian Soldiers."

The "evil empire" speech was not well received in Moscow or, for that matter, in some quarters in the US. The *New York Times* reported that "Tass called the speech an example of Mr. Reagan's 'pathological hatred of Socialism and Communism' and a revival of 'the worst rhetoric of the cold war.'"[15] Anthony Lewis, a Pulitzer Prize–winning liberal commentator, concluded that "the real Ronald Reagan was speaking in Orlando. The exaggeration and the simplicities are there not only in the rhetoric but in the process by which he makes decisions."[16] Lewis had a point when he said the speech reflected the real Reagan. Reagan recorded in his memoir that he had made the "evil empire" speech "with malice aforethought; I wanted to remind the Soviets that we knew what they were up to."[17]

Two weeks after the Orlando speech, Reagan mixed rhetoric with substance in his "star wars" speech, in which he proposed the development of the ballistic missile-defense system that was officially known as the Strategic Defense Initiative. Biden criticized both the tone and the substance of the star-wars speech; the substance would later bedevil Gorbachev.

Biden's split with Reagan on the merits of SDI did not surface until later. But he immediately criticized Reagan's rhetoric, this time as the spokesman for a bipartisan group of fifteen senators urging Reagan to show good faith on the issue of INF reductions by unilaterally removing largely obsolete tactical (short-range) nuclear weapons from Europe. As the chairman of the NATO Special Committee, Biden was acutely aware of the strength of the antinuclear movement: As far as Biden was concerned, Reagan's rhetoric about nuclear weapons had needlessly aroused the antinuclear movement in the US and abroad. Biden made it plain that he recognized the importance of countering the Soviet SS-20 with Tomahawk and Pershing II missiles (or by negotiating the removal of all three weapons). He was also aware of a real possibility that the European antinuclear movement might get enough traction to prevent deployment of US INF weapons in Europe, leaving the Russians with precisely the advantage they hoped to gain by deploying the SS-20.

Because it was not an election year, 1983 would have been a good year to make some real headway in arms control—the kind of headway that requires national leaders to put some of their political capital on the line. That was not to be. As the year wore on, Andropov got steadily weaker and was increasingly under close medical care. In September, a Soviet fighter plane shot down a Korean Airlines airliner that had strayed off course into Soviet airspace enroute from Anchorage to Seoul, killing all 269 passengers and crew. And by the end of November, the first Pershing II and Tomahawk missiles were in place in Western Europe—the Pershings in West Germany and the Tomahawks in Belgium, Germany, Italy, the Netherlands, and the UK.

The deployment of these INF weapons was precisely what Carter and Reagan (to say nothing of the young senator from Delaware) had in mind to set the table for serious arms-control negotiations. As Reagan recorded, both he and Paul Nitze (as chief US arms-control negotiator) were convinced "that the Soviets wouldn't budge on removing the SS-20 missiles aimed at Europe unless and until we deployed our INF missiles."[18] Nitze's experience and intellect ran very deep. He had been vice chairman of the strategic bombing survey at the end of World War II and principal author of NSC-68. For good reason, Reagan had complete confidence in Nitze's ability to deal with the Russians.

In January 1984, Reagan used a nationally televised speech to hold out the olive branch to the Kremlin. In February, Biden and his Republican senate colleague, William Cohen, hand-carried that olive branch to Moscow. Reagan's speech was as conciliatory—and as emphatic about arms control—as anything he had ever said about the Soviet Union: "Nuclear arsenals are far too high, and our working relationship with the Soviet Union is not what it must be. . . . Neither we nor the Soviet Union can wish away the differences between our two societies and our philosophies, but we should always remember that we do have common interests and the foremost among them is to avoid war and reduce the level of arms."[19]

Andropov died less than a month after Reagan's speech. A plenum of the Central Committee promptly turned to Chernenko. The election of Chernenko (seventy-two years old) to succeed Andropov (sixty-nine when he died) indicated to Dmitri Simes, of the Carnegie Endowment, that "they wanted a caretaker, there was no heir apparent among the younger men and the old guard wanted continuity and stability."[20] As it happened, before Andropov died, Biden and Cohen had been invited by the Soviet Academy of Sciences to visit Moscow to discuss the US arms-control initiatives.[21] Arriving in Moscow a few days after Chernenko took office, they explained US proposals to the Academy of Sciences' other high-ranking Soviet officials.[22] By Biden's account: "We found a great deal more common ground than the Soviets thought beforehand was there."[23]

Chernenko's thirteen months in office amounted to another interregnum, this one presided over by a general secretary who was, as described by Yegor Ligachev, "a classic apparatchik—from head to toe, to his very marrow."[24] (Ligachev, who became second secretary after Gorbachev was elected general secretary, would later have equally unflattering things to say about Gorbachev.) Less than a week after Chernenko took office, Western diplomats began to wonder about his health.[25] Chernenko died two months after Reagan's second inauguration and seven months after Reagan said, jokingly, and unaware that he was speaking into a live microphone: "I am pleased to tell you I just signed legislation which outlaws Russia forever. The bombing begins in five minutes."[26] To their credit, Soviet leaders chose not to criticize this gaffe too harshly, but antinuclear groups, including the Greens in West Germany, found it useful.

Chapter 15

Mikhail Sergeivich Gorbachev: Viewed from East and West

By Ligachev's account, at the hastily called Politburo meeting, held a few hours after Chernenko died in March 1985, the question of who would chair the funeral commission hung heavily in the air—because, by tradition, that would be the "first, unambiguous step toward selecting a general secretary."[27] Gorbachev won that election. The next day, at the recommendation of the Politburo and on motion of Foreign Minister Gromyko, Mikhail Gorbachev was unanimously elected general secretary by the Central Committee of the CPSU. Gorbachev would be the last incumbent in a party office created in 1922 by Lenin specifically for the benefit of Stalin. He had the distinction of having been the principal author of the last chapter of the history of a nation that no longer exists—and having lived to tell about it.

Gorbachev was young, energetic, and eloquent. Impatient with the USSR's stagnation and underdevelopment, he was painfully aware of how life for average families in Western Europe compared with life in the Soviet Union. Gorbachev's reform initiatives are famously capsulized under the headings of perestroika (restructuring) and glasnost (openness). Volumes have been written—not the least of which is Gorbachev's own memoir—about Gorbachev's tenure as general secretary, then as the first president of the Soviet Union, and finally as the signatory on the document that ended the existence of the USSR. New and newly relevant information makes it worthwhile to take another look at some of the pivotal events between March 1985, when Gorbachev was elected general secretary, and December 1991, when the flag of the Soviet Union was lowered for the last time.

Although Gorbachev is maligned in many quarters (and most vehemently of all in his own country), any fair assessment of his leadership must begin with an understanding that the Soviet Union he was called upon to lead in 1985 was not on a sustainable path. Consequently, the likelihood is vanishingly small that, at the end of 1991, *any* leader could have successfully presided over a nation having any real resemblance to the Soviet Union as it existed in March 1985.

It was, of course, inevitable that a new generation would eventually take over; the Brezhnev dynasty could not go on forever. Even so, it is remarkable that George Kennan—writing six years before Brezhnev died and nine years before Gorbachev took office—predicted the arrival of a new generation that would be "more pragmatic [and] less confined by ideological rigidities."[28] Gorbachev was well aware from day one that the country he now led was not on a sustainable path, either domestically or geopolitically. Military expenditures amounted to 40 percent of the state budget.[29] This, combined with the USSR's vulnerability to wide swings in oil prices on the world market, left Gorbachev with very few good options as he contemplated how his country could respond to Reagan's massive military buildup. Despite—or more likely because of—the tight spot he was in, Gorbachev did not delay in opening the door to serious dialogue with Reagan. In June, Gorbachev sent Reagan a letter expressing, as he put it, his "positive attitude to a personal meeting" with Reagan.[30] Foreshadowing controversy to come, Gorbachev insistently criticized Reagan's SDI plans, arguing—as Biden and some of his senate colleagues later would—that the development of the missile-defense system could violate the 1972 Anti-Ballistic Missile Treaty. Reagan firmly believed that the weapon system envisioned by SDI could only be thought of as defensive. That, of course, was in the eye of the beholder. Gromyko made it plain to Nitze that, as far as the Kremlin was concerned, SDI was a "sword of Damocles, designed to deny the Soviet Union the ability to retaliate after an initial attack."[31]

By the time they had their first summit meeting in Geneva in November 1985, Gorbachev had had nearly five years to take the measure of Reagan as president. Reagan's resolve when confronted with a stark choice between right and wrong—or between good and evil as he saw it—was well known to Gorbachev. Reagan's resolve and his ideology were a potent combination, as the world learned during his first year as president, when he summarily fired more than eleven thousand air traffic controllers who, in violation of federal law (and their oaths), went on strike for better pay and working conditions. Secretary of State George Shultz was heard to say that Reagan's decision to fire the striking controllers "was the most important foreign policy move Ronald Reagan ever made."[32] It is reasonable to give both Reagan and Gorbachev credit for their personal resolve. There may have been no real difference between them on that score. But resolve is tested by pressure, and the pressures that ultimately confronted Gorbachev far exceeded anything Reagan ever had to worry about.

Reagan's briefing materials for the Geneva summit undoubtedly included the substance of a National Intelligence Estimate rendered on November 18, 1985, titled "Domestic Stress on the Soviet System." The NIE concluded that "Soviet domestic problems are a constraint on Soviet capabilities for military technological competition with the West, especially with respect to mass production of high-technology items."[33] This was not lost on Reagan. In the memorandum he dictated just before the summit, Reagan observed that Gorbachev "doesn't want to face the cost of competing with us" in defense spending.[34]

The main product of the Geneva summit was rapport between Reagan and Gorbachev. In terms of documents signed, there was not much substance, mostly because of the impasse on SDI. From Gorbachev's perspective, there could be no real progress on arms control as long as Reagan refused to abandon SDI. And if Gorbachev had hoped that, at long last, the Americans would stop harping on human rights, he was disappointed. In a one-on-one session on the second day of the summit, Reagan's focus on human rights could only have impressed on Gorbachev that human rights under communist rule were a serious issue with Reagan—at least as serious as they had been with Henry Jackson. But, unlike Jackson, Reagan chose to broach the topic privately. He understood the folly of publicly putting Gorbachev on the spot.[35]

As for rapport, Gorbachev recorded (echoing Prime Minister Margaret Thatcher's assessment of Gorbachev) that he came out of the Geneva summit with an understanding that "Ronald Reagan too was a man 'you could do business with.'"[36] Reagan's assessment of Gorbachev was the same.[37] Though Reagan was happy that he and Gorbachev had gotten off to a good start, Biden's take on the summit was that "if he were to rate the summit on a scale of good, bad or indifferent, he would choose 'indifferent.'"[38] (One thing we don't yet know is whether Biden would, at least privately, apply that word to his June 2021 summit with Vladimir V. Putin.)

The mediocre grade Biden gave the Reagan-Gorbachev summit was doubtless a result of the fact that he opposed SDI (albeit not for the same reasons Gorbachev opposed it) but had no trouble agreeing with deployment of the Pershing II. He wholeheartedly subscribed to the proposition that, in dealing with the Russians, the only answer to strength was strength. As Reagan traveled to Geneva, Biden told a college audience that "we now have the ability two and a half times over to knock out every single Soviet land-based system for the first time since they've had their big missiles. That's why they're back at the table. That's why they're talking about major reductions." He was unconcerned about the Kremlin's ability to answer SDI: "The Soviet Union is a Third World nation in terms of technology. . . . It is a country in the mid-1950s in every sense but in the nuclear war-making capability."[39] By this time, just short of his forty-third birthday, Biden was no neophyte on the Foreign Relations Committee, having served on the committee for ten years.

By the spring of 1986, a few months after the "indifferent" summit, Biden was actively positioning himself to run in the 1988 presidential election. A *Wall Street Journal* article, noting that Biden "fancies himself an expert on the North Atlantic Treaty Organization," quoted him as criticizing both Carter and Reagan on their approaches to the Soviet Union: "The central theme of their foreign policies has been, 'How do we modify Soviet behavior?' where I think it ought to be, 'How do we manage the conflict?'" Howard Baker, a Tennessee Republican who had served as senate majority leader and would soon be Reagan's chief of staff, opined that "there is real substance to Joe. He dares to think some unconventional thoughts." The article concluded that "there is little doubt that Joe Biden has the potential to play in the big leagues. But it would be a shame if he were pushed up too quickly."[40] (This was 1986.)

As a presidential candidate, Biden stayed with his argument that the United States should hold an olive branch in one hand and a big stick in the other. He pressed the Reagan administration on arms control, describing the administration as being "at war with itself" because it couldn't decide whether it really was committed to arms control.[41] As for the big stick, Biden partook of Harry Truman; conscious of Iran's humiliation of Jimmy Carter in the hostage crisis, he understood that no Democrat who was squishy in his support for US military power, or irresolute in its use, had ever been elected (or re-elected) president. He thought the Democratic Party should be unabashed in its support for military power, contending that Americans "are afraid the Republicans are too tough. But they think we [Democrats] are not tough enough."

Voters, Biden said, have favored "what they perceive as the firmer hands."[42] This theme continued into the postmortems after Vice President George H. W. Bush won the 1988 presidential election (decisively defeating Michael Dukakis, who won the Democratic nomination after Biden and others dropped out or lost in the primaries). On the day Bush was inaugurated in January 1989, Biden was quoted as lamenting, again, that the voters did not trust the Democrats' "willingness to be tough." "We have to argue that military power is important. . . . [We] must maintain our defenses even if it comes at the price of some social programs."[43]

No mere chronological account can do justice to the long arc of events from the first Reagan-Gorbachev summit in Geneva, in late 1985, to their last substantive meeting in Moscow in the spring of 1988. In the thirty months between those summits, Reagan's domestic situation—at least as it might have any real effect on his geopolitical leverage—remained essentially unchanged. To be sure, episodes such as the Iran-Contra affair came and went, but they seemed only to burnish Reagan's reputation as the "Teflon president." On the other side of the divide, manageable reform morphed into an unmanageable (and ultimately terminal) crisis as events within the USSR—especially in the Russian Republic—and the Warsaw Pact fed on each other, leading to the demise of the multinational empire that was the Union of Soviet Socialist Republics. That chain of events was driven in part by strategies conceived and implemented by Reagan and his national security team. But, in the end, the proximate cause of the demise of the empire came from within rather than from without. For his part, Reagan, a retired actor, played the role Kennan had scripted for US leaders thirty-eight years before Reagan and Gorbachev met in Geneva. The effect of Reagan's strategy was that the Soviet Union was, as Kennan had prescribed, "contained by the adroit and vigilant application of counter-force at a series of constantly shifting geographical and political points."[44] Thus, external pressure played a role; internal forces wrote the last act of the drama.

Going into the summit, Gorbachev had more reason than ever to persist in his opposition to SDI. Between October 1985 and June 1986, the price of the benchmark Brent crude oil had fallen by two-thirds, to less than ten dollars a barrel, putting a nine billion–ruble hole in the Soviet budget. Gorbachev had no desire to commit billions of rubles to a

Soviet version of SDI. But Reagan remained steadfast in support of SDI, signing National Security Decision Directive 238, which unequivocally endorsed SDI research, a few weeks before the summit.[45]

In ten hours of talks in Reykjavik, Reagan and Gorbachev arrived at the basic terms of an INF agreement—ultimately finalized fourteen months later.[46] But the byproduct of the summit was frustration rather than agreement. Gorbachev correctly recorded (and Reagan agreed) that "success was a mere step away, but SDI proved an insurmountable stumbling-block."[47]

The impasse over SDI played directly into Biden's dual role as a member of both the Foreign Relations Committee and the Judiciary Committee. In 1986, he was the ranking minority member of the Judiciary Committee—and was again in the majority in 1987, after the voters gave control of the Senate to the Democrats in the 1986 elections. As for the wisdom of letting SDI be a dealbreaker, there was a consensus but not unanimity among Democrats. Opposing SDI, Biden "shared the deep disappointment of people around the world" and was, he said, "puzzled by the decision to pass up a real opportunity to destroy a large portion of the Soviet nuclear arsenal."[48] In contrast, Zbigniew Brzezinski, Jimmy Carter's former national security advisor, thought the Reykjavik summit was a trap for the unwary, arguing that giving in on SDI would have been a serious mistake.[49]

Biden's legal objection to SDI was as emphatic as his policy opposition. His legal argument—which had substantial support, including respectable academic support—was twofold. First, Biden insisted that the 1972 Anti-Ballistic Missile treaty prohibited development and testing of *any* anti-ballistic missile system. He did not mince words: "Unilateral executive action to implement a new interpretation of the ABM Treaty would represent not only [1] cavalier arrogance toward international law, but [2] a direct challenge to the Constitution's delineation of the treaty power."[50] The first issue—interpretation of the ABM treaty—was a pivotal issue for US-Soviet relations and, equally, for relations within the NATO alliance.[51] America's NATO allies in Europe were not interested in living in the shadow of the Russian SS-20s if the only thing keeping those warheads aimed at European capitals was Reagan's insistence on a not-yet-invented weapon system that might, at some future date, intercept ICBMs headed for New York and Chicago.

Biden's "treaty power" argument was a matter altogether separate from the international law argument. The gist of the treaty-power argument was that, when the 1972 ABM treaty was considered by the Foreign Relations Committee and ratified by the full Senate, there was no suggestion that the document would permit the development of a space-based anti-missile system using any technology not existing at that time. Ergo, the argument went (as aired in a *joint* meeting of the Foreign Relations and Judiciary committees in mid-March 1987), any contrary interpretation of the treaty would undermine the Senate's prerogative of granting or withholding ratification of a treaty based on the meaning of the document as understood at the time it was presented to the Senate for ratification. This was originalism, Biden-style. Biden's view of Senate prerogatives ultimately prevailed—and is now institutionalized as the "Biden-Byrd Condition" to Senate ratification, which typically provides that a treaty must be interpreted in accordance with the common understanding of the treaty as shared by the president and the Senate at the time of ratification. But SDI survived the immediate post-Reykjavik controversy.

Reagan was fortunate—as were the American people—to have the services of George P. Shultz as his secretary of state from mid-1982 to the end of his presidency. Shultz matched Reagan in depth of convictions but not in stridence of rhetoric. In April 1987, about midway between the Reykjavik summit and the next summit (in Washington, in December of that year), Shultz, Nitze, and Ambassador Jack Matlock had a long meeting with Gorbachev in Moscow. Gorbachev complained, not without reason, that as soon as it began to look like the ABM treaty limits were too tight for the US side, they called in the lawyers to come up with a broad interpretation.[52] Shultz and Gorbachev just kept talking. Then there was some movement. As recorded in the State Department's memorandum of the conversation, "If the administration was that committed to SDI," Gorbachev said, then he "proposed to record the Soviet side's agreement to the U.S. side's conducting laboratory research." That is, research "conducted without launching an object into outer space."[53] This was a major breakthrough.

With the progress made in the spring of 1987, insiders in Washington and Moscow understood that no major obstacles remained in the way of an INF treaty, to bring about the removal and destruction of the Pershing IIs, the Tomahawks, and the SS-20s. Reagan had enough confidence in the momentum of the INF negotiations to refer to the negotiations in a speech he gave while standing in front of the Berlin Wall, near the Brandenburg Gate, in mid-June: "Because we remained strong, today we have within reach the possibility, not merely of limiting the growth of arms, but of eliminating, for the first time, an entire class of nuclear weapons from the face of the earth." While he was at it, he made the speech famous by addressing Gorbachev directly: "General Secretary Gorbachev, if you seek peace—if you seek prosperity for the Soviet Union and Eastern Europe—if you seek liberalization, come here, to this gate. Mr. Gorbachev, open this gate. Mr. Gorbachev, tear down this wall."[54] On the same day, the North Atlantic Council, meeting in Reykjavik, endorsed the proposed INF treaty.

The treaty was initialed by Shultz and Soviet foreign minister Eduard Shevardnadze in Geneva on November 24, just in time for formal signing at the Washington summit set to begin on December 8. Reagan and Gorbachev finally had something to celebrate at a summit meeting, and they made the most of it in an elaborate ceremony in the East Room at the White House. More than 2,600 US and Soviet missiles were, as the *New York Times* put it, to be "smashed, exploded, crushed, burned or launched to be destroyed."[55] But not before the US Senate had its say.

Though the INF treaty enjoyed public support across a wide political spectrum, it had to be steeped in a witch's brew of politics during the senate ratification process. The treaty had been negotiated by a *Republican* administration. It would be ratified, if at all, by a Senate controlled by the *Democrats.* (It had been fifteen years since the Senate had ratified an arms-control treaty.) The most ardent opponent of the treaty was a *Republican*, Senator Jesse Helms. Its most active senate supporter was a *Democrat* named Joe Biden. But Biden fully intended to attach to the treaty—over Republican opposition—the "Biden-Byrd condition," to preclude later reinterpretation of the treaty by the executive branch. And it was a presidential election year; Democratic support for the treaty would amount to an explicit admission that the Republican administration had done something right.

With the Foreign Relations Committee hearings set to start in late January 1988, Biden—as chairman of the Subcommittee on European Affairs—would play a major role in the committee's deliberations on the treaty and in the subsequent floor debate.[56] He laid the groundwork for the ratification process by going to London, Bonn, Paris, and Brussels to gauge support for the treaty among NATO allies, capping the trip with a meeting with Gromyko (then the chairman of the Presidium of the Supreme Soviet) in Moscow in mid-January. (This was his third trip to the Soviet Union.) Biden liked what he heard from NATO allies: "Everywhere I went, with every single political leader that I met, there was absolute unanimity about the need for us to see to it that the Senate quickly and in an unencumbered way ratify the INF agreement."[57] As for the Russian attitude, Biden "said he found the political atmosphere very different" from his previous visits. "They concluded they have a Third World economy and that they're in deep, deep trouble. And I believe they want a halt in the competition in effect for the next 15 or so years."[58]

This was, to be sure, not Biden's first day in the sun as a voice worthy of national and international note in international affairs. But it is unmistakable that his successful advocacy of the INF treaty, both at home and abroad, marked a significant milestone in the inherently incremental process by which this player earned national stature in the foreign policy arena. This was not lost on Pulitzer Prize–winning *Washington Post* columnist David Broder. Broder sat down with Biden for a two-hour conversation in anticipation of the committee hearings, resulting in a nationally syndicated column, "The Education of Joe Biden." Biden told Broder that he hoped the hearings would serve to "reestablish an essential bipartisan center . . . that can sustain foreign policy on a stable basis." As for the significance of that moment in the East-West relationship, Biden recognized that "the next five years can be as important, for good or ill, as the first five years after World War I or World War II." Broder was impressed. A few months before, Biden had withdrawn from the presidential race, but Broder was not ready to write Joe Biden off: "As gifted as he is at 45, I think the Democrats will find him better presidential material at 49 or 53 or 57 or 61. And meantime, Delaware and the nation have a senator who is providing no small service by taking on some of the most important challenges we face."[59] Biden was in for a busy winter and spring.

After he returned from his visit to the European capitals, Biden authored an op-ed in the *New York Times*. He made four interrelated points: (1) SDI is a bad idea, and is "dispiriting" to our NATO allies because it implies "decoupling" from Europe "by seeking sanctuary beneath an antinuclear astrodome," (2) the administration's proposed reinterpretation of the ABM treaty—so as to permit SDI development and testing—made the US look like an unreliable ally, willing to destroy the bedrock of arms control "in pursuit of a Presidential whim," (3) at Reykjavik, Reagan "appeared willing to discard nuclear weapons and NATO doctrine with little thought and no consultation," and (4) the INF treaty should promptly be ratified.[60]

The Foreign Relations Committee hearings, filling five volumes of testimony, ran into May, with the result that the floor debate on ratification didn't begin until May 17. This put the administration in a squeeze, because Reagan was due in Moscow at the end of May for a summit, the high point of which was to be the exchange of instruments of ratification of the INF treaty. For Biden, the prolonged committee hearings were time well spent. The committee reported favorably on the treaty, *but* with a draft instrument of ratification that included the Biden-Byrd condition, limiting interpretation of the treaty to "the common understanding of the Treaty shared by the President and the Senate at the time the Senate gave its advice and consent to ratification."[61] To reinforce his point about post-ratification reinterpretation, Biden elicited from Secretary of State Shultz a confirmation that "the Reagan administration will in no way depart from the INF treaty as we are presenting it to the Senate."[62]

It was not until Reagan was en route to Moscow that he learned, as he recorded, that "the Senate had overwhelmingly ratified the INF treaty after weeks of brinksmanship that made it uncertain Gorbachev and I could complete the ratification papers while I was in Moscow."[63] The final vote, taken with a packed Senate gallery looking on, was 93 to 5. Ironically, Biden had to miss the vote because he was recovering from surgery.

All was now in order for the Moscow summit. Though the exchange of instruments of ratification certainly was the high point, Gorbachev was not happy that Reagan insistently returned to the subject of human rights. Discussion of human rights—especially emigration—was perhaps a bit more irritating to Gorbachev now than at the Geneva or Reykjavik summits because of the restiveness that was developing within the communist hierarchy. Going into the summit, Reagan knew that Gorbachev was contending with growing domestic political turmoil. It was increasingly apparent that Second Secretary Yegor Ligachev, less willing than Gorbachev to stray from traditional communist economic doctrine, was (along with others) pushing back against some of Gorbachev's reforms. As Richard Sakwa puts it, though Ligachev "endorsed a constrained type of reform communism," he "suffered genuine moral torment at seeing the achievements of 'socialist construction' being torn down."[64] And the economic situation was getting tighter. Reagan's briefing book for the summit disclosed that a decline in annual Soviet GNP growth had produced "stagnation and malaise and threatens to bring the USSR into the 21st century well behind the West."[65] The price of oil was not much over half of what it had been when Gorbachev took office in March 1985.

An understanding of how the US-Soviet relationship played out from 1988 until the Soviet Union ceased to exist on December 25, 1991, requires an understanding of the pressures Gorbachev faced domestically as he pushed for reform. Moving the Soviet Union to a market-based economic system was central to Gorbachev's reform strategy. As far as Gorbachev was concerned, the Politburo could debate all day about the design of a social safety net to protect those who came out on the short end of the conversion to a market economy. But it was essential to move resolutely away from the centrally planned command economy. The problem for Gorbachev was that, though the CPSU retained a firm grip on the levers of power in the USSR, the cleavage between the reformist and conservative ideological camps was getting more obvious by the day. For Ligachev and his fellow conservatives, the move away from a planned economy portended nothing good for the Soviet Union. Ligachev lamented that the "'contractual freedom' that gave enterprises the right to dispose immediately of a considerable part of their products at their own discretion was essentially the spontaneity of market relations." (He had that exactly right.) As Ligachev saw it, this "flareup of group selfishness [i.e., free enterprise] led to a situation in which unprofitable goods started being removed from production everywhere."[66] That, of course, was (and is) one of the key functions of a market economy. That movement toward a market economy was complicated enormously by the fact that, as Ligachev accurately observed: "An attempt was made to implant contractual, in essence commodity-market relations in a planned system without the legal and economic groundwork, without creating a tax system and a market infrastructure."[67]

There is room for debate as to when Gorbachev irretrievably lost control of the cascade of events that ended with his political demise. Some of the skeptics of glasnost were retired from the Politburo in the fall of 1988; Ligachev was relieved of his duties as ideologist and given the agriculture portfolio. And as early as December 1988, Gorbachev found it necessary to comment in a meeting of the Politburo on the perception in other parts of the world that (as recorded in the minutes) "the country is sliding toward chaos."[68] Although Gorbachev was still the man in charge, when he and Reagan sat down in Moscow in May 1988, Reagan's headaches in dealing with the Democrats who controlled both houses of Congress were trifling compared with the mounting pressures on Gorbachev.

One thing Gorbachev wanted, and got, from the Moscow summit was Reagan's retraction of the "evil empire" label for the Soviet Union. In March, the Soviet side had informally requested (through Dobrynin and an intermediary) that the president acknowledge a change in his estimation of the Soviet Union *before* the summit.[69] That didn't happen, but while on a walking tour of the Kremlin grounds, and with Gorbachev at his side, Reagan told reporters that "he no longer sees the Soviet Union as 'the evil empire.'"[70] Gorbachev was pleased: "For me, Ronald Reagan's acknowledgement was one of the genuine achievements of his Moscow visit."[71] And while in Moscow, Reagan strolled the Arbat—almost an obligatory stop for any American tourist—and chatted with ordinary Muscovites. His conclusion was one that would likely be shared by anyone who might have an opportunity to get to know Russian people: "The Soviet people were the warmest, friendliest, nicest people you could ever meet."[72]

The Moscow summit was the last Reagan-Gorbachev meeting with anything substantive on the agenda. (Their meeting on Governor's Island in New York Harbor six months later, on the occasion of a UN speech by Gorbachev, was essentially an occasion for sentimental farewells.) But Gorbachev had good reason to call Reagan's expressed change of attitude a "genuine achievement." It helped set the stage for the next chapter in the bilateral relationship as that unfolded during the presidency of George H. W. Bush.

Bush, as president-elect, attended the Governor's Island meeting, with the result that Reagan, by his account, "enjoyed watching, now almost as an outsider, as Gorbachev and George started to get to know each other."[73] Bush assured Gorbachev that he "would like to build on what President Reagan had done," and Gorbachev, equally unsurprisingly, commented that his "country had become a different one. It would never go back to what it had been three years before, regardless of whether he or someone else were leading it."[74] The ratification of the INF treaty earlier in the year had been a major accomplishment, but *strategic* arms reduction—ICBMs, submarine-launched ballistic missiles, and long-range bombers—remained very much a work in progress. The world was reminded of that fact in late November 1988, with the rollout of the US B-2 stealth bomber, which promised to render much of the Soviet air defense system obsolete, and there is no reason to doubt that Gorbachev's defense advisors would have informed him of that fact. (Although Mathias Rust, a West German teenager, arguably stole that march when he flew his light plane without interference from Helsinki to Moscow in May 1987, circling Red Square before successfully landing his Cessna 172 next to the Kremlin wall.[75])

Reagan's success in his dealings with Gorbachev had several ingredients, not the least of which was the fact that Gorbachev was impressed with the fact that a man of Reagan's deep convictions nevertheless abhorred even the thought of nuclear war and thus recognized, as did Gorbachev, the need to seek common ground. Reagan's personal rapport with Gorbachev made a difference, as did his military buildup, which presented the Kremlin with the prospect of an arms competition that the Kremlin knew quite well was unwinnable for the USSR.[76] Although Bush, not Reagan, was the president during the last years of the existence of the Soviet Union and the glacis, Reagan and his presidency made an indelible impression on the peoples of Eastern Europe. Nowa Huta was a communist-era development, built around a steel plant in Krakow in southern Poland. The spacious central square in Nowa Huta had been home to a large statue of Lenin. In 2004, the Krakow councillors voted to give the square a new name. The new name was Ronald Reagan Central Square (Plac Centralny im. Ronalda Reagana).[77]

George H. W. Bush, not Joe Biden, took the oath of office as president on January 20, 1989. But the Senate was still in Democratic hands, with Biden second only to the chairman among the Democrats on the Foreign Relations Committee. Perhaps because he was thought of as a "relentless conceptualizer,"[78] and one who rarely hesitated to speak his mind, Biden was a Democrat who was heard from with greater frequency on foreign policy issues than the chairman, Claiborne Pell. And in 1989, there was plenty of conceptualizing to be done by all who had any interest in East-West relations.

Just before the end of December 1988, the Politburo paused to consider the prospect of the Bush presidency. Gorbachev had had the opportunity to size up Bush at the Governor's Island meeting earlier that month, which was, of course, aside from the fact that Bush's long career in public service (including as director of the CIA) had produced plenty of material for Soviet intelligence services to analyze. Gorbachev's take on Bush, as he told the Politburo, was that Bush was "a very cautious politician. They say his idiosyncratic feature is the 'natural caution' of Bush." US Ambassador Jack Matlock was quoted to the Politburo as opining that "Bush is more professional, better informed, but at the same time is more cautious."[79] Gorbachev and his comrades could hardly have expected another Ronald Reagan; they clearly understood that they were not getting one.

Bush, in turn, had the benefit of a close evaluation of the evolving situation in the Soviet Union. A National Intelligence Estimate was rendered in the spring of 1989, "Soviet Policy Toward the West: The Gorbachev Challenge," which took an in-depth look at Gorbachev and where he and his nation were headed. Although that NIE predicted a continuation of "vigorous efforts to protect and advance Soviet geopolitical interests," it assessed that Gorbachev's policy changes were getting some traction, noting that "Moscow wants to shift competition with the West to a largely political and economic plane."[80] That assessment was squarely on point with Biden's prescription, as he articulated it a few weeks before the NIE was issued. He urged adoption of a strategy "with the objectives to reduce risks, encourage a focus on economic growth and move the competition with the Soviets, if we can, into the economic sphere as opposed to the military sphere."[81] It is easily discernible from Biden's observations in early 1989 that he thought the US approach to relations with the Russians should be predicated on three interrelated propositions, as he formulated them: (1) isolation of the USSR from the international economic community,[82] which will (2) lead the Russians to the conclusion that communism is defunct as a worldwide economic model, while bearing in mind that, as Biden put it, (3) "military parity is essential—absolutely essential."[83]

It is not much of an oversimplification (if oversimplification at all) to say that Bush's approach to the momentous events that unfolded in Eastern Europe during his first year as president partook of a time-honored maxim of domestic US politics: when the other side is self-destructing, get out of the way and let it happen. That first year, 1989, was the year it became obvious that the Soviet satellites—the outer layer of the glacis—were destined to break free of domination from Moscow. The inner layer—the Baltics, Ukraine, Belorussia, Moldova, and the Transcaucasian and Central Asian republics—would be independent nations by the end of the third year.

After the Kremlin-dominated regime in East Germany held sham elections in May 1989 (the Erich Honecker dictatorship got 98.85 percent of the vote, triggering massive demonstrations), the Poles showed their neighbors in Eastern Europe how to do it. Lech Wałęsa's Solidarity movement overwhelmed the communists in the popular vote in national elections in June. Gorbachev didn't have to wait for the Berlin Wall to fall (in November) to see the trend. In a speech to the Council of Europe in Strasbourg, on July 6, he knocked on the door of what he called the "common European home." His speech touched on geopolitics, economics, and (most worthy of note in the third decade of the present century) shared liberal democratic values. As for geopolitics, Gorbachev proclaimed that the "realities of today and the prospects for the foreseeable future are obvious: the Soviet Union and the United States are a natural part of the European international and political structure." Gorbachev's Europe was, as he put it, "that part of the world to which we, the Soviet Union, belong, and with which we have been tied most closely over the centuries." This was "our common European home."[84]

As for liberal democratic values, Gorbachev's comments in Strasbourg were noteworthy even though he found it necessary to be a little vague. He praised parliamentary government in general and the Parliamentary Assembly of the Council of Europe in particular. He alluded to the possibility of establishing consular relations with the Council of Europe. He did have some room to talk about parliamentary government with a straight face, but, at that point in the evolution of perestroika, Gorbachev still had one foot in both worlds. On one hand, the Soviet Union had had its first-ever truly contested multicandidate elections in March, and about 20 percent of the seats had been won by independents, including Nobel Peace Prize winner (and dissident nuclear scientist) Andrei Sakharov. Those elections led, in May, to the first Congress of People's Deputies, replacing the USSR Supreme Soviet, and intended by Gorbachev to give perestroika a large dose of legitimacy. Genuinely competitive electoral politics had thus gotten a toehold in the Soviet Union. On the other hand, Article 6 of the 1977 Soviet Constitution was still on the books. It expressly guaranteed the political primacy of the CPSU. Article 6 would not be amended to eliminate the provision for the communist monopoly until early 1990.

A "peaceful and democratic" Europe maintaining "its diversity and common humanistic ideas" was Gorbachev's vision; it was "in such a Europe that we visualize our own future."[85] Gorbachev was convinced, as Vladislav Zubok puts it, "that his romantic schemes of common interests, nonuse of force, and the 'common European home' amounted to a ticket for him and the USSR to join the community of 'civilized nations.'"[86] It was not to be.

On November 9, 1989, a hapless GDR official mistakenly declared at a press conference that the border had been opened to East-West travel. Crowds immediately began dismantling the Berlin Wall. The next day, Anatoly Chernyaev, a principal foreign policy advisor to Gorbachev, recorded in his diary that "this entire era in the history of the socialist system is over. . . . This is the end of Yalta . . . of the Stalinist legacy."[87] Less than a month later, an angry crowd advanced on the Dresden office of the Stasi—the GDR's secret police—and then on the local headquarters of the KGB across the road. This would be a turning point in the life of Vladimir Vladimirovich Putin, the KGB Lieutenant Colonel in charge in Dresden. By his account, he "called our group of forces and explained the situation. And I was told: 'We cannot do anything without orders from Moscow. And Moscow is silent.'"[88] The report that "Moscow is silent" gave Putin "the feeling then that the country no longer existed." Putin's country had what he called "a terminal disease;" specifically, a "paralysis of power."[89]

When the wall came down, Senator Joe Biden, ten years older than Putin, was a little further along in his career in public service than Putin was in his. As the second-ranking Democrat on the Foreign Relations Committee, Biden's standing with the chairman was such that he chaired a one-on-one meeting of the Foreign Relations Committee (no other senators having returned from holiday recess) with eighty-five-year-old George Kennan. Seated opposite Kennan with a few reporters looking on, Biden "gushed like a rookie in the presence of Babe Ruth."[90] Kennan did not disappoint. He saw "a situation of great difficulty and danger for Gorbachev, who is viewed as personally responsible" for political instability and the failure of perestroika to meet "even the normal demands of consumers in large cities." Kennan saw the problems Gorbachev was facing as so serious that it was "questionable whether there is any among his potential rivals who would like, at the present time, to assume this burden in his place."[91]

Although Kennan offered no specific warnings as to the possibility of a resurgence of authoritarianism, it is noteworthy that, even at that stage in the cascade of events in the Soviet Union and Eastern Europe, expert opinion held that it was possible that Russian politics could take a radical turn. In January 1990, James Billington, the Librarian of Congress and an eminent authority on Russian history and culture, raised the possibility that one or the other of two extremes might squeeze out the middle path Gorbachev was attempting to tread. For Billington, the moral high ground was occupied by those who might "build a pluralistic multiparty democracy based on the rule of law following essentially Western models." The darker possibility was "a resurgence of Great Russian chauvinism, which sees a strong, Russian-dominated political machine as the only glue that can hold together an otherwise fragmented and potentially anarchic imperial domain." The key question, for Billington, was whether the Russians could find "a way of feeling good about themselves without feeling hostile to others."[92]

The fall of the Berlin Wall was the first major physical manifestation of the forces that ultimately led to the independence of the Soviet satellites, the unraveling of the Warsaw Pact and the movement—beginning with the Baltic republics—culminating in the dissolution of the Soviet Union. The wall came down in November 1989. But the restiveness was not limited to Germany. In a massive demonstration in August, protesters formed a human chain from Tallinn in Estonia to Riga in Latvia to Vilnius in Lithuania, to remind the world that the fate of those Baltic lands had been sealed fifty years before, on that late night in August 1939, when Ribbentrop and Molotov (with a pleased Stalin looking on) signed the Molotov-Ribbentrop nonaggression pact and its secret protocols. It should thus come as no surprise that, in the late 1980s, the first strong movement toward independence among the Soviet republics began in the Baltics. This makes for an interesting study in how US and Soviet leaders dealt with their domestic constituencies and with each other.

On March 11, 1990 (the fifth anniversary of Gorbachev's election to the office of general secretary), the Lithuanian parliament—having been elected in free multiparty elections in February—voted 124 to 0 to declare Lithuania's independence from Moscow. What had been the Lithuanian Soviet Socialist Republic was now, by parliamentary decree, the Lithuanian Republic. This put Gorbachev on a political tightrope, as witness the fact that, two days after the Lithuanian vote, the Congress of People's Deputies, sitting in Moscow, voted to end the Communist Party's political monopoly and to grant expanded powers to Gorbachev as the first president of the USSR. But to solidify broad support from the Congress on those propositions, Gorbachev found it necessary to unequivocally reject the Lithuanian declaration of independence as "illegitimate and invalid." Gorbachev was in a bind. Legislation was pending to create a powerful new executive presidency. To keep that initiative afloat, he needed to appease conservatives by staving off any controversial action on the Baltic question.[93]

Though the presidential legislation was enacted, Gorbachev's legislative victory was the precarious success of a poker player who had successfully drawn to an inside straight. As the Lithuanian crisis unfolded, Ambassador Jack Matlock cabled to Secretary of State James Baker that Gorbachev's "position is imperiled not by conservative apparatchiki or men on white horses, but rather by the powerful social forces he has unleashed." Matlock's conclusion: "Standing at the center of a crumbling political order, Gorbachev looks less a man in control and more an embattled leader."[94] Matlock was prescient. Aside from the unrest in the Baltics, Ukrainian nationalism was ascendant, even in Russified eastern Ukraine. It is a tribute to Gorbachev's political skills that he remained in office for nearly two years after the Baltics were in open revolt. It would get worse; Gorbachev was due in Washington at the end of May for a summit with Bush. It was increasingly obvious that East and

West Germany were headed for unification and that Bush's position on NATO membership for a unified Germany would carry decisive weight within NATO. The specter of a unified Germany in NATO was a problem of an entirely different order than the crisis in the Baltics. Gorbachev recorded that his Kremlin colleagues "were genuinely convinced that our security could be guaranteed only by perpetuating the division of Germany at all costs."[95]

Lithuania's push for independence generated robust debate within the US foreign policy community, bringing Senator Joe Biden once again into the spotlight. In late March, Soviet troops seized the Communist Party headquarters in Vilnius and were hunting down Lithuanian deserters from the Soviet Army, raising the possibility of a more muscular Soviet military intervention. The day after the seizure of the party headquarters, Biden was a guest on the *MacNeil/Lehrer News Hour,* along with Senator Bill Armstrong of Colorado. In one of those recurring paradoxes of Cold War politics, Biden concurred with Bush's cautious approach to the Baltic crisis while Armstrong, a Republican, rejected any reaction that might seem passive, arguing that the US should not "give any appearance of vacillating or leaving open in some way how we feel about the status of Lithuania." But Biden praised Bush for "erring on the side of giving time for negotiation. . . . How do we allow Gorbachev a way out and save a little bit of face?"[96] On September 6, 1991, in the wake of a failed coup against Gorbachev, and as the disintegration of the Soviet Union was entering its final stages, the State Council of the USSR recognized the independence of all three of the Baltic states. They gained de facto and de jure independence, for the first time in five decades, with a minimum of bloodshed.

Meanwhile, with the satellites—to say nothing of the Baltic republics—in ferment, the May–June 1990 summit was approaching. Gorbachev was feeling the heat from conservatives in the party hierarchy, with tension growing by the day. On March 17, just as Gorbachev was assuming the newly created office of president of the Soviet Union, Ligachev could stand it no more. He wrote a long letter to Gorbachev, in his capacity as general secretary, intended for the eyes of the Central Committee. Ligachev remonstrated about the trend of perestroika, concluding that "under the flag of democracy and glasnost, the ideological and moral pillars of society are being washed away."[97] To put Gorbachev in the right frame of mind for the summit with Bush, Ligachev reminded Gorbachev that "the German question is a priority," lamenting that "the socialist community is falling apart and NATO is growing stronger." Although Ligachev asked Gorbachev to distribute the letter to the Politburo and the Central Committee, the letter, by Ligachev's account, "simply fell into a crevasse." Ligachev explained: "This was Gorbachev's method. Under Stalin, you would have lost your head for a letter like that. Under Khrushchev, you would have been fired. Under Brezhnev, you would be made an ambassador to Africa. And under Gorbachev, you were simply ignored."[98] Had he written his letter one day later, Ligachev would have had one more cause for concern. On March 18, in the first free elections in East Germany since Hitler came to power in 1933, the voters routed the Communist Party in favor of a coalition led by the Christian Democrats, who were actively supported by West German Chancellor Helmut Kohl. German unification was now inevitable.

In preparation for the summit, Secretary Baker met with Gorbachev and Foreign Minister Shevardnadze in the Kremlin in mid-May. The declassified memorandum of that long conversation makes it plain that the status of a reunified Germany—in or out of NATO—was uppermost in Gorbachev's mind. This may well have been more of an indication of conservative pressure on Gorbachev than a reflection of Gorbachev's personal agenda. Baker's arguments to Gorbachev were both practical and legal. The practical argument was that the Russians would be better off with Germany in NATO (relying on the US nuclear umbrella) than with Germany making its way as an untethered free agent in Central Europe.[99] Baker's legal argument was equally uncomplicated: "Neutrality or nonalignment cannot be forced upon a nation. . . . [The] Helsinki [accord] makes it very clear that every country will have the right to participate and to chose [sic] its own alliance."[100] (Baker's argument would be echoed by Biden on the floor of the Senate eight years later, in the context of ratification of the admission of Poland, Hungary, and the Czech Republic to NATO: "Every country must have the right to choose its own security arrangements . . . including whether or not to join the alliance."[101]) Attempting to match legality with legality, Shevardnadze admonished Baker that "when you say Germany will be in NATO you forget all about the Potsdam agreement."[102] The foreign minister did not explain how any agreement reached at Potsdam in 1945 would preclude a unified Germany (which did not exist—and which Stalin intended never to exist—at the time of the Potsdam conference) from making a free choice to join NATO (which also did not exist in 1945).[103]

After his long meeting with Gorbachev, Baker reported to Bush (unsurprisingly) that "Germany definitely overloads [Gorbachev's] circuits right now" and that Gorbachev "had no good answer" to Baker's explanation of the logic of admission of a unified Germany to NATO, including Baker's reminder that "the Helsinki principle . . . gives each state the right to choose its alliances."[104] Equally unsurprising, and highly relevant in the present decade, is the fact that Gorbachev was under pressure to protect ethnic Russians—in this instance in Lithuania. In the wake of the declaration of independence, several thousand ethnic Russians had massed outside the Lithuanian parliament building "to condemn the independence declaration."[105] Gorbachev told Baker that he would bring to the summit "all the telegrams he was receiving asking him to protect the Russians in Lithuania."[106] This would not be the last time a US diplomat would hear about the (soon to be) ethnic Russian diaspora.

At the Washington summit, Gorbachev started by proposing dual membership for Germany—in both NATO and the Warsaw Pact—maintaining that this would be "a forerunner of the new European structures."[107] That was a nonstarter, mainly because Bush insisted, as had Baker, that it was not for the United States and the USSR to dictate to Germany what alliance it must join. For the sake of discussion, Bush acknowledged the possibility that a united Germany might reject NATO, "choose a different path," and tell NATO to get its troops out. This led to Bush's proposed formulation: "The United States is unequivocally in favor of united Germany's membership in NATO, however, if it makes a different choice, we would not contest it, we will respect it." Gorbachev's response: "I agree. I accept your formulation."[108] Slightly over four months later, a united Germany was a member of NATO.[109] Among other consequences, the unification spelled the end of any pretense that France stood on an equal footing with Germany within the European Community.

Though the summit produced little by way of immediate substantive results (mainly due to the lingering standoff between the USSR and Lithuania), it did lay the groundwork for economic cooperation, including legislation sponsored by Biden—still the chairman of the

Subcommittee on European Affairs—to provide funding for technical assistance to the USSR and Eastern European nations. At this point in Gorbachev's tenure, his main defense against attacks from either direction within the Soviet hierarchy was his eminent standing in the international community. Consequently, from Gorbachev's perspective, it was all to the good that, as reported by Ambassador Matlock, "The official assessment of the Washington summit, as exemplified by Gorbachev's June 12 report to the Supreme Soviet, is very positive. . . . This summit is seen as truly marking the end of the cold war, opening a 'new epoch' in Soviet-American relations." Although Gorbachev did get a modest boost from the summit itself, that didn't amount to much when compared with domestic concerns over the food supply and the news of the election of Boris Yeltsin to the presidency of the Russian Republic.[110] Yeltsin had been elected to the presidency of the Russian Republic while Gorbachev was en route to Washington for the summit. As Gorbachev's political rival, Yeltsin would be seen, as aptly described by William J. Burns, as "the heroic destroyer of the old, calcified Soviet system."[111] With Yeltsin's election, over Gorbachev's opposition, Gorbachev was flanked on both the right (Ligachev) and the left by critics with clout.

For our purposes, we need only take a wide-angle view of Gorbachev's final months in office. October 1990 was a momentous month for Gorbachev, who was now both the general secretary of the party and the first president of the USSR. Early in the month, East Germany merged into the Federal Republic of Germany, and, thus, into NATO. On the fifteenth, Gorbachev was awarded the Nobel Peace Prize, which only sharpened the contrast between his stature as an international statesman and his rapidly declining domestic political fortunes. His arrival at the apex of international eminence coincided with (and was not unrelated to) a new low in his domestic standing. Gorbachev recorded that, when the prize was announced, "the situation in our country had come to a head, with all-out attacks launched at me from all sides."[112] Because of the hostile domestic reaction to the award of the prize, he concluded that he could not even travel to Oslo for the ceremony, sending, instead, a deputy foreign minister to deliver a letter of thanks and receive the award. He was not able to travel to Oslo to deliver the customary Nobel lecture until June 1991, about two months before he endured the humiliation of an amateurish (and ultimately unsuccessful) putsch.

The putsch, in August, was attempted by "a motley group of Soviet conservatives."[113] Gorbachev was placed under house arrest, mostly incommunicado, for a few days while vacationing in Crimea (as Russian leaders have done since the days of Catherine II). For Gorbachev, the upside of the putsch was that it was unsuccessful; the downside was that Yeltsin, working tirelessly on Gorbachev's behalf in Moscow, was instrumental in ensuring that it would fail. As Ambassador Burns put it: "Yeltsin was the man of the hour. The failed putsch had stripped bare the fecklessness of the conservative opposition, opening the way for radical democratic and market reform and a range of independence movements."[114] International opposition to the putsch was, of course, all but unanimous. Never before had Western leaders of all political stripes been so passionate in calling for strict adherence to a communist constitution.

In early December 1991, the leaders of the Eastern Slavic republics of the USSR—Russia (represented by Yeltsin), Ukraine, and Belarus—met at a government dacha in Belavezha Forest, Belarus, where they signed an agreement providing for the dissolution of the USSR and the creation of the Commonwealth of Independent States. On the twenty-first, leaders of those republics, the five Central Asian republics,[115] and two of the three Transcaucasian republics,[116] as well as Moldova, met in Kazakhstan to sign the documents expanding the CIS to eleven constituent members, the final step in the dissolution of a multinational empire. With the eleven CIS members, the Baltics and Georgia, there were now fifteen nations instead of one.

Gorbachev put a final coda on the dissolution in a televised address on December 25, announcing his resignation as president of what had been the Union of Soviet Socialist Republics. Authority over the former Soviet nuclear arsenal was transferred to Yeltsin, the president of the Russian Federation. With the assent of the other CIS member states, Russia succeeded to the USSR's position as a member of the United Nations (and as one of the five permanent members of the Security Council).

Gorbachev's address was gracious, not overly boastful, and almost entirely free of self-pity.[117] One sentence deserves attention here: "And today I watch apprehensively the loss of the citizenship of a great country by our citizens—the consequences of this could be grave, for all of us."[118] In one stroke, at least *145 million people*—now living in fourteen of the new sovereign nations—were no longer governed from Moscow. In a Chatham

House publication in 1993, the ethnic Russian portion of that 145 million was credibly estimated at 25 million.[119] It included 12 million ethnic Russians in the newly minted Ukrainian state. As was noted in the prologue, in 2005, President Vladimir V. Putin described the collapse of the Soviet Union as the greatest geopolitical catastrophe of the twentieth century. He elaborated: "As for the Russian nation, it became a genuine drama. Tens of millions of our co-citizens and compatriots found themselves outside Russian territory." Gorbachev's concern for the Russian diaspora at the end of 1991, as echoed in substance by Putin fourteen years later, was not pulled out of thin air. These concerns—rooted in a sense of obligation traceable largely to ethnic affinity—pervade the population of the Russian Federation, including tens of millions of Russians who are otherwise indifferent, at best, to the stewardship of Mr. Putin.

Gorbachev was still a communist on December 25, 1991. In his memoirs, he maintained that "in its essence communism is a humanist ideology," while acknowledging that, in the USSR, "communism was used to camouflage a totalitarian regime."[120] In 1991, that regime was no longer totalitarian, with the result that it could hold a multinational empire together only by common consent, rather than by force. As for domestic politics, not explained by Gorbachev in 730 pages is how he could reasonably have expected to reconcile the market reforms he genuinely desired to implement with any recognizable version of Marxist-Leninist ideology. As political analyst Richard Sakwa puts it, "the Soviet party-state could adapt to society, but in doing so it stopped being the Soviet system."[121] The transformation set in motion by Gorbachev was anathema to the conservatives but could not happen fast enough for the liberals, with the result that Gorbachev was, in the end, unable to control the cascade of events he set in motion. The outcome in December 1991 was not the result he sought. But, at a minimum, he must be given credit, as the first and last president of the Soviet Union, for his role in preserving the peace while forces he could not control dismembered the empire.

Conclusion

The central thesis of this book is that the Cold War was a period in which hundreds of years of history on both sides of the East-West divide were fused into historical memory and popular consciousness, with consequences which undeniably persist to this day. That premise leads to three concluding propositions:

First: We disregard the lessons of history and geography only at our peril.
Second: Those who believe democratic reform in Russia can be coerced or induced from without will be disappointed.
Third: In the long run, don't bet against the Russian people.

Time will tell whether the present and future administrations concur with the three concluding propositions we will now address.

In late 1988, Senator Joe Biden had some good words for James A. Baker, who was preparing to take office as President George H. W. Bush's secretary of state. Biden's advice: "You have a great chance to reinvigorate a bipartisan foreign policy. Everybody here likes you and George Bush—in spite of your tough campaign. We have respect for you both. I want you to know I'm ready to be enlisted in a bipartisan foreign policy approach."[1] The foreign policy challenges now confronting the

United States are far more varied, in some ways far more complex—and no less momentous—than the challenges Bush and Baker faced as they prepared to take office.

To start with the obvious, for President Biden, the point of departure was January 2021, not January 2017, let alone January 1989. Biden and his secretary of state, Antony Blinken, took office with a tall order in front of them in terms of relations with US allies and coalition partners. The internationalist approach of the new administration was the polar opposite of the isolationism of Donald Trump, who, like Putin, had built his base by offering shamelessly reductionist solutions rooted in xenophobic nationalism. Biden and Blinken were well aware that the status quo ante Trump could not be resurrected quickly—and recognized, too, that it might not be politically feasible, even if desirable, to accomplish that restoration in all respects. As for relations with Russia, Biden, having been appointed to the Senate Foreign Relations Committee forty-six years before he took the oath as President of the United States, brought to the table the experience and discernment to understand that Russia is *sui generis.* We can hope that Biden's successors have in common with Biden an understanding that regardless of who is in charge in the Kremlin, Russia's culture and history mean that dealing with Russia is like dealing with no other country.

Equally noteworthy is the fact that, on day one of the Biden administration, the US presidency was in the hands of a president from a generation that experienced American power and influence at its height, a generation that in its heyday was scarcely able to conceive of a world in which the United States would not be seen as the unrivaled global leader and force for good, whatever missteps there may have been along the way. Of course, in the decades since Biden first gained prominence in the foreign policy arena, US leaders have repeatedly run up against the limitations of US influence. Of surpassing importance in the post-Trump and post-Biden era will be the way successive administrations navigate the divide between the legacy of US foreign policy in the Cold War era versus contemporary realities. Intertwined with all the other substantive issues will be hard choices as to the pace of normalization after Putin's catastrophic war finally ends.

Conclusion

We Disregard the Lessons of History and Geography Only at our Peril.

The only reason for all the attention in these pages to the Cold War and its antecedents is that we can't devise a viable strategy for getting where we want to go without understanding how we—and Russia—got to where we are. The challenge now is to prepare for the post-Putin era.

There is in the United States a wide gamut of predictions—from well-qualified experts—as to what post-Putin Russia will look like. The short answer, of course, is that there is not a person in the world who knows the answer to that question. But even a hard-bitten realist (and Russia expert) such as Robert Gates was willing to write—in the wake of Putin's attack on Ukraine—that "a different Russia could emerge" when Putin passes from the scene.[2] Millions of Russians in the educated, urban middle class, concentrated in Moscow, St. Petersburg, and a handful of other major cities, would love to see Russia do what it takes to return to the community of civilized nations committed to free enterprise, a functional democracy (with real political competition), freedom of expression, and the rule of law. But there is no way to know whether or when Russia's democratic believers will have a genuine opportunity to win the rest of the population (or, at least enough of them to prevail in a fair election) over to their worldview.

Before February 24, 2022, a strong argument could have been made that a policy premised on greater sensitivity to Russia's understandable interest in its "near abroad" would not pose an unacceptable risk (and might actually mitigate the risk) that Russia would engage in actual or threatened aggression against noncompliant neighbors. Running counter to that view was (and is) the more pessimistic conviction that Russia is a revanchist power dead set on relitigating the post–Cold War Euro-Atlantic security order by any available means short of all-out nuclear war. The former policy, emphasizing sensitivity and accommodation, might well have been a good prescription for working toward at least a tolerable modus vivendi with a Russia governed by democratically elected leaders with some semblance of a commitment to a rules-based international order. But that, alas, is not the Russia we have. As long as Russia is ruled by Putin or anyone of his ilk, the only strategy with a proven record of success will be one based on military might, Western unity, and resolve. This could be called Nitze-style containment. Kennan would protest mightily, but Kennan, long-lived though he was, did not live long enough to see Putin's butchery in Ukraine. As much as we may sympathize with the Russian population at large (especially those millions for whom emigration is not a realistic option and who devoutly desire democratic reform with all its trappings), Russia must be regarded as an aggressive, revanchist power as long as it has a governing regime that answers that description.

Either way, risk is unavoidable. The risk of an accommodative policy is that the ruling regime—whomever the ruler may be—won't get the hint and will answer perceived Western weakness with more aggression directed at the former Soviet republics and satellites. The risk of the hard-nosed policy of containment advocated here is twofold. In the United States, the risk of unyielding containment is that the American public (not remembering and in any event unmoved by the resolve Truman was able to inspire in the first five years of his presidency) will balk at putting lives and treasure on the line with anything like the unity and resolve of the late 1940s. Internationally, the risk of a hard-nosed policy of containment is the risk that Kennan was right when he warned against the perils of introduction of Western military prowess into the former Soviet space. A renewed commitment to hard-nosed containment would benefit from accession of Finland and Sweden into NATO—which, as these pages are written, appears highly likely.

With the understanding that Putin himself made a compelling case for the accession of Finland and Sweden, we should understand also that NATO membership for Ukraine would likely be a bridge too far. This requires an understanding of the Russian concept of the "near abroad."

The near abroad: A concept rooted in and nourished by Russian history. The English phrase *near abroad* is traceable to the early 1990s, as a translation of the Russian *blizhneye zarubezhye* (near beyond border).[3] After the dissolution, Russian politicians used that phrase to refer to the newly independent nations that had been Soviet republics. Russia asserts a "privileged interest" in its near abroad. In the West, that concept is anathema to those who contend that the very notion of spheres of influence—let alone anything smacking of the post-Yalta Soviet hegemony—should be relegated to the dustbin of history. And it is worthy of note here that, with the on-and-off exception of Belarus, the nations Russia would influence within its sphere of privileged interests are not noticeably eager to fall into Russia's slipstream. But as Putin made clear in February 2022, Russia's desire to fortify its standing vis-à-vis a sphere of privileged interests is not premised on the consent of the countries that find themselves within that sphere.

The Russian concept of the near abroad includes both *land* and *people.* Importantly, Russian interest in the near abroad exists independently of (and predates) Putin's fear of comparison of life in Russia with life in, say, a thriving, democratic Ukraine. From the Russian perspective, the "land" part of that concept is all about defending Russia; the "people" component is all about defending Russians. As for the land, George Kennan observed in 1960—after the United States and the Soviet Union had each developed the ability to obliterate the other in an hour's time—that "the history of Europe has been such that danger to the nation, within the period of historical memory, has generally been associated with the movement of armies over land frontiers."[4] It should come as no surprise that geography remains especially relevant to the Russians. Geographer and geopolitical analyst Tim Marshall puts it well: "From the Grand Principality of Moscow, through Peter the Great, Stalin, and now Putin, each Russian leader has been confronted by the same problems. It doesn't matter if the ideology of those in control is czarist, communist, or crony capitalist—the ports still freeze, and the European Plain is still flat."[5] In that mix also is the indelible Russian historical memory of the fact that Russia, as a nation, owes its very existence to time and distance, specifically (as Napoleon and Hitler, among others, found out) the *time* it takes an army to cover the *distance* across the East European Plain from Western Europe to Moscow. Thus, the fact that the Cold War ended with the disintegration of the Soviet empire (which lasted some seventy years) is not nearly as historically significant as the fact that the Cold War ended with the disintegration of the *Russian* empire, which lasted for more than three hundred years. In December 1991, Russia was essentially reduced to the lands encompassed by its borders as they existed in the time of Peter the Great.

The "people" component of the near abroad involves some demographic facts that have gotten short shrift in the Western press. The case of Ukraine vividly illustrates the Russian perspective. Of the twenty-five million ethnic Russians who, overnight, found themselves living "abroad" from Russia on December 26, 1991, more than eleven million lived in Ukraine.[6] Russian speakers were (and are) concentrated in the east and south of Ukraine, Ukrainian speakers in the west.[7] This Russian population in Ukraine amounted to 20 percent of the whole Ukrainian population—the largest ethnic minority in Europe.[8] To put just a little finer point on it, the Russian population in *Crimea*, as counted in the 1989 census, amounted to just over 68 percent of the population of that region (with ethnic Ukrainians accounting for about 26 percent).[9]

The tensions arising from the distribution of ethnic Russians on various sides of the newly relevant international boundaries of the fifteen former Soviet republics are exacerbated by the fact that, to begin with, the citizens of the Soviet Union did not have a strong sense of national identity.[10] For Russians living in Russia during the last years of the USSR, the pull of the Soviet Union as a source of national identity was far weaker than the pull of *Russia*. But the problem was that the newly relevant boundaries of the fifteen newly sovereign nations did a very poor job of defining where Russians lived, worked, spoke their mother tongue and raised their families. In the case of Ukraine, it gets worse. As we were repeatedly reminded in 2021 and 2022, millions in Russia—Putin foremost among them—reject any notion that Ukraine even has a legitimate historical claim to nationhood. More than seven decades before Putin invaded Ukraine, Zbigniew Brzezinski wrote that "Soviet historicism is currently engaged in proving conclusively the fact that the Ukrainian nation as such is but a branch of the great Russian nation."[11] This exemplified, as Ambassador Jack Matlock put it, a "Russian tendency to look at Ukrainians as wayward relatives rather than as neighbors of equal status."[12]

Consequently, for both the land and the people components of the near abroad, Putinism rejects the notion that Ukraine should even be considered "abroad." No short summary of Putin's historical manifesto "On the Historical Unity of Russians and Ukrainians," delivered on July 12, 2021, can do it justice.[13] In its five thousand words, the document covers a litany of grievances and plainly challenges Ukraine's claim to sovereignty. And Putin doubled down on his idée fixe about the very existence of Ukraine in a speech to the Russian nation on February 21, 2022, three days before he invaded Ukraine, proclaiming, in substance, that the Ukrainian nation and its people were in essence squatters on Russian land.

Even though the West should be entirely unmoved by Putin's legally and morally bankrupt denial of Ukraine's right to exist as a sovereign neighbor of Russia, Russia's history and culture confront us—independently of anything Putin ever said or did—with two realities relating to Ukraine. First, it is not likely that Crimea will ever be returned to Ukraine. Second, it will be a long time, if ever, before geopolitical conditions, and conditions within Ukraine, are conducive to accession of Ukraine into NATO.

Crimea. In March 2014, Russian special forces in unmarked uniforms, augmenting Russian naval infantry forces already stationed in Crimea by agreement, took control of strategic locations in the peninsula, setting in motion the chain of events that led to the completion of the annexation of Crimea by Russia before the end of that month. This, as former Foreign Service Officer William Hill has noted, "was the first time since World War II that any European state had taken and annexed territory from another European state through the use of force."[14]

Russia originally annexed Crimea from Turkey in 1783, after the First Turkish War. The annexation was recognized by Turkey in 1792, thus establishing, as it was put in a leading history of Russia, "what appeared to be [Russia's] natural boundaries in the south."[15] As discussed in chapter 10, Khrushchev signed Crimea over to the Ukrainian Soviet Socialist Republic in 1954—a few months after Vladimir Putin's first birthday—in a move that was politically astute for Khrushchev and, at the time, devoid of geopolitical significance. In consequence, the Russians have a respectable argument, whether anyone in the West likes it or not, that the real territorial amputation occurred in 1954, not in 2014. As Hill noted, the notion that Crimea would one day become a permanent appendage of an independent Ukraine was "surely not a possibility that Khrushchev envisioned when he transferred the peninsula from the Russian Soviet Federative Socialist Republic to the Ukrainian SSR in 1954."[16] For his part, of course, Putin takes a back seat to no one as a critic of Khrushchev's gift of Crimea to Ukraine. In his July 2021 manifesto, Putin denounced the transfer as a "gross violation of the legal norms that were in force at that time."[17]

To be sure, unlike ancient Russian cities such as Pskov or Novgorod, Crimea is not primordially Russian. But Russians make no bones about the fact that they retain a special interest in lands that are predominantly Russian, culturally, linguistically, ethnically, and religiously. They will also point out that land that has been redeemed with blood, as Crimea has been redeemed more than once with Russian blood, is not soon forgotten by its redeemers.

The political meaning that all this carries within Russia is consequential for the West, even—or especially—in the wake of Putin's attack on Ukraine. In contending with the Putin regime (or one like it), it is logical for Western strategists to be restrained when the issue is one on which the regime enjoys broad popular support at home, and to be emboldened when addressing issues on which the Russian population is deeply divided. There is no such deep division in Russia when the subject is Crimea. For the Kremlin, and, of equal significance, for major segments of the Russian population, keeping Crimea Russian is an obligation of existential magnitude. Russia, without Crimea, its majority ethnic Russian population, and the warm water port of Sevastopol, is not Russia as conceived by scores of millions of Russians.

In a 1994 monograph for Chatham House, Neil Melvin wrote that "by the end of 1992 a willingness to champion the rights of Russian-speakers [in the near abroad] had become a prerequisite for almost all shades of political opinion in Russia. Neither politicians nor military leaders deemed that the protection of the Russian-speaking communities should be the sole responsibility of their host states and all the main political groupings had begun to pursue active policies as regards the Russian-speaking populations."[18] A premise for those policies was, as Melvin put it, the proposition that "Russia has the right to intervene to protect [Russian-speaking communities] in neighbouring states."[19] It is, thus, unsurprising that the Russian public's support for the annexation of Crimea started strong and stayed strong. It was at 88 percent in March of 2014, and 86 percent in March 2019, as gauged in polling by the Levada Center, the most widely respected independent polling organization in Russia.[20]

This exceptionally broad-based sense of kinship—and inclination to act on that sense—is no mere matter of political belief for Russians. It rises above that. That fact was brought home to me when I was in a major city in the Volga region in April 2014, a few weeks after Russia annexed Crimea by force. I had a long conversation with a lawyer who was a confirmed pacifist—and emphatically no fan of the Putin regime. Her summation of the Crimea situation: "Stephen, the procedure was questionable, but the result was obligatory. These are Russian people." That was that.

More broadly, and on a geopolitical level, the Russian attitude toward the ethnic Russian diaspora nurtured "the so-called Russian Monroe Doctrine: the claim that the territories of the former USSR constitute a natural and exclusive Russian sphere of influence."[21] Thus, in March 1993, President Boris Yeltsin had no reason to be squeamish about declaring that it was time to give Russia "special powers as the guarantor of peace and stability on the territory of the former USSR."[22] Notably, Yeltsin's proposal met with no pushback from the administration of President Bill Clinton. To the contrary, as *New York Times* columnist Leslie Gelb wrote, "key Clinton Administration officials are cheering their Russian hero on. . . . 'What's wrong with a Russian Monroe Doctrine?' one high Clinton official asked rhetorically."[23] Most Russians would not easily discern fine distinctions between Russian concern for the near abroad and the 2019 affirmation of the Monroe Doctrine, as expressed by John Bolton, one of Trump's US national security advisors ("This is our hemisphere. It's not where the Russians ought to be interfering."[24]) or by the January 2022 version articulated by Biden's National Security Advisor Jake Sullivan: "If Russia were to move in that direction [deploying forces in Latin America], we would deal with it decisively."[25]

Russian solicitude for the near abroad, as ardent now as it was in the early 1990s, is tightly intertwined with Russia's attitude toward NATO. Not long after Russia annexed Crimea, Alexander Lukin, vice president of the Diplomatic Academy of the Russian Ministry of Foreign Affairs, explained it thus: "Russia annexed Crimea in response to the aspirations of a majority of its residents and to NATO's obvious attempt to push Russia's navy out of the Black Sea. . . . It was only a matter of time before Russia finally reacted to Western encirclement."[26] Putin put it more concisely: "I simply cannot imagine that we would travel to Sevastopol to visit NATO sailors. Of course, most of them are wonderful guys, but it would be better to have them come and visit us, be our guests, rather than the other way around."[27] The combination of (1) history, (2) geography (i.e., encirclement), (3) the Russian diaspora (people) and (4) the centuries-old Russian imperative of access to a warm-water port

(Sevastopol—a city of immense emotional as well as strategic significance) should tell us that voluntary Russian relinquishment of Crimea is not in the cards.

As for the legality of the 2014 annexation, not much need be said. The short version is that the arid logic of the law is no match for a perceived national-security imperative rooted in history (a thousand years of it), culture, and values. There is, consequently, no need here to get into a chapter-and-verse analysis of the international commitments Russia plainly breached when it annexed Crimea. The relevant documents express the renunciation of force and the principles of noninterference and territorial integrity with varying degrees of specificity, using language ranging from aspirational to very explicit. The documents include the UN Charter, the Helsinki Final Act of 1975, the Budapest Memorandum of 1994, the NATO-Russia Founding Act of 1997, and the Rome Declaration of 2002. History on both sides of the East-West divide tells us that international law, let alone a conventional understanding of international morality, often exists only at the sufferance of great powers.

The status of Crimea is far more important to Russia than it is to any Western power or to the NATO alliance. As Nikolas Gvosdev put it in 2019 (referring to the annexation): "Russian control of Crimea did not have much impact on the day-to-day interests of any major world power."[28] That remains true, and leads to the reality that military conflict over the status of Crimea, as a stand-alone issue, is unlikely because, for starters, the Western nations that would have to decide whether to commit blood and treasure to support the return of the peninsula to Ukraine know very well that winning any such conflict would be much more important to Russia than to any Western power (and we know how conflicts like that usually turn out).

In March 2022, a month after Putin mounted his full-on invasion, no less an authority than Michael Kimmage (formerly a Russia-Ukraine specialist in the State Department's Office of Policy Planning) wrote that "Russia, and not just Putin's Russia, is unlikely to ever return [Crimea] to Ukraine."[29] True enough, but there is, at the same time, no need for the West to recognize, let alone condone, Russia's ownership of Crimea. As for where Crimea would fit into an overall effort to reconstitute East-West relations in the aftermath of Putin's catastrophic war, Thomas Graham, formerly senior director for Russia on the National Security

Council, quite plausibly suggested (also a month after the invasion) an internationally monitored referendum as a component of an overall settlement, though, as he and his coauthor observed, "such a vote would likely affirm Crimea as a part of Russia."[30] That would likely be as close as we would ever get to returning Crimea to Ukraine.

Expansion of NATO to include Ukraine would be counterproductive, unnecessary, and conducive to open conflict.

Putin has probably been reminded (if he ever forgot) that, as vice president, Joe Biden traveled to Ukraine in July 2009 to express strong US support for Ukraine's bid for NATO membership, proclaiming from Kyiv, after meeting with Ukrainian President Viktor Yushenko, that "we do not recognize—and I want to reiterate it—any sphere of influence."[31] This was essentially a reprise of Senator Biden's remarks in October 1997 as the ranking member of the Foreign Relations Committee, when he left no doubt as to where he stood on the question of admission of Poland, the Czech Republic, and Hungary to NATO. He stated that admitting them to NATO "will extend the zone of security to central Europe in a way that, if left undone, will leave a gray zone and insecurity in that region. . . . If we were not to enlarge, the countries between Germany and Russia would inevitably seek other means to protect themselves, creating bilateral or multilateral alliances as they did in the 1930's with, I predict, similar results."[32]

Between 1990 and 2004, when the Baltic states joined the alliance, NATO's eastern frontier moved nearly a thousand miles northeast, from central Germany to the Estonian-Russian border. It is at least arguable that NATO expansion in the 1990s and 2004 presupposed that Russia—neutered by every measure other than its inventory of nuclear warheads—was weak and would stay weak. That, of course, was a supposition that contradicted the entire rationale for NATO in the first place.

The accession of the Baltics left St. Petersburg seventy-five miles from a NATO country. Russia's western line of defense had not come that close to Moscow in a long time. Four US presidents have signed off on NATO expansion since 1999, with the result that the alliance's membership has grown from sixteen to thirty nations, the most recent accession having been North Macedonia in 2020. It surely cannot sit well with Putin that four of the five most recent tranches (and five of the six most recent when the accession of Finland and Sweden is completed) of

NATO expansion took place on his watch. Rubbing salt into that wound is the fact that, under Putin, Russia became the only non-NATO member on the eastern or southern shores of the Baltic Sea.

Russia was vocal but not vitriolic in opposition to the inclusion of the Czech Republic, Hungary, and Poland in NATO in 1999, bringing a years-long accession process to a conclusion. As we have seen, Senator Biden supported the inclusion of the three former Soviet satellites. When that round of expansion was debated on the floor of the Senate, Biden made clear his conception of the historical significance of the proposed expansion. For him, this was about "erasing a line," and "the line I am talking about erasing is Yalta."[33] George Kennan opposed expansion. He argued that this expansion "would be the most fateful error of American policy in the entire post-cold-war era." As for the negative consequences of expansion, Kennan wrote that it "may be expected to inflame the nationalistic, anti-Western and militaristic tendencies in Russian opinion; to have an adverse effect on the development of Russian democracy; to restore the atmosphere of the cold war to East-West relations, and to impel Russian foreign policy in directions decidedly not to our liking."[34]

On March 12, 1999, exactly fifty-two years after President Truman enunciated the Truman Doctrine in an address to a joint session of Congress, the foreign ministers of the three new NATO members delivered their instruments of accession, formalizing their entry into the alliance. Lest anyone miss the point, the ceremony was held at the Truman Presidential Library and Museum in Independence, Missouri. On the last day of that year, Vladimir Putin became president of Russia. In April 2008, as Putin prepared to temporarily hand off the Russian presidency to Dmitry Medvedev, the leaders of the NATO nations, meeting in Bucharest, formally declared that "NATO welcomes Ukraine's and Georgia's Euro-Atlantic aspirations for membership in NATO. We agreed today that these countries will become members of NATO."[35] In Georgia the following August, post–Cold War triumphalism collided with reality. The collisions continue.

As a legal proposition, the decisions of the former Soviet republics and satellites to join NATO, as ten of them did in the thirteen years after the dissolution of the USSR, and of the incumbent members to accept them, are unassailable. On that score, we can look at antecedents as old as the Peace of Westphalia (1648), originating the modern concept of state sovereignty, or as new as the explicit language of the Helsinki Final Act. And there is no need here to relitigate the wisdom of the post–Cold War accessions to date. Debate as to the net effect of those accessions on stability and security could go on endlessly and tends in the final analysis to revert to the unanswerable fact that the new NATO members had the right to seek membership if they saw fit to do so. What *is* in issue is whether the collective-security interests of the NATO allies would be served by expansion to include Ukraine (a historic member, with Russia and Belarus, of the triune Rus).

As has been discussed, every Russian who cares about these things understands (regardless of personal political inclinations) that strategic depth was indispensable to Russia's ability to defeat Germany in World War II. For that reason, "Russian security has thus traditionally been partly predicated on moving outward, in the name of preempting external attack."[36] Movement of NATO's eastern boundary farther east to encompass Ukraine—adding nearly 1,500 miles to the frontier between Russia and NATO—would have all the makings of another geopolitical collision, regardless of the outcome of Putin's war. For geographic, geopolitical, and historical reasons, accession of Ukraine would differ materially from accession of Finland and Sweden. As for domestic Russian politics, even though it is not likely that Putin perceives a real threat of invasion of Russia by NATO, he knows how to play to the predispositions of broad segments of the Russian population by making *them* feel threatened by NATO.

The short of the matter is that, rightly or wrongly, Russia would consider accession of Ukraine to be an existential threat, and that is a matter wholly apart from Putin's need to avoid any possibility that a prosperous, democratic Ukraine might make his fellow Russians wonder what's wrong with Russia. On that score, we should recall Ambassador Harriman's advice to Roosevelt in 1943 (chapter 2): With respect to the USSR's "border countries," the Russians will "keep us informed," but they will "take unilateral action in respect to those countries in the establishment of relations satisfactory to themselves." There is no reason to believe, eight decades later, that the Russians have discerned any reason to take a more relaxed stance. William Burns—the former US ambassador to Russia, more recently director of the CIA under President

Biden—recognized this geopolitical reality in early 2008, in an email to Secretary of State Condoleezza Rice: "Ukrainian entry into NATO is the brightest of all red lines for the Russian elite (not just Putin)."[37] For decades, Burns has been singularly qualified to assess what makes the Russians tick and what they would regard as an existential threat or an intolerable geopolitical concession. Burns reported in his 2008 message to Secretary Rice that he had found no one, even among Putin's liberal critics, who viewed Ukraine in NATO as anything other than a direct challenge. Robert Gates, then the secretary of defense, agreed. He thought NATO membership for Ukraine would be "a huge provocation,"[38] even though he recognized and applauded the value of the expansions during the Clinton and second Bush administrations (primarily the Baltic states and the former satellite nations) as important in "deterring and containing a resurgent, revanchist Russia."[39] These two observations by Gates are not inconsistent; it is hard to argue with either of them.

Anyone, with a map in one hand and a history book in the other, should be able to understand why, for the foreseeable future, it is unlikely that any Russian leader will find it acceptable for Ukraine to join NATO (or politically tenable to acquiesce in that result). To be sure, comparisons between Finland and Sweden, on one hand, and Ukraine, on the other, are inevitable. But again, history, ethnicity and even geography explain why Ukraine is different from Finland and Sweden. For Ukraine, general alignment with the West, as by membership in the European Union, should be another matter, as witness the accelerated Ukraine-EU accession process initiated soon after Russia's 2022 assault on Ukraine. That possibility—distinguishable in every material way from joining a military alliance—should be vouchsafed in any East-West settlement to close out the Russia-Ukraine war.

Much Western thinking and policy-making is founded on the implicit premise that the West can and should bring Russia to a different understanding of where its vital interests lie—a different understanding of the importance of Russia's near abroad to Russian security in the twenty-first century. But no combination of friendly persuasion or coercive diplomacy can erase history or historical memory. The upshot of all this is that if NATO pushes farther east to include Ukraine, Russia can be expected to push back (regardless of the outcome of Putin's war on Ukraine), and there is no assurance that the pushback would be limited to Ukraine. In that event, the Russians could be forgiven if they were to suggest that George Kennan would have called it containment.

It is also true that a postwar Ukraine, unprotected by NATO membership, cannot be left defenseless. Ukraine will survive Putin's murderous assault. Postwar Ukraine will need, and should get (preferably with the help of reparations payable directly or indirectly from Russia's frozen reserves), the armaments necessary to deter the Kremlin from repeating Putin's catastrophic miscalculation. (It is difficult to conceive of a morally and politically defensible use for Russia's frozen assets other than to support Ukraine's civilian and military reconstruction.)

NATO, without Ukraine and with or without Finland and Sweden, is an essential deterrent and stabilizing force. Before his 2022 invasion of Ukraine, Putin could only have been emboldened by his recollection of the Obama and Trump administrations, during which he saw polarization, increasing political paralysis, and tangible evidence of weak US resolve, all augmented, during the Trump administration, by obvious presidential disdain for NATO. For his part, Obama seemingly didn't spend much time thinking about Russia, and when he did, he didn't take Russia seriously—dismissing a nation armed with thousands of nuclear warheads as a "regional power."[40] In contrast, Trump spent too much time thinking about how much he admired Putin's style. The net result of the Obama and Trump administrations was that the Kremlin's perception of American resolve was seriously eroded during the Obama administration, which, unfortunately, only served as the set up for the damage Trump inflicted on NATO.

With his assault on Ukraine, Putin singlehandedly unified and strengthened NATO—in one stroke finishing the job, started by Biden, of repairing the damage done by Trump. On the European side of the NATO map, perhaps the most striking consequence of the invasion is that it knocked Germany out of its complacent mercantilism. And for reasons that could scarcely have been imagined when the Soviet Union disintegrated, the need for a strong NATO alliance is more acute now than ever. Aside from Putin's murderous revanchism, we have to face the fact that Russia's development of unquestionable competence in pressing hybrid forms of aggression, and the emergence of nonstate actors, using cyberweapons and other asymmetric tools, are threats to the vital interests of NATO members.

The key thing to bear in mind is that stability results from *deterrence* of bad behavior, to the end that a conflict, conventional or hybrid, will not have to be fought and won (or maybe lost). An essential prerequisite of deterrence is *power*, consisting of (1) the ability to mobilize people and resources in support of a strategy and (2) the actual and perceived will to use those people and resources, resulting in (3) the credible threat of consequences to the target state (especially its ruling elite). When power is measured that way, the combined power of the United States and its allies and coalition partners far exceeds the power of the United States alone. Michael Mandelbaum puts it succinctly: "Working with partners exploits Washington's greatest strength: its ability to attract allies and create powerful coalitions against isolated opponents. Coordinating with other countries also endows American foreign policy with a legitimacy it would otherwise lack, showing that the United States is not simply acting for itself but defending broad principles of international order that many others support."[41] What Putin wants is Dulles-style rollback, albeit from east to west rather than vice versa. By invading Ukraine, the regime has cast a dark shadow across the Baltic states. Regardless of the ultimate outcome in Ukraine, the deterrent power (translation: credibility) of NATO is as important now as at any time since the alliance was formed in 1949.

There is just one catch in all of this. We are no longer basking in the afterglow of "winning" (that was always a bad word for it and still is) the Cold War. Even with the war in Ukraine, it is no longer obvious to millions of American voters that full-throated support of our alliance relationships, especially with an open checkbook, is in their own personal interest. The American people will want to see some tangible benefit to be derived from a renewed and sustained commitment to expensive military deterrence. In the same sense that NATO's stabilizing and deterrent influence depends on international (including Russian) confidence that the United States will honor its Article 5 commitment, the credibility of that commitment depends on whether US voters perceive that they and their country will benefit from putting US assets on the line in support of collective security. It comes as no surprise, then, that Nikolas Gvosdev, of the US Naval War College, sounds a note of caution: "A foreign policy that takes as its starting point an a priori American obligation to contain and roll back the influence of Russia, China and other revisionist powers, particularly at the behest of allies and partners, without clear linkages as to how this will generate improvements in security or prosperity for Americans will not rest on a steady foundation of public support."[42] This reminds us once again (as discussed in chapter 5) that the actual language of Article 5 of the North Atlantic Treaty is cold comfort. To borrow Prince von Metternich's apt expression from another era, Article 5 is one of those "phrases which on close examination dissolve into thin air."[43]

The unmistakably vague assurance embodied in Article 5 derives its geopolitical meaning from—and only from—the credibility of the commitments of the nations that have subscribed to that language. On that score, we can learn from the fact that bank deposits always seem safe until the morning that depositors are to be seen lined up, down the street and around the corner. It would not take much—perhaps not much more than we saw during the Trump administration—to trigger a "run" on the Article 5 "bank." Hence, the still-incomplete task of removing NATO from the shadow of the Trump presidency is at least as much a domestic challenge as an international challenge. Trump tapped into some rich veins in the electorate, many of which are traceable, at least in part, to economic stresses disproportionately affecting middle-class and working-class voters. An economically stressed voter is a voter who will be strongly inclined to view international commitments as liabilities rather than assets. Consequently, post-Trump US leaders who would seek to repair the damage done between January 2017 and January 2021 would do well to attend to the domestic issues that enabled Trump to get traction in the first place, bearing in mind the oftrepeated dictum that foreign policy starts at home.

Kotkin refers to the "bipartisan resolve of containment" as having been crucial in bringing the Cold War to a conclusion.[44] It is not at all a stretch to say that what we might think of as "resolve" cannot pass for resolve if it is not bipartisan. Whether the American people are now represented in Congress by individuals possessing the wisdom, foresight, and bipartisan spirit essential to forming and maintaining the extraordinarily successful (at least in East-West terms) post-World War II order is very much an open question.

Those Who Believe Democratic Reform in Russia Can Be Coerced or Induced from Without Will be Disappointed.

About a year after the dissolution of the Soviet Union, Warren Christopher was preparing to take office as secretary of state, having been nominated by newly elected president Bill Clinton. William J. Burns—then the State Department's director of policy planning, and much later, as has been noted, director of the CIA under President Biden—drafted a twenty-two-page memorandum giving Christopher a tour d'horizon of the foreign policy issues the new administration would face. On the first page of the memo, Burns wrote of the possibility of "a breakdown of reform in Russia and a reversion to some form of authoritarian rule."[45] This was 1993.

Seven years later, on December 31, 1999, President Boris Yeltsin stunned his nation and the world with a New Year's Eve resignation, appointing Vladimir Putin to serve as acting president, making Putin the runaway favorite to win election to the presidency in an election to be held in March. In a reassuring New Year's Eve address to the people of Russia, Putin pledged that "the state will stand firm to protect the freedom of speech, the freedom of conscience, the freedom of the mass media, ownership rights, these fundamental elements of a civilised society."[46] Four years later, in his inaugural address to launch his second term as president, Putin cited the need for "a broad base for developing democracy in our country," noting his "conviction that a mature civil society is the best guarantee that this development will continue." Putin was emphatic: "Only free people in a free country can be genuinely successful."[47]

To put it mildly, Putin's stated views as to personal freedom—the balance between the rights of the individual and the coercive power of the state—evolved over time. In a June 2019, interview with *Financial Times*, on the eve of a G20 summit, Putin told his interviewer that "the liberal idea has become obsolete. It has come into conflict with the interests of the overwhelming majority of the population."[48] Nationalism and social conservatism are ascendant in Russia. The duration of that trend is for Russians to determine, and this should be understood in light of one sobering fact. In rejecting some core Western values, Putin is as much a follower as he is a leader. As Kimmage puts it, Russian society "is expressing and cultivating a national identity that would exist with or without Putin. That identity has created Putin more than he has created it."[49] Kimmage's astute observation is supported by no less a Russophile than Tolstoy: "The will of the historic hero does not control the actions of the mass but is itself continually controlled."[50]

The efforts made by Western governments and civil-society organizations—too numerous to list here—over the last thirty years to assist with democratic development in Russia are laudable. But it was one thing for Westerners to assist with, or incentivize, democratic development when Russians were writing on a relatively clean slate during the first few years after the dissolution. The slate is no longer clean, and the narrative that has been written on that slate by the Putin regime—with the concurrence of large segments of the Russian polity—can only be changed by the Russian people, when and if they are ready to do so. This brings to mind the line (discussed earlier in these pages) written by Kennan a year before Putin was born and two years before Stalin died. Referring to the ways by which Russians might "advance toward dignity and enlightenment in government," Kennan concluded that "there is nothing less understandable to foreigners, nothing in which foreign influence can do less good."[51]

There have been some credible voices on the other side of Kennan's prescription of noninterference. In her 2010 book, *Lonely Power*, Lilia Shevtsova argues in favor of Western incentives—somewhat vaguely defined—designed to encourage liberalization in Russia. But that was 2010. Now, more than a decade on, with the prospect of years of East-West estrangement resulting from Putin's war, the contrast between what the West can induce and what the Russian polity must produce for itself is far more stark.

Even though Shevtsova argues that "without the support of the West, primarily the European community, Russia's transformation is unlikely,"[52] she also recognizes, echoing Kennan (and putting it rather tartly), that "there have been many examples in recent history when the West has tried to force-feed bliss to a country without understanding what was really going on there."[53] Even if the West had an opportunity to attempt to "force-feed bliss," that effort would be doomed to fail as long as personalized rule continues in Russia. When a nation finds itself in the grip of increasingly personalized rule, that "person" has no incentive to get that nation out of that rut—and has every incentive to frustrate the democratic processes which might, on paper, offer a way forward to a new day. Putin understands quite well, as the ruler of a personalist authoritarian state, that any autocrat's overriding priority must be the suppression—ruthlessly if necessary—of alternatives. Nothing else comes close. Consequently, as the Putin regime becomes increasingly entrenched in self-preservation mode, getting into an ever tighter downward spiral of short-sighted and self-serving tactics, the notion that the West can effectively promote democratic reform becomes increasingly fanciful. The short version of that is that we are no longer living in the early 1990s.

One other aspect of personalized rule is relevant here (and may not be widely understood in the West). Anything the United States may do that is interpreted in the Kremlin as an attempt to bring about regime change is likely to be regarded by the Putin regime—for its own reasons—as being fully equivalent in gravity to a move against the Russian state itself, with the potential for a response commensurate with a threat of that magnitude.

All of this is not to say that the West should stand completely aloof to a nation armed with several thousand nuclear warheads. Grassroots-cultural and educational exchanges—if they ever resume—could serve valuable purposes, as long as we don't fool ourselves into thinking they promise to produce quick, tangible results. Another passive, yet powerful influence is the increasingly devastating persuasiveness of simple comparison between life for the average Russian citizen versus life in the West—including, especially, life in Western Europe. As for more assertive measures, the Putin regime has given the United States and the European Union every reason to consider the effects of his harsh repression of Russian citizens when deciding whether, when, and to what extent the sanctions imposed in 2022 should be relaxed. In sum, it should be more evident now than at any time since 1991 that the necessary transition from brooding discontent to overt political action is not something that can (or even should) be induced from outside the borders of the Russian Federation. We should remember that the United States or, more broadly, the West, didn't eliminate communism in Russia. The Russians did. The West is no more likely to take down the Putin regime or reinvigorate Russian democracy from the outside than it was to defeat Soviet communism from the outside.

In the Long Run, Don't Bet Against the Russian People

It is likely that the long arc of history will bend toward freedom and democracy in any country that has (1) a nearly 100 percent literacy rate, (2) a well-developed educational system producing an exceptionally well-educated urban middle class, (3) a per-capita GDP well above the subsistence level, (4) access to information about what is happening in the country and the world (even if some extra effort is required), and (5) significant cultural ties with Western democracies. Russia answers this description. So what is the problem?

The Challenges Russians Face

Once they get past the suffocating oppression of the Putin regime and the moral and economic impoverishment resulting from Putin's war, Western observers tend to focus on Russia's endemic corruption when commenting on the challenges confronting that nation and its people. That concern is well founded; corruption is as demoralizing to the citizenry as it is insidiously destructive to Russian institutions. That corruption is variously a contributing cause or a consequence of other challenges with which the Russian people must contend, individually and collectively. We address some of those other challenges here.

State domination of the economy. Writing in 1994, Yevgenia Albats, a Russian journalist and political scientist (educated at Moscow State University and Harvard University), predicted that "monopolistic state capitalism is likely to be the economic model for this regime. Private property and small business will be tolerated, but the economy will be dominated by large monopolies, which will operate under rigid state control and hand over 90 percent of their profits to the government."[54] Regardless of what the exact numbers may be, it is a fact, in the fourth decade after the dissolution of the Soviet Union, that an extraordinarily large portion of the productive capacity of Russia is directly or indirectly controlled by state actors. Accurate estimation of the percentage of Russia's GDP that is accounted for by a combination of the federal budget and the operations of the myriad state-owned and state-controlled enterprises is treacherous business, fraught with the potential for double counting. There is, consequently, room for debate as to the accuracy of some frequently cited estimates. That said, in 2018, Konstantin Sonin (an economics professor with impeccable credentials) noted that, under Putin, the privatization process came to a halt, with the result that almost three-quarters of Russia's GDP is derived from state-controlled enterprises. Sonin's point was that state-controlled enterprises breed corruption and that the private sector must be strengthened if Russia is to have any hope of competing successfully on a global scale.[55]

The Putin regime is determined to perpetuate state control of the commanding heights of the economy as a matter of political survival—as an essential tool in the service of the regime's objectives of minimizing political competition, promoting all the while the narrative that only the current regime can deliver the stability Russia needs. This control fits quite well with Russia's dependence, for hard currency, on exports of oil, gas, and military wares—all firmly in the regime's control. The *economic* effect of a statist economy is equally telling. Russian economic growth averaged 7 percent for the first several years after Putin became president, a growth rate fueled largely by the tremendous increase in oil prices between 2000 and 2008. GDP growth has not, in more recent years, come close to that rate, and continuing declines in per-capita GDP will be an inevitable consequence of Putin's war—resulting in a steady decline in Russian citizens' real disposable income. It will be difficult to turn these trends around as long as Russia's major productive enterprises are largely arms of the state, controlled by state decision-makers whose incentives do not run in the direction of the innovation and efficiency necessary (along with human and financial capital) to make Russia a player in the top tier of the global economy.

The brain drain. "I swear to you that not for anything in the world would I change my country for another, nor have any history other than that of our ancestors, such as it has been given us by God."[56] So wrote Alexander Pushkin to philosopher Pyotr Chaadev in 1836. Many Russians still feel that way about their country, but many do not, which led President Putin to tell the nation in his 2012 annual address to the Federal Assembly that Russia "needs smart, educated, hard-working people who do not just want to make some money here and leave."[57] It is telling that a head of state was moved to make that sort of a comment in a formal address to his nation. In the fall of 2019, a Levada Center poll of 1,601 Russians in all regions indicated that 21 percent of respondents desired to emigrate. The age breakdown was more unsettling. Just over 50 percent of respondents aged eighteen to twenty-four, and 30 percent of those aged twenty-five to thirty-nine, wanted to leave.[58] Annual emigration increased almost tenfold, to 350,000, between 2011 and 2015. And in just the first few weeks after the February 24 invasion, more than 300,000 emigrated (*fled* would not be too strong a word for it), most not expecting to return to Russia any time soon, if ever. As Andrei Kolesnikov puts it, the Russians who emigrated in the wake of the Russian attack on Ukraine "are motivated less by fear of persecution than by a lack of belief in Russia's prospects and disgust at what the regime has become."[59]

Most of the émigrés in the current wave are younger than forty years old. They tend to be well educated, as witness the fact that, in 2021, the Russian Academy of Sciences disclosed that annual emigration of Russian scientists had increased fivefold, to seventy thousand, between 2012 and 2020.[60] Well over ten thousand Russian émigrés have made their way to Silicon Valley. It was surely not lost on then-President Dmitri Medvedev, speaking at Stanford University in the heart of Silicon Valley in 2010, that, when it was time for the president to take questions, many of the attendees spoke in their native Russian to put their questions to him.[61] This is the type of talent Russia cannot afford to lose.

As debilitating as the accelerating hemorrhage of educated Russians is, it may also be true that Putin's most chilling thought is the thought of a growing cohort of intelligent, engaged, and politically aware independent thinkers, not beholden to the government for their economic livelihood, and who increasingly feel like exiles in their own country but are *not* inclined to leave. The practicalities of life in Russia (or, for that matter, anywhere else) tell us that most of the millions of young Russians who might want to vote with their feet will actually end up staying in Russia—as voters. As for those who do leave, the more recent emigration by individuals who are intelligent, energetic, proactive, and anti-Putin may—as was the case with Jewish emigration in the last stages of the Soviet era—be good news for the Putin regime even as it depletes Russia's stock of precious human capital.

Dependence on oil and gas production. In the late 1960s, when Vladimir Putin was a teenager, his future political career got a major boost.

Phenomenally productive oil and gas fields were discovered in western Siberia. Putin had excellent political timing vis-à-vis the price of oil. From the day he took over at the end of 1999 to mid-2008, he rode the price of oil from under $30 per barrel to higher than $125—surely a discouraging trend for potential opponents. By the time the price of oil crashed in the fall of 2008, Putin had temporarily parked the presidency with Dmitri Medvedev. When Putin successfully reclaimed the presidency in the March 2012 election, the price of a barrel of Urals crude again exceeded $120—a nice cushion for a Russian federal budget that was, for 2012, based on a Urals crude price of $100.[62]

Experts in political economy can debate all day whether Russia's oil and gas wealth has been used as a political opiate—a "resource curse," as it has been called. But it is hard to argue with Fiona Hill's conclusion, in the early years of Putin's presidency, that "the high oil prices and budget surplus have alleviated the pressure on the Russian government to restructure the economy and to tackle the hard reforms remaining from the agenda outlined by Putin's economics team in 2000."[63] Writing in 2010, Lilia Shevtsova was a little more blunt about this: "Money accumulated from the sale of energy and raw materials is the most effective method for keeping Russia in a state of sleepy oblivion."[64]

The good news, of course, is that, in a high commodity-price environment, oil and gas reserves in the ground come close to being wealth that is there for the taking. This is wealth that in a state-controlled economy is there for the political elite (whom Russian economics professor Oleg Komolov calls the "oligarchic-bureaucratic ruling class"[65]) to spread around in the manner best calculated to meet the objectives of that elite. In Russia, the bad news includes the fact that many erstwhile customers for Russian hydrocarbons in Western Europe and elsewhere are weaning themselves away from Russian supplies. To be sure, there will be a market of sorts for Russian oil and gas. (On that score, Russia is headed in the direction of becoming an economic colony of China, a vassal state valued in Beijing for its natural resources and not much else.) But the market for Russian product is shrinking, with the result that, due to reduced volume being sold at increased discounts to world prices, the hydrocarbon opiate will not, for a very long time (if ever), serve the interests of the ruling regimes the way it did for nearly a hundred years before February 24, 2022.

More to the present point, there is a collateral political effect of the fact that Russia's GDP, and, hence, federal revenues, have been so substantially tied directly or indirectly to production and sale of oil and gas. That collateral effect is this: For the current regime, it is all to the good (and not a coincidence) that, thanks to oil and gas revenues and the value-added tax, the Russian federal budget has enjoyed a relatively high degree of independence from income taxes directly paid by individual Russians. Out-of-pocket payment of taxes tends to cause the taxpayers to demand accountability; conversely, reliance on hydrocarbon rents helps to keep large segments of the population docile, dampening the prospects for genuine political competition. One notable consequence of this is that the Putin regime has felt itself relatively insulated from the demands of small, independent entrepreneurs—a segment of the polity that is typically one of the most politically engaged in fully functioning democracies. Declining oil and gas revenues are sure to put pressure on the regime to extract revenues from sources that are more keenly felt by everyday Russians.

Capital flight. Russians who have enough money to be in a position to send chunks of it abroad have been voting with their rubles. This is not a new phenomenon, and it was forthrightly addressed by Putin in his 2012 message to the Federal Assembly.[66] The net outflow of private capital from Russia is subject to wide year-to-year swings, but it averaged over $60 billion annually from 2008 through 2018.[67] After the invasion of Ukraine, capital flight rose so fast that the regime found it necessary, in short order, to impose strict controls on international transfers. Worse yet, the oligarchs' ability to stash their riches offshore has seriously eroded any incentive they might have had to push for domestic reforms.

With or without international sanctions, Putin's war guarantees a capital-starved Russia for the foreseeable future. That capital shortage amounts, at base, to a shortage of trust. One result of that shortage of trust is that even Russia's domestic capital markets require a much higher return on investment in Russia than is commonly found in Western democracies. For anyone employed in the private sector in Russia, that risk premium amounts to a tax on being a Russian living in Russia.

The Russian people have a decent chance of overcoming these challenges in the long run—but the long run may be painfully long. Looking at the trend in Russia in 1999, Martin Malia wrote that "if the existing situation continues, the predominance of private property and the market (that is, a 'normal' modern society) will in the long run produce the same effects in Russia that they have everywhere in the contemporary world: the formation of a civil society and a pluralistic culture." Comforting though that may be, Malia was quick to add: "the real question is: how long will the long run take?" His answer: "Given Russia's heavy heritage of poverty and despotism, it could be quite long indeed. But given also the fact that in the twentieth century history moves much faster than in earlier ages—and at the end of the century even faster than at its beginning—Russia's current long run may turn out to be not so long after all."[68] And on this point, we would do well to bear in mind Kennan's advice to Ambassador Harriman in 1944 (chapter 3): "The strength of the Kremlin lies largely in the fact that it knows how to wait. But the strength of the Russian people lies in the fact that they know how to wait longer."

Malia, who died in 2004, would be disappointed that, in the third decade of the twenty-first century, the end of the "long run" is not in sight, and doubly disappointed that Russia now has nothing resembling the nascent democracy of the 1990s. But Malia's basic premise was that the long arc of history does not bend in favor of authoritarian leaders in societies in which the basic ingredients of functional democracy, with true political competition, exist (or are within reach). In Russia, some of those ingredients do exist; others are within reach. Only the Russian people can do the reaching. A lot depends on the ability of the educated urban middle class to convince other segments of the Russian polity that democracy, transparency, and true political competition can coexist with a strong central government (and that the transition will be worth the effort, for themselves, their children, and their grandchildren). "The main problem with Russian modernisation, says Mr. [Kirill] Rogov [a Russian political economist], is that the new, competitive urban middle class that has emerged as the economy has developed has no place in the current authoritarian model, which is designed for those who depend on the state but cannot compete."[69] The flip side of that astute observation is the fact that the very presence of Rogov's "competitive urban middle class" in Russian society (even though it is a minority within the whole population) makes it hard for Putin to comfort himself with any notion that he represents a monolithic "Russian" view of the world.

Those who will be at the heart of the movement for transformation once Russia begins, however haltingly, to recover from Putin's relentless repression and disastrous war will be those who are not dependent on the federal budget for their livelihoods and have no reason to be apathetic about corruption, political overreach, or mistreatment of individuals who are deemed disloyal to the regime. These are the independent thinkers who never bought into the tacit agreement by which Putin provided stability and a semblance of prosperity in return for pervasive apathy. It is devoutly to be desired that those independent thinkers will be joined increasingly by believers in democratic reform who—like many in the Soviet-era *nomenklatura*—have nonetheless found it necessary to remain politically passive. There are those who are politically passive out of necessity, and those who are simply apathetic. As for the latter group, it is fair to say that when a governing cadre finds it necessary to rely on apathy to bolster its sense of political security, there is always a potential for sudden change. If the Putin regime were to guess wrongly about the threshold of indifference of major segments of the population, the consequences of the bad guess could be serious.

Some will argue that Russia's historical affinity for a strong central government headed by a strong leader is, and will continue to be, fatal to democratic reform. On that score, it is certainly true that a sizable segment of the Russian population believes that, in the natural order of things, Russia must be governed by a heavy-handed executive. That in and of itself is unremarkable, especially considering the fact that in the United States, Congress has been steadily ceding power to the executive for more than eight decades. More unsettling is the fact that, in Russia, there is a widespread expectation that the executive in exercising that power will enjoy a level of deference from the other branches that would be foreign to the United States and most European systems. Consequently, there are those who would contend that if full-fledged Western-style constitutionalism, complete with a robust tradition of judicial review of executive and legislative acts, is a prerequisite to admission of Russia into the ranks of liberal democracies, the "long run" will be long indeed.

Granting that the long run may be longer than many would hope, it would be a serious mistake to assume that the Russian polity is permanently mired in what Lilia Shevtsova (quoting Ambassador Thomas

Graham) refers to as "the old tradition of the Russian state." Shevtsova's explanation: "This can be interpreted in only one way: Russians carry a special gene that precludes them from living in a rule of law state that abides by international conventions. This means that we Russians are a predatory nation that can live only by being subjugated by our rulers and by subjugating other nations. If so, this is not merely a condescending way of looking at Russians, but a racist one as well."[70] Shevtsova's pungently expressed view is cogently supported by Timothy Frye, who demonstrates that, in Russia, a preference for a strong executive cannot be equated with a desire for something other than democratic rule based on free and fair elections.[71] Shevtsova's faith in the Russian people is shared by former Ambassador Michael McFaul, an astute observer who has spent much of his adult life in Russia and who wrote in 2018 that he found it "hard to believe that Russia will defy the odds of modernization."[72] Putin's war made those odds longer. We don't yet know whether the odds have become prohibitive.

We should also bear in mind Malia's observation, quoted above, that history moves much faster than in earlier ages. This, of course, is largely a result of advances in communication technology, and it invites a comparison. Totalitarian communist rule lasted seven decades in Russia—in an era in which cross-border movement of people, information, and ideas was much more tightly restricted than has been the case at any time since the early 1990s. Thus, one major difference between Russia and China is that, in Russia, the internet cat is out of the bag. The Russian government—to put it mildly—does have inordinate influence over the legacy channels of communication (especially television). And after the invasion of Ukraine, the regime blocked many (but not all) internet-based sources of independent reporting. But Russian city dwellers are among the most internet-savvy and internet-reliant populations in the world (perhaps, consciously or not, in reaction to the government's success in isolating the population from international media during the Soviet era). For Russian city dwellers keenly interested in unfettered internet access, virtual private network (VPN) capability has been a godsend. As reprehensible as the post-invasion internet blockages have been, if anything could trigger a nationwide response in Russia, it would be a China-style government clampdown on internet access. A wholesale cutoff of internet access would be an extraordinarily risky move. It is unlikely that Russians would, for long, meekly accept being reduced to passing samizdat (bootlegged magazines and manually reproduced political and cultural commentary) from hand to hand as they did in the Soviet era. In Russia, unlike China, the internet and a serious attempt at democracy arrived within a few years of each other. Russians have tolerated (so far) deep compromise of the democracy contemplated by their 1993 constitution, but they are unlikely to be willing to give up *both* the internet *and* democracy, especially in an era in which it will no longer be possible to buy them off with the benefits of a robust resource-based economy.

Finally, as Kennan wrote in 1951, "above all, it behooves us Americans, in this connection, to repress, and if possible to extinguish once and for all, our inveterate tendency to judge others by the extent to which they contrive to be like ourselves."[73] We would do well to remember these words, written while the Soviet Union had forty years yet to go. Meaningful democratic reform in Russia, when it comes, will be democratic reform, Russian-style. Russia is unique, just as every Western democracy is unique. If we are waiting for democratic reform in Russia to produce something approaching a fully replicated version of democracy as practiced in the United States (assuming, just for the sake of discussion, that that would be a desirable outcome), the wait will be long indeed.

Russia confronts the United States, its allies, and partners with two formidable challenges: (1) dealing with Putin and (2) dealing with Russia after Putin. Western leaders can hope that the second challenge will not be identical to the first, but they will have to bear in mind, all the while, that Russia's unique national identity will exist with or without Putin. Normal East-West relations will be impossible as long as Putin remains in power. That possibility vanished on February 24, 2022. Putin does not think in terms of the Cold War rules of engagement, the rules which kept human civilization from destroying itself. The "stable and predictable" relationship to which Secretary of State Antony Blinken aspired early in the Biden administration will be attainable, if at all, only after Putin leaves the scene.

This brings us back to the initial premise that the Cold War and its historical antecedents remain relevant because they continue to have a profound effect on popular consciousness in the United States and

Russia. As I wrote at the outset, popular consciousness, nourished by history, goes far, on both sides of the East-West divide, to determine what the constituencies expect of their leaders, what risks they will consider acceptable, what they will and will not tolerate, and what they are willing or unwilling to sacrifice in the service of the national interest as they see it, and as their leaders seek to define it. All of this leaves US leaders with work to do, both domestically and in dealing with Russia.

Domestically, the combined effect of historical memory of the Cold War and Putin's war has been to leave large swaths of the US population in a frame of mind to detest everything Russian, with no differentiation between the Putin regime and the Russian people. But it would be a serious mistake, even now, to equate the Russian people with the Kremlin regime. On that score, we would do well to accord at least a little plausibility to the 2019 prediction of Andrei Kozyrev, Russia's first post-dissolution foreign minister, as recorded in the final sentence of his masterful memoir: "Sooner or later the Russian people will rise up again and reclaim the Russia they deserve."[74] Yes, it has often been said that people get the government they deserve. That is a fair comment about a mature democracy (though some would argue, based on recent experience, that that maxim should not inflexibly be applied even to a democracy that is well into its third century). It is also true that, as a practical matter, the population of any nation, Russia included, must unavoidably bear the consequences of the sometimes-catastrophic decisions made by national leaders. But policy toward Russia should, wherever possible, differentiate (as Biden and other western leaders have done) between the Russian people on one hand and the Kremlin elite on the other. US leaders should be at pains to make that point with the American people. Western leaders should also make clear at every opportunity that support for Ukraine's sovereignty and independence does not imply ill will toward the Russian people.

Another challenge on the domestic side lies in the fact that in the United States xenophobic nationalism is in some ways ascendant in parallel with rising social conservatism in Russia—and with similar effects. Depending on how far back we might look, that xenophobia is either supported—or not—by historical memory. We have yet to find out whether that xenophobia, now resident on the right side of the political spectrum, is a passing fever or a long-term trend. If it is a long-term trend, it does not portend well for the US commitment under Article 5 of the North Atlantic Treaty. On the left side of the spectrum, the Article 3 commitment of all NATO allies to "maintain and develop their individual and collective capacity to resist armed attack" may become increasingly inconvenient at a time of soaring domestic demands on the federal treasury.

For all these domestic challenges, it boils down to a question of political leadership and political will, leadership and will of the kind demonstrated by Harry S. Truman in the early years of the Cold War. NATO is all about deterrence. That deterrence depends at least as much on the Kremlin's *perception* of political will as on the size and disposition of forces in the field.

As for the challenges of dealing with the Putin regime, we have the fact, as a beginning point, that the United States has had five presidents since President Putin took office at the end of 1999. Otto von Bismarck believed, as recorded by his preeminent biographer, that the key to success in dealing with other states lay in the ability to "deal with realities, calculations of probabilities, assessing the inevitable missteps and sudden lurches by the other actors, states, and their statesmen."[75] So it is with Vladimir Putin, who is also driven, in part, by an abiding sense of historical injustice—producing a deep reservoir of unspent rancor. As far as Putin is concerned, after the dissolution, Russia was treated like a scruffy boy relegated to the kids' table at Thanksgiving Dinner—treatment ill-befitting a nation with nuclear weapons, a Security Council veto, and a thousand years of history.

Internationally as well as domestically, Putin is a skilled practitioner of a raw form of the politics of memory. Because he doesn't have anything resembling the Politburo to rein him in, he practices his raw politics without meaningful domestic guard rails. Internationally, he has a nose for weakness. Because he understands that power, unaccompanied by the political will to use it, is weakness, he is the living embodiment of Churchill's dictum, in his Iron Curtain speech, that there is "nothing [the Russians] admire so much as strength, and there is nothing for which they have less respect than for weakness, especially military weakness" (chapter 1). Although Putin does understand that Russia's global reach has its limits, he can be counted on—even, or especially, after the war in Ukraine—to relentlessly reinforce Russia's role as a geopolitical player, to the end that when any major international problem is addressed, Russia will be recognized as a necessary party at the table, with deference fully equal to that accorded the Soviet Union at the height of the Cold War. Putin's successors will likely be no different. Arrayed against Putin's, and Russia's, resolve is the fact that Putin has succeeded, as did Stalin and Khrushchev, in persuading Americans and their elected representatives (at least for now) that there is, once again, a reason to push back against the Kremlin and to provide the resources necessary to do that.

It took more than four decades for the Cold War to cycle through the phases of disengagement, belligerent rhetoric, deep mistrust, diplomatic and military standoff and, finally, re-engagement. But the spirit that animated the re-engagement during the Gorbachev and Yeltsin years is now a distant memory. Russia faces economic stagnation (at best) and an era of international isolation of uncertain duration. And all of this with an increasingly embittered population in which the devoutly-to-be-desired influence of the educated urban middle class will be on the wane for a while. Even so, and despite that there are some things about Russia and Russians that aren't going to change, it would be a mistake to look at Russia through a narrow aperture and see only the present regime in the Kremlin. Sooner or later, and notwithstanding the regime's efforts to control the narrative, major segments of the Russian population will come to the realization that the only victory Putin can deliver to his country by force of arms is a Pyrrhic victory. Western leaders cannot know when that inflection point will arrive, but it is essential that they be prepared to recognize it and act on it with a view, at least, to putting the East-West relationship on a less perilous trajectory.

The main beneficiary, by far, of continuation of the adversarial relationship between the United States and Russia is China. As counterintuitive as this may seem, the good news here is that a workable relationship may, in the long run, be more likely between the United States and Russia than between the United States and China. The relationship between Russia and China is predominantly transactional—more a product of geographic convenience and economic necessity than any real affinity. As Ivan Timofeev puts it, "Moscow and Beijing have developed unprecedented constructive relations at the political level. But human contacts between the Russians and the Chinese are not yet comparable with those with Western countries."[76] Russian oligarchs have never lain awake at night scheming to get their daughters into lyceums and universities in China. When student visas again become readily available, Natasha will be much more likely to matriculate in Zurich than in Zhengzhou.

Most members of the Russian elite, though politically at odds with the West in many ways, do not viscerally dislike the West. That remains true even though polling in early 2021 by the Levada Center indicated that a declining percentage of the Russian population considers Russia to be a European country.[77] The takeaway here is that the Western cultural affinity of Russian elites, though not unbounded, remains a priceless asset. To be sure, that affinity does not translate directly into geopolitical stabilization, never mind genuine cooperation. But, as a door opener, that affinity presents opportunities unlike anything China will enjoy in the foreseeable future.

It may fairly be concluded from these pages that, at the government-to-government level, there will be nothing approaching a cordial relationship between the United States and Russia any time soon. But, ultimately, and in the interest of the American people, it will become necessary to resume the search for common ground wherever it may be found. That common ground can and should be found by leaders who understand that the adversarial relationship between the two countries cannot be wished away and, consequently, must be competently managed. What is needed is a pragmatic strategy, founded on firm resolve, informed by a good understanding of history, and implemented by a unified West, all aimed at accommodation when possible and, if you will pardon the expression, containment when and where containment is required.

Notes

Preface

1. George F. Kennan, "America and the Russian Future," *Foreign Affairs*, Apr. 1951, 356. Of all Kennan's writings penned while he was in public service, it is perhaps in this article that he drew the most pointed distinctions between the Soviet government, on one hand, and the Russian people, on the other. Later in this article, Kennan wrote of Russia's satellite states that "they must, and will, recover their full independence."

2. Oleg Barabanov, "Foreword: Memory of War and Wars of Memory," in Valdai Discussion Club report *Forgive but Not Forget? The Image of War in Culture and Historical Memory* (Moscow: Valdai Discussion Club, May 2020), 3, https://valdaiclub.com/files/30027/.

Prologue

1. Tocqueville, *Democracy in America*, 475–76.

2. National Security Council, "Report to the National Security Council by the Executive Secretary on United States Objectives and Programs for National Security" (NSC-68), Washington, DC, Apr. 14, 1950, declassified by order of Henry A. Kissinger, Feb. 27, 1975, 4.

3. Vladimir V. Putin, "Annual Address to the Federal Assembly of the Russian Federation," President of Russia, Apr. 25, 2005, http://en.kremlin.ru/events/president/transcripts/22931. According to the official translation of this passage, he said, "Above all, we should acknowledge that the collapse of the Soviet Union was a major geopolitical disaster of the century." He elaborated: "As for the Russian nation, it became a genuine drama. Tens of millions of our co-citizens and compatriots found themselves outside Russian territory." The words often attributed to Putin are to the effect that he said that the dissolution of the Soviet Union was *the* greatest geopolitical *catastrophe* of the twentieth century. See, for example, Associated Press, "Putin: Soviet Collapse a 'Genuine Catastrophe,'" *NBC News*, April 25,

2005, http://www.nbcnews.com/id/7632057/ns/world_news/t/putin-soviet-collapse-genuine-tragedy/. As a matter of literal translation, he did call it a catastrophe. He said: катастрофой. Although the reference to "the" greatest geopolitical "catastrophe" is a bit more sensational, that difference is immaterial to the present discussion.

4. Lawrence S. Eagleburger to Warren Christopher (memorandum), Jan. 5, 1993, Carnegie Endowment for International Peace, https://carnegieendowment.org/pdf/back-channel/1993MemotoChristopher.pdf.

5. Miller, *Who Are the Russians?*

6. Martin, *Affirmative Action Empire.*

7. Michael Kimmage, "The People's Authoritarian: How Russian Society Created Putin," *Foreign Affairs*, July–Aug. 2018, 176.

8. Barbara A. Anderson and Brian D. Silver, "Growth and Diversity of the Population of the Soviet Union," *Annals of the American Academy of Political and Social Science* 510, no. 1 (July 1990): 156.

9. Pipes, "Reflections on the Nationality Problems," 457. The ethnic Russian population of the Soviet Union amounted to 54.5 percent in 1959 and 53.5 percent in 1970.

10. Pipes, 459.

11. Gail Warshofsky Lapidus, "Ethnonationalism and Political Stability: The Soviet Case," *World Politics* 36, no. 4 (July 1984): 555.

12. *Pravda*, Feb. 24, 1981, 7.

13. Smith, *Russians*, 484.

14. Jerry Z. Muller, "Us and Them: The Enduring Power of Ethnic Nationalism," *Foreign Affairs*, Mar.–Apr. 2008, 35.

15. Kedourie, *Nationalism*, 68.

16. Tolstoy, *War and Peace*, 549.

17. Frye, *Weak Strongman*, 32, 200.

Chapter 1

1. "Speech Delivered by Stalin at a Meeting of Voters of the Stalin Electoral District, Moscow," 42, Feb. 9, 1946, Wilson Center Digital Archive, http://digitalarchive.wilsoncenter.org/document/116179 (from the pamphlet collection, J. Stalin, *Speeches Delivered at Meetings of Voters of the Stalin Electoral District* [Moscow: Foreign Languages Publishing House, 1950]). These were the first elections for the Supreme Soviet since 1937. There was only one candidate for each position.

2. "Speech Delivered by Stalin," 22.

3. "Speech Delivered by Stalin," 22–23.

4. "Stalin Sets a Huge Output under New Five-Year Plan; Expects to Lead in Science," *New York Times*, February 10, 1946. The text of the speech was printed on page 30 of the same edition.

5. Acheson, *Present at the Creation*, 150.

6. Chace, "Day the Cold War Started," 4.

7. Churchill, speech at Fulton, Missouri, March 5, 1946, in *Never Give In!* 420, 423.

8. Sivachev and Yakovlev, *Russia and the United States*, 219. (This book is a remarkable piece of Cold War writing.)

9. Brzezinski, *Grand Failure*, 39.

10. Moynahan, *Claws of the Bear*, 9.

11. Moss, *History of Russia*, 1:341. Present-day Russia encompasses about an eighth of the world's land area. It has borders, nearly 36,000 miles, inclusive of land and sea borders, longer than any other nation. Its border with Kazakhstan alone is longer than that between Canada and the lower forty-eight states of the United States.

12. Edward D. MacMorland, "Our First War with the Russians," *Collier's*, Oct 13, 1951, 19.

13. Moss, *History of Russia*, 2:211.

14. John Fischer, "The Scared Men in the Kremlin," *Harper's Magazine*, Aug. 1946, 103.

15. Biden, *Promises to Keep*, 145.

16. Moynahan, *Claws of the Bear*, 9. Spanning a different period (1800 to 1946), the number of invasions from the West has been put at fourteen. Fischer, "Scared Men in the Kremlin," 100.

17. Miller, *Who Are the Russians?* 21.

18. Salisbury, *American in Russia*, 290.

19. Hitler memorandum to naval chief of staff, Sept. 29, 1941, Sec. II, as quoted in Payne, *Life and Death*, 437.

20. Snyder, *Bloodlands*, 174.

21. Payne, *Life and Death*, 431.

22. Snyder, *Bloodlands*, 395.

23. Sakwa, *Soviet Politics in Perspective*, 257.

24. Moss, *History of Russia*, 2:289.

25. George Kennan, "Russia—Seven Years Later" (memorandum), Sept. 1944, Wilson Center Digital Archive, http://digitalarchive.wilsoncenter.org/document/123185.

26. Anonymous, "Russia and Germany—Political and Military Reflections," *Foreign Affairs*, Jan. 1942, 312.

27. Snyder, *Bloodlands*, 116.

28. Bohlen, *Witness to History*, 82.

29. Felix Chuev, *Molotov Remembers*, 13. *Molotov Remembers* is, in substance, a memoir, though Molotov did not leave memoirs under his own name. The book is the product of 139 conversations between Molotov and Russian poet and biographer Felix Chuev, beginning in 1969 and ending with Molotov's death in 1986. Chuev states that Molotov understood that Chuev would write a book about him. Chuev, vii. Molotov was not the only Russian foreign minister to deny the existence of the protocols. Writing in 1989, Andrei Gromyko, who was, in 1939, the director of the American section of the Commissariat of Foreign Affairs, also emphatically denied the existence of the protocols. Gromyko, *Memories*, 38.

30. Moynahan, *Claws of the Bear*, 98.

31. Churchill, *Grand Alliance*, 472.

32. The gist of the revision to the secret protocol was that "almost all of Lithuania could become part of the Soviet sphere in exchange for allowing Germany a slightly larger share of Poland." Moss, *History of Russia*, 2:289.

33. Chuev, *Molotov Remembers*, 27. Molotov's description of the pact as a delaying tactic bears out Churchill's statement that both Hitler and Stalin were aware that the pact "could only be a temporary expedient." Churchill, *Gathering Storm*, 393.

34. As recounted in detail in Moynahan, *Claws of the Bear*, 91.

35. Harriman and Abel, *Special Envoy*, 67.

36. John F. Kennedy, "Commencement Address at American University, Washington, D.C., June 10, 1963," John F. Kennedy Presidential Library and Museum, https://www.jfklibrary.org/Research/Research-Aids/JFK-Speeches/American-University_19630610.aspx.

37. McCullough, *Truman*, 262. Stalin had had thoughts quite like Truman's comment about Germany versus Russia. In 1935, when it appeared that alliances were emerging, consisting of Italy with France and Britain with Germany, Stalin wrote to Molotov and Lazar Kaganovich: "The bigger the brawl between them, the better for the USSR. We can sell bread to both sides, so that they would continue to fight." Zubok, *Failed Empire*, 17.

38. Miller, *Who Are the Russians?* 170.

39. Merridale, *Ivan's War*, 118.

40. Kennan, "America and the Russian Future," 364.

41. Krivosheev, *Soviet Casualties*, 93.

42. LaFeber, *America, Russia, and the Cold War*, 17. Snyder puts the death toll at "about one million people," an estimate that probably also includes lives lost to the bombardment. Snyder, *Bloodlands*, 173.

43. Salisbury, *American in Russia*, 8.

44. Moynahan, *Claws of the Bear*, 134.

45. Moynahan, *Claws of the Bear*, 150.

46. Baime, *Accidental President*, 149. The "up-to-that-point" qualification was probably unnecessary. Paul H. Nitze (who, as vice chairman of the US Strategic Bombing survey, was virtually unexcelled in his knowledge of the effects of strategic bombing in World War II) recorded in his memoir that a single firebombing raid on Tokyo in March 1945 destroyed nearly sixteen square miles of the city and killed more people than the nuclear bombing of Hiroshima or Nagasaki. Nitze, *Hiroshima to Glasnost*, 43.

47. "Mitchell Monument," United States Department of Agriculture, Forest Service (undated historical brochure), https://www.fs.usda.gov/Internet/FSE_DOCUMENTS/stelprdb5374039.pdf.

48. Ziemke, *Stalingrad to Berlin*, 500.

49. Snyder, *Bloodlands*, 411.

50. Sakwa, *Communism in Russia*, 77–78.

51. Sakwa, *Communism in Russia*, 77.

52. Merridale, *Ivan's War*, 3.

53. Merridale, *Ivan's War*, 147, 188.

54. Snyder, *Bloodlands*, 181.

55. Riasanovsky and Steinberg, *History of Russia*, 518; Zubok, *Failed Empire*, 1.

56. Vladimir V. Putin, "On Memory of Great Patriotic War" (TASS interview), President of Russia, Mar. 10, 2020, en.kremlin.ru/d/62963.

57. Merridale, *Night of Stone*, 215.

58. Jacoby, *Moscow Conversations*, 194.

59. Smith, *Eisenhower in War and Peace*, 451. On this flight, Eisenhower asked Zhukov how he minimized losses of Russian tanks as they crossed German minefields. "It wasn't complicated," Zhukov replied. "He sent the infantry through first."

60. Sokolovskiy, *Soviet Military Strategy*, 176.

61. Kennedy, *Freedom from Fear*, 647.

62. Gorbachev, *Memoirs*, chap. 2.

63. Toal, *Near Abroad*, 276.

64. Krivosheev, *Soviet Casualties*, 92.

65. Merridale, *Ivan's War*, 290.

66. Kennedy, *Freedom from Fear*, 584.

67. Zhukov, *Marshal of Victory*, xv.

68. Churchill, *Grand Alliance*, 383.

69. Churchill, *Grand Alliance*, 384–85.

70. "Press Release Issued by the White House, June 11, 1942," Office of the Historian, https://history.state.gov/historicaldocuments/frus1942v03/d483.

71. "Press Release Issued." As described by Charles Bohlen, the 1942 commitment was included in the communiqué because "Roosevelt and his advisors in the White House, including, I am sorry to say, [Harry] Hopkins, were head-down in their desire to make the Soviets happy." Bohlen, *Witness to History*, 124.

72. Harriman and Abel, *Special Envoy*, 139.

73. Chuev, *Molotov Remembers*, 6.

74. Zhukov, *Marshal of Victory*, 457.

75. Zhukov, *Marshal of Victory*, 261.

76. Rick Atkinson, "The Road to D-Day," *Foreign Affairs*, July–Aug. 2013, 59.

77. Truman, *Year of Decisions*, 229.

78. As recounted firsthand in Speer, *Inside the Third Reich*, 463.

79. Beevor, *Fall of Berlin*, 189.

80. Robinson, "Composing for Victory," 73.

81. Beevor, *Fall of Berlin*, 190.

82. Kotkin, *Armageddon Averted*, 190.

Chapter 2

1. Alfred Vagts, "Capitalist Encirclement: A Russian Obsession—Genuine or Feigned?" *Journal of Politics* 18, no. 3 (Aug. 1956): 499–500 (emphasis in original).

2. Snyder, *Bloodlands*, 71.

3. Smith, *Three Years in Moscow*, 113.

4. Vagts, "Capitalist Encirclement," 500.

5. Sherwood, *Roosevelt and Hopkins*, 815.

6. J. H. Burns to Harry Hopkins (memorandum), Aug. 10, 1943, Office of the Historian, https://history.state.gov/historicaldocuments/frus1943/d317.

7. Joseph W. Ballentine and Max W. Bishop to Secretary Hull (memorandum), August 19, 1943, Office of the Historian, https://history.state.gov/historicaldocuments/frus1943/d318.

8. Isaacson and Thomas, *Wise Men*, 46.

9. As Walter Bedell Smith, US ambassador to Russia from 1946 to 1948 (Harriman's successor as ambassador), put it, in a slightly different context: "Any Russian official has been trained how to deal with a capitalist, but, apparently, he has not been trained how to deal with a hybrid." Smith, *Three Years in Moscow*, 206.

10. Harriman and Abel, *Special Envoy*, 250.

11. Letter no. 402 from L. D. Wilgress, Canadian Embassy, Moscow, to the Secretary of State for External Affairs, W. L. Mackenzie King, 9 Nov. 1944 (orig. in W. L. Mackenzie King Papers, 1944, Correspondence, Primary Series, Public Archives of Canada [renamed the National Archives of Canada in 1987]), 2.

12. George F. Kennan to Averell Harriman (memorandum), Moscow, July 26, 1944, as reprinted in Kennan, *Memoirs, 1925–1950*, 206.

13. "Record of Meeting at the Kremlin, Moscow, 9 Oct. 1944, at 10:00 p.m.," 2, Wilson Center Digital Archive, http://digitalarchive.wilsoncenter.org/document/123186.

14. "Record of Meeting," 5.

15. "Record of Meeting at the Kremlin, Moscow, 17 Oct. 1944 at 10:00 p.m.," 4, Wilson Center Digital Archive, http://digitalarchive.wilsoncenter.org/document/123190.

16. Eisenhower, *Eisenhower*, 650.

17. Merridale, *Ivan's War*, 337.

18. Churchill, *Triumph and Tragedy*, 366.

19. Stern, *Water's Edge*, xii.

20. Churchill, *Triumph and Tragedy*, 368.

21. Halle, *Cold War as History*, 65.

22. Sivachev and Yakovlev, *Russia and the United States*, 196.

23. Garthoff, *Soviet Strategy*, 57. (Soviet armed forces as of May 1945.)

24. Churchill, *Triumph and Tragedy*, 353. Churchill may have been in error in writing that Roosevelt said this at the first (February 4) session. The available minutes of the February 4 session show no discussion of the duration of the occupation. But notes from the *second* plenary session (February 5), kept separately by two members of the US delegation, confirm that Roosevelt made the statement attributed to him by Churchill.

25. Neiberg, *Potsdam*, 164.

26. Harriman and Abel, *Special Envoy*, 271.

27. Eisenhower, *Eisenhower*, 659.

28. Gromyko, *Memories*, 91–92 (emphasis added).

29. Letter, Franklin D. Roosevelt to Marshal Stalin (Yalta, February 6, 1945). Volume available at the University of Wisconsin–Madison, per "Foreign Relations of the United States, Diplomatic Papers, Conferences at Malta and Yalta, 1945" Office of the Historian, https://history.state.gov/historicaldocuments/frus1945Malta/d3778.

30. Minutes (by Charles E. Bohlen, Special Assistant to the Secretary, US Department of State), Meeting of Churchill, Roosevelt and Stalin, Yalta, Feb. 9, 1945, Office of the Historian, https://history.state.gov/historicaldocuments/frus1945Malta/d423.

31. Minutes (by H. Freeman Matthews, Director of Office of European Affairs, US Department of State), Meeting of Churchill, Roosevelt, and Stalin, Yalta,

Feb. 9, 1945, Office of the Historian, https://history.state.gov/historicaldocuments/frus1945Malta/d424.

32. Winston S. Churchill, Franklin D. Roosevelt, and Josef Stalin, "Report of the Crimea Conference," Pt. VI, February 11, 1945, https://history.state.gov/historicaldocuments/frus1945Berlinv02/d1417.

33. Chuev, *Molotov Remembers*, 51.

34. Kennan, *Memoirs 1925–1950*, 212.

35. Phillip S. Meilinger, "The USSBS' Eye on Europe," *Air Force Magazine*, Oct. 2011, 74–78.

36. Baime, *Accidental President*, 11–12.

37. Baime, *Accidental President*, 12. See also Neiberg, *Potsdam*, 12 (they met "privately" only twice).

38. Isaacson and Thomas, *Wise Men*, 254.

39. Letter, Harry S. Truman to Bess Truman, France, Nov. 11, 1918, Harry S. Truman Presidential Library and Museum, https://www.trumanlibrary.gov/library/truman-papers/correspondence-harry-s-truman-bess-wallace-1910-1919/november-11-1918.

40. Neiberg, *Potsdam*, xii.

41. Truman, *Year of Decisions*; Truman, *Trial and Hope*.

42. Isaacson and Thomas, *Wise Men*, 371.

43. Yergin, *Shattered Peace*, 72.

44. Churchill, *Triumph and Tragedy*, 634.

45. "Memorandum of Conversation, by Charles E. Bohlen, Assistant to the Secretary of State," Washington, DC, Apr. 20, 1945, Office of the Historian, https://history.state.gov/historicaldocuments/frus1945v05/d190.

46. "Minutes of the Secretary of State's Staff Committee, Saturday Morning, April 21, 1945," Office of the Historian, https://history.state.gov/historicaldocuments/frus1945v05/d633.

47. Stalin, *Great Patriotic War*, 154.

48. Sherwood, *Roosevelt and Hopkins*, 837.

49. Djilas, *Conversations with Stalin*, 114. To the same effect: Harriman and Abel, *Special Envoy*, 334.

50. Chuev, *Molotov Remembers*, 51.

51. Truman, *Year of Decisions*, 82.

52. Churchill had weighed in earlier in May in a long message to Truman, lamenting "the great movements of American armies out of Europe," and concluding that "an iron curtain has been drawn down upon [the Russian army's] front." Churchill, *Triumph and Tragedy*, 573, available as "No. 6: Prime Minister Churchill to President Truman," Office of the Historian, https://history.state.gov/historicaldocuments/frus1945Berlinv01/d6. This is the earliest recorded use of "iron curtain" by Churchill.

53. Baime, *Accidental President*, 273.

54. Neiberg, *Potsdam*, 251.

55. Churchill, *Triumph and Tragedy*, 636.

56. Chuev, *Molotov Remembers*, 55.

57. Gromyko, *Memories*, 108.

58. Zhukov, *Marshal of Victory*, 449.

59. Dobrynin, *In Confidence*, 23.
60. Clifford, *Counsel to the President*, 181–82.
61. George F. Kennan, "Peaceful Coexistence," *Foreign Affairs*, Jan. 1960, 178.
62. Bohlen, *Witness to History*, 192.
63. Malia, *Russia under Western Eyes*, 358.
64. Stern, *Water's Edge*, xii.
65. "Books and Authors," *New York Times Book Review*, Apr. 17, 1921, 26.
66. James Reston, "Khrushchev Asks World Rule of the Satellite and Missiles If Part of Wide U.S.-Soviet Pact," *New York Times*, Oct. 8, 1957.
67. Harriman and Abel, *Special Envoy*, 159.
68. Stalin held a meeting of the Politburo in December 1945, the first meeting after a five-year interlude. Zubok and Pleshakov, *Inside the Kremlin's Cold War*, 119. For purposes of the present discussion, there is no need to differentiate between the State Committee of Defense and the Politburo. Until 1941, when Stalin became head of government, he ruled the USSR through the party.
69. Trister, "Traditionalists, Revisionists," 215–16.
70. Harriman and Abel, *Special Envoy*, 536.
71. Smith, *Three Years in Moscow*, 29.
72. Fischer, "The Scared Men in the Kremlin,"105.
73. Moynahan, *Claws of the Bear*, 193.

Chapter 3

1. McCullough, *Truman*, 488.
2. Sivachev and Yakovlev, *Russia and the United States*, 219.
3. Churchill, speech at Fulton, Missouri, March 5, 1946, in *Never Give In!* 420, 423.
4. Sivachev and Yakovlev, *Russia and the United States*, 219.
5. LaFeber, *America, Russia, and the Cold War*, 40.
6. Brzezinski, "Competitive Relationship," 159–60.
7. Khrushchev, *Khrushchev Remembers*, 393.
8. Kennan, *Century's Ending*, 31.
9. Kennan, *Sketches from a Life*, 22.
10. Kennan, *Sketches from a Life*, 90.
11. Office of the Historian, Bureau of Public Affairs, United States Department of State, file no. 861.00/1246, cited at "The Chargé in the Soviet Union (Kennan) to the Secretary of State," Feb. 22, 1946, Office of the Historian, https://history.state.gov/historicaldocuments/frus1946v06/d475, n. 44.
12. Isaacson and Thomas, *Wise Men*, 351.
13. Kennan, *Memoirs, 1925–1950*, 293.
14. Isaacson and Thomas, *Wise Men*, 352.
15. "The Chargé in the Soviet Union," reprinted in Jensen, *Origins of the Cold War*. A scanned image of the original document may be found at the National Archives Catalog, https://catalog.archives.gov/id/2642322. An HTML version is available at https://nsarchive2.gwu.edu/coldwar/documents/episode-1/kennan.htm.

16. Telegram from Nikolai V. Novikov, Soviet Ambassador to the US, to the Soviet Leadership, trans. Gary Goldberg (Paris, Sept. 27, 1946). The text of the telegram may be found in English and Russian at the Wilson Center Digital Archive, http://digitalarchive.wilsoncenter.org/document/110808.pdf?v=a8c1bf9f79f04aa2227394087a767c2a. In English translation, Novikov's telegram is just over five thousand words in length. The Russian version runs to slightly over four thousand words.

17. Zubok and Pleshakov, *Inside the Kremlin's Cold War*, 101.

18. Malkov, "Commentary," in Jensen, *Origins of the Cold War*, 73.

19. Telegram from Nikolai Novikov to the Soviet Leadership, Sept. 27, 1946, trans. John Glad and Kenneth Jensen, in Jensen, *Origins of the Cold War*, 14. The Novikov Telegram is available online, in a slightly different translation, at the Wilson Center Digital Archive, https://digitalarchive.wilsoncenter.org/document/110808.pdf?v=a8c1bf9f79f04aa2227394087a767c2a.

20. Arthur Schlesinger Jr., "Some Lessons from the Cold War," *Diplomatic History* 16, no. 1 (Jan. 1992): 49.

21. Kennan, *Century's Ending*, 110.

22. Anonymous [Kennan], "The Sources of Soviet Conduct," *Foreign Affairs*, July 1947, 566.

23. Nitze, *Hiroshima to Glasnost*, 51.

24. Anonymous [Kennan], "Soviet Conduct," 574.

25. Anonymous [Kennan], "Soviet Conduct," 575, 576.

26. Anonymous [Kennan], "Soviet Conduct," 582.

27. Anonymous [Kennan], "Soviet Conduct," 582.

28. In the translation of the X Article that was initially given to Stalin by the Ministry of State Security (MGB), "containment" was translated as "strangulation." It may have been provident that language specialists ultimately prevailed in providing the correct translation. Zubok, *Soviet Intelligence*, 7, https://www.wilsoncenter.org/sites/default/files/media/documents/publication/ACFB84.pdf.

29. Kennan, *Century's Ending*, 38.

30. Kennan, *Memoirs, 1925–1950*, 511.

31. See note 1 from the preface.

32. The Reith Lectures, BBC Radio, https://www.bbc.co.uk/programmes/b00729d9.

33. Kennan, *Century's Ending*, 38.

Chapter 4

1. Isaacson and Thomas, *Wise Men*, 370.

2. Tokaev, *Stalin Means War*, 115. Stalin could have added that Truman was not a successful gentleman shopkeeper.

3. Zubok, *Failed Empire*, 15.

4. McCullough, *Truman*, 478.

5. Letter, Harry S. Truman to James F. Byrnes, Washington, DC, Jan. 5, 1946, https://www.trumanlibrary.gov/library/truman-papers/longhand-notes-presidential-file-1944-1953/january-5-1946?documentid=NA&pagenumber=11. In *Shattered Peace*,

Daniel Yergin suggests that Truman summarized the letter in his meeting with Byrnes, rather than reading it. Yergin, *Shattered Peace,* 160. But Truman recorded unequivocally that "I read it to [Byrnes] as he sat at my desk." Truman, *Year of Decisions,* 551. Either way, the letter's significance lies in what it tells us about Truman's thinking.

6. Chace, "Day the Cold War Started," 6.

7. Truman, *Trial and Hope,* 95, and Zubok, *Failed Empire,* 44 (Soviet tank formation moving toward Tehran).

8. Truman, *Trial and Hope,* 95.

9. Truman, *Trial and Hope,* 95.

10. Zubok and Pleshakov, *Inside the Kremlin's Cold War,* 121.

11. Yergin, *Prize,* 403.

12. LaFeber, *America, Russia, and the Cold War,* 44.

13. Churchill, *Triumph and Tragedy,* 634–35.

14. Secretaries of War and Navy and Under Secretary of State (Acheson), to President Truman (memorandum), Washington, DC, Aug. 15, 1946, as quoted in "The Acting Secretary of State to the Secretary of State, at Paris" (telegram), Office of the Historian, https://history.state.gov/historicaldocuments/frus1946v07/d659.

15. Chace, *Acheson,* 154.

16. "Acheson Hints U.S. Is Firm on Straits," *New York Times,* Aug. 17, 1946.

17. Thomas J. Hamilton, "Turk's U.N. Speech Taken as Defiance on Straits Demand," *New York Times,* Oct. 27, 1946.

18. Lewis Wood, "Truman Silences Wallace Until After Paris Parley; Secretary Will Keep Post," *New York Times,* Sept. 19, 1946.

19. McCullough, *Truman,* 522.

20. "Fulbright Invites Truman to Resign," *New York Times,* Nov. 7, 1946. (The secretary of state would succeed to the presidency because the office of vice president was vacant, Vice President Truman having become the president when Roosevelt died.)

21. "Pravda Analyzes Election Results," *New York Times,* Nov. 8, 1946.

22. "Good Show by Political Actors Brings Crowds," The Watchman, *Los Angeles Times,* Sept. 18, 1946.

23. Ralph Barstow, "Thinking Out Loud" (editorial), *Covina [Cal.] Argus-Citizen,* Nov. 1, 1946.

24. "Nixon Debates with Voorhis," *Los Angeles Times,* Sept. 14, 1946.

25. Aide-Mémoire, "The British Embassy to the Department of State," Washington, DC, Feb. 21, 1947, Office of the Historian, https://history.state.gov/historicaldocuments/frus1947v05/d24.

26. "Memorandum by the Under Secretary of State (Acheson) to the Secretary of State," Feb. 21, 1947, Office of the Historian, https://history.state.gov/historicaldocuments/frus1947v05/d23.

27. Truman, *Trial and Hope,* 100.

28. Truman, *Trial and Hope,* 101.

29. George Washington, "Washington's Farewell Address 1796," Philadelphia, Sept. 1796, The Avalon Project, http://avalon.law.yale.edu/18th_century/washing.asp.

30. Thomas Jefferson, "First Inaugural Address," Washington, DC, Mar. 4, 1801, The Avalon Project, http://avalon.law.yale.edu/19th_century/jefinau1.asp.

31. Tocqueville, *Democracy in America*, 147.

32. Isaacson and Thomas, *Wise Men*, 395.

33. Bohlen, *Witness to History*, 261.

34. "Address of the President of the United States," 80th Cong., 1st Sess., House of Representatives, document 171, Mar. 12, 1947.

35. Clifford, *Counsel to the President*, 177 (emphasis in original).

36. Hopkins, "Containing Challenges," 70.

37. Harry S. Truman, "Executive Order 9835 Prescribing Procedures for the Administration of an Employees Loyalty Program in the Executive Branch of the Government," (Washington, DC, March 21, 1947). https://www.trumanlibrary.gov/library/executive-orders/9835/executive-order-9835.

38. Executive Order 9835 (Mar. 21, 1947), pt. II (2).

39. 1947 Cong. Rec. 8958 (July 15, 1947) (debate on H.R. 3813).

40. "The President[']s News Conference" (White House, Washington, DC, April 3, 1947), https://www.trumanlibrary.gov/library/public-papers/67/presidents-news-conference.

41. Thompson, *Frustration of Politics*, 39.

42. 1947 Cong. Rec. 2835 (Mar. 28, 1947).

43. Yergin, *Shattered Peace*, 283.

44. Isaacson and Thomas, *Wise Men*, 401.

45. Djilas, *Conversations with Stalin*, 182.

46. Isaacson and Thomas, *Wise Men*, 402.

Chapter 5

1. Melvyn P. Leffler, "Divide and Invest—Why the Marshall Plan Worked," *Foreign Affairs*, July–Aug. 2018, 172.

2. An audio recording of the speech is available at "Life and Legacy," George C. Marshall Foundation, https://www.marshallfoundation.org/marshall/the-marshall-plan/marshall-plan-speech/.

3. "Life and Legacy."

4. Bohlen, *Witness to History*, 265.

5. As quoted (in translation) in Smith, *Three Years in Moscow*, 176.

6. *New York Times*, Oct. 6, 1947.

7. LaFeber, *America, Russia, and the Cold War*, 70.

8. Thomas, *Being Nixon*, 44.

9. Brands, *Reagan*, 81.

10. Powers, *Not Without Honor*, 218.

11. "Message from the President of the United States," Washington, DC, Dec. 19, 1947, in *The Marshall Plan* (Washington, DC: U.S. Government Printing Office, 1967), 16, available at https://www.marshallfoundation.org/library/wp-content/uploads/sites/16/2014/05/Section_01.pdf.

12. Truman, *Trial and Hope*, 241.

13. Address, Harry S. Truman to U.S. Congress, Washington, DC, Mar. 17, 1948, Harry S. Truman Presidential Library and Museum, https://www.trumanlibrary.gov/library/public-papers/52/special-message-congress-threat-freedom-europe.

14. 1947 Cong. Rec. 164–66 (Jan. 10, 1945).

15. Borgwardt, *New Deal for the World*, 161.

16. Bohlen, *Witness to History*, 266.

17. Senate Res. 239, 80th Cong., June 11, 1948, https://static.history.state.gov/frus/frus1948v03/medium/0153.png.

18. United Nations Charter, Chap. VII, Art. 51 (emphasis added), https://www.un.org/en/sections/un-charter/chapter-vii/index.html.

19. Large, "Great Rescue," 26.

20. Truman, *Trial and Hope*, 123.

21. House, *Military History*, 121.

22. Large, "Great Rescue," 25.

23. Chuev, *Molotov Remembers*, 58.

24. Bailey, *America Faces Russia*, 324.

25. Harrington, *Air Force Can Deliver Anything*, 106

26. Yergin, *Shattered Peace*, 384.

27. Powers, *Not Without Honor*, 222.

28. C. P. Trussell, "Red 'Underground' in Federal Posts Alleged by Editor," *New York Times*, Aug. 4, 1948.

29. Trussell.

30. C. P. Trussell, "Truman Calls Spy Inquiries a Republican 'Red Herring,'" *New York Times*, Aug. 6, 1948.

31. Trussell.

32. United Press, "New Witnesses May Prove Who Lied in Spying Inquiry," *Los Angeles Times*, Aug. 19, 1948.

33. "Red Spy Hearings Ordered Reopened," *Los Angeles Times*, Dec. 5, 1948.

34. United States Department of State, *History of the Bureau of Diplomatic Security of the United States Department of State* (Washington, DC: Global Publishing Solutions 2011), 90.

35. "Grand Jury to Get Chambers Papers," *Los Angeles Times,* Dec. 12, 1948.

36. Powers, *Not Without Honor*, 225.

37. Phillips, *Truman Presidency*, 197.

38. Clark Clifford, "Memo, Clark Clifford to Harry S. Truman, November 19, 1947," Harry S. Truman Presidential Library and Museum, https://www.trumanlibrary.gov/library/research-files/memo-clark-clifford-harry-s-truman.

39. The Clifford memorandum was in fact the product of the joint efforts of Clifford and James H. Rowe, another Washington lawyer. Clifford described Rowe as "one of the most brilliant political thinkers of the New Deal era." Clifford, *Counsel to the President,* 189–90. It has been suggested that the memorandum is more the intellectual product of Rowe than Clifford, because the version given to Truman so closely tracks the draft Rowe gave to Clifford. Gary A. Donaldson, "Who Wrote the Clifford Memo? The Origins of Campaign Strategy in the Truman Administration," *Presidential Studies Quarterly* 23, no. 4 (Fall 1993): 747. But that question—immaterial for present purposes—cannot be answered without knowing how much guidance Rowe got from Clifford before Rowe put pen to paper or as he wrote the first draft.

40. "Memo, Clark Clifford," 14.

41. "Dewey's Cleveland Talk Scoring Truman Policy on Soviet," *New York Times*, Oct. 28, 1948.

42. "Memo, Clark Clifford," 13.

43. "Memo, Clark Clifford," 13.

44. United Press, "Concedes Dewey Victory," *New York Times*, Oct. 28, 1948.

45. James A. Hagerty, "Final Survey of Nation Gives Dewey a Commanding Lead," *New York Times*, Oct. 31, 1948.

46. The Radio Moscow endorsement did not carry the day for Wallace. He got slightly over 2 percent of the popular vote and no electoral votes.

47. Truman, *Trial and Hope*, 253.

48. Acheson, *Present at the Creation*, 280.

49. Belgium, Canada, Denmark, France, Iceland, Italy, Luxembourg, the Netherlands, Norway, Portugal, the United Kingdom, and the United States.

50. Hearings Before the Committee on Foreign Relations, United States Senate (Eighty-First Congress, First Session), on the North Atlantic Treaty, pt. 1 (Washington, DC: Government Printing Office, 1949), 528 (hereafter Hearings on the North Atlantic Treaty).

51. Hearings on the North Atlantic Treaty, 11.

52. Hearings on the North Atlantic Treaty, 547–48.

53. House, *Military History*, 129.

54. Holloway, *Stalin and the Bomb*, 272.

55. Bohlen, *Witness to History*, 286.

56. Nye, *Paradox of American Power*, 33.

57. Executive, USAF Directorate of Intelligence to Commanding General, Air Materiel Command and Commanding General, Strategic Air Command (memorandum), July 13, 1949, transmitting report dated July 1, 1949, https://nsarchive2.gwu.edu/nukevault/ebb286/doc04.PDF. Discussed in Steven L. Rearden, *Council of War*, 98.

Chapter 6

1. Kissinger, *Diplomacy*, 465.

2. Halle, *Cold War as History*, 115.

3. Acheson, *Present at the Creation*, 195.

4. Superbly portrayed by Isaacson and Thomas, in *Wise Men*.

5. Sell, *Washington to Moscow*, 337.

6. The reality of American life in the first half of the twentieth century was such that women simply did not have the opportunity to earn their way into a pantheon such as the one discussed here. The same was true of racial minorities. In 1945, future secretaries of state Madeleine Albright (the first woman) and Colin Powell (the first Black person) were eight years old. Future secretaries of state Condoleezza Rice and Hillary Clinton had not yet been born.

7. Brinkley, *Liberalism and Its Discontents*, 209.

8. Isaacson and Thomas, *Wise Men*, 740.

9. Dwight D. Eisenhower, Installation Address, Oct. 12, 1948, in Clark, *Eisenhower in Command*, 52.

10. Alexander Heffner, "Former Supreme Court Justice Sandra Day O'Connor on the Importance of Civics Education," *Washington Post Magazine*, Apr. 12, 2012.

Chapter 7

1. David Alan Rosenberg, "American Atomic Strategy and the Hydrogen Bomb Decision," *Journal of American History* 66, no. 1 (June 1979): 63.

2. Bohlen, *Witness to History*, 290.

3. Gregg Herken, "'A Most Deadly Illusion': The Atomic Secret and American Nuclear Weapons Policy, 1945–1950," *Pacific Historical Review* 49, no. 1 (Feb. 1980): 58.

4. Beevor, *Fall of Berlin*, 138.

5. Holloway, *Stalin and the Bomb*, 222.

6. Kotkin, *Armageddon Averted*, 79.

7. Hugh Baillie, "Stalin Says Soviet Lacks Atom Bomb," *New York Times*, Oct. 29, 1946.

8. Baillie.

9. George F. Kennan, "Two Hundred Years of American Policy: The United States and the Soviet Union, 1917–1976," *Foreign Affairs*, July 1976, 681.

10. Telegram from Nikolai Novikov to the Soviet Leadership, in Jensen, *Origins of the Cold War*, 16.

11. Holloway, *Stalin and the Bomb*, 132.

12. Holloway, *Stalin and the Bomb*, 218.

13. "Churchill Holds Atom Bomb Saved Europe from Soviet," *New York Times*, Apr. 1, 1949. Churchill's March 31 speech, reproduced in the Congressional Record. Appendix to Cong. Rec., Apr. 1, 1949, A1933 (extension of remarks of Rep. Hobbs). It was printed in full in the *New York Times* on April 1, 1949.

14. Harry S. Truman, "Statement by President Truman in Response to First Soviet Nuclear Test," Sept. 23, 1949, Wilson Center Digital Archive, https://digitalarchive.wilsoncenter.org/document/134436.

15. Anthony Leviero, "Atom Blast in Russia Disclosed," *New York Times*, Sept. 24, 1949.

16. Hanson W. Baldwin, "The Effects of Russia's Bomb on Our Military Strategy," *New York Times*, Sept. 25, 1949.

17. Baldwin.

18. Truman, *Trial and Hope*, 308.

19. Nitze, *Hiroshima to Glasnost*, 91.

20. Nitze, *Hiroshima to Glasnost*, 92.

Chapter 8

1. Kissinger, *Years of Upheaval*, 1151.

2. National Security Council, "Report to the National Security Council on United States Objectives and Programs for National Security" (NSC-68), Washington, DC, Apr. 14, 1950, Wilson Center Digital Archive, https://digitalarchive.wilsoncenter.org/document/116191.pdf?v=2699956db534c1821edefa61b8c13ffe.

3. House, *Military History*, 221.

4. Yergin, *Shattered Peace*, 402.

5. NSC-68, 4, 7.

6. NSC-68, 6.

7. NSC-68, 9.
8. NSC-68, 20.
9. NSC-68, 49.
10. NSC-68, 12.
11. NSC-68, 21–22.
12. NSC-68, 56 (emphasis added).
13. NSC-68, 62.
14. NSC-68, 60.
15. NSC-68, 25.
16. Sivachev and Yakovlev, *Russia and the United States*, 230.

Chapter 9

1. Truman, *Trial and Hope*, 290.
2. Spanier, "Choices We Did Not Have," 138.
3. *Toomey v. Farley*, 138 N.E.2d 221 (N.Y. 1956); *Utah State Farm Bureau Federation v. National Farmers Union Serv. Corp.*, 198 F.2d 20 (10th Cir. 1952); and *Grant v. Reader's Digest Ass'n*, 151 F.2d 733 (2d Cir. 1945).
4. Concurrent Resolution of Congress, S. Con. Res. 11, Reaffirming Friendship of the American People for All Peoples of the World, Including the Peoples of the Soviet Union, 81st Cong., 1st Sess., June 26, 1951.
5. Pope Pius XI, *Encyclical: Divini Redemptorus* (Rome: March 19, 1937), ¶ 3.
6. Oleg Barabanov, "Foreword: Memory of War," 4.
7. Bosley Crowther, "'The Red Menace,' Dealing with Communist Party in U.S., Shown at the Mayfair," *New York Times*, June 27, 1949.
8. "Russia's Plans for World War III Bared by Former Staff Officer of Red Army in Warning to West," *St. Louis Post-Dispatch*, Jan. 14, 1949.
9. Girgori A. Tokaev, "Stalin Means Business—World Domination by Any Means, Including War," *St. Louis Post-Dispatch*, January 16, 1949.
10. Malia, *Russia under Western Eyes*, 364.
11. Caballero, *McCarthyism v. Clinton Jencks*, 25, et seq.
12. Joseph R. McCarthy, "Enemies from Within," speech delivered to the Ohio County, West Virginia Republican Women's Club, Feb. 9, 1950, Ohio County Public Library, https://www.ohiocountylibrary.org/wheeling-history/5655. Advance copies of the speech put the number at 205, not 57. In the transcript McCarthy submitted to the Congressional Record, he put the number at 57.
13. "M'Carthy Insists Truman Oust Reds," *New York Times*, Feb. 12, 1950.
14. Tanenhaus, *Whittaker Chambers*, 482.
15. "The President's News Conference at Key West" (transcript), Mar. 30, 1950, The American Presidency Project, https://www.presidency.ucsb.edu/documents/the-presidents-news-conference-key-west-4.
16. William S. White, "Communism as an Issue Baffles Both Parties," *New York Times*, June 18, 1950.
17. 1950 Cong. Rec. 7894–95 (June 1, 1950).
18. William S. White, "Seven GOP Senators Decry 'Smear' Tactics of McCarthy," *New York Times*, June 2, 1950.

19. Malia, *Russia under Western Eyes*, 382.

20. Austin Stevens, "General Removed Over War Speech," *New York Times*, Sept. 2, 1950.

21. Elizabeth Gurley Flynn, "A Better World," *Daily Worker*, Apr. 19, 1951.

22. Walter H. Waggoner, "U.S. Cancels Visas for Entering Here," *New York Times*, Oct. 13, 1950.

23. Editorial, "Abuse of the Classroom," *San Francisco Examiner*, Sept. 23, 1950.

24. Lewis Wood, "Oaths of Loyalty by Lawyers Asked," *New York Times*, Sept. 23, 1950.

25. American Bar Association, *Proceedings of the House of Delegates: 1950*, 36 ABAJ 948, 972 (1950).

26. 1946 Cong. Rec. 2856–57 (Mar. 29, 1946).

27. "Mrs. Douglas' View of Reds Challenged," *Los Angeles Times*, Aug. 30, 1950.

28. Editorial, "Red Herring Keeps on Growing," *Los Angeles Times*, Aug. 31, 1950.

29. Editorial, "The Four Big Senatorial Races," *Los Angeles Times*, Oct. 31, 1950.

30. "Nixon and Douglas Views Contrasted," *Los Angeles Times*, Oct. 26, 1950.

31. "Nixon Hits Foe's Policy on Red China," *Los Angeles Times*, Nov. 4, 1950.

32. Editorial, "Last and Most Important Act: Vote!" *Los Angeles Times*, Nov. 5, 1950.

33. Nixon Presidential Materials Staff, *Tape Subject Log*, 68 (conversation nos. 10–120), Richard Nixon Presidential Library and Museum, https://www.nixonlibrary.gov/sites/default/files/forresearchers/find/tapes/finding_aids/tapesubjectlogs/wht010.pdf. Jack Nelson, "Nixon Targeted the Times, Tapes Show," *Los Angeles Times*, Mar. 22, 1997.

34. Richard M. Nixon, conversation nos. 10–118, Oct. 7, 1971. Recording at UVA Miller Center, https://millercenter.org/the-presidency/secret-white-house-tapes/10–118.

35. Nelson, "Nixon Targeted the Times."

36. James Reston, "Moderate Liberals Appear Favored by Nation's Voters," *New York Times*, Oct. 30, 1951.

37. James Preston (not to be confused with James "Scotty" Reston), "Rival Parties Resort to McCarthyism," *Atlanta Constitution*, Oct. 31, 1950.

38. James Reston, "U.S. Arming on Premise Soviet Will Avoid '51 War," *New York Times*, Jan. 5, 1951.

39. Allan Michie, "Russia Could Take Europe in Three Weeks," *Collier's*, Dec. 30, 1950, 11.

40. Michie.

41. Editorial, "Why Russia Can't Be Trusted," *Collier's*, Jan. 27, 1951, 22–23.

42. "The Bill for Defense" (appropriation) and "Father's Little Watchman" (bombers), *Time*, Aug. 20, 1951, 11, 28.

43. "The Unwanted War," *Collier's*, Oct. 27, 1951, 17.

44. 1951 Cong. Rec. 6602 (June 14, 1951).

45. Casey, "Confirming the Cold War Consensus," 90.

46. "Republican Party Platform of 1952" (see under "Foreign Policy"), July 7, 1952, The American Presidency Project, https://www.presidency.ucsb.edu/documents/republican-party-platform-1952.

47. "McCarthy Urges Tough Attitude Toward Reds," *Los Angeles Times*, July 10, 1952.

48. Fletcher Knebel, "Potomac Fever," *Des Moines Register*, Sept. 19, 1952.

49. W. H. Lawrence, "Eisenhower to Back M'Carthy if Named, But Assails Tactics," *New York Times*, Aug. 23, 1952.

50. W. H. Lawrence, "Eisenhower Scores President on Reds: Supports M'Carthy," *New York Times*, Oct. 4, 1952.

51. Lawrence.

52. "Text of Eisenhower's Speech on Red 'Penetration of Government,'" *New York Times*, Oct. 4, 1952.

53. W. H. Lawrence, "General for Peaceful Drive to Let Captive Nations Determine Own Rule," *New York Times*, Aug. 14, 1952, (emphasis added).

54. Lawrence.

55. Russell Porter, "Dulles Gives Plan to Free Red Lands," *New York Times*, Aug. 28, 1952.

56. Porter.

57. LaFeber, *America, Russia, and the Cold War*, 136.

58. W. H. Lawrence, "Eisenhower for Repudiation of Yalta to Give Poland Hope," *New York Times*, Oct. 12, 1952.

59. Lawrence.

60. Elie Abel, "Stevenson Called Appeaser by Nixon," *New York Times*, Oct. 17, 1952.

61. Editorial, "Home Stretch," *New York Times*, Nov. 2, 1952.

62. Editorial, "Repudiation of Yalta," *New York Times*, Oct. 19, 1952.

63. Toal, *Near Abroad*, 278.

64. "The President's Farewell Address to the American People," Jan. 15, 1953, Harry S. Truman Presidential Library and Museum, https://www.trumanlibrary.gov/library/public-papers/378/presidents-farewell-address-american-people.

65. "Cohn, Veteran Investigator at 25, Will Aid McCarthy in Inquiries," *New York Times*, January 3, 1953.

66. *In the Matter of Roy M. Cohn*, 118 A.D.2d 15, 17 (N.Y. 1986).

67. Margot Hornblower, "Roy Cohn Is Disbarred by New York Court," *Washington Post*, June 24, 1986.

68. William S. White, "Senators Approve Dulles in Cabinet," *New York Times*, Jan. 16, 1953.

69. John Foster Dulles, "United States Foreign Policy" (address), 1953 Cong. Record 676–77 (Jan. 30, 1953). Reprinted in full in *New York Times*, Jan. 28, 1953.

70. Nichols, *Ike and McCarthy*, 15.

71. "This Beets Everything!" *Miami Daily News*, Mar. 6, 1953.

72. Bohlen, *Witness to History*, 314.

73. William S. White, "Bohlen Defends Yalta Pact; Stresses Russia Violated It," *New York Times*, Mar. 3, 1953.

74. Bohlen, *Witness to History*, 323. Bohlen was generous to George Kennan in this comment. Kennan—never famous for sheer diplomatic skill, at home or abroad—had a history of fairly sharp policy differences with Dulles, with the result that Dulles chose not to retain Kennan in the State Department.

75. 1953 Cong. Record 2292 (Mar. 25, 1953).

76. 1953 Cong. Record 2294.

77. 1953 Cong. Record 2285.

78. William S. White, "President Terms Bohlen Best Man," *New York Times*, Mar. 27, 1953.

79. Bohlen, *Witness to History*, 334.

80. Whitfield, *Culture of the Cold War*, 38.

81. *Executive Sessions of the Senate Permanent Subcommittee on Investigations*, vol. 2, Aug. 31, 1953, S. Prt. 107–84, p. 1628 (Washington, DC: Government Printing Office, made public Jan. 2003).

82. *Executive Sessions*, p. 1633 (testimony of Doris Walters Powell).

83. *Executive Sessions*, p. 1632.

84. Charles Grutzner, "Army Drops Clerk M'Carthy Accused," *New York Times*, Sept. 17, 1953.

85. 1954 Cong. Rec. 2886 (Mar. 9, 1954).

86. Transcript of the *See It Now* presentation was obtained upon request from the University of California at Berkeley, Media Resources Center,

87. Val Adams, "Praise Pours in on Murrow Show," *New York Times*, Mar. 11, 1954.

88. Transcript of Presidential Press Conference, *New York Times*, Mar. 11, 1954.

89. W. H. Lawrence, "Army Charges M'Carthy and Cohn Threatened It in Trying to Obtain Preferred Treatment for Schine," *New York Times*, Mar. 12, 1954.

90. Nichols, *Ike and McCarthy*, 216.

91. *Hearings Before the Special Subcommittee on Investigations, Committee on Government Operations, June 9, 1954* (Washington, DC: Government Printing Office, 1954), 2428 (statement of Joseph Welch).

92. United States House of Representatives Report No. 3123, 81st Cong., 2d Sess., *Report on the National Lawyers Guild—Legal Bulwark of the Communist Party* (Washington, DC: Sept. 21, 1950), 1.

93. Joseph N. Welch, "The Lawyer's Afterthoughts," *Life*, July 26, 1954, 100.

94. Dwight D. Eisenhower, Address, Columbia University, May 31, 1954, https://www.presidency.ucsb.edu/documents/address-the-columbia-university-national-bicentennial-dinner-new-york-city.

95. "Text of Statement on Reds," *New York Times*, June 3, 1954.

96. *Hearings before the Special Subcommittee on Investigations of the Committee on Government Operations, June 2, 1954* (Washington, DC: Government Printing Office, 1954), 1947.

97. *Hearings*, 2426 (June 9, 1954).

98. Thomas, *Man to See*, 76.

99. *Hearings*, 2426–27.

100. W.H. Lawrence, "M'Carthy to Shun Inquiry till Group Acts in News 'Leak,'" *New York Times*, April 16, 1954.

101. *Hearings*, 2428–29.

102. W.H. Lawrence, "Welch Assails M'Carthy's 'Cruelty' and 'Recklessness' in Attack on Aide," *New York Times*, June 10, 1954.

103. W.H. Lawrence, "M'Carthy Hearings End on 36th Day," *New York Times*, June 18, 1954.

104. "McCarthy Plans to Seize U.S. in '56, Moscow Says," *New York Times*, July 30, 1954.

105. 1954 Cong. Rec. 14210 (Aug. 12, 1954).

106. Wallace Mitchell, "Bjornson Hits Humphrey as Leftist Leader," *Minneapolis Star*, Aug. 5, 1954.

107. 1954 Cong. Rec.

108. C.P. Trussel, "Congress Passes Softened Version of Communist Ban," *New York Times*, Aug. 20, 1954.

109. 1954 Cong. Rec. 15105–07, 15118–20 (Aug. 19, 1954).

110. Joseph A. Loftus, "Eisenhower Signs Red Control Bill, Citing Protection," *New York Times*, Aug. 25, 1954.

111. Harry S. Truman, *Veto of Internal Security Bill,* Washington, DC, Sept. 22, 1950, Harry S. Truman Presidential Library and Museum, https://www.trumanlibrary.gov/library/public-papers/254/veto-internal-security-bill.

112. Title 50 United States Code §§ 841–844.

113. 1954 Cong. Rec. 15105 (Aug. 19, 1954).

114. *Blawis v. Bolin*, 358 F. Supp. 349 (D. Ariz. 1973).

115. *Commonwealth of Pennsylvania v. Nelson*, 350 U.S. 497 (1956).

116. "The Censure of Joe McCarthy," *Time*, Oct. 4, 1954, 21.

117. "Statement of Senator McCarthy," 1954 Cong. Rec. 15953 (Nov. 10, 1954).

118. Anthony Leviero, "Final Vote Condemns McCarthy, 67–22," *New York Times*, Dec. 3, 1954.

119. Schlesinger, *Thousand Days*, 12.

120. Kennan, *Memoirs, 1925–1950*, 191.

121. Kennan, *Memoirs, 1925–1950*, 223.

Chapter 10

1. Winterton, *Inquest on an Ally,* 268.

2. Message, Josef Stalin to Kim Il Sung (Mar. 18, 1950), trans. Kathryn Weathersby, in Kathryn Weathersby, "New Russian Documents on the Korean War," *Bulletin*, Cold War International History Project (Washington, DC: Woodrow Wilson Center for Scholars), nos. 6–7 (Winter 1995–96): 37.

3. Telegram from Josef Stalin to N. V. Roshchin (July 5, 1950), trans. Kathryn Weathersby, in Weathersby, "New Russian Documents," 43.

4. "U.S. Troops Land in South Korea," *New York Times,* July 1, 1950.

5. Khrushchev, *Khrushchev Remembers*, 369.

6. Gromyko, *Memories,* 164.

7. U.N. Document S/1511, "Resolution concerning the Complaint of Aggression upon the Republic of Korea," June 27, 1950.

8. Josef Stalin to Soviet Ambassador in Prague, trans. Gary Goldberg (cable), Moscow, Aug. 27, 1950, Wilson Center Digital Archive, https://digitalarchive.wilsoncenter.org/document/112225. Source: Russian State Archive of Socio-Political History (RGASPI), fond 558, opis 11, delo 62, listy 71–72.

9. Gromyko, *Memories,* 102.

10. Khrushchev, *Khrushchev Remembers*, 371.

11. Khrushchev, 371.

12. Evgueni Bajanov, "Assessing the Politics of the Korean War, 1949–51," *Bulletin,* Cold War International History Project (Washington, DC: Woodrow Wilson Center for Scholars), nos. 6–7 (Winter 1995–96), 89.

13. "U.S. Envoy Expects War to End Soon," *New York Times*, Nov. 2, 1950.

14. Michael James, "Long Winter War Feared in Korea," *New York Times*, Nov. 1, 1950.

15. James Reston, "Revitalized G.O.P. in Scientific Drive," *New York Times*, Nov. 1, 1950.

16. Lawrence E. Davies, "California Tests Communism Issue," *New York Times*, Nov. 1, 1950.

17. James Reston, "Intellectual Left Silent in Campaign," *New York Times*, Nov. 2, 1950.

18. Boyne, *Beyond the Wild Blue*, 79.

19. Anthony Leviero, "President Warns We Would Use Atom Bomb in Korea, If Necessary," *New York Times,* Dec. 1, 1950. In this article, the president's answers at the press conference were "paraphrased, as required by White House rules."

20. "Marshall Limits M'Arthur Advance North of Parallel," *New York Times*, Mar. 28, 1951.

21. Telegram from Josef Stalin to Mao Zedong (June 5, 1951), trans. Kathryn Weathersby, in Weathersby, "New Documents on the Korean War," 59.

22. W.H. Lawrence, "Truman Announces He Will Not Run Again," *New York Times*, Mar. 30, 1952.

23. Truman, *Trial and Hope*, 488.

24. The Twenty-Second Amendment to the Constitution became effective in February 1951. Under that amendment, no person could be elected to the presidency more than twice, nor more than once if he had succeeded (as Truman did) to more than two years of another president's term. But the amendment, by its terms, did not apply to the person holding the office on the effective date of the amendment. Truman was legally free to run in 1952.

25. "Republican Party Platform, 1952."

26. "Text of General Eisenhower's Speech in Detroit on Ending the War in Korea," *New York Times*, Oct. 25, 1952.

27. "Text of Stevenson's Boston Speech on 'Old Guard' and Communism," *New York Times*, Oct. 26, 1952.

28. Lindesay Parrott, "Eisenhower Visits Korea Front," *New York Times*, Dec. 6, 1952.

29. National Security Council, "Report to the National Security Council by the Executive Secretary" (NSC-68/2), Washington, DC, Sept. 30, 1950, https://history.state.gov/historicaldocuments/frus1950v01/d129.

30. Walker, *Cold War*, 77.

31. Nitze, *Hiroshima to Glasnost*, 109.

32. National Security Council, *Memorandum for the President*, Washington, DC, Nov. 24, 1950, 5. (Provided to author by request by the Harry S. Truman Presidential Library and Museum.)

33. Hanson W. Baldwin, "Why They Picked General Ike," *New York Times Magazine*, Dec. 24, 1950.

34. North Atlantic Treaty Organization, Final Communiqué, Brussels, Dec. 19, 1950, https://www.nato.int/docu/comm/49–95/c501219a.htm.

35. Kennan, *Memoirs, 1925–1950*, 186.

36. Dwight D. Eisenhower, "The Chance for Peace," Address Delivered Before the American Society of Newspaper Editors (April 16, 1953).

37. William B. Pickett, ed., *George F. Kennan and the Origins of Eisenhower's New Look: An Oral History of Project Solarium* (Princeton, NJ: Princeton Institute for International and Regional Studies, 2004), 10.

38. NSC-162/2, 11, 22 and 4.

39. John Foster Dulles, "Policy for Security and Peace," *Foreign Affairs*, Apr. 1954, 358, 362, 364.

40. "The Kremlin," *Time*, Apr. 30, 1956, 28.

41. Department of State, "Khrushchev Reaches the Top After Long, Steady Rise," Washington, DC, Feb. 17, 1955, Office of the Historian, http://history.state.gov/historicaldocuments/frus1955-57v24/d8.

42. Zubok, *Failed Empire*, 99.

43. "Kremlin Makes Crimea Part of Ukraine Republic," *St. Louis Post-Dispatch*, Feb. 27, 1954.

44. Gorbachev, *Memoirs*, 61.

45. "The News of the Week in Review," *New York Times*, June 10, 1956.

46. "Pravda Names Stalin 101 Times on a Page," *New York Times*, Jan. 4, 1951.

47. As described by Khrushchev in a conversation with Averell Harriman in the Kremlin on June 23, 1959. Dispatch, Conversation between N. S. Khrushchev and Governor Harriman, Moscow, June 26, 1959, Office of the Historian, https://history.state.gov/historicaldocuments/frus1958-60v10p1/d75.

48. "Interview With Oleg Troyanovski" (transcript), Episode 8, George Washington University National Security Archive, Nov. 15, 1998, https://nsarchive2.gwu.edu/coldwar/interviews/episode-8/troyanovski1.html.

49. Raleigh, *Soviet Baby Boomers*, 56.

50. "The Kremlin," *Time*, Apr. 30, 1956, 29.

51. "Dulles Attacks Red 'Despotism,'" *Charlotte [NC] News*, June 21, 1956. See also "The Contest Between Freedom and Despotism" (Address by the Secretary of State), *Department of State Bulletin* 35, no. 888 (July 2, 1956), 4.

52. Nikita S. Khrushchev, "On Peaceful Coexistence," *Foreign Affairs*, Oct. 1959, 3 (emphasis added).

53. Kotkin, *Armageddon Averted*, 2.

Chapter 11

1. See the main page of the Communist Party USA, www.cpusa.org. The party's online magazine is *Political Affairs*, www.politicalaffairs.net.

2. 18 U.S.C. § 2385.

3. 341 U.S. 494 (1951).

4. 354 U.S. 298 (1957).

5. 367 U.S. 203 (1961).

6. *Dennis v. United States*, 341 U.S. 494, 574–55 (1951) (Jackson, J., concurring).

7. The original version of the Smith Act, under which the *Dennis* defendants were convicted, had its own conspiracy provision. 54 Stat. 671, § 3 (1940). Unlike the general federal conspiracy statute, 18 U.S.C. § 371, the conspiracy provision in the original Smith Act did not require proof of an overt act in furtherance of the conspiracy.

8. Tocqueville, *Democracy in America*, 310.

9. *Dennis v. United States,* 341 U.S. 494, 554–55 (1951) (Frankfurter, J., concurring), quoting from George F. Kennan, "Where Do You Stand on Communism?" *New York Times,* May 27, 1951.

10. Robert C. Doty, "High Court Upholds Guilt of 11 Top Communists; Other Prosecutions Are Set," *New York Times*, June 5, 1951.

11. Cray, *Chief Justice*, 272.

12. Michal R. Belknap, "Why Dennis?" *Marquette Law Review* 96 (2013): 1013, 1015 n. 16.

13. Welles Hangen, "Pravda Modifies Khrushchev Slur," *New York Times,* Nov. 20, 1956.

14. Cray, *Chief Justice*, 330.

15. *Yates v. United States*, 354 U.S. 298, 324–25 (1957).

16. Cray, *Chief Justice*, 333.

17. *Bary v. United States*, 248 F.2d 201 (10th Cir. 1957).

18. 354 U.S. 178 (1957).

19. 354 U.S. 234 (1957).

20. 354 U.S. 363 (1957).

21. *Watkins*, 354 U.S. at 185.

22. "Assignments in Orient Marked Service's Career in Government," *New York Times,* June 18, 1957.

23. The government officer defending the case in the Supreme Court was Acheson's successor, John Foster Dulles, because the government litigant was, technically, the secretary of state in his official capacity, even if the challenged action had been taken by his predecessor.

24. *New York Times*, June 18, 1957.

25. James Reston, "Supreme Court Declares Rights of Individuals Must Be Protected," *New York Times,* June 18, 1957.

26. "Supreme Court Confuses Matters," *Los Angeles Times*, June 19, 1957.

27. 1959 Cong. Rec. 7471 (May 5, 1959).

28. 1959 Cong. Rec. 3377 (Mar. 5, 1959).

29. Pub.L. 87–486 (June 19, 1962).

30. Letter, Byron R. White to James O. Eastland, Washington, DC, Jan. 31, 1962, appended to S. Rep. No. 1410, 87th Cong., 2d Sess. 1962.

31. "Text of Bar Association's Stand on Communists," *New York Times*, Feb. 28, 1959.

32. *Jencks v. United States*, 353 U.S. 657 (1957). See Caballero, *McCarthyism v. Clinton Jencks* for a superb account of the *Jencks* case.

33. Luther A. Huston, "Bar Unit Assails High Court Trend," *New York Times*, July 26, 1957.

34. American Bar Association, "Supplemental Report of the Special Committee on Communist Tactics, Strategy and Objectives," reproduced in 1958 Cong. Rec. 19132–39 (Aug. 22, 1958).

35. *Sheiner v. State*, 82 So.2d 657 (Fla. 1955); *State v. Sheiner*, 112 So.2d 571 (Fla. 1959).

36. *Communist Party of the United States v. Subversive Activities Control Board*, 367 U.S. 1 (1961); *Albertson v. Subversive Activities Control Board*, 382 U.S. 70 (1965).

37. *Barenblatt v. United States*, 360 U.S. 109 (1959).

38. *United States v. Robel*, 389 U.S. 258 (1967).

39. *Aptheker v. United States*, 378 U.S. 500 (1964).

40. *Scales v. United States*, 367 U.S. 203 (1961).

41. *Noto v. United States*, 367 U.S. 290 (1961).

42. "A Political Prisoner," *New York Times*, June 14, 1962.

43. Hoffer, et al., *Federal Courts*, 363.

44. Sheft, "The End of the Smith Act Era: A Legal and Historical Analysis of Scales v. United States," *American Journal of Legal History* 36, no. 2 (Apr. 1992): 182.

45. Sheft.

46. "The Court on Communism," *New York Times*, June 7, 1961.

Chapter 12

1. T. Gerhard Bidlingmaier, "The Strategic Importance of the Baltic Sea," *Proceedings, U.S. Naval Institute*, Sept. 1958, 24.

2. Bidlingmaier, 24.

3. "Memorandum of Discussion at the 249th Meeting of the National Security Council, May 19, 1955," in vol. 5, *Foreign Relations of the United States, 1955–1957* (Washington, DC: Government Printing Office, 1988), 184.

4. Toal, *Near Abroad*, 97.

5. William Griffith to Richard J. Condon, "Policy Review of Voice for Free Hungary Programming, 23 October–23 November 1956," ¶ (A)(2) (memorandum), Washington, DC, Dec. 5, 1956, National Security Archive, https://nsarchive2.gwu.edu/NSAEBB/NSAEBB76/doc10.pdf. The outlet for RFE broadcasts into Hungary was called Voice of Free Hungary.

6. "Foreign Relations," *Time*, Apr. 30, 1956, 20.

7. Clayton Knowles, "Stevenson Warns of a Split in West," *New York Times*, Nov. 1, 1956.

8. "Policy Review of Voice," ¶ (A)(3).

9. "Working Notes from the Session of the CPSU CC Presidium on 31 October [1956] (see under "On Hungary"; compiled by V.N. Malin), The National Security Archive, https://nsarchive2.gwu.edu/NSAEBB/NSAEBB14/doc9.htm.

10. "Minutes of the Nagy Government's Fourth Cabinet Meeting, November 1, 1956" (trans. Csaba Farkas), ¶ 2(a). The National Security Archive, https://nsarchive2.gwu.edu/NSAEBB/NSAEBB76/doc7.pdf.

11. John MacCormac, "Nagy Quits Warsaw Pact, Declares Hungary Neutral," *New York Times*, Nov. 2, 1956.

12. "Policy Review of Voice," ¶ (A)(4).

13. "The Choice of a Candidate," *New York Times*, Oct. 16, 1956.

14. Bohlen, *Witness to History*, 418.

15. Adams, *Firsthand Report*, 255.

16. "Interview with Oleg Troyanovski," Episode 8, George Washington University National Security Archive (Nov. 15, 1998).

17. Allen Drury, "House Study Says U.S. 'Inaction' Hurt Freedom in Hungary Revolt," *New York Times*, May 17, 1957.

18. Peter Edson, "U.S. Lacks Policy on Hungary," *Pittsburgh Press*, March 25, 1957.

19. "After Democratic Sweep," *New York Times*, Nov. 9, 1958.

20. "'We Will Bury You.' Khrushchev Says; West's Envoys Walk Out," *St. Louis Post-Dispatch*, Nov. 19, 1956.

21. Barry M. Goldwater, "Official Report of the Proceedings of the Twenty-Eighth Republican National Convention" (acceptance speech), Washington, DC, Republican National Committee, 1964, 416.

22. Goldwater, 419.

23. Bohlen, *Witness to History*, 437.

24. Douglas Aircraft Company, "Preliminary Design of an Experimental World-Circling Spaceship," Report No. SM-11827, Santa Monica, CA, May 2, 1946, 2.

25. Nitze, *Hiroshima to Glasnost*, 167.

26. Holloway, *Stalin and the Bomb*, 234.

27. G. A. Tokaty, "Soviet Rocket Technology," *Technology and Culture* 4, no. 4 (Autumn 1963): 525. (G. A. Tokaty was also known as G. A. Tokaev.)

28. Tokaty.

29. Testimony of Dr. Vannevar Bush, Dec. 3, 1945, quoted in "Inquiry into Satellite and Missile Programs," *Hearings Before the Preparedness Investigating Committee*, pt. 1, (Washington, DC: Government Printing Office, 1958), 822–23.

30. Figes, *Natasha's Dance*, 512.

31. Jacoby, *Inside Soviet Schools*, 11.

32. Brzezinski, "Russo-Soviet Nationalism," 130.

33. Jacoby, *Inside Soviet Schools*, 98.

34. Central Intelligence Agency, "Current Intelligence Weekly Review" Washington, DC, Apr. 11, 1957, National Security Archive, https://nsarchive.gwu.edu/dc.html?doc=6763150-National-Security-Archive-Doc-16-Central.

35. Nitze, *Hiroshima to Glasnost*, 167.

36. "Text of Soviet Statement," *New York Times*, Aug. 27, 1957.

37. John F. Kennedy, "A Democrat Looks at Foreign Policy," *Foreign Affairs*, Oct. 1957, 47.

38. John Foster Dulles, "Challenge and Response in United States Policy," *Foreign Affairs*, Oct. 1957, 35.

39. "Adm. Bennett Scoffs," *New York Daily News*, Oct. 5, 1957.

40. "'Silly Bauble in Sky,' Ike Aide Calls Satellite," *Boston Globe*, Oct. 22, 1957.

41. "Let It Remind Us That Goals Are Reached by Hard Effort—And of *Our* Goals," *Life*, Oct. 21, 1957.

42. Allen Drury, "Congress Steps Up Missile Pressure," *New York Times*, Nov. 4, 1957.

43. "Text of President's Talk in Oklahoma Citing Need for Rise in Funds for Science," *New York Times*, Nov. 14, 1957. See also "Radio and Television Address to the American People on 'Our Future Security,'" The American Presidency Project,

https://www.presidency.ucsb.edu/documents/radio-and-television-address-the-american-people-our-future-security.

44. Zubok and Pleshakov, *Inside the Kremlin's Cold War*, 192.

45. "Report to the President by the Security Resources Panel of the ODM Science Advisory Committee on Deterrence and Survival in the Nuclear Age," NSC 5724, Washington, DC: November 7, 1957, pt. B(3), Office of the Historian, https://history.state.gov/historicaldocuments/frus1955-57v19/d158.

46. Public Law 85-864, signed by the president on September 2, 1958.

47. Leonard Buder, "Rickover Calls Education 'Race' Main Battle of U.S. and Soviet," *New York Times*, Aug. 9, 1959.

48. George F. Kennan, "The Internal Soviet Scene," *Reith Lectures 1957: Russia, the Atom and the West*, London, BBC, Nov. 10, 1957, https://www.bbc.co.uk/programmes/poohg1nt.

49. Drew Middleton, "Khrushchev Says Soviet Will Make H-Bomb Missile," *New York Times*, April 24, 1956.

50. Dobrynin, *In Confidence*, 40.

51. "Aquatone Briefing Paper for the Joint Chiefs of Staff re Guided Missiles, Atomic Energy, and Long Range Bombers," TCS-1881-57, Washington, DC, Central Intelligence Agency, Aug. 28, 1957, 1, 4, 5, National Security Archive, https://nsarchive.gwu.edu/dc.html?doc=6763156-National-Security-Archive-Doc-22-Central.

52. James Q. Reber (CIA) to Project Director (memorandum), Washington, DC, Oct. 9, 1957, National Security Archive, https://nsarchive.gwu.edu/dc.html?doc=6763166-National-Security-Archive-Doc-30-James-Q-Reber.

53. Bohlen, *Witness to History*, 466.

54. "Text of the U.S. Statement on Plane," *New York Times*, May 6, 1960.

55. Jack Raymond, "Soviet Downs American Plane," *New York Times*, May 6, 1960.

56. Osgood Caruthers, "Khrushchev Charges Jet Was 1,200 Miles from the Border," *New York Times*, May 8, 1960.

57. James Reston, "U.S. Concedes Flight Over Soviet," *New York Times*, May 8, 1960.

58. "Text of the U.S. Statement on Plane," *New York Times*, May 8, 1960.

59. James Reston, "Washington Is Upset and Humiliated by Spy Developments," *New York Times*, May 9, 1960.

60. Smith, *Eisenhower in War and Peace*, 753.

61. "Herter Statement on U-2 Flight," *New York Times*, May 10, 1960.

62. Bohlen, *Witness to History*, 468.

63. Khrushchev, *Khrushchev Remembers*, 458.

64. Nitze, *Hiroshima to Glasnost*, 168.

65. National Security Council, *Memorandum for the President*, Washington, DC, Nov. 24, 1950, 4. Available at Harry S. Truman Presidential Library and Museum.

66. Holloway, *Stalin and the Bomb*, 344.

67. "Report to the President by the Security Resources Panel of the ODM Science Advisory Committee on Deterrence and Survival in the Nuclear Age," NSC 5724, Washington, DC, Nov. 7, 1957, pt. 1, Office of the Historian, https://history.state.gov/historicaldocuments/frus1955-57v19/d158.

68. "Text of Communiqué Issued by NATO," *New York Times*, May 4, 1957.

69. National Security Council, "Report to the National Security Council by the Executive Secretary" (NSC162/2), Washington, DC, Oct. 30, 1953, 20.

70. United States Department of State, "Memorandum of Conversation with the President and the Congressional Leadership" Washington, DC: June 6, 1961, Office of the Historian, https://history.state.gov/historicaldocuments/frus1961-63v13/d231.

71. *Hearing Before the Committee on Foreign Relations, United States Senate (Eighty-Sixth Congress, First Session), on the Nomination of Christian Herter to Be Secretary of State* (Washington, DC: Government Printing Office, 1959), 10.

72. Department of State, "Circular Telegram from the Department of State to the Embassies in the North Atlantic Treaty Organization Countries," Washington, DC, July 10, 1959, Office of the Historian, https://history.state.gov/historicaldocuments/frus1958-60v07p1/d215.

73. H. Scott and W. Scott, *Soviet Art of War*, 10.

74. Sokolovskiy, *Soviet Military Strategy*, 249.

75. Marshall Rodion Y. Malinovsky, "Report to the XXII Congress of the Communist Party of the Soviet Union by the Minister of Defense," Moscow, Oct. 23, 1961, in H. Scott, *Soviet Military Doctrine*, 88.

76. Garthoff, *Soviet Strategy*, 79 (emphasis in original).

77. Central Intelligence Agency, "Intelligence Memorandum—Soviet Concepts of War in Europe: Transition from Conventional to Nuclear Conflict," Washington, DC, May 1971, 16, https://ia601904.us.archive.org/16/items/1971-05-01b-cia/1971-05-01b.pdf.

78. Garthoff, *Soviet Strategy*, 89.

79. *The Priority Tasks of the Development of the Armed Forces of the Russian Federation* (Moscow: Voeinform Agency of the Defense Ministry of the Russian Federation, 2003), 51.

80. *Priority Tasks*, 61.

81. Zubok and Pleshakov, *Inside the Kremlin's Cold War*, 167.

82. House, *Military History*, 382.

83. Robert S. McNamara to President Kennedy re: Recommended Long Range Nuclear Delivery Forces 1963–1967 (memorandum), Washington, DC, Sept. 23, 1961, Pt. 2, National Security Archive, https://nsarchive.gwu.edu/dc.html?doc=6895259-National-Security-Archive-Doc-11-Memorandum-to.

84. Zbigniew Brzezinski, "How the Cold War Was Played," *Foreign Affairs*, October 1972, 204.

85. Memorandum for the Assistant to the President for National Security Affairs [from Secretary of Defense Harold Brown], Washington, DC, Apr. 25, 1977, U.S. National Archives and Records Administration, https://www.archives.gov/files/declassification/iscap/pdf/2010-082-doc1.pdf.

Chapter 13

1. Public Law 86–90 (July 17, 1959).

2. "Nixon Presses Hard on the Need for Experience in Standing Up to the Menace of Communism," *New York Times*, Oct. 23, 1960.

3. "Nixon Won't List Campaign Issues," *New York Times*, Feb. 7, 1960.

4. Thomas W. Ottenad, "Kennedy Ends Western Tour, Assails Nixon," *St. Louis Post-Dispatch*, Sept. 24, 1960.

5. Isaacson and Thomas, *Wise Men*, 603.

6. Zubok and Pleshakov, *Inside the Kremlin's Cold War*, 238.

7. Joseph Alsop, "Mortgaging the Future," *Hartford Courant*, Aug. 10, 1960.

8. Powaski, *Cold War*, 123.

9. Westad, *Cold War*, 289; John T. Correll, "High Noon," *Air Force Magazine*, October 2012.

10. Benjamin Welles, "Khrushchev Bangs His Shoe on Desk," *New York Times*, Oct. 13, 1960.

11. Thomas W. Ottenad, "Kennedy Gives Russia Excuse in Cuba, Nixon Says," *St. Louis Post-Dispatch*, Oct. 23, 1960.

12. "Excerpts From Castro's Speech Denouncing the U.S. in the General Assembly," *New York Times*, Sept. 27, 1960.

13. "Americans Have the Courage to Meet Communist Threat," *Miami Herald*, Oct. 18, 1960; "Text of Statement by Kennedy on Dealing with Castro Regime," *New York Times*, Oct. 21, 1960.

14. Harrison E. Salisbury, "Nixon Says Kennedy Plan on Cuba Risks World War," *New York Times*, Oct. 23, 1960.

15. James Reston, "The Bees Are Settling Along the Potomac," *New York Times*, Oct. 23, 1960.

16. "The President's News Conference of August 24, 1960," in *Public Papers of the Presidents of the United States, 1960–61* (Washington, DC: Government Printing Office, 1961), 658.

17. Dwight D. Eisenhower, "Farewell Address," Washington, DC, Jan. 17, 1961, National Archives, https://www.archives.gov/milestone-documents/president-dwight-d-eisenhowers-farewell-address.

18. Powaski, *Cold War*, 141.

19. "Text of President Kennedy's News Conference on World and Domestic Affairs," *New York Times*, Apr. 13, 1961.

20. House, *Military History*, 402.

21. Nitze, *Hiroshima to Glasnost*, 184.

22. Schlesinger, *Thousand Days*, 267.

23. Schlesinger, 259.

24. "Excerpts from Statements Made by Roa and Stevenson to U.N. Political Committee," *New York Times*, April 18, 1961.

25. "Interview With Oleg Troyanovski" (transcript), Episode 10, George Washington University National Security Archive, Nov. 29, 1998, https://nsarchive2.gwu.edu/coldwar/interviews/episode-10/troyanovski1.html.

26. Bird, *Color of Truth*, 201. Bohlen agrees with this assessment. Bohlen, *Witness to History*, 479.

27. Jervis, *Logic of Images*, 78.

28. Anna Kasten Nelson, "Operation Northwoods and the Covert War Against Cuba, 1961–1963," *Cuban Studies* 32 (2001): 151.

29. Weiner, *Legacy of Ashes*, 229.

30. United States Senate Report No. 94-465, 94th Cong., 1st Sess., "An Interim Report of the Select Committee to Study Governmental Operation with Respect to

Intelligence Activities," Washington, DC, Nov. 20, 1975, 157–58 (bracketed material in original).

31. "Interim Report," 255.

32. Drew Middleton, "East Berlin 'Votes' Defiance of Soviet," *New York Times*, Oct. 13, 1950.

33. Mikhail Pervukhin, "On Several Issues Regarding Economic and Political Situation in Democratic Berlin" (Dec. 10, 1959), quoted in Harrison, *Ulbricht and the Concrete 'Rose,'* 26.

34. Nikita S. Khrushchev, "On Peaceful Coexistence," *Foreign Affairs*, Oct. 1959, 6.

35. Halle, *Cold War as History*, 367.

36. Joseph Alsop, "Military Buildup in East Germany Bodes a Cold Fall," *Detroit Free Press*, Sept. 6, 1962.

37. United States Department of State, "Memorandum of Conversation," Vienna, June 3, 1961, Office of the Historian, https://history.state.gov/historicaldocuments/frus1961-63v05/d83.

38. United States Department of State, "Memorandum of Conversation," Vienna, June 4, 1961, 10:15 a.m., U.S. Department of State Archive, https://2001-2009.state.gov/r/pa/ho/frus/kennedyjf/xiv/15856.htm.

39. United States Department of State, "Memorandum of Conversation" Vienna, June 4, 1961.

40. "Savaged," as said by Kennedy to James Reston of the *New York Times*; David E. Sanger, "A Cold War Summit Offers Lessons for Trump Before Putin Meeting," *New York Times*, July 5, 2017.

41. Sanger.

42. Bohlen, *Witness to History*, 483.

43. "Measuring Mission," *Time*, June 9, 1961, 11.

44. Dean Acheson to John F. Kennedy (memorandum), Washington, DC, June 28, 1961, Office of the Historian, https://history.state.gov/historicaldocuments/frus1961-63v14/d49.

45. Acheson memorandum.

46. Acheson memorandum.

47. John F. Kennedy, "The Berlin Crisis," Washington, DC, July 25, 1961, U.S. Diplomatic Mission to Germany, https://usa.usembassy.de/etexts/speeches/rhetoric/jfkberli.htm.

48. Kennedy.

49. Zubok and Pleshakov, *Inside the Kremlin's Cold War*, 248.

50. Zubok and Pleshakov, 4.

51. Nitze, *Hiroshima to Glasnost*, 202.

52. Zbigniew Brzezinski, "How the Cold War Was Played," *Foreign Affairs*, October 1972, 205.

53. Kennedy, *Thirteen Days*.

54. "Rodion Malinovsky and Matvei Zakharov to the Chairman of the Defense Council on Deployment of Soviet Forces to Cuba" (memorandum), Moscow, May 24, 1962, Wilson Center Digital Archive, https://digitalarchive.wilsoncenter.org/document/113038.

55. Khrushchev, *Khrushchev Remembers*, 496.

56. Isaacson and Thomas, *Wise Men*, 621.

57. Paul Lashmar, "The Real Doctor Strangelove," *Guardian* (UK), Oct. 8, 1996.

58. "Anatoly Dobrynin to Soviet Foreign Ministry" (cable), Washington, DC, Oct. 27, 1962, George Washington University National Security Archive, https://nsarchive2.gwu.edu/nsa/cuba_mis_cri/moment.htm.

59. John F. Kennedy, "Address During the Cuban Missile Crisis," Oct. 22, 1962, John F. Kennedy Presidential Library and Museum, https://www.jfklibrary.org/node/11861.

60. "Anatoly Dobrynin to Soviet Foreign Ministry."

61. Khrushchev, *Khrushchev Remembers*, 498.

62. Westad, *Cold War*, 309.

63. John F. Kennedy, "Address to the Nation" [draft], Oct. 1962, John F. Kennedy Presidential Library and Museum, https://www.jfklibrary.org/asset-viewer/archives/RFKAG/217/RFKAG-217–001.

64. "Russia: The Adventure," *Time*, Nov. 9, 1962.

65. Bernard Gwertzman, "Soviet Announces Khrushchev Death in Cool Language," *New York Times*, Sept. 13, 1971.

66. Zubok and Pleshakov, *Inside the Kremlin's Cold War*, 236–37.

67. "Dulles Is Assured 2-Party Support on Geneva Parley," *New York Times*, Apr. 21, 1954.

68. Kissinger, *Diplomacy*, 694.

69. Isaacson and Thomas, *Wise Men*, 648.

70. Kissinger, *Diplomacy*, 624.

71. "Truman Statement on Korea," *New York Times*, Dec. 1, 1950.

72. "Transcript of President Eisenhower's Press Conference, With Comment on Indo-China," *New York Times*, Apr. 8, 1954.

73. *New York Times*, Aug. 3, 1964.

74. Lyndon B. Johnson, "Special Message to the Congress on U.S. Policy in Southeast Asia," Aug. 5, 1964, The American Presidency Project, https://www.presidency.ucsb.edu/documents/special-message-the-congress-us-policy-southeast-asia. The SEATO Treaty was the Manila Pact of September 1954, which did not include South Vietnam.

75. Pub.L. 88-408 (Aug. 10, 1964), govinfo (United States Government Publishing Office), https://www.govinfo.gov/content/pkg/STATUTE-78/pdf/STATUTE-78-Pg384.pdf.

76. Kissinger, *Diplomacy*, 743.

77. Lee Winfrey and Michael Schaffer, "America's 'Most Trusted,'" *Philadelphia Inquirer*, July 18, 2009.

78. Winfrey and Schaffer.

79. Tom Wicker, "Johnson Says He Won't Run," *New York Times*, Apr. 1, 1968.

80. Moynahan, *Claws of the Bear*, 307.

81. "Conversation Between President Nixon and His Assistant for National Security Affairs," Washington, DC, Apr. 19, 1972, Office of the Historian, https://history.state.gov/historicaldocuments/frus1969-76v14/d126.

82. Bernard Gwertzman, "Kissinger Asserts That 'Peace is at Hand,'" *New York Times*, Oct. 27, 1972.

83. Ulam, *Understanding the Cold War,* 152.
84. Powaski, *Cold War,* 157.

Chapter 14

1. "Versions of the Two Sides," *New York Times,* Aug. 21, 1968,
2. Leonid Ilyich Brezhnev, Speech to Polish Communist Party Congress, Warsaw, Nov. 12, 1968, as quoted from TASS International Service, Nov. 12, 1968, in Stephen G. Glazer, "The Brezhnev Doctrine," *International Lawyer* 5, no. 1 (Jan. 1971): 169.
3. Glazer, 170.
4. Malia, *Russia under Western Eyes,* 385.
5. "Interview with Oleg Troyanovski," Episode 8, George Washington University National Security Archive (Nov. 15, 1998).
6. "Conversation Between President Nixon and His Assistant for National Security Affairs," Washington, DC, Apr. 19, 1972, Office of the Historian, https://history.state.gov/historicaldocuments/frus1969-76v14/d126.
7. "Conversation."
8. "Memorandum of Conversation," Washington, DC, Dec. 4, 1987, in *Foreign Relations of the United States,* vol. 6 (Washington, DC: Department of State, 2016), 598, Office of the Historian, https://history.state.gov/historicaldocuments/frus1981-88v06/d104.
9. "Basic Principles of Relations Between the United States of America and the Union of Soviet Socialist Republics," Moscow, May 29, 1972, Office of the Historian, https://history.state.gov/historicaldocuments/frus1969-76v01/d116.
10. Richard Nixon, "Reagan and Gorbachev: Superpower Summitry," *Foreign Affairs,* Fall, 1985, 9.
11. Nitze, *Hiroshima to Glasnost,* 337.
12. Kissinger, *Years of Upheaval,* 288.
13. Louis Harris, "Majority See Summit as Breakthru [sic]," *Chicago Tribune,* June 23, 1973.
14. Harris.
15. Kissinger, *Diplomacy,* 741.
16. Zubok, *Failed Empire,* 230.
17. Brent Scowcroft was appointed to serve as national security advisor in November 1975, but Kissinger continued as secretary of state.
18. "Conference on Security and Co-Operation in Europe Final Act," Helsinki, Aug. 1, 1975, Art. 1(a)(III), Organization for Security and Co-operation in Europe, https://www.osce.org/files/f/documents/5/c/39501.pdf.
19. Sell, *Washington to Moscow,* 66.
20. Zubok, *Failed Empire,* 238.
21. Dobrynin, *In Confidence,* 351.
22. Dobrynin, *In Confidence,* 351.
23. "Conference on Security and Co-Operation," Art. 1(a)(I).
24. White, *Making of the President,* 154.
25. White, 154.
26. White, 155.

27. White, 156.

28. Charles E. Bohlen, "Bohlen Minutes," Tehran, Dec. 1, 1943, Office of the Historian, https://history.state.gov/historicaldocuments/frus1943CairoTehran/d378.

29. "Bohlen Minutes."

30. Moshe Decter, "The Status of the Jews in the Soviet Union," *Foreign Affairs*, Jan., 1963, 420.

31. Gitelman, "Meanings of Jewishness," 198.

32. Sell, *Washington to Moscow*, 175.

33. Pipes, "Reflections on the Nationality Problems," 458.

34. Albats, *State Within a State*, 145.

35. Zubok, *Failed Empire*, 232.

36. "Minutes of a Cabinet Meeting," Washington, DC, Oct. 18, 1973, Office of the Historian, https://history.state.gov/historicaldocuments/frus1969–76v38p1/d20.

37. "Minutes."

38. Theodore C. Sorensen, "Dilemmas of Détente: Most-Favored-Nation and Less Favorite Nations," *Foreign Affairs*, Jan. 1974, 278–79.

39. Zubok, *Failed Empire*, 233.

40. Stern, *Water's Edge*, xix.

41. Dobrynin, *In Confidence*, 371.

42. Sell, *Washington to Moscow*, 60.

43. Dobrynin, *In Confidence*, 274.

44. Dobrynin, 339.

45. "Text of Letters Exchanged by Kissinger and Jackson," *New York Times*, Oct. 19, 1974.

46. Dobrynin, *In Confidence*, 340.

47. "Text of Letters."

48. Stern, *Water's Edge*, 163.

49. Bernard Gwertzman, "Kissinger Leaves Moscow Hopeful on Arms Accord," *New York Times*, Oct. 28, 1974.

50. "Gromyko's Letter," *New York Times*, Dec. 19, 1974.

51. Bernard Gwertzman, "Soviet Denies Any Pledge to Ease Emigration Curb to Win U.S. Trade Benefit," *New York Times*, Dec. 19, 1974.

52. Bernard Gwertzman, "Export Bank Credit Curbs Are Said to Anger Moscow," *New York Times*, Dec. 20, 1974.

53. Ronald Reagan, "Memorandum Dictated by Reagan: 'Gorbachev,'" Nov. 1985, National Security Archive, https://nsarchive.gwu.edu/dc.html?doc=3242109-Document-1-Gorbachev-Memorandum-dictated-by.

54. Matlock, *Reagan and Gorbachev*, 152.

55. Stern, *Water's Edge*, 198.

56. Kissinger, *Diplomacy*, 836.

Chapter 15

1. Nitze, *Hiroshima to Glasnost*, 374.

2. George F. Kennan, "Two Hundred Years of American Policy: The United States and the Soviet Union, 1917–1976," *Foreign Affairs*, July 1976, 688.

3. Gorbachev, *Memoirs*, 443.

4. Sell, *Washington to Moscow*, 107.

5. Gaddis, *New History*, 192.

6. Zubok, *Failed Empire*, 254.

7. "Republican Party Platform of 1980," July 15, 1980, The American Presidency Project, https://www.presidency.ucsb.edu/documents/republican-party-platform-1980.

8. United States Department of Defense (Defense Intelligence Agency), *Soviet Military Power* (Washington, DC, 1981), 27.

9. "Our Childish View of Moscow," *Chicago Tribune*, Jan. 7, 1982.

10. Ronald Reagan, "Address to the Houses of Parliament," London, June 8, 1982. See also "Text of President Reagan's Address to Parliament on Promoting Democracy," *New York Times*, June 9, 1982.

11. Dobrynin, *In Confidence*, 557.

12. "Resolution on Nuclear Weapons in Europe," North Atlantic Assembly, Nov. 18, 1982, in *Second Interim Report on Nuclear Weapons in Europe*, annexed to *Report to the Committee on Foreign Relations*, S. Prt. 98–3 (Washington, DC: Government Printing Office: Jan. 1983).

13. *Second Interim Report*, "Statement by Senator Joseph R. Biden, Jr. (USA), Chairman, Special Committee on Nuclear Weapons in Europe" (emphasis added).

14. "Excerpts from President's Speech to National Association of Evangelicals," *New York Times*, Mar. 9, 1983.

15. Serge Schmemann, "Soviet Says Reagan Has 'Pathological Hatred,'" *New York Times*, Mar. 10, 1983.

16. Anthony Lewis, "Onward, Christian Soldiers," *New York Times*, Mar. 10, 1983.

17. Reagan, *American Life*, 569.

18. Reagan, 571.

19. Ronald Reagan, "Address to the Nation and Other Countries on United States–Soviet Relations," Washington, DC, Jan. 16, 1984, Ronald Reagan Presidential Library and Museum, https://www.reaganlibrary.gov/archives/speech/address-nation-and-other-countries-united-states-soviet-relations.

20. "American Experts' Comments on the Appointment of Chernenko," *New York Times*, Feb. 14, 1984.

21. Suzanne M. Schafer, "Biden, Cohen Say Soviet Officials Receptive to Movement Toward Arms Talks" (Associated Press, Feb. 23, 1984).

22. "Time to Test Russ 'Intentions': Shultz," *Indianapolis News*, Feb. 24, 1984.

23. Schafer.

24. Ligachev, *Inside Gorbachev's Kremlin*, 34. Ligachev served as the Central Committee's second secretary under Gorbachev. As his memoir reflects (almost from cover to cover), Ligachev, though recognizing the need for reform, soured on Gorbachev's approach to perestroika. His book surely ranks as one of the angriest memoirs ever written.

25. John F. Burns, "World Attention Turns to Chernenko's Health," *New York Times*, Feb. 16, 1984.

26. "Reagan Jokes on Bombing Soviets," *Los Angeles Times*, Aug. 13, 1984.

27. Ligachev, *Inside Gorbachev's Kremlin*, 69.

28. George F. Kennan, "Two Hundred Years of American Policy: The United States and the Soviet Union, 1917–1976," *Foreign Affairs*, July 1976, 689.

29. Gorbachev, *Memoirs*, 215.

30. Mikhail Gorbachev, "Letter from Soviet General Secretary Gorbachev to President Reagan" (June 10, 1985), in *Foreign Relations of the United States*, vol. 5 (Washington, DC: Department of State, 2020), 145.

31. Nitze, *Hiroshima to Glasnost*, 405.

32. Sell, *Washington to Moscow*, 146–47.

33. National Intelligence Estimate, "Domestic Stress on the Soviet System," Washington, DC, Central Intelligence Agency, Nov. 18, 1985, 20.

34. "Memorandum Dictated by Reagan," Nov. 1, 1985, George Washington University National Security Archive, https://nsarchive.gwu.edu/document/22396-document-1-gorbachev-memorandum-dictated. Personal observations in this memorandum leave no doubt that it is, in fact, Reagan's product.

35. Sell, *Washington to Moscow*, 202.

36. Gorbachev, *Memoirs*, 405.

37. Reagan, *American Life*, 641.

38. Lawrence L. Knutson, "Summit Reviews: 'Polite Applause but Not a Standing Ovation'" (Associated Press, Nov. 21, 1985).

39. "Domestic News," United Press International, Nov. 19, 1985 (speech at Wooster College).

40. Albert R. Hunt, "A Senator Strives to Make the Big Leagues," *Wall Street Journal*, Apr. 7, 1986.

41. Barry Schweid, "Washington Dateline" (Associated Press, March 31, 1986).

42. Melissa Healy, "Democrats Hardening New Foreign Policy," *U.S. News and World Report*, June 23, 1986.

43. David Shribman, "The Inauguration (A Special Report After You . . . Democrats Say They'll Let Bush Take the Lead in Risky Initiatives)," *Wall Street Journal*, Jan. 20, 1989.

44. Anonymous [Kennan], "The Sources of Soviet Conduct," *Foreign Affairs*, July 1947, 576.

45. Ronald Reagan, "Basic National Security Strategy," Washington, DC, Sept. 2, 1986, 8, declassified Aug. 2, 2013, National Security Archive, https://nsarchive.gwu.edu/dc.html?doc=6895275-National-Security-Archive-Doc-27-National.

46. Reagan, *American Life*, 683.

47. Gorbachev, *Memoirs*, 418. Reagan's agreement: Reagan, *American Life*, 677.

48. "Democrats Disappointed Over Reagan's Near Miss," *Los Angeles Times*, Oct. 13, 1986.

49. "Democrats Disappointed."

50. Charlotte Saikowski, "ABM Treaty as Legal Issue," *Christian Science Monitor*, Mar. 12, 1987.

51. Nitze, *Hiroshima to Glasnost*, 445.

52. United States Department of State, "Memorandum of Conversation," Moscow, Apr. 14, 1987, Office of the Historian, https://history.state.gov/historicaldocuments/frus1981-88v06/d42.

53. "Memorandum of Conversation."

54. "Excerpts From Reagan's Talk at the Berlin Wall," *New York Times*, June 13, 1987.

55. Michael R. Gordon, "How to Destroy the 2,611 Missiles," *New York Times*, Dec. 8, 1987.

56. Michael R. Gordon, "Democrat Outlines Arms-Pact Strategy," *New York Times*, Jan. 25, 1988.

57. Anita Huslin, "Biden Says European Allies, Soviets Support Arms Reduction Treaty" (Associated Press, Jan. 17, 1988).

58. Huslin.

59. David S. Broder, "The Education of Joe Biden," *Washington Post*, Jan. 6, 1988.

60. Joseph R. Biden Jr., "Calming the Allies' Jitters," *New York Times*, Feb. 3, 1988.

61. 1988 Cong. Rec. 12849 (May 27, 1988). See, generally, Joseph R. Biden Jr. and John B. Ritch III, *The Treaty Power: Upholding a Constitutional Partnership*, 137 U. Pa.L.Rev. 1529 (1989).

62. "Responses of Secretary of State Shultz to Questions Asked by Senator Biden," in *Hearings Before the Committee on Foreign Relations, United States Senate*, pt. 1 (Washington, DC: Government Printing Office, 1988), 446.

63. Reagan, *American Life*, 705.

64. Sakwa, *Communism in Russia*, 116.

65. "Background Book: President Reagan's Meetings with General Secretary Gorbachev, May 29–June 2, 1988." George Washington University National Security Archive, https://nsarchive2.gwu.edu/NSAEBB/NSAEBB251/10.pdf.

66. Ligachev, *Inside Gorbachev's Kremlin*, 346.

67. Ligachev, *Inside Gorbachev's Kremlin*, 345.

68. "Minutes of the Meeting of the Politburo of the Central Committee of the Communist Party of the Soviet Union," Dec. 27, 1988, trans. Vladislav Zubok, Wilson Center Digital Archive, https://digitalarchive.wilsoncenter.org/document/112478.

69. National Security Council, "Memorandum of Conversation," Washington, DC, Mar. 11, 1988, George Washington University National Security Archive, https://nsarchive2.gwu.edu/NSAEBB/NSAEBB251/4.pdf.

70. Stanley Meisler, "Regan Recants 'Evil Empire' Description," *Los Angeles Times*, June 1, 1988.

71. Gorbachev, *Memoirs*, 457.

72. "Remarks and a Question-and-Answer Session at a Luncheon with Radio and Television Journalists," June 8, 1988, Ronald Reagan Presidential Library and Museum, https://www.reaganlibrary.gov/archives/speech/remarks-and-question-and-answer-session-luncheon-radio-and-television-journalists.

73. Reagan, *American Life*, 720.

74. "Memorandum of Conversation," Dec. 7, 1988, *Foreign Relations of the United States, 1981–1988*, vol. 6 (Washington, DC: Government Printing Office, 2016), 1234, 1235.

75. Felicity Barringer, "Lone West German Flies Unhindered to the Kremlin," *New York Times*, May 30, 1987.

76. Sell, *Washington to Moscow*, 334.

77. "City Honors Reagan by Renaming Square," *Chicago Tribune*, Sept. 9, 2004.

78. Thomas Oliphant, "Small Thinking That Hurts the US," *Boston Globe*, May 7, 1989.

79. "Minutes of the Meeting of the Politburo of the Central Committee of the Communist Party of the Soviet Union," Dec. 27, 1988, trans. Vladislav Zubok, Wilson Center Digital Archive, https://digitalarchive.wilsoncenter.org/document/112478.

80. "Soviet Policy Toward the West: The Gorbachev Challenge," National Intelligence Estimate No. 11489 (Washington, DC: Central Intelligence Agency, April 1989), George Washington University National Security Archive, https://nsarchive2.gwu.edu/NSAEBB/NSAEBB261/us11.pdf.

81. John Wilkens, "Biden Cites Foreign Policy Opportunity," *San Diego Union-Tribune*, Jan. 12, 1989.

82. Thomas Oliphant, "Small Thinking That Hurts the US," *Boston Globe*, May 7, 1989.

83. Wilkens, "Biden Cites Foreign Policy Opportunity."

84. Mikhail S. Gorbachev, "Address Given by Mikhail Gorbachev to the Council of Europe," Strasbourg, July 6, 1989, cvce.eu, https://www.cvce.eu/obj/address_given_by_mikhail_gorbachev_to_the_council_of_europe_6_july_1989-en-4c021687-98f9-4727-9e8b-836e0bc1f6fb.htm.

85. "Address Given by Mikhail Gorbachev."

86. Zubok, *Failed Empire,* 330–31.

87. "Excerpt from the Diary of Anatoly Chernyaev," Nov. 10, 1989, trans. Vladislav Zubok, (Archive of the Gorbachev Foundation), Wilson Center Digital Archive, https://digitalarchive.wilsoncenter.org/document/111535.

88. Putin, *First Person,* 79.

89. Putin, *First Person,* 79.

90. Sandy Grady, "George Kennan Looks at the World," *Philadelphia Daily News*, Jan. 18, 1990.

91. 1990 Cong. Rec. 757 (Jan. 30, 1990).

92. James H. Billington, "The Soviet Drama—Looking to the Past," *Washington Post*, Jan. 22, 1990. Reprinted in 1990 Cong. Rec. 762 (Jan. 30, 1990).

93. Esther B. Fein, "Lithuania Move Is 'Illegitimate,' Gorbachev Says," *New York Times*, Mar. 11, 1990.

94. Jack Matlock, "Gorbachev Confronts a Crisis of Power," Moscow, May 11, 1990, George Washington University National Security Archive, https://nsarchive2.gwu.edu/NSAEBB/NSAEBB320/01.pdf.

95. Gorbachev, *Memoirs,* 517.

96. "Lithuania-Forcing the Issue," *MacNeil/Lehrer News Hour* (Educational Broadcasting Corp., Mar. 27, 1990).

97. Ligachev, *Inside Gorbachev's Kremlin*, 115.

98. Ligachev, *Inside Gorbachev's Kremlin*, 117–18.

99. "Memorandum of Conversation [between Baker and Gorbachev]," 11, Moscow, May 18, 1990, National Security Archive, https://nsarchive.gwu.edu/document/22563-document-16-gorbachev-baker-memcon-may-18-1990.

100. "Memorandum of Conversation," 15–16.

101. 1998 Cong. Rec. S3641 (Apr. 27, 1998).

102. "Memorandum of Conversation," 17.

103. By Gorbachev's account, in a meeting in Moscow in February 1990, Baker posed the question of whether Gorbachev would prefer a united Germany outside NATO or a united Germany in NATO "but with the guarantee that NATO jurisdiction or troops would not extend east of the current line?" Gorbachev, *Memoirs,* 529. That statement (or rather a question) has triggered decades of debate as to just what Baker intended to suggest and as to whether Gorbachev acted on Baker's question as a guarantee against eastward expansion of NATO. Because that subject has generated an extensive literature of its own (easily discoverable in an online search), there is no need to attempt here to improve on those writings.

104. James Baker to George H.W. Bush, ¶¶ 13, 17 (cable), Moscow, May 19, 1990, National Security Archive, https://nsarchive.gwu.edu/document/20370-national-security-archive-doc-08-secretary.

105. James Rosen, "Lithuanian Leader Hails Negotiations" (UPI, Apr. 4, 1990).

106. Baker Cable, ¶ 6.

107. "Excerpt from the Second Conversation Between M. S. Gorbachev and G. Bush," 4, Washington, DC, May 31, 1990, National Security Archive, https://nsarchive.gwu.edu/sites/default/files/documents/6935347/National-Security-Archive-Doc-15-Record-of.pdf.

108. "Excerpt from the Second Conversation," 9.

109. Unification was a result that Khrushchev had predicted thirty-one years before it occurred. "As for Germany's unity, I am convinced that Germany will be united sooner or later." Nikita S. Khrushchev, "On Peaceful Coexistence," *Foreign Affairs*, Oct. 1959, 12.

110. Jack Matlock to James Baker, ¶ 2 (cable), Moscow, June 12, 1990, National Security Archive, https://nsarchive.gwu.edu/document/20384-national-security-archive-doc-22-soviet.

111. Burns, *Back Channel*, 90.

112. Gorbachev, *Memoirs*, 549.

113. Burns, *Back Channel*, 76.

114. Burns, *Back Channel*, 76.

115. Kazakhstan, Kyrgyzstan, Tajikistan, Turkmenistan, and Uzbekistan.

116. Armenia and Azerbaijan. Georgia joined in 1993.

117. Full text at Gorbachev, *Memoirs*, xxvi. (Online sources provide various English translations.)

118. Gorbachev, *Memoirs,* xxviii.

119. Anthony Hyman, "Russians Outside Russia," *World Today,* Nov. 1993, 205.

120. Gorbachev, *Memoirs,* 680.

121. Sakwa, *Communism in Russia*, 117.

Conclusion

1. Baker, *Politics of Diplomacy*, 49.

2. Robert Gates, "We Need a More Realistic Strategy for the Post-Cold War Era," *Washington Post*, March 2, 2022.

3. Toal, *Near Abroad*, 3

4. Kennan, "Peaceful Coexistence," *Foreign Affairs*, Jan. 1960, 184.

5. Tim Marshall, "Russia and the Curse of Geography," *Atlantic*, Oct. 31, 2015, https://www.theatlantic.com/international/archive/2015/10/russia-geography-ukraine-syria/413248/.

6. Melvin, *Forging the New Russian Nation*, 3.

7. Elise Giuliano, "Is the Risk of Ethnic Conflict Growing in Ukraine?" *Foreign Affairs*, March 18, 2019, https://www.foreignaffairs.com/articles/ukraine/2019-03-18/risk-ethnic-conflict-growing-ukraine.

8. Kotkin, *Armageddon Averted*, 4.

9. Melvin, *Russians Beyond Russia*, 90.

10. Melvin, *Russians Beyond Russia*, 5.

11. Brzezinski, "Russo-Soviet Nationalism,"137.

12. Matlock, *Autopsy on an Empire*, 701.

13. Vladimir V. Putin, "On the Historical Unity of Russians and Ukrainians," President of Russia, July 12, 2021, http://en.kremlin.ru/events/president/news/66181.

14. Hill, *No Place for Russia*, 352.

15. Riasanovsky and Steinberg, *History of Russia*, 247.

16. Hill, *No Place for Russia*, 69.

17. Putin, "On the Historical Unity," note 16.

18. Melvin, *Forging the New Russian Nation*, 36.

19. Melvin, 27.

20. "Crimea: Five Years," Levada Center, Apr. 11, 2019, https://www.levada.ru/en/2019/04/11/crimea-five-years.

21. Melvin, *Forging the New Russian Nation*, 50.

22. Bohuslav Litera, "The Kozyrev Doctrine: A Russian Variation on the Monroe Doctrine," *Perspectives* (Institute of International Relations) 4 (Winter 1994–95): 50.

23. Leslie H. Gelb, "Yeltsin as Monroe," *New York Times*, Mar. 7, 1993.

24. Leslie Wroughton and Andrew Osborn, "Tension Grows between U.S. and Russia over Venezuela Standoff," *Reuters World News*, May 1, 2019.

25. "Press Briefing by Press Secretary Jen Psaki and National Security Advisor Jake Sullivan," Jan. 13, 2022, The White House, https://www.whitehouse.gov/briefing-room/press-briefings/2022/01/13/press-briefing-by-press-secretary-jen-psaki-and-national-security-advisor-jake-sullivan-january-13-2022/.

26. Alexander Lukin, "What the Kremlin Is Thinking: Putin's Vision for Eurasia," *Foreign Affairs*, July–Aug. 2014, 87–88.

27. Vladimir V. Putin, "Address by President of the Russian Federation," President of Russia, Mar. 18, 2014, http://en.kremlin.ru/events/president/news/20603.

28. Nikolas K. Gvosdev, "Where Will Ukraine Go from Here?" *National Interest*, Oct. 13, 2019, https://nationalinterest.org/feature/where-will-ukraine-go-here-87936?page=0%2C1.

29. Liana Fix and Michael Kimmage, "What If Russia Makes a Deal?" *Foreign Affairs*, Mar. 23, 2022, https://www.foreignaffairs.com/articles/ukraine/2022-03-23/what-if-russia-makes-deal.

30. Thomas Graham and Rajan Menon, "How to Make Peace with Putin," *Foreign Affairs*, Mar. 21, 2022.

31. Maria Danilova, "Biden Assuages Ukraine's Fears," *Miami Herald*, July 22, 2009.

32. *Hearings Before the Committee on Foreign Relations: Strategic Rationale for NATO Enlargement* (S. Hrg. 105-285, Oct. 7, 1997), 5, govinfo (United States Government Publishing Office), https://www.govinfo.gov/content/pkg/CHRG-105shrg46832/html/CHRG-105shrg46832.htm.

33. 1998 Cong. Rec. S3637, Apr. 27, 1998 (remarks of Sen. Biden).

34. George F. Kennan, "A Fateful Error," *New York Times*, Feb. 5, 1997.

35. "Bucharest Summit Declaration," NATO, Apr. 3, 2008, https://www.nato.int/cps/en/natolive/official_texts_8443.htm.

36. Stephen Kotkin, "Russia's Perpetual Geopolitics: Putin Returns to the Historical Pattern," *Foreign Affairs*, May–June 2016, 4.

37. Burns, *Back Channel*, 233.

38. Gates, *Exercise of Power*, 274.

39. Gates, *Exercise of Power*, 291.

40. Michael Shear and Peter Baker, "Obama Answers Critics, Dismissing Russia as a 'Regional Power,'" *New York Times*, Mar. 25, 2014.

41. Michael Mandelbaum, "The New Containment: Handling Russia, China, and Iran," *Foreign Affairs*, Mar.–Apr. 2019, 127.

42. Nikolas K. Gvosdev, in "What Now? A Symposium on the Future of the United States," *National Interest*, Jan.–Feb. 2021, 37, 38.

43. Metternich, *Nachgelassenen Papieren*, 3:365, as quoted in Kissinger, *Diplomacy*, 86.

44. Kotkin, *Armageddon Averted*, 170.

45. Lawrence S. Eagleburger (drafted by W. J. Burns) to Secretary of State–Designate Warren Christopher, "Parting Thoughts: U.S. Foreign Policy in the Years Ahead" (memorandum), Washington, DC, Jan. 5, 1993, https://carnegieendowment.org/pdf/back-channel/1993MemotoChristopher.pdf.

46. Vladimir V. Putin, "New Year Address by Acting President Vladimir Putin," President of Russia, Moscow, Dec. 31, 1999, http://en.kremlin.ru/events/president/transcripts/22280.

47. Vladimir V. Putin, "Address to the Nation at the Presidential Inauguration Ceremony," President of Russia, Moscow, May 7, 2004, http://en.kremlin.ru/events/president/transcripts/22452 .

48. Lionel Barber, Henry Foy, and Alex Barker, "Vladimir Putin Says Liberalism Has 'Become Obsolete,'" *Financial Times*, June 27, 2019, https://www.ft.com/content/670039ec-98f3-11e9-9573-ee5cbb98ed36.

49. Michael Kimmage, "The People's Authoritarian: How Russian Society Created Putin," *Foreign Affairs*, July–Aug., 2018, 176.

50. Tolstoy, *War and Peace*, 1062.

51. Kennan, "America and the Russian Future," *Foreign Affairs*, April 1951, 356.

52. Shevtsova, *Lonely Power*, 302.

53. Shevtsova, 209.

54. Albats, *State within a State*, 332.

55. Konstantin Sonin, "Russia's Economic Stagnation Is Here to Stay," Project Syndicate, Feb. 1, 2018, https://www.project-syndicate.org/commentary/russia-economic-stagnation-structural-reform-by-konstantin-sonin-2018-02?barrier=accesspaylog.

56. Letter (in French) from Pushkin to Chaadev, Oct. 19, 1836, in *Sochineniia Pushkina Perepiska*, 3 vols. (St. Petersburg, 1906–11), 3:388, quoted in Figes, *Natasha's Dance*, 368.

57. Vladimir V. Putin, "Address to the Federal Assembly," President of Russia, Dec. 12, 2012, http://en.kremlin.ru/events/president/news/17118.

58. "Emigration Sentiments" (in Russian), Levada Center, Nov. 11, 2019, https://www.levada.ru/2019/11/26/emigratsionnye-nastroeniya-4/print.

59. Andrei Kolesnikov, "Russians at War," *Foreign Affairs*, Apr. 18, 2022.

60. "Exodus of Russian Researchers Grew Fivefold Since 2012," *Moscow Times*, Apr. 21, 2021.

61. Joshua Falk, "Medvedev Seeks to Learn from Silicon Valley's Successes," *Stanford Daily*, July 1, 2010, https://www.stanforddaily.com/2010/07/01/medvedev-seeks-to-learn-from-silicon-valleys-successes/.

62. Ministry of Economic Development of the Russian Federation, "Statements of Minister Elvira Nabiullina," Apr. 3, 2012. HSE University, https://www.hse.ru/en/news/50411837.html.

63. Fiona Hill, "Energy Empire: Oil, Gas and Russia's Revival" (The Foreign Policy Centre, Sept. 2004), 43, Brookings, https://www.brookings.edu/wp-content/uploads/2016/06/20040930.pdf.

64. Shevtsova, *Lonely Power*, 338.

65. Oleg Komolov, "Capital Outflow and the Place of Russia in Core-Periphery Relationships," *World Review of Political Economy* 10, no. 3 (Fall 2019): 329.

66. Vladimir V. Putin, "Address to the Federal Assembly," President of Russia, Dec. 12, 2012, http://en.kremlin.ru/events/president/news/17118.

67. Komolov, "Capital Outflow," 330 (figure 1). It must be admitted that estimation of real net capital outflow is complicated by the fact that some of the outbound rubles, euros, or dollars quickly get recycled into Russia by Russian investors who, for various reasons, are more comfortable when their funds enter Russia via foreign entities.

68. Malia, *Russia under Western Eyes*, 419.

69. "Inside the Bear," *Economist*, Oct. 22, 2016, (special report insert) 8.

70. Lilia Shevtsova, "Humiliation as a Tool of Blackmail" June 2, 2015, Brookings, https://www.brookings.edu/opinions/humiliation-as-a-tool-of-blackmail/.

71. Frye, *Weak Strongman*, 67.

72. McFaul, *Cold War to Hot Peace*, 426.

73. Kennan, "America and the Russian Future," *Foreign Affairs*, April 1951, 356.

74. Kozyrev, *Firebird*, 339.

75. Steinberg, *Bismarck*, 472.

76. Ivan Timofeev, "Russia and the US: Where Will the Growing Alienation Lead To?" Valdai Discussion Club, Nov. 26, 2019, https://valdaiclub.com/a/highlights/russia-and-the-us/.

77. "Russia and Europe," Levada Center, Mar. 22, 2021, https://www.levada.ru/en/2021/03/22/russia-and-europe/.

Bibliography

Acheson, Dean. *Present at the Creation: My Years in the State Department.* New York: W. W. Norton, 1987.

Adams, Sherman. *Firsthand Report.* New York: Harper, 1961.

Albats, Yevgenia. *The State within a State: The KGB and Its Hold on Russia—Past, Present, and Future.* Translated by Catherine A. Fitzpatrick. New York: Farrar, Straus and Giroux, 1994.

Bailey, Thomas A. *America Faces Russia: Russian-American Relations from Early Times to Our Day.* Gloucester, MA: Peter Smith, 1964.

Baime, A. J. *The Accidental President: Harry S. Truman and the Four Months That Changed the World.* New York: Houghton Mifflin Harcourt, 2017.

Baker, James A., III. *The Politics of Diplomacy.* New York: Putnam, 1995.

Beevor, Antony. *The Fall of Berlin 1945.* New York: Penguin, 2003.

Biden, Joe. *Promises to Keep: On Life and Politics.* New York: Random House, 2008.

Bird, Kai. *The Color of Truth.* New York: Touchstone, 1998.

Bohlen, Charles E. *Witness to History 1929–1969.* New York: W. W. Norton, 1973.

Borgwardt, Elizabeth. *A New Deal for the World: America's Vision for Human Rights.* Cambridge, MA: Harvard University Press, 2005.

Boyne, Walter J. *Beyond the Wild Blue: A History of the U.S. Air Force, 1947–2007.* 2nd ed. New York: Thomas Dunne, 2007.

Brands, H. W. *Reagan: The Life.* New York: Doubleday, 2015.

Brinkley, Alan. *Liberalism and Its Discontents.* Cambridge, MA: Harvard University Press, 1998.

Brzezinski, Zbigniew. "The Competitive Relationship." In *Caging the Bear: Containment and the Cold War,* edited by Charles Gati, 157–99. Indianapolis, IN: Bobbs-Merrill, 1974.

———. *The Grand Failure: The Birth and Death of Communism in the Twentieth Century.* New York: Scribner's, 1989.

———. "Russo-Soviet Nationalism." MA thesis, McGill University, 1950. https://escholarship.mcgill.ca/concern/theses/vx021k06b.

Burns, William J. *The Back Channel: A Memoir of American Diplomacy and the Case for Its Renewal.* New York: Random House, 2019.

Caballero, Raymond. *McCarthyism v. Clinton Jencks*. Norman: University of Oklahoma Press, 2019.

Casey, Steven. "Confirming the Cold War Consensus: Eisenhower and the 1952 Election." In *US Presidential Elections and Foreign Policy*, edited by Andrew Johnstone and Andrew Priest, 82–104. Lexington: University Press of Kentucky, 2017.

Chace, James. *Acheson: The Secretary of State Who Created the American World*. New York: Simon & Schuster, 1998.

———. "The Day the Cold War Started." In *The Cold War: A Military History*, edited by Robert Cowley, 3–12. New York: Random House, 2005.

Chuev, Felix. *Molotov Remembers: Inside Kremlin Politics: Conversations with Felix Chuev*. Edited by Albert Resis. Chicago: Ivan R. Dee, 1993.

Churchill, Winston S. *The Gathering Storm*. Boston: Houghton Mifflin, 1948.

———. *The Grand Alliance*. Boston: Houghton Mifflin, 1950.

———. *Never Give In! The Best of Winston Churchill's Speeches*. New York: Hyperion, 2003.

———. *Triumph and Tragedy*. Boston: Houghton Mifflin, 1953.

Clark, Douglas E. *Eisenhower in Command at Columbia*. Lanham, MD: Lexington Books, 2013.

Clifford, Clark. *Counsel to the President*. New York: Anchor Books, 1992.

Cray, Ed. *Chief Justice: A Biography of Earl Warren*. New York: Simon & Schuster, 1997.

Djilas, Milovan. *Conversations with Stalin*. Translated by Michael B. Petrovich. San Diego: Harcourt Brace, 1962.

Dobrynin, Anatoly. *In Confidence: Moscow's Ambassador to America's Six Cold War Presidents (1962–1986)*. New York: Times Books, 1995.

Eisenhower, David. *Eisenhower: At War 1943–1945*. New York: Random House, 1986.

Figes, Orlando. *Natasha's Dance: A Cultural History of Russia*. New York: Picador, 2002.

Frye, Timothy. *Weak Strongman: The Limits of Power in Putin's Russia*. Princeton, NJ: Princeton University Press, 2021.

Gaddis, John Lewis. *The Cold War: A New History*. New York: Penguin, 2005.

Garthoff, Raymond L. *Soviet Strategy in the Nuclear Age*. New York: Praeger, 1962.

Gates, Robert M. *Exercise of Power: American Failures, Successes, and a New Path Forward in the Post-Cold War World*. New York: Knopf, 2020.

Gitelman, Zvi. "The Meanings of Jewishness in Post-Soviet Russia and Ukraine." In *Contemporary Jewries: Convergence and Divergence*, edited by Eliezer Ben-Rafael, Yosef Gorny, and Yaacov Ro'i, 194–215. Leiden, Netherlands: Brill, 2003.

Gorbachev, Mikhail. *Memoirs*. Translated by Georges Peronansky and Tatjana Varsavsky. New York: Doubleday, 1995.

Gromyko, Andrei. *Memories*. Translated by Harold Shukman. London: Hutchinson, 1989.

Halle, Louis J. *The Cold War as History*. New York: Harper & Row, 1967.

Harriman, W. Averell, and Elie Abel. *Special Envoy to Churchill and Stalin, 1941–1946*. New York: Random House, 1975.

Harrington, Daniel F. *The Air Force Can Deliver Anything: A History of the Berlin Airlift*. Ramstein, Germany: United States Air Force, 1998.

Harrison, Hope M. *Ulbricht and the Concrete 'Rose': New Archival Evidence on the Dynamics of Soviet-East German Relations and the Berlin Crisis, 1958–1961*. Washington, DC: Woodrow Wilson Center, 1993.

Hill, William H. *No Place for Russia: European Security Institutions since 1989*. New York: Columbia University Press, 2018.

Hoffer, Peter Charles, William James Hull Hoffer, and N. E. H. Hull. *The Federal Courts: An Essential History*. New York: Oxford University Press, 2016.

Holloway, David. *Stalin and the Bomb: The Soviet Union and Atomic Energy, 1939–1956*. New Haven, CT: Yale University Press, 1994.

Hopkins, Michael F. "Containing Challenges: The Triumphs of Harry Truman in the Presidential Election of 1948." In *US Presidential Elections and Foreign Policy*, edited by Andrew Johnstone and Andrew Priest, 61–81. Lexington: University Press of Kentucky, 2017.

House, Jonathan M. *A Military History of the Cold War, 1944–1962*. Norman: University of Oklahoma Press, 2012.

Isaacson, Walter, and Evan Thomas. *The Wise Men: Six Friends and the World They Made*. New York: Simon & Schuster, 1986.

Jacoby, Susan. *Inside Soviet Schools*. New York: Schocken Books, 1975.

———. *Moscow Conversations*. New York: Coward, McCann & Geoghegan, 1972.

Jensen, Kenneth M., ed. *Origins of the Cold War: The Novikov, Kennan, and Roberts "Long Telegrams" of 1946*. Washington, DC: United States Institute of Peace, 1993.

Jervis, Robert. *The Logic of Images in International Relations*. New York: Columbia University Press, 1989.

Kedourie, Elie. *Nationalism*. 4th ed. Oxford: Blackwell, 1993. First published in 1960.

Kennan, George F. *At a Century's Ending: Reflections, 1982–1995*. New York: W. W. Norton, 1996.

———. *Memoirs, 1925–1950*. Boston: Little, Brown, 1967.

———. *Memoirs, 1950–1963*. New York: Pantheon Books, 1972.

———. *Sketches from a Life*. New York: W. W. Norton, 2000.

Kennedy, David M. *Freedom from Fear: The American People in Depression and War, 1929–1945*. New York: Oxford University Press, 1999.

Kennedy, Robert F. *Thirteen Days: A Memoir of the Cuban Missile Crisis*. New York: W. W. Norton, 1969.

Khrushchev, Nikita. *Khrushchev Remembers*. Edited and translated by Strobe Talbott. Boston: Little, Brown, 1970.

Kissinger, Henry. *Diplomacy*. New York: Simon & Schuster, 1994.

———. *Years of Upheaval*. New York: Simon & Schuster, 1982.

Kotkin, Stephen. *Armageddon Averted: The Soviet Collapse, 1970–2000*. Oxford: Oxford University Press, 2008.

Kozyrev, Andrei. *Firebird: A Memoir*. Pittsburgh: University of Pittsburgh Press, 2019.

Krivosheev, G. F., V. M. Andronikov, P. D. Burikov, M. V. Filimoshin, V. V. Gurkin, A. I. Kruglov, and Ye. I. Rodionov. *Soviet Casualties and Combat Losses in the Twentieth Century*. Edited by G.F. Krivosheev. London: Greenhill Books, 1997.

LaFeber, Walter. *America, Russia, and the Cold War, 1945–1996*. 8th ed. New York: McGraw-Hill, 1997.

Large, David Clay. "The Great Rescue." In *The Cold War: A Military History*, edited by Robert Cowley, 20–34. New York: Random House, 2005.

Ligachev, Yegor. *Inside Gorbachev's Kremlin: The Memoirs of Yegor Ligachev*. Translated by Catherine A. Fitzpatrick, Michele A. Berdy, and Dobrochna Dyrcz-Freeman. New York: Pantheon Books, 1993.

Malia, Martin. *Russia under Western Eyes: From the Bronze Horseman to the Lenin Mausoleum*. Cambridge, MA: Belknap Press of Harvard University Press, 1999.

Malkov, Viktor L. "Commentary." In *Origins of the Cold War: The Novikov, Kennan and Roberts "Long Telegrams" of 1946*, edited by Kenneth M. Jensen. Washington, DC: United States Institute of Peace Press, 1993.

Martin, Terry. *The Affirmative Action Empire: Nations and Nationalism in the Soviet Union, 1923–1939*. Ithaca, NY: Cornell University Press, 2002.

Matlock, Jack F., Jr. *Autopsy on an Empire: The American Ambassador's Account of the Collapse of the Soviet Union*. New York: Random House, 1995.

———. *Reagan and Gorbachev: How the Cold War Ended*. New York: Random House, 2005.

McCullough, David. *Truman*. New York: Simon & Schuster, 1992.

McFaul, Michael. *From Cold War to Hot Peace: An American Ambassador in Putin's Russia*. New York: Houghton Mifflin Harcourt, 2018.

Melvin, Neil. *Forging the New Russian Nation: Russian Foreign Policy and the Russian-Speaking Communities of the Former USSR*. London: Royal Institute of International Affairs, 1994.

———. *Russians Beyond Russia: The Politics of National Identity*. London: Royal Institute of International Affairs, 1995.

Merridale, Catherine. *Ivan's War: Life and Death in the Red Army, 1939–1945*. New York: Metropolitan Books, 2006.

———. *Night of Stone: Death and Memory in Twentieth-Century Russia*. New York: Viking, 2001.

Miller, Wright. *Who Are the Russians? A History of the Russian People*. London: Faber & Faber, 1973.

Moss, Walter G. *A History of Russia*. Vol. 1, *To 1917*. 2nd ed. London: Anthem Press, 2005.

———. *A History of Russia*. Vol. 2, *Since 1885*. 2nd ed. London: Anthem Press, 2005.

Moynahan, Brian. *Claws of the Bear: The History of the Red Army from the Revolution to the Present*. Boston: Houghton Mifflin, 1989.

Neiberg, Michael. *Potsdam: The End of World War II and the Remaking of Europe*. New York: Basic Books, 2015.

Nichols, David A. *Ike and McCarthy: Dwight Eisenhower's Secret Campaign Against Joseph McCarthy*. New York: Simon & Schuster, 2017.

Nitze, Paul H. *From Hiroshima to Glasnost: At the Center of Decision: A Memoir*. With Ann M. Smith and Steven L. Reardon. New York: Grove Weidenfeld, 1989.

Nye, Joseph. *The Paradox of American Power: Why the World's Only Superpower Can't Go It Alone*. London: Oxford University Press, 2002.

Payne, Robert. *The Life and Death of Adolph Hitler*. New York: Praeger, 1973.

Phillips, Cabell. *The Truman Presidency: The History of a Triumphant Succession*. New York: Macmillan, 1966.

Pipes, Richard. "Reflections on the Nationality Problems in the Soviet Union." In *Ethnicity: Theory and Experience*, edited by Nathan Glazer and Daniel P. Moynihan, 453–65. Cambridge, MA: Harvard University Press, 1975.

Powaski, Ronald E. *The Cold War: The United States and the Soviet Union*. New York: Oxford University Press, 1998.

Powers, Richard Gid. *Not Without Honor: The History of American Anticommunism*. New Haven, CT: Yale University Press, 1998.

Putin, Vladimir V. *First Person: An Astonishingly Frank Self-Portrait by Russia's President*. Translated by Catherine A. Fitzpatrick. New York: Public Affairs, 2000.

Raleigh, Donald J. *Soviet Baby Boomers: An Oral History of Russia's Cold War Generation*. New York: Oxford University Press, 2012.

Reagan, Ronald. *Ronald Reagan: An American Life*. New York: Simon & Schuster, 1990.

Rearden, Steven L. *Council of War: A History of the Joint Chiefs of Staff, 1942–1991*. Washington, DC: Joint History Office, Joint Chiefs of Staff, 2012.

Riasanovsky, Nicholas V., and Mark D. Steinberg. *A History of Russia*. 7th ed. New York: Oxford University Press, 2005.

Robinson, Harlow. "Composing for Victory: Classical Music." In *Culture and Entertainment in Wartime Russia*, edited by Richard Stites, 62–76. Bloomington: Indiana University Press, 1995).

Sakwa, Richard. *Communism in Russia: An Interpretative Essay*. Basingstoke, UK: Palgrave Macmillan, 2010.

———. *Soviet Politics in Perspective*. 2nd ed. London: Routledge, 1998.

Salisbury, Harrison E. *American in Russia*. New York: Harper, 1955.

Schlesinger, Arthur M., Jr. *A Thousand Days: John F. Kennedy in the White House*. Boston: Houghton Mifflin, 1965.

Scott, Harriet Fast. *Soviet Military Doctrine: Its Continuity, 1960–1970*. Menlo Park, CA: Stanford Research Institute, 1971.

Scott, Harriet Fast, and William F. Scott. *The Soviet Art of War: Doctrine, Strategy and Tactics*. Boulder, CO: Westview Press, 1982.

Sell, Louis. *From Washington to Moscow: US-Soviet Relations and the Collapse of the USSR*. Durham, NC: Duke University Press, 2016.

Sherwood, Robert E. *Roosevelt and Hopkins: An Intimate History*. 1948. Reprinted, New York: Enigma Books, 2001.

Shevtsova, Lilia. *Lonely Power: Why Russia Has Failed to Become the West and the West Is Weary of Russia*. Translated by Antonina W. Bouis. Washington, DC: Carnegie Endowment for International Peace, 2010.

Sivachev, N. V., and N. N. Yakovlev. *Russia and the United States*. Translated by O.A. Titelbaum. Chicago: University of Chicago Press, 1979.

Smith, Hedrick. *The Russians*. New York: Times Books, 1983.

Smith, Jean Edward. *Eisenhower in War and Peace*. New York: Random House, 2012.

Smith, Walter Bedell. *My Three Years in Moscow*. Philadelphia: Lippincott, 1950.
Smith, Zadie. *Swing Time*. New York: Penguin, 2016.
Snyder, Timothy. *Bloodlands: Europe between Hitler and Stalin*. New York: Basic Books, 2010.
Sokolovskiy, V. D. *Soviet Military Strategy*. 3rd ed. Edited and translated by Harriet Fast Scott. New York: Crane, Russak, 1975. First published in 1968.
Spanier, John. "The Choices We Did Not Have: In Defense of Containment." In *Caging the Bear: Containment and the Cold War*, edited by Charles Gati, 128–58. Indianapolis, IN: Bobbs-Merrill, 1974.
Speer, Albert. *Inside the Third Reich*. Translated by Richard and Clara Winston. New York: Macmillan, 1970.
Stalin, Joseph. *The Great Patriotic War of the Soviet Union*. New York: International Publishers, 1945.
Steinberg, Jonathan. *Bismarck, A Life*. New York: Oxford University Press, 2011.
Stern, Paula. *Water's Edge: Domestic Politics and the Making of American Foreign Policy*. Westport, CT: Greenwood Press, 1979.
Tanenhaus, Sam. *Whittaker Chambers: A Biography*. New York: Random House, 1997.
Thomas, Evan. *Being Nixon: A Man Divided*. New York: Random House, 2015.
———. *The Man to See*. New York: Simon & Schuster, 1991.
Thompson, Francis H. *The Frustration of Politics: Truman, Congress and the Loyalty Issue 1945–1953*. Cranbury, NJ: Associated University Presses, 1979.
Toal, Gerard. *Near Abroad: Putin, the West, and the Contest Over Ukraine and the Caucasus*. New York: Oxford University Press, 2017.
Tocqueville, Alexis de. *Democracy in America*. Translated by Arthur Goldhammer. New York: Library of America, 2004.
Tokaev, G. A. *Stalin Means War*. London: Weidenfeld & Nicolson, 1951.
Tolstoy, Leo. *War and Peace*. Translated by Louise and Aylmer Maude. Oxford: Oxford University Press, 2010.
Trister, Toby. "Traditionalists, Revisionists, and the Cold War." In *Caging the Bear: Containment and the Cold War*, edited by Charles Gati, 211–22. Indianapolis, IN: Bobbs-Merrill, 1974.
Truman, Harry S. *Memoirs by Harry S. Truman*. Vol. 1, *Year of Decisions*. Garden City, NY: Doubleday, 1955.
———. *Memoirs by Harry S. Truman*. Vol. 2, *Years of Trial and Hope*. Garden City, NY: Doubleday, 1956.
Ulam, Adam B. *Understanding the Cold War: A Historian's Personal Reflections*. Charlottesville, VA: Leopolis Press, 2000.
Walker, Martin. *The Cold War: A History*. New York: Macmillan, 1995.
Weiner, Tim. *Legacy of Ashes: The History of the CIA*. New York: Anchor Books, 2008.
Westad, Odd Arne. *The Cold War: A World History*. New York: Basic Books, 2017.
White, Theodore H. *The Making of the President, 1972*. New York: Atheneum, 1973.
Whitfield, Stephen. *The Culture of the Cold War*. 2nd ed. Baltimore: Johns Hopkins University Press, 1996.
Winterton, Paul. *Inquest on an Ally*. London: Cresset Press, 1948.
Yergin, Daniel. *The Prize: The Epic Quest for Oil, Money & Power*. New York: Free Press, 2009.

———. *Shattered Peace: The Origins of the Cold War.* New York: Penguin, 1990.
Zhukov, Georgy. *Marshal of Victory.* Vol. 2, *The WWII Memoirs of General Georgy Zhukov, 1941–1945.* Edited by Geoffrey Roberts. Mechanicsburg, PA: Stackpole Books, 1974.
Ziemke, Earl F. *Stalingrad to Berlin: The German Defeat in the East.* New York: Dorset Press, 1968.
Zubok, Vladislav M. *A Failed Empire: The Soviet Union in the Cold War from Stalin to Gorbachev.* Chapel Hill: University of North Carolina Press, 2009.
———. *Soviet Intelligence and the Cold War: The "Small" Committee of Information, 1952–53.* Washington, DC: Woodrow Wilson International Center for Scholars, 1992.
Zubok, Vladislav, and Constantine Pleshakov. *Inside the Kremlin's Cold War: From Stalin to Khrushchev.* Cambridge, MA: Harvard University Press, 1996.

Index

References to illustrations appear in italic type.

Index